INTERNATIONAL ECONOMICS

(INTERNATIONAL ECONOMIC RELATIONS)

Late Dr. S. S. M. DESAI

M.A., Ph.D.
Former Head of the Department of Economics,
Nawrosjee Wadia College,
Pune.

Dr. (Mrs.) NIRMAL BHALERAO

M.A., Ph.D.
Head of the Department of Economics,
Fergusson College,
Pune.

Himalaya Publishing House
ISO 9001:2015 CERTIFIED

FIRST EDITION : 2008
REPRINT : 2020
REPRINT : 2023

Published by	:	Mrs. Meena Pandey for **HIMALAYA PUBLISHING HOUSE PVT. LTD.,** Ramdoot, Dr. Bhalerao Marg, Girgaon, Mumbai - 400 004 **Phone:** 022-23860170/23863863; **Fax:** 022-23877178 **E-mail:** himpub@bharatmail.co.in; **Website:** www.himpub.com
Branch Offices	:	
New Delhi	:	Pooja Apartments, 4-B, Murari Lal Street, Ansari Road, Darya Ganj, New Delhi - 110 002. Phone: 011-23270392, 23278631; Fax: 011-23256286
Nagpur	:	Kundanlal Chandak Industrial Estate, Ghat Road, Nagpur - 440 018. Phone: 0712-2738731, 3296733; Telefax: 0712-2721216
Bengaluru	:	Plot No. 91-33, 2nd Main Road, Seshadripuram, Behind Nataraja Theatre, Bengaluru - 560 020. Phone: 080-41138821; Mobile: 09379847017, 09379847005
Hyderabad	:	No. 3-4-184, Lingampally, Besides Raghavendra Swamy Matham, Kachiguda, Hyderabad - 500 027. Phone: 040-27560041, 27550139
Chennai	:	No. 34/44, Motilal Street, T. Nagar, Chennai - 600 017. Mobile: 09380460419
Pune	:	First Floor, Laksha Apartment, No. 527, Mehunpura, Shaniwarpeth (Near Prabhat Theatre), Pune - 411 030. Phone: 020-24496323, 24496333; Mobile: 09370579333
Cuttack	:	Plot No 5F-755/4, Sector-9, CDA Market Nagar, Cuttack - 753 014, Odisha. Mobile: 09338746007
Kolkata	:	3, S.M. Bose Road, Near Gate No. 5, Agarpara Railway Station, North 24 Parganas, West Bengal - 700 109. Mobile: 09674536325
DTP by	:	HPH Editional Office, Bhandup (Shobha)
Printed at	:	Trinity Academy, Mumbai. On behalf of HPH.

PREFACE TO THE FIRST EDITION

The subject of INTERNATIONAL ECONOMICS (INTERNATIONAL ECONOMIC RELATIONS) has been assuming importance in recent years.

The world has been experiencing radical transformation during the second half of the 20th century. Revolutions in transport and communication have for all practical purposes annihilated distance and that has brought one hundred and fifty and odd countries of the world closer together as never before. The consequence is that any major or even a minor development in any part of the world produces almost instantaneous consequences in other parts of the world. Thus, failure of crops in the United States might mean death to millions in countries in Africa; war in Korea sent price level in India shooting upward, spelling increasing misery for the vast Indian masses even in the remotest part of rural India; and oil crisis of 1970s seriously upset balance of payments position of most of the countries.

Thus, on the one hand, different countries in the world are coming closer to one another and there is increasing realisation, that some of the common problems confronting the mankind (such as world food problem, population problem, problem of environmental balance, menace of drugs and epidemics, exploitation of sea-bed, energy problem, etc.) can be solved only by close international cooperation; on the other hand, there appears to be developing confrontation between North and South and West and East and the gap between developed and developing countries appears to be widening, threatening increasing economic conflicts between the two groups of countries.

It is, therefore, not enough to know only what is taking place in the economic sphere in one's own country; it is equally essential to know the various economic changes that are taking place in other countries of the world and their possible repercussions on the economy of one's own country.

An attempt has been made in this book to analyse various problems and issues concerning international trade and international economic relations. All the relevant concepts and theories relating to international trade and international economic relations, have been analysed with as much clarity as possible. Attempt has been made to cover practically all the topics included in the syllabi of most of the universities in India, as also those topics which are of interest to wider reading public.

Special attention has been given in this book to international trading problems and international economic relations concerning India, in a fairly exhaustive chapter which includes latest statistical data relation to the subject and also indicating India's relative position *vis-a-vis* other countries of the world.

The author is confident that the book will be useful to Graduate and Post-Graduate students of Arts and Commerce Faculties of various Indian universities, as also to candidates preparing for various Public Service Commission examinations and to others who are concerned with or interested in the subject of International Trade and International Economic Relations.

I am thankful to Shriman D.P. Pandey of Himalaya Publishing House, Mumbai, for inviting me to write on this subject and undertaking to publish this book. I feel confident that like my previous book 'Industrial Economy of India' this book will also be enthusiastically received by the teaching and student community in India and also by the wider public interested in the subject.

Pune

Ist January, 1990. **Authors**

PREFACE TO THE FOURTH REVISED EDITION

I am very happy to bring out the fourth revised edition of ***' International Economics'.*** While doing so I missed my father late Dr. S.S.M. Desai.

Last 2 decades were marked by drastic and far-reaching changes in the Indian economy, while according to me, should be reflected in any International Economics textbook written today. I have tried my best to stick to this view while preparing this fourth edition. Doing so, has meant substantial revision of text as well as data. In addition, to maintain the flow in topics the whole book has been reorganized.

Section I –This section covers theories of International trade, gains from trade and tariffs and import quotas.

Section II —It includes balance of trade and payments, gold standard, foreign exchange rates policy, exchange control etc.

Section III — This section includes all the topics covering the subject of 'Trade and Development'.

Section V — is devoted for India's international trade.

I am thankful to my colleagues from 'Economic Department' for supporting me all the time. While preparting this fourth edition, Dr. Mrs.Sharmishtha Satav, a colleague and friend from my department helped me adding valuable material in the theory chapters. I am thankful to her for the help.

I am also thankful to Shree D. P. Pandey of the Himalaya Publishing House, Mumbai for giving me opportunity to work for him and showing confidence in me.

I am sure that the teaching and student community in India will appreciate this edition of ***'International Economics'.***

Pune

August 24, 2008. **Dr. Mrs. N.D. Bhalerao**

CONTENTS

SECTION I

THEORY OF INTERNATIONAL TRADE

SECTION II

INTERNATIONAL FINANCE

SECTION III

TRADE AND DEVELOPMENT

SECTION IV

THE WORLD ECONOMY

SECTION V

INDIA'S INTERNATIONAL TRADE

SECTION I

THEORY OF INTERNATIONAL TRADE

1. Scope of International Economics
2. Characteristic Features of International Trade
3. The Classical Theory of International Trade
4. Haberler's Opportunity Cost Theory of International Trade
5. Heckscher-Ohlin's Theory of International Trade
6. Gains from Trade
7. Terms of Trade
8. Free Trade: Case for and Against
9. Tariffs and Import Quotas

CHAPTER 1

SCOPE OF INTERNATIONAL ECONOMICS

Structure:

1.1 INTRODUCTION

For some centuries 'the National State' is an acknowledged and dominant political institution. The national state has at present come to be accepted as a political entity with vast economic implications.

And yet, most national states or countries are economically closely linked with one another and these economic links among nations of the world are growing as years go by, and especially after the World War II. With revolutionary changes in means of transport and communications and with annihilation of distance, economic links among nations of the world are growing more and more intimate with the consequence that any major economic change in any part of the world has almost immediate economic impact on the rest of the world.

This means in modern times, for all practical purposes, countries have become parts of the world closely linked with one another. It may be observed that only a few big countries like the United States, former Soviet Union, China and India may conceivably cut themselves off from the rest of the world economy without catastrophic disaster befalling them. But for most countries (and even for countries mentioned above) cutting off of their economic relations with the rest of the world and trying to be economically self-sufficient would certainly result in drastic lowering of standard of living of their peoples and also drastic changes in their pattern of living.

The degree of economic interdependence among nations of the world through international trade is continually on the increase. For example, world trade in commodities increased annually by about 8 per cent during 1951 to 1971. Since then there has been taking place 'Informational Revolution' and international trade appears to be growing at a much faster rate than during the earlier decades. India is no exception to this phenomenon of growing economic interdependence among nations through international trade. For example, value of India's imports rose from Rs. 1,140 crores in 1960-61 to Rs. 22,243, crores in 1987-88 and her exports during the same period from Rs. 660 crores to Rs. 15,719 crores. This would show that while in 1960-61 India's total international commodity trade amounted to Rs. 1,800 crores, in 1987-88 India's commodity imports have gone up by nearly 20 times, her exports by 28 times and her total commodity trade by 21 times. It appears that the annual growth rate of international trade has been much faster than the annual growth rate in world output and income.

That there is increasing interdependence among nations of the world is also indicated by increasing amounts of annual capital flow among countries as also from increasing number of travellers visiting different countries in the world. International transfer of managerial skills and technology has also assumed vast dimensions. There is also taking place considerable migration of labour force from one country to another.

Before the Ist World War (1914-18), there were no doubt, fewer restrictions on movement of labour and capital from one country to another as compared to increasing restrictions on capital movements by way of tariffs, quotas and other trade barriers. But in those times there were natural obstacles in the form of poor communication systems and higher transport costs compared to the present day. And, therefore, in spite of various restrictions and trade barriers which are being enforced at present, volume of international trade and economic interdependence among nations of the world have been growing at a much faster rate than ever before.

There is another notable development intimately linking different nations of the world. Though multinational industrial and commercial or trading corporations existed and functioned before 1914, the emergence of truly international or multinational corporations is a post-World War II development.

Compared to their position and functioning before 1914, there is phenomenal increase in the number, size and dimensions of their activities in different countries of the world. The multinational corporations have been dealing in the production and distribution of not only minerals and crude oil but also in various capital and consumer goods on a world-wide scale quickly responding to opportunities in developed as well as in developing countries.

Most countries are having at present comprehensive national economic policies, mainly aiming at maintaining full employment and stable and, if possible rising level of income for people in the country. Before 1914 and during the days of the gold standard, any disturbance in balance of payments of a country used to be automatically corrected by deflation, decline in prices and rise in the level of unemployment. With more active national economic policies dealing with the problem of unfavourable balance of payments, deflation and rising level of unemployment in the deficit country to correct adverse balance of payments of a country are almost unthinkable during the post-World War II period. Naturally, the present national economic policies aiming at full employment and steadily rising level of income of people in the country have implications for international trading transactions. Increasing international economic dependence raises a number of complicated domestic issues. If fuller advantage is to be taken of international division of labour (which is what international trade is based on), then certain domestic economic adjustments become necessary. Naturally, this dilemma must be solved satisfactorily. 'International Economics' devotes considerable attention to this problem.

While on the one hand, international economic dependence among nations of the world is increasing, on the other hand, there are also emerging various groups of countries such as the European Economic Community, the Organisation for European Cooperation and Development (OECD) and Council for Mutual Economic Aid (COMECON) consisting of East European communist countries. There are also groups of African countries. Then there are developing countries which have constituted (through informal) groups distinct from the EEC, the OECD and COMECON such as the South Asian Association for Regional Cooperation (SAARC), Organisation of Petroleum Exporting Countries (the OPEC) and so on. Though international trade is of increasing importance to these different groups of countries, the problems in carrying on their international trade differ in the cases of above mentioned different groups of countries. For example, developing countries aiming at raising the annual growth rates of their economies are required to import capital goods and technology; but often they cannot earn through their exports enough foreign currencies to pay for such imports. Often such developing countries borrow from abroad to make payments for imports of capital goods. Some of the developing countries in South America have borrowed abroad so heavily that they have to borrow abroad additional funds to pay annual interest on foreign debts already raised. Though 'International Economics' (or International Economic Relations) is of great significance, it does not follow that this subject should be or can be studied separately or independently of other branches of economies.

Though the subject of International Economics is in one sense 'Applied Economics', where many policy problems of empirical nature are elucidated and examined with the help of economic theories, there are good many reasons why International Economics should be studied as a separate subject and not just as a part of general economics.

For example, though the theories of comparative cost advantage and of factor price equalisation are in a sense part of general theory of values or price, they need to be studied separately to understand all their vast international implications. Thus, we find that "(International) trade theory is a distinct part of economic theory with a rich body of theorems. These results are not part of general economics theory as it is commonly understood and thought."[1]

---

1. Bo Soderton, *International Economics,* (Macmillan, 1979), p. 5.

In the case of international economics, there appear many policy issues which are not at all encountered in other fields of economics — for example, exchange rate policy, commercial policy, problems of balance of payments and various measures advocated to correct external imbalance. While knowledge of general economic theory would serve as a good and necessary background, it is felt that to get proper understanding of the subject, it is useful and necessary to study International Economics separately and not just merely as a minor branch of general economic theory.

1.2 COVERAGE OF INTERNATIONAL ECONOMICS

International Economics covers analysis and study of pure theory of comparative cost or advantage (which would explain in the first instance why international trade takes place), modern theory of international trade (which will help students to understand the basic principles of general equilibrium), and the modern version of the pure theory of international trade (which is a fruitful application of the general equilibrium theory). The theory of comparative cost advantage will explain why a country exports certain commodities and why it imports certain other commodities.

But the theory of comparative cost advantage is basically a static theory. Gradually dynamic variables like capital inflows and outflows, new technology, increase in population and labour force and economic growth of countries are introduced and their effects on international trade of a country are traced as also rebound effects of growth of international trade of a country on employment and level of income of the people in a country and on its economic growth.

One important aspect that distinguishes internal or domestic trade from international trade is that the latter is carried out mostly with the help of different currencies. This open up a vast field of study of foreign currencies — how the rates of exchange of one currency into other currencies are determined and what happens when rates of exchange are managed artificially.

A substantial part of International Economics may be said to be 'Applied Economic'. International Economics concern itself with various policy measures such as commercial policy, quota fixation, price stabilisation of commodities (by developing countries), formation of regional groups of countries like the European Economic Community and international trade policies adopted by such groups of countries.

A large number of countries in Asia, Africa and Latin America have become independent after the end of World War II (1939-45), and they are all trying to develop their economies rapidly so that they can be in a position to solve their age-old problems of unemployment and mass poverty. The subject of International Economics makes an attempt to study how and to what extent international trade can be an effective instrument to help developing countries to attain the above objectives.

1.3 INTERNATIONAL TRADE, A BRANCH OF GENERAL ECONOMICS

Though International Economics is a separate study in the sense that the problems of International Economics need to be studied separately, it needs to be emphasised that International Economics is not an independent discipline or subject but is only a branch of General Economics. General Economics has several branches such as theory of consumption, theory of value, of exchange and distribution, theories of money and banking, of public finance, etc. In the same way International Economics is also a branch of General Economics and not an independent discipline to be studied apart from other branches of General Economics. In fact, the above different branches of General Economics and International Economics are closely interlinked and knowledge of other branches of General Economics is absolutely essential to properly understand problems studied in International Economics. Knowledge of the theory of value, of money and banking, of public finance, etc. is essential to properly understand problems and policies studied in International Economics. And, therefore, it would be correct to say that International Economics is only a branch of General Economics, though it requires a separate study.

1.4 THE SUBJECT OF INTERNATIONAL ECONOMICS

International Economics *per se* might seem to be a mixture of many other economic disciplines like Public Finance, Money and Banking, Labour Economics and so on. This is somewhat true. Take any branch of economics and International Economics deals with the international aspects of it. It also considers the intertwining of the domestic market and the international markets. Do farmers from Madhya Pradesh know whether the wheat they sell will be exported? When you buy a handkerchief, do you inspect it closely for label indicating manufacture abroad, say China? International transactions are indeed related with the domestic markets. Ultimately our explanation of International Trade must be a part of an explanation of each national market.

Nevertheless International Economics does have its own flesh as well as bones and hence must be treated as a separate branch of study. Following are the two most important reasons for doing so.[2]

The Power of International Economic Theory

The most useful models for explaining international trade are those, which are simple but elegant and general. They not only explain international trade patterns, but also tell much about patterns of production, income distribution, and so on within countries. One might think why do we require separate models to explain international trade and domestic trade? The traditional answer to this question is that the factors of production–labour and capital–are perfectly mobile in the long run within the national economy, but their mobility between countries is sharply limited. For example, labour and capital move freely between Delhi and Mumbai, whenever workers or lenders feel that such movement will have favourable effect on their real incomes. However, the effect of such movement on their native endowments does not lend itself to an interesting analysis. On the other hand, if little movement of labour and capital takes place between the European Union and India, the commodities they trade and the benefits from exchange become both interesting and important.

The Importance of Nationhood for Policy

Trade occurs between two sovereign nations. Two governments with potentially clashing objectives can apply their policies to the trade between them, and against each other's interest. More importantly, the deep-rooted fear of outsiders repeatedly prompts the debate whether trade is really beneficial to the nation or its just another channel for the foreigners to plunder us of our precious wealth. This fear is much more marked in India, which happens to be former colony of the United Kingdom.

The Swadeshi lobby keeps on propagating its ideas of the Western design to loot India and indeed they find many buyers. This shows the power of the deep-rooted xenophobia and only highlights the need for separately analysing the issues in international trade and policy to help the governments of today engage in sensible policy making. Here the critical role of theory is to clearly spell out the gains from trade and their distribution. Only objectivity and scientific rigour can allay the fears carried over from colonial times but unfit in the modern world.

---

2. This part is based upon Ch. 1 of Caves R.E., Frankel J.A. and Jones R. W. (1990), *"World Trade and Payments — An Introduction",* Harper Collins Publishers, (5th Ed.).

In short, international economics as a separate branch of study aims to do the following:

(1) To show how international exchange and improvements in economic policies can result in gains;

(2) To identify the bases for conflict over international economic policy, both within nations (between interest groups) and among them;

(3) To point out ways in which the conflicting groups or nations can resolve their differences for mutual benefit.

1.5 THE SCOPE AND NATURE OF INTERNATIONAL ECONOMICS

As mentioned earlier, international economics studies how independent economies of the world interact with one another in the process of allocating scarce resources to satisfy human wants. International economics concentrates on the problems of two or more economies. Thus, it examines the same problems as the general economic theory, but in their international setting. Clearly, international economics is more general than the economics of closed economy. Rather, the economics of a closed economy is a special case where the number of trading countries is reduced from many to one — a situation termed as autarky in international economics.

The subject matter of international economics can be divided into two parts: (1) international trade and (2) international finance.

International Trade[3]

This part of international economics deals with the long-run static-equilibrium theory of barter. In this part, money is assumed to play the true classical role of a veil. The approach taken in this part is micro-economic in nature. It relies heavily on the concepts of demand, supply, indifference curves, opportunity cost, etc., from micro economics to explain why nations trade with each other, what are the gains from trade and what kinds of trade patterns would emerge. What are the pros and cons of protectionism?

The Gains from Trade: Everybody understands that some trade is beneficial. Nobody expects that the Arabian countries grow their own food gains or India should use oil to the extent it is available with itself. However, we always find argument "Be Indian, Buy Indian" emotionally appealing. Probably the most important insight in all of international economics is the idea that there are gains from trade, i.e. that when countries sell goods and services to one another, this is usually for their mutual benefit. Moreover, the range of circumstances under which international trade is beneficial is much wider than most people think. Demonstrating these situations with powerful theories is one of the tasks of the international trade theory.

The Pattern of Trade: Economists cannot be confident in commenting on effects of international trade or recommend changes on government policies unless they are sure that their theory explains what is observed in reality fairly well. Thus, attempts to explain the pattern of international trade — who sells to whom — have been a major preoccupation of international economics.

Some patterns are fairly obvious and can be explained with the help of climate and resource availability. For example, the answer to why Brazil exports coffee or Saudi Arabia exports oil is clear once we look at their climate or the resource availability. However, instances like Japan exporting

3. This section draws on Krugman Paul and Maurice Obstfeld (2000), *International Economics,* Addison Wesley, pp. 3-8.

automobiles or America exporting aircrafts are not that easier to explain. Attempts to predict patterns of trade *a priori* go back to David Ricardo whose explanation that trade occurs due to international differences in labour productivity remains a powerful insight even today but unfortunately inadequate. Then we have theories put forth by Eli Hechscher and Bertil Ohlin, the specific factors model and so on. Though each of these models does not offer a complete answer, it individually contributes important insights, only bettering our understanding of patterns of trade. Nonetheless, this is in fact one of the important objectives of the international trade theory.

Protectionism: If the concept of gains from trade is the most important theoretical concept in international economics, the seemingly eternal battle between free trade and protection is its most important policy theme. Since the emergence of nation states in the sixteenth century, governments have worried about the effects of international competition on the progress of domestic industries and hence have either tried to shield them from foreign competition by placing limits on imports or to help them in world competition by subsidizing exports. The single most consistent mission of international economics has been to analyze the effects of these so called protectionist policies and usually, though not always, to demonstrate the superiority of freer international trade over protectionism.

Commercial Policy: Though one accepts the superiority of freer international trade over any protectionist stance, countries continue to use different instruments to control trade. Tariffs and Quotas are the most common of such instruments and are indeed extensively used. What are the effects of these instruments? Which instrument is better if some control over trade is necessary? These are some of the questions, which can be answered with the help of theoretical constructs. This is another important area where economists have taken pains to analyze effects of such instruments under varying sets of circumstances. It's an important subject matter of the international economics.

International Finance

International finance theory focuses on the monetary aspects of international economic relations. Its approach is primarily macro economic in nature. It deals with the foreign exchange market and studies the short-run problems of balance of payments, disequilibrium and adjustment. It is also concerned with the economic policies that may be necessary for achievement of international equilibrium when the automatic processes do not work properly.

International finance deals with the international monetary system, which is so much necessary for the smooth working of the international economy. Determination of exchange rates, choice of a exchange rate system, and choosing appropriate policy mix (fiscal and monetary policy) to achieve external as well as internal balance are some of the areas dealt with under international finance. To analyze the problems and issues it uses various macroeconomic models, notably the IS-LM one. The specific areas into which this part of international economics can be divided are as follows:

Balance of Payments: India mostly runs a trade deficit with most of its trading partners. In 1990, both Japan and Brazil ran large trade surpluses — each sold more to the rest of the world than it bought in return. What does it mean when a country runs a deficit or a surplus? To make sense of this we have to place these numbers in the broader context of the whole nation's international transactions. The record showing all these international transactions of a country is nothing but the balance of payments. Explaining the balance of payments and diagnosing its significance is a main theme of international economics. Such a diagnosis emerges in number of contexts like that of international capital movements and international aspects of monetary policy.

Exchange Rate Determination: A few years ago one US Dollar traded for 35 Indian Rupees. Today it trades for almost 50 Indian Rupees. This change had effects that reached far beyond financial markets. Those industries which found it impossible to sell their product at the rate of US$ 1 = Rs. 35 might find it easier to push through the international market at the today's much depreciated rate. On the other hand, industries using imported inputs might have felt the pinch because of these exchange rate movements.

One of the important differences between international economics and other branches of economics is that countries have different currencies. Though, it is possible to convert one currency into another, as the above example of Rupee-Dollar exchange rate suggests relative prices of currencies may change over time and sometimes drastically. Hence, it becomes important to study exchange rate determination. However, such a study is relatively a new part of international economics and this is for purely historical reasons. For most of the twentieth century, exchange rates have been fixed by the governments rather than determined in the market place. Before World War I the values of the world's major currencies were fixed in terms of gold, while for the generation after World War II the values of most currencies were fixed in terms of the US dollar. Thus, the analysis of international monetary systems that fix exchange rates forms an important subject matter of international economics.

International Policy Coordination

The international economy comprises of sovereign nations, each free to choose its own economic policies. Unfortunately, in an integrated world one country's economic policies affect other countries as well. For example, when Germany's Bundesbank raised interest rates in 1990 in order to control the possible inflationary impact or reunification of West and East Germany, it helped precipitate a recession in the rest of the Western Europe. Thus, differences in goals often lead to conflict, but similarities might also create problems if policies are not properly coordinated. A fundamental problem in international economics is how to produce an acceptable degree of harmony among international trade and monetary policies of different countries without a world government that tells countries what to do. This motivates us to study the evolution of GATT and the WTO as an international organization. However, it should be noted that this only concentrates on cooperation on international trade policies. Coordination of macroeconomic policies remains an area, which is not so much explored.

1.6 INDIA IN THE INTERNATIONAL ECONOMY

Are all these issues relevant to India? If someone had to answer this question before 1990s, the answer would have been a qualified negative. However, in the present scenario in which India is a member of the World Trade Organization and has followed policies leading to its increasing integration in the international economy, the answer is a definite positive.

Though, India's share in world trade is almost negligible, trade (exports + imports) as percentage of its Gross Domestic Product is continuously rising (see Chart 1 below). This ratio is generally taken as a sign of openness of an economy.

CHART I

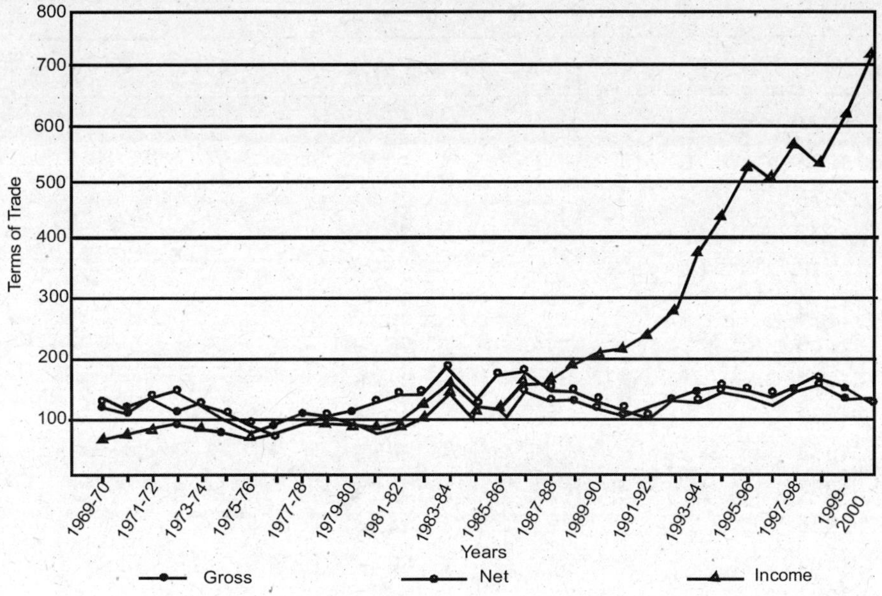

Source: Nayar (2001).[4]

Another indicator of the openness of an economy is the tariff level. High levels of tariffs signify a higher degree of protection accorded to local production against imports from the world economy. Hence, lower tariffs would signify an open regime. Table 2 gives import duties as percentage of Total imports over the years. From 1988, onwards this has shown a continuous decline highlighting the reduction in the protection accorded to the domestic production. This again signifies increasing openness of the Indian economy.

4 Nayar Baladev Raj (2001), Opening Up and Openness of Indian Economy, *Economic and Political Weekly,* September 15.

Table 1.1

India's Tariff Levels

Year	*Import Duties as % of Imports*
1974	29.42
1975	29.11
1976	29.51
1977	28.21
1978	29.76
1979	29.01
1980	26.39
1981	31.48
1982	37.14
1983	36.85
1984	39.71
1985	44.14
1986	50.84
1987	53.07
1988	47.92
1989	45.44
1990	42.18
1991	45.88
1992	36.92
1993	26.87
1994	23.26
1995	24.82
1996	24.58
1997	21.96
1998	24.20

Thus, the exciting subject of international economics becomes much more relevant to India with its increasing openness and integration in the world economy.

CHAPTER 2

CHARACTERISTIC FEATURES OF INTERNATIONAL TRADE

Structure:

2.1 Definition of International Trade

2.2 Definition of Regional Trade

2.3 Distinguishing Features of International Trade

2.1 DEFINITION OF INTERNATIONAL TRADE

By the term 'trade' is meant mercantile transaction or exchange of goods and services among people or associations of people.

When exchange of goods and services take place between two individuals or firms or institutions in the same country, such trade is called 'domestic' or 'internal' trade.

When exchange of goods and services between individuals living in different countries take place, such trade is called 'international trade.' To be more specific, international trade in goods and services may take place between two individuals of different countries, or between two firms or companies, between two countries or between Governments of any two countries. Such trade transaction is called 'international trade.' Thus, under the title international trade, India may buy or sell goods and services to or from other countries, may borrow capital or lend capital to or from other countries; may buy technical services from other countries or sell such services to any country. All such trading transactions between peoples of any two countries constitute international trade.

2.2 DEFINITION OF REGIONAL TRADE[1]

In contrast to international trade is what is called or referred to by Bertil Ohlin as 'inter-regional, or 'Inter-local, or 'domestic' or 'internal' trade. The concept of inter-regional trade may be clarified here. For example, India is divided into several geographical regions such as northern region, southern region, north-eastern region and western region. Trade between or among these different regions of India is called 'inter-regional' trade, which is another name for 'internal' or 'domestic' trade.

It may be pointed out here that economists like Bertil Ohlin and G. A. Haberler hold the view that there is no fundamental difference between 'Inter-regional Trade, and 'International Trade' and if there is any difference between the two, according to them, the difference is only of degree and not of kind.

On the other hand, the classical economists like Adam Smith and David Ricardo held the view that there are some fundamental differences between inter-regional (i.e., internal or domestic) trade and international trade. And, therefore, the English Classical School provided a separate theory to explain international trade known as the theory of comparative cost advantage.

2.3 DISTINGUISHING FEATURES OF INTERNATIONAL TRADE

Following are the distinguishing features of international trade. These features may be said to distinguish international trade from domestic or internal or inter-regional trade.

(1) ***Immobility of Factors of Production:*** The classical school favoured formulation of a separate theory of international trade on the ground that while within a country factors of production like labour and capital are freely mobile as between different areas or regions of the country as also among different occupations in the country, these factors of production are immobile between countries entering into international trade.

1. Bertil Ohlin had defined the concept of 'Region' as a district or area which fulfills two essential conditions: (i) The district or the area should be different from other districts or areas in respect of the conditions that govern production of different goods and services; and (ii) the differences between parts of such district or an area should be smaller than those differences that exist between the two districts themselves. According to Bertil Ohlin, different regions are differently supplied with productive factors and hence their specialisation in the production of different goods and services which forms the basis of 'Regional Trade' as distinguished from International Trade.

This would mean that wage and interest differentials in a country produce almost immediate response from various factors of production like labour and capital which tend to move from areas of relatively low wage and interest rates to areas where they are relatively high and this movement goes on until wage rates and other factor-prices attain the same level eliminating all the differentials. This means within a country factor movements go on taking place fairly quickly until factor prices tend towards equality.

But in the case of different countries, there is no such free mobility and movement of factors of production from a country of low factor prices to a country of relatively high factor prices. This immobility of factors of production among countries is due to reasons like differences in languages, cultural and social environment, differences in customs, in climate, desire to live among family members and close friends, fear of the unknown surroundings in foreign countries, heavy travelling expenses and above all restrictions imposed by different states on the movements of labour and capital into their countries. Even a factor of production like capital is relatively immobile in regard to its movement from country to country because of legal restrictions and procedural difficulties, changing rate of foreign exchange, ignorance about investment opportunities abroad, mistrust about investments in foreign countries and tendency to invest capital in companies in the home state due to feeling of relatively greater safety and certainty about returns on such investments. While a number of legal and other restrictions are placed on the movements of labour and capital by a number of countries, there are no such problems in regard to their movements from region to region in the same country.

(2) ***Geographical and Climatic Differences and Differences in Natural Resource Endowments:*** Different countries have different climatic conditions that favour production of certain commodities and not of other commodities. For example, the climate of Bangladesh is favourable to production of raw jute, of Sri Lanka that of tea, of Brazil that of coffee, of Cuba that of sugar and so on. Because of the peculiarities of geographical and climatic conditions, no country is in a position to produce all the commodities it needs. Thus, geographical and climatic conditions favour specialisation of certain commodities and giving up production of certain other commodities.

Nature has endowed different countries with different types of natural resources. Thus the Middle East countries are rich in crude oil but lack adequate fertile agricultural lands to produce necessary food grains. Australia, on the other hand, has abundant supply of agricultural land, while England, while having abundant capital, suffers from relative scarcity of land. Each country tries to produce those commodities in the production of which factors which are abundant with them play a major role. Thus, Australia specialises in the production of agricultural commodities like wheat, wool and mutton, all of which require relatively more land, and in return of their export, import from England commodities like manufactured goods and machinery in the production of which capital plays a major role relative to land. The Middle East countries have specialised in the production of crude oil and petroleum products because of extremely favourable natural endowments in that field and in return for their exports, import from various countries all the essential supplies (including sometimes water). Thus differences in natural resources determine to a great extent the line in which each country is going to specialise and export goods and in return what commodities the country is going to import.

(3) ***Differences in Market Conditions:*** Markets in different countries of the world are separated or distinguished by differences in languages, tastes and fashions, systems of weights and

measures and so on. This is not so in the case of markets in a country. For example, right-hand driving cars manufactured in India may not be sold in the United States where there is left-hand driving; ready-made garments which Indian manufacturers make and are in a position to sell in the domestic market may be unable to sell their goods, say in South American countries where clothes of bright colour and of different fashions are generally preferred. Machinery manufactured on the basis of inches and feet may not be in demand in countries where decimal system of weights and measures is adopted.

(4) ***Different Currency Systems in Different Countries:*** While in the case of a single country like India, there is only a single currency system where Indian rupee is a legal tender which is accepted in all parts of India for trading purposes, that is not the case when international trade is involved. For goods imported from England, West Germany, France, the United States and Japan, Indians are required to make payments in terms of pound sterling, marks, francs, US dollars and yen, respectively. It should also be noted that since the abandonment of the gold standard in 1930s, rates of exchange between Indian rupee and the above foreign currencies often go on changing, creating complicated problems in the sphere of international trade. "When monetary units of different currencies are not subject to gold conversion, exchange rates may vary by much greater amounts than those under gold standard. Calculations and execution of monetary exchange transactions incidental to international trading constitute costs and risks of a kind that are not ordinarily involved in domestic trade."[2]

Another difficulty is that whereas some currencies like US dollars, marks, yen etc. are easily convertible into any other currency, there are some currencies which are not so easily convertible into other currencies which are referred to as hard currencies. This naturally creates problems in the field of international trade, especially for those countries with soft currencies (i.e., currencies which are easily available but are not easily convertible into hard currencies).

Also according to Kindleberger, different countries adopt and follow different monetary and foreign exchange policies and "It is this difference in policies rather than the existence of different national moneys which distinguishes foreign trade from domestic trade."[3]

(5) ***Higher Transfer Costs:*** Compared to local, domestic or inter-regional trade, international trade among countries involves heavier transport costs because of vast distances over which goods are to be transported.

(6) ***Different Political Systems:*** In the case of domestic or inter-regional trade, all the trading units belong to the same political unit and all the domestically trading people, though speaking different languages and differing in caste and religion, share a common sense of belonging to the same nation and common concern for the welfare of the country and its people and are prepared to make necessary adjustments in the national interest. But in the case of trade between two independent countries, the question of common loyalty does not arise and the basic idea behind international trade is to gain as much as possible from the other trading partner. In the case of international trade, a country may not at all mind, under certain circumstances, harming the other country to gain its national and political objectives. As Freidrich list pointed out in his *National System of Political Economy* published in 1841, "Domestic trade is among us, international trade is between us and them."

2. H. B. Killough and L. W. Killough, *Economics of International Trade.*
3. C. B. Kindleberger, *International Economics* (1973).

(7) ***Different International Trade Policies:*** In the case of domestic trade, the nation concerned follows a single national trade policy in respect of commerce, taxation exports, imports, tariffs and so on. There is thus a single national policy affecting domestic trade.

But in the case of international trade, participating countries may and do adopt and follow different national policies in respect of exports, imports, capital inflows and outflows, exchange control, quota fixation and putting various barriers on the movement of goods and services from one country to another. Also, in the case of international trade there may be laid down elaborate customs procedures, packing arrangements and requirements giving detailed information regarding contents of the packages all having unfavourable impact on the movement of goods from one country to another. But such discriminating restrictions do not exist in the case of internal or domestic trade. Thus, in the case of internal trade, movement of goods from one centre to another in the same country is much faster than in the case of international trade. Thus, while international trade is characterised by different national trade policies, in the case of domestic or internal trade there is just one commercial policy for the entire country.

(8) ***Problem of Balance of Payments:*** An important feature that distinguishes international trade from internal or domestic or regional trade is the problem of balance of payments that arises in the case of international trade while there is no such problem in the case of domestic trade.

The point can be illustrated with an example. A developing country like India needs, say from the United States, a number of capital goods and essential industrial raw materials. All these imports from the United States must be paid for by India's exports of goods of equal value as that of imports. But it is possible that the United States may not want to purchase goods from India to the extent that would enable India to make full payment for all the imports from the United States. India begins to face the problem of adverse balance of trade and payments *vis-à-vis* the United States. India can temporarily meet this deficit between the value of imports and of exports by borrowing from the United States. But soon the funds borrowed from the United States will have to be paid back with interest and this payment will have to be made in US dollars which India can earn only by exporting more goods to the United States. But as already noted, the United States may not want all the exports from India which India is eager to send to the United States. The deficit between India's imports from the United States and India's exports to that country may be filled by using the reserve of US dollars which India may have built in the past. But if the deficit occurs again and again, such reserves are bound to get exhausted sooner or later forcing India to borrow from the United States. Thus, with a view to correct adverse balance of trade and payments, India may be forced to adopt policies such as restricting imports from the United States (which may, however, slow down the process of her economic development) or adopt policy of devaluation or quota fixation of imports from the United States and so on. All such restrictive trade policies would raise a host of complex problems in the sphere of India's international trade. Such problems of balance of trade and payments do not arise in the case of internal or domestic trade.

On account of the above characteristics or features which distinguish international trade from internal or domestic or internal or inter-regional trade, the English classical school formulated a separate theory of comparative cost advantage to explain the phenomenon of international trade.

CHAPTER

3 THE CLASSICAL THEORY OF INTERNATIONAL TRADE

Structure:

3.1 INTRODUCTION

While studying the problems of international trade, two questions need answers: Why does or under what conditions does international trade take place? And secondly, what are the terms of trade on which international trade takes place and how do these terms of trade get determined?

The classical economists (Adam Smith and David Ricardo) held the view that international trade takes place because of differences in costs. While Adam Smith emphasised 'absolute cost differences', Ricardo demonstrated that even in the case of 'comparative cost advantage' international trade can take place to the mutual advantage of participating countries.

But both Adam Smith (1723-1790) and David Ricardo (1772-1823) based their doctrine of international trade on the labour theory of value. Later economists, the marginalists like Prof. Haberler, developed opportunity cost theory of international trade in place of labour cost theory. The marginalist school emphasised that while analysing international trade theory, labour is not the only factor of production that has to be considered but other factors of production must also be taken into consideration.

In recent years, the Swedish economists were critical of the opportunity cost theory of international trade and in its place they developed a new version of international trade known as Heckscher-Ohlin version of comparative cost.

While the classical economists explained that international trade takes place because of absolute or comparative cost advantage, they did not offer any explanation of the causes of such absolute or comparative cost advantage, or in other terms international cost differentials. It was Bertil Ohlin who argued that cost differences arise because of differences in factor endowments of different countries.

Attempt will be made in this chapter to state and critically examine the classical theory of international trade as developed by Adam Smith and Ricardo, as also contribution to the theory by another classical economist John Stuart Mill (1806-1873). After that will be explained international trade theories as expounded by Heckscher and Bertil Ohlin as also contribution made by a number of economists to the theory of international trade.

3.2 PRE-CLASSICAL THEORY OF INTERNATIONAL TRADE

Since Adam Smith, the founder of the classical school, formulated his theory of international trade to rebut the pre-classical international trade theory, knowledge of the pre-classical international trade theory would help appreciate in a better way the classical theory of international trade.

Some three hundred years before Adam Smith published his Wealth of Nations in 1776, there prevailed a system of economic thoughts commonly designated as Mercantilism. Mercantilists were essentially practical men of affairs and not theoreticians. Hence Mercantilism was not a comprehensive body of economic theory concerning various aspects of economic activities of the people but contained only practical views on them concentrating on policy measures.

The background against which Mercantilism gradually emerged must be taken into consideration, if their theory (i.e., pre-classical theory) of international trade is to be properly appreciated.

There were two significant developments taking place after the breakdown of Feudalism in Western Europe by 15th century. One was that national states had begun to emerge. England, Spain, Portugal, Germany and France were hereafter not mere geographical areas but peoples in those countries were being united by the emergence of the spirit of nationalism based on common territory of habitation, common language, common heritage and common culture and close blood-relationship. Nationalism then had two aspects. On the one hand, nationalism was a unifying force; on the other hand, nationalism led to fierce national rivalries among nations and national wars and from that point of view, nationalism was a dividing force. Thus, some three hundred years before Adam Smith there was bitter rivalry among different national states that were newly emerging. War between Spain and England and final defeat of the Spanish armada at the hands of Queen Elizabeth I would illustrate the point of national rivalry prevailing in those centuries.

The second aspect was that the agricultural, self-sufficient and non-monetary economies of the feudal age were gradually being transformed into monetary economies. Instead of barter exchanges, trading transactions started taking place with the help of money which then consisted mainly of gold and silver.

The emergence of gold and silver as money-metals acquired for the national states greater importance. If only a nation had a sufficiently big share in the world stock of gold and silver, the country could raise armies (which could now be paid in money), build navy, buy commodities that it wanted from any place in the world and thus become a politically strong nation. Thus, nationalism, national rivalries and acquisition of more gold and silver assumed great significance during the Mercantilist period. A nation's strength came to be generally measured by the stock of gold and silver which the country possessed. Thus, stock of gold and silver (i.e., precious metals) which a country possessed became the index of national strength.

There were two ways of acquiring and increasing the stock of gold and silver with a nation. One way was that if a country possessed mines of gold and silver, the government could see that the gold and silver produced in the country did not leave the borders of the country.

But what about countries like Britain, France, Germany and Spain which did not possess gold mines? It was this question which gave rise to the Mercantilist or pre-classical theory of international trade.

According to the pre-classical theory of international trade, the way to acquire gold by countries without gold mines was through the medium of international trade.

According to this theory, a country should export goods and services to the maximum possible extent and it should import from other countries as small quantities of goods and services as possible. Thus, the excess of total value of a country's exports over the total value of the country's imports would be paid in terms of gold and silver. Greater the total value of exports of a country and smaller the total value of that country's imports, larger would be the difference between the two and greater the quantity of gold the country would receive.

Thus, according to the pre-classical theory of international trade, the main objective of that trade was to acquire increasing quantities of gold and silver. According to that theory, in international trade one country (acquiring gold and silver through excess of exports over its imports) would be the gainer whereas the country losing gold would be a loser to that extent in her international trading transactions. The idea that international trade benefits both the participating countries could not be conceived by the pre-classical economists.

With a view to promote exports to the maximum possible extent and cut imports to the minimum, the Mercantilists suggested a number of measures. Development of industries should be encouraged and domestic consumption of all types of goods should be reduced to the minimum to build up exportable surplus. To develop industries, government should regulate prices of raw materials and wage rates and give other aids to domestic industries by insisting on the use of domestic products for home consumption. Government should help build and expand mercantile marine to carry goods to other countries for which service the country would get paid in gold and silver.

To cut down imports to the minimum, government should prohibit imports on non-essential goods and cut down to the minimum imports of other goods by imposing heavy import duties. The high import duties would provide protection domestic industries which could develop due to tariff protection and assured domestic markets.

Thus, according to the pre-classical theory of international trade, the main objective of trade between any two countries was to acquire gold; this could be done by exporting goods and services to the maximum possible extent and cutting down imports to the minimum, compelling the other country to pay the difference in gold and silver. In international trade the country acquiring gold gained from such trade and the country losing gold was to that extent the loser; exports were to be pushed up by regulating prices of raw materials and wage rates and compelling people to use domestically produced goods. Imports were to be reduced by prohibiting imports of some goods and reducing imports of some goods by imposing tariff duties which not only would cut down imports but also provide protection to domestic industries and help their expansion by guaranteeing them domestic markets.

According to the Mercantilists, if a country's exports exceeded her imports, the excess of exports over her imports was referred to as 'favourable balance of trade', because the country with such a favourable balance would be acquiring gold which was the main objective of international trade; if on the contrary, a country's imports exceeded her exports, then the country with excess of imports over her exports was said to have 'unfavourable balance of trade' as the country would be losing gold. These terms 'favourable balance of trade' and 'unfavourable balance of trade' introduced by the Mercantilists under the peculiar environment have continued to be in use even to this day, though the context is different.

The Mercantilist or pre-classical theory of international trade is criticised on the following grounds: Acquisition of gold is not the main objective of international trade; it would be an absurd and illogical position to lay down the policy that all countries should only export and no country should import or cut down imports to the minimum; and that in international trade the country acquiring gold gains from the trade while the country losing gold loses from such trade is to misunderstand the purpose of international trade. As we shall see, Adam Smith was extremely critical of the Mercantilist or pre-classical theory of international trade.

J.M. Keynes on Mercantilist Theory of International Trade

Though the Mercantilist or the pre-classical theory of international trade has been criticised on the above-mentioned groups, J.M. Keynes brought out the significance of this theory in the following passage which he wrote: "This ... the preoccupation on the part of the authorities with a favourable balance of trade served both purposes; and was furthermore, the only available means of promoting them. At the same time when the authorities had no direct control over domestic rate of interest or the other inducements to home investments, measures to increase the favourable balance of trade were the only direct means at their disposal for increasing investment; and at the same time, the effect of a favourable balance of trade on the influx of the precious metals was their only indirect means of reducing the domestic rate of interest and so increasing the inducement to home investment."

3.3 VIEWS OF PHYSIOCRACY ON INTERNATIONAL TRADE

About the middle of the 18th century, a group of French thinkers evolved a system of economic thought that has come to be known as Physiocracy. While in England the period of Mercantilism was followed by the English Classical School of Adam Smith and Ricardo, in the case of France, between Mercantilism and the French Classical School, there was an intervening period (roughly from 1770 to 1775) when Physiocracy dominated the French economic thinking and government's economic policies.

According to the Physiocratic thinkers, only those activities in the economic sphere were productive which produced 'material surplus.' This means that according to the Physiocrats, only agriculture was productive and all other occupations were non-productive.

According to the Physiocrats, all exchanges were unproductive. According to them "Exchange is a concept of equality, equal value being given in exchange for equal value. Consequently it (international trade) is not a means of increasing wealth, for one gives as much as the other receives." According to them, "It may, however, happen that the parties to the exchange are of unequal strength and this may result in one party gaining at the expense of the other. In giving a bottle of wine in exchange for a loaf of bread, there is double displacement of wealth, which certainly affords a fuller satisfaction of human wants in both cases; but there is no wealth created."

It is interesting to note that the Physiocrats are to be regarded as the founders of Free Trade, "not because of any desire to favour trade as such, but because their attitude towards it was one of disdainful *laissez-faire."* They probably believed that the policy of *laissez-faire* of free trade would lead to the disappearance of international trade which was essentially unproductive in the sense it produced no real wealth.

There was also another reason for their advocacy of free trade policy in the sphere of international trade. The 'Natural Order' implied that each one should be free to buy or sell wherever he chooses within or outside the country. It is only through such liberty that 'good price' would be secured by sellers. The 'good price' meant the highest price and not the lowest. Free competition with foreign merchants can alone secure the best possible price.

The fallacy lurking behind the Mercantilist policy of striving for a favourable balance of trade was fully exposed by the Physiocrats: "Suppose that I give you all the money which circulates among the nations with whom you trade. Imagine it all in your possession. What would you do with it?" The argument goes on to show how not a single foreign country will any longer be able to buy goods from the country which possesses all the money and consequently all exportation will stop. The result of this excessive dearness will be that buying from the foreign countries will be resorted to and result in the exportation of gold or metallic money.

The Physiocrats have also successfully repudiated the argument of the Mercantilists that all import duties are always paid by the foreigners. If a country wants a commodity very urgently from a foreign country and still imposes an import duty on such a commodity, an import duty on such a commodity will only increase the price which the exporter will demand and this import duty will be paid by those who purchase the commodity.

3.4 ADAM SMITH'S THEORY OF ABSOLUTE COST DIFFERENCE

Assumptions: Adam Smith based his 'Absolute Cost Advantage' theory of international trade on the following assumptions:

(1) Labour is the only factor of production; and therefore, exchange between goods was determined by the relative amounts of labour embodied in them;

(2) There is full employment in the country;

(3) Labour is mobile within the country but perfectly immobile between the countries; and

(4) The Law of Constant Returns is in operation.

On the basis of these assumptions, according to Adam Smith, exchange of goods will take place (assuming two countries and only two commodities), if each of the two countries can produce a commodity at an absolutely lower labour cost of production than the other country.

According to Adam Smith, because of climate and other natural advantages, a country should produce that commodity for which it is best fitted and exchange the surplus of that commodity for another commodity which the country finds it costlier to produce. According to Adam Smith, division of labour and specialisation at the international level requires 'absolute' difference in costs. In this connection Adam Smith wrote: "Whether the advantage which one country has over another be natural or acquired is in this respect of no consequence."

The following example illustrates the case of absolute difference in costs as the basis of international trade:

Let us assume that X number of mandays can produce:

In England: 100 units of cloth or 50 units of wheat; and

In Australia: 50 units of cloth or 100 units of wheat.

In the above illustration, England enjoys absolute cost advantage in the production of cloth.

And, therefore, Adam Smith maintained that England should specialize in the production of cloth and Australia in the production of wheat. Both the countries would gain by this specialisation in cloth and wheat by England and Australia, respectively and by exchanging their products. International trade, thus, provides scope for international division of labour and specialisation whereby production increases and it also provides vent for surplus — England can exchange her surplus of cloth for Australian wheat and Australia in turn can exchange her surplus of wheat for English cloth.

From the above illustration, it is clear that to produce one unit of wheat, England will have to sacrifice 2 units of cloth. And, therefore, England will be ready to get in exchange for her one unit of cloth anything above ½ unit of wheat.

On the other hand, from the above illustration, it is clear that to produce one unit of cloth, Australia will have to sacrifice 2 units of wheat. This means, Australia will be ready to give anything up to 2 units of wheat for one unit of cloth from England.

Thus, England for 1 unit of cloth wants in exchange anything above ½ unit of wheat, and Australia is prepared to give for 1 unit of English cloth anything up to 2 units of wheat. And, therefore, international trade between England and Australia would be possible and both the countries will gain by specialising in the production of that commodity in which she has absolute cost advantage over the other country, as in the above illustration England having absolute cost advantage over Australia in the production of cloth, and Australia absolute advantage over England in the production of wheat.

3.5 DAVID RICARDO'S THEORY OF COMPARATIVE COST ADVANTAGE

According to Ricardo, it is not the absolute cost advantage but comparative cost advantage that forms the basis of international trade between any two countries. Comparative cost advantage may arise due to geographical or natural advantages and specialisation of production on that basis. Thus due to the advantage of geographical situation or efficiency of labour, a country may have greater advantage in the production of one commodity than in the production of the other commodity. According to Ricardo, each country should specialise in the production on that commodity in which she has the greatest comparative advantage or the least comparative disadvantage.

The above Ricardian principle can be illustrated with the following example:

Let us assume that X number of mandays can produce:

In England, either 200 units of cloth or 200 units of wheat, and in Australia, either 80 units of cloth or 160 units of wheat.

It is clear from the above illustration that England has absolute cost advantage over Australia in the production of both the commodities, namely, cloth and wheat; and Australia has absolute cost disadvantage *vis-à-vis* England in the production of both cloth and wheat (as is clear from the figures, namely, X number of mandays can produce in England 200 units of cloth or 200 units of wheat as compared to 80 units of cloth and 160 units of wheat in Australia).

Under such circumstances, according to Ricardo, the rule is that England should specialise in the production of that commodity where she has the greatest comparative cost advantage; and in the case of Australia, though she is at absolute disadvantage *vis-à-vis* England in the production of both cloth and wheat, it would be beneficial from the point of view of both England and Australia, that Australia should specialise in the production of that commodity where her comparative cost disadvantage is the least. In such circumstances, England should specialise in the production of cloth (200:80) where her comparative cost advantage over Australia is the greatest; and Australia should specialise in the production of wheat because, though she is at an absolute disadvantage *vis-à-vis* England in the production of both cloth and wheat, Australia's cost disadvantage is the least in the production of wheat (200:160) compared to cloth (200:80).

In England X number of mandays can produce either 200 units of cloth or 200 units of wheat. This means, in exchange of 1 unit of cloth, England would be prepared to accept anything above 1 unit of cloth, England would be prepared to accept anything above 1 unit of wheat (but not less, because by sacrificing 1 unit of cloth, England herself can produce 1 unit of wheat in her own country).

On the other hand in Australia, since X number of mandays can produce either 80 units of cloth or 160 units of wheat, it follows that in order to get 1 unit of cloth from England, Australia would be willing to give in exchange anything up to 2 units of wheat, she can offer upto 2 units of wheat (but not more because by sacrificing 2 units of wheat, Australia herself can produce 1 unit of cloth in the country).

Thus, for 1 unit of her cloth England wants in exchange at least something more than 1 unit of wheat, whereas Australia to get 1 unit of cloth from England is willing to give in exchange anything up to 2 units of her wheat. From this it follows that international trade between England and Australia can take place and that it will be to the advantage of both the countries.[1]

3.6 ASSUMPTIONS OF THE CLASSICAL (RICARDIAN) THEORY OF INTERNATIONAL TRADE

The classical or the Ricardian theory of international trade is strictly based on the following assumptions:

(a) There are only two countries;

(b) There are only two commodities which those two countries can produce;

(c) Labour is the only factor of production involved in the production of those two commodities;

(d) All the units of labour are homogenous (which means any one worker is a perfect substitute for any other worker);

(e) There is perfect competition in labour and product markets;

(f) There is supposed to be full employment in both the countries (which implies that an additional unit of a commodity can be produced only by sacrificing something of the other commodity);

(g) Labour is perfectly mobile within the country but is perfectly immobile between the two countries;

(h) The law of constant returns is operating in both countries (which means application of a given input will always produce the same amount of output);

(i) No technological changes take place in both the countries;

(j) There are no transport costs in moving goods from one country to the other; and

(k) There is freedom of trade which means international trade between the two countries is free from governmental intervention and regulation of any type.

---

1. There is the possibility of 'Equal Cost Differences.' For example, in the case of England, X number of mandays, let us assume, can produce either 200 units of cloth or 200 units of wheat. In the case of Australia, let us assume that X number of mandays can produce either 100 units of cloth or 100 units of wheat. Let us suppose that England specialises in the production of cloth and Australia in the production of wheat.

In England 1 unit of wheat can be produced by sacrificing 1 unit of cloth. This means that England in exchange of 1 unit of cloth wants at least something more than 1 unit of wheat. But Australia will not be ready to give more than 1 unit of wheat in exchange of 1 unit of cloth, because by sacrificing 1 unit of wheat, Australia herself can produce 1 unit of cloth. Thus for 1 unit of cloth England wants something more than 1 unit of wheat, whereas Australia is not prepared to give anything more than 1 unit of wheat in exchange of 1 unit of English cloth. And, therefore, in the event of 'Equal Cost Difference', international division of labour or specialisation and, hence, international trade will not take place. It is only in the case of 'Absolute Cost Advantage' and 'Comparative Cost Advantage' that international specialisation and international trade will take place.

3.7 CRITICISM OF THE CLASSICAL (RICARDIAN) THEORY OF INTERNATIONAL TRADE

The classical (Ricardian) theory of international trade, though accepted for long as the valid basis of international trade, has come to be subjected to severe criticism by economists like Bertil Ohlin and Graham. According to them, the main point of criticism is the extremely unrealistic and restrictive assumptions which for all practical purposes render the theory of little theoretical and practical use of significance.

Following are the main points of criticism:

(1) The first assumption of the classical theory, namely, existence of the only two countries and only two commodities is highly unrealistic. In fact, there are more than 150 countries and thousands of commodities. Under such circumstances, calculations of comparative cost advantage will not be as simple as in the above illustration of two-country, two commodity model. With hundreds of countries and thousands of commodities involved, calculations of even approximately accurate comparative cost differentials would be practically impossible. The classical theory of international trade would, therefore, be of very little practical use in the real world.

(2) The classical theory has assumed labour as the only factor of production and the labour theory of value according to which values of commodities are determined by labour embodied in them. In fact, there are other factors of production like land, capital and organization which along with labour go to determine cost of production of commodities and, therefore, the rate of exchange between any two commodities. The classical theory has not taken note of the part played by capital and organization in the process of production of commodities in determining their exchange rates.

(3) The classical theory assumed that all units of labour are homogeneous and one worker can be perfect substitute for any other worker. This is a highly unrealistic assumption. Some workers are more efficient and labour is not perfectly homogeneous as assumed in the classical theory. Labour efficiency may be different and one worker in country A may produce twice that of a worker in country B. The classical theory has, therefore, made an unrealistic assumption regarding homogeneous nature of all labour.

(4) The classical theory assumed full employment of labour in both the participating countries. But, in fact, there might be a certain amount of unemployment in both the countries. This means in England, in addition to cloth, certain amount of wheat may also be produced with the help of labour that was lying unemployed. The same would be true of Australia in our above illustration.

(5) The classical theory made another unrealistic assumption, namely, labour is perfectly mobile within a country and perfectly immobile between any two countries. There can be two objections to this assumption. For example, in England some labour may be specific and can produce only wheat and not cloth; and similarly, in Australia there might be some workers who can produce only cloth and not wheat. And therefore, the position in England is not either cloth or wheat but it can be cloth plus some wheat; and similarly in Australia, the position would be wheat plus some cloth. Thus, labour in both the countries being to some extent occupationally immobile, the assumption of cloth or wheat in England and wheat or cloth in Australia is

unrealistic. That is why we find countries always producing some quantity of a commodity which that country also imports in substantial quantity. The second criticism that labour is perfectly mobile within a country but perfectly immobile between any two countries is also unrealistic. A large number of workers have migrated from England to Australia and from Australia to England, thus falsifying the classical assumption in this respect. There is, at present, increasing migration of labour within the EEC countries.

(6) The classical theory of international trade assumed that in the case of cloth industry in England and in the case of wheat production in Australia, it is the law of constant returns that operates. But there is always the possibility that in England the law of constant returns is not always operating and there might come into operation the law of increasing or decreasing returns. The consequence of this would be that in England the production cost of a unit of cloth in terms of wheat and in Australia production cost of wheat in terms of cloth will go on changing, depending upon whether the law of increasing returns or decreasing returns is in operation in those countries. Finally, a state may be reached in which in England production cost of cloth in terms of wheat and in Australia production cost of wheat in terms of cloth would be such as not to allow any more benefit from international trade between England and Australia. The classical school assuming that the law of constant returns will always be operating in both the countries did not take this possibility into consideration rendering its theory unrealistic and unsatisfactory.

(7) The classical theory makes another assumption that no technological changes would be taking place. But it so happened that during the past century and especially in the second half of the 20th century extremely rapid technological changes have been taking place. Thus, in England with the help of high-breed seeds and chemical fertilizers wheat may come to be produced comparatively more cheaply than in Australia where technological changes may be slow; it is also possible that due to technological changes in Australia and adoption of automatic looms, cost of production of cloth in Australia may be much cheaper than in England. This means that the classical theory was static.

(8) The assumption that no transport costs are involved in international movements of goods is highly unrealistic. In fact heavy transport costs play an important role in determining the pattern of international trade and exchange of goods. Thus, because water transport was cheaper than land transport for quite some time, textile mills in Mumbai used to get their coal from England instead of from Bihar coal-mines in the country.

(9) The classical theory makes another unrealistic assumption that there will be free international trade which will not be facing any governmental barriers to such trade. The fact is that for centuries international trade barriers such as total prohibition of import of some commodities and of export of some items, heavy import duties, export subsidies, quota fixation, etc. have been in operation and continue to do so even at present. This limits the practical use of the classical theory of international trade.

(10) The classical theory appears to have laid emphasis only on the supply side of goods and on their cost of production. As Bertil Ohlin has pointed out, "It is indeed nothing more than an abbreveated account of the conditions of supply." The unstated classical assumption appears to be that demand for each other's commodity would be of equal intensity and there will not be any changes in the elasticity of demand for each other's commodity.

But the assumption is unrealistic because elasticity of demand for each other's commodity depends on so many factors that there is likely to be change of different degrees in elasticity of demand for each other's commodity.

(11) Frank Graham has pointed out that complete specialisation on the basis of comparative cost advantage is impossible, if one of the two trading countries is small and the other a big one. The smaller country will be in a position to completely specialise and dispose of its surplus commodity in the bigger country; but if the bigger country completely specialises in the production of one commodity on the basis of comparative cost advantage, it will not be in a position to dispose of all its surplus production in the small country.

(12) The classical theory will not hold good, if any country does not want to import any essential commodity (like arms and defence goods) from other country due to strategic reason or due to political considerations. For achieving self-reliance in defence goods, most countries try to produce defence goods, though comparative cost difference is against such production.

(13) The classical theory of international trade based as it is on labour theory of value fails to take into account time-element for storage which gives rise to interest. This makes the theory unrealistic as the classical theory excludes interest from cost of production.

(14) The classical theory is based on the implicit assumption that imports and exports of the two trading countries will exactly balance each other and there will be no deficit or surplus in the balance of trade. The theory thus ignores the important issue of capital inflows and outflows which are of vital importance to small as well as big trading countries.

(15) According to the classical theory, the gains from international trade would be to the country as a whole. But Sodersten has pointed out that gains from international trade to a country do not necessarily mean that all citizens gain from that trade. It is quite likely that while some citizens become better off because of international trade, some others may not get the benefit at all or may even suffer on account of such trade.

Concluding Remarks

The classical two-country-two-commodity model with labour alone as a factor of production and with law of constant returns in operation and assumption of labour immobility and of free trade appears to be a very simple model to satisfactorily explain the complex phenomenon of international trade which is influenced by far too many variables in the real world.

And yet the basic structure of the classical theory of comparative cost advantage appears to have remained intact. As Prof. Samuelson has pointed out, "Yet for all its simplifications, the theory of comparative advantage has in it the most important glimpse of truth. Political economy has found few more pregnant principles. A nation that neglects comparative advantage may have to pay a heavy price in terms of lowering standards and potential rate of growth."

3.8 J.S. MILL'S THEORY OF RECIPROCAL DEMAND

David Ricardo formulated his theory of international trade in terms of comparative cost advantage. But Ricardo did not pay attention to the ratio or rate at which one commodity would exchange for the other commodity (in our illustration a unit of cloth against how many units of wheat and *vice versa*).

Ricardo failed to pay adequate attention to rate of exchange of the two commodities, because of the manner in which he explained the principle of comparative cost advantage. Ricardo took in his illustration the total quantity of English cloth exchanged against the total quantity of Australian wheat (45 units of English cloth against 60 units of Australian wheat) and, therefore, failed to pay attention to the problem of terms of trade and the factors that determine terms of trade.

Ricardo's Illustration:

X number of mandays produce:

In English 200 units of cloth or 200 units of wheat, and

In Australia 80 units of cloth or 160 units of wheat.

Ricardo explained that though England enjoyed absolute cost advantage over Australia in the production of both cloth and wheat, England's comparative advantage was greater in respect of cloth than in the case of wheat, as is clear from the following ratios:

	England		*Australia*
Cloth	200	:	80
Wheat	200	:	160

Ricardo concluded that England should specialise in the production of that commodity where her comparative cost advantage is the highest. Though Australia is at a disadvantage compared to England in the production of both cloth and wheat, Australia's disadvantage is the least in the case of wheat. And, therefore, Ricardo concluded that Australia should specialise in the production of the commodity where her disadvantage is the least.

In England X number of mandays can produce either 200 units of cloth or 200 units of wheat. This means by sacrificing one unit of cloth, England in her own country can produce one unit of wheat. Similarly X number of mandays can produce in Australia either 80 units of cloth or 160 units of wheat. That means Australia by sacrificing two units of wheat can in her own country produce one unit of cloth.

Let us now assume that with X number of mandays at their disposal, both England and Australia want to be self-sufficient and, therefore, they produce both the commodities in the following way:

England: 150 units of cloth 50 units of wheat, and

Australia: 40 units of cloth 80 units of wheat.

Now let us assume that England specialises in cloth and Australia in the production of wheat. X number of mandays will produce in England 200 units of cloth and in Australia 160 units of wheat.

Then Ricardo proceeded to assume that both England and Australia specialise in the production of cloth and wheat, respectively, so that England with X number of mandays produces 200 units of cloth and Australia with X number of mandays produces 160 units of wheat and international trade takes place between the two countries. Ricardo says, let us assume that England exchanges 45 units of cloth in exchange for 60 units of Australian wheat.

Exchanging 45 units of English cloth for 60 units of Australian wheat is an advantageous position for both England and Australia. This is so because England for one unit of cloth is getting something more than one unit of wheat (in fact England is getting for 1 unit of her cloth $1^1/_3$ units of Australian wheat).

After specialising, England in cloth and Australia in wheat and after exchanging 45 units of English cloth in exchange of 60 units of Australian wheat, the position of England and Australia will be:

England: 155 units of cloth 60 units of wheat, and

Australia: 45 units of cloth 100 units of wheat.

If this position is compared with the position when with X number of mandays England tried to be self-sufficient with 150 units of cloth and 50 units of wheat and Australia with X number of mandays and trying to be self-sufficient producing 40 units of cloth and 80 units of wheat, it will be noticed that England by specialising in cloth and Australia in wheat and by exchanging 45 units of English cloth in exchange of 60 units of Australian wheat, both England and Australia are better off as a result of specialisation and international trade than when they tried to be self-sufficient, each with X number of mandays at their disposal.

While formulating international trade theory on the basis of comparative cost advantage, Ricardo did not explain the terms of trade or the rate of exchange at which the two countries would exchange their goods. Ricardo thus failed to explain the phenomenon of terms of trade and factors that influence those terms of trade between the two participating countries.

The credit for discussing the problem of terms of trade in terms of reciprocal demand goes to John Stuart Mill (1806-1873).

From Ricardo's illustration, namely, X number of mandays in England producing either 200 units of cloth or 200 units of wheat and X number of mandays producing in Australia either 80 units of cloth or 160 units of wheat, it follows that England for her 1 unit of cloth wants from Australia a little above 1 unit of wheat, whereas Australia to get 1 unit of cloth from England is ready to give in exchange anything up to 2 units of wheat. Thus, the lower most and the upper most limits of terms of trade come to be fixed by the comparative cost difference.

Between the lower most and the upper most limits, where exactly would the terms of trade lie at any particular time? It is here that J.S. Mill comes into the picture as he drew attention to the problem of terms of trade and factors that would determine the actual terms of trade.

In modern terms the term of trade or the rate of exchange between cloth and wheat will be determined (between the above lower most and the upper most limits) on the basis of England's elasticity of demand for English cloth. J.S. Mill used the phrase 'reciprocal demand' to explain the determination of terms of trade. According to J.S. Mill, reciprocal demand explains "the determination of the equilibrium terms of trade." Reciprocal demand indicates urgency or elasticity of demand for Australian wheat and what England is prepared to give in terms of cloth in exchange of 1 unit of Australian wheat and *vice versa*.

In general terms 'reciprocal demand' explains a country's demand for a commodity in terms of quantity of the commodity it is ready to give in exchange. According to J.S. Mill, it is the reciprocal demand that will determine the terms of trade and it is these terms that will explain whose gains (e.g.,

England's or Australia's) will be relatively greater from international trade (i.e., from international exchange of goods). According to J.S. Mill, "Equilibrium would be established at that rate of exchange (i.e., terms of trade) between the two commodities at which quantities demanded by each country would be sufficient to pay for the other." In other terms, reciprocal demand will establish equilibrium rate of exchange at that level at which exports of each country would be exactly sufficient to pay for her imports. According to J.S. Mill, reciprocal demand would establish the equilibrium rate of exchange that would result in each country importing from the other country such quantity that export of each country would be sufficient to pay for the imports by each country.[2]

In the case of J.S. Mill's reciprocal demand theory, the terms of trade refer to 'barter terms of trade' between the two countries (i.e., the number of units of cloth which England would give in exchange of 1 unit of Australian wheat and *vice versa*); and as already stated, according to J.S. Mill "... the limits to the possible barter terms of trade are set by the domestic exchange ratio set by the relative efficiency of labour in each country."

J.S. Mill has summarised his theory of reciprocal demand as follows: "(1)... the possible range of barter terms is given by the respective domestic terms of trade as set by comparative efficiency in each country; (2) within this range, the actual terms of trade depend on intensity of each country's demand for the other country's produce, and (3) finally, only those barter terms of trade will be stable at which the exports offered by each country just suffice to pay for the imports it desires."

Criticism of Mill's Theory of Reciprocal Demand

J. S. Mill's theory of reciprocal demand has made all the assumptions which Ricardian theory of comparative cost has done. And, therefore, J.S. Mill's theory of reciprocal demand suffers from the same defects or points of criticism as Ricardian theory of comparative cost does.

This theory is explained further by Marshall Edgeworth.

2. J. S. Mill's Theory of Reciprocal Demand has also made a number of assumptions such as existence of only two countries and only two commodities, operation of the law of constant returns, absence of transport costs, perfect competition in the market and existence of freedom of trade, etc.

APPENDIX A

Causes of Cost-Differences

As already observed international trade takes place because of either absolute cost difference (as stated by Adam Smith) or comparative cost difference or advantage (as emphasised by David Ricardo).

The question that arises is why do these absolute or comparative cost differences arise?

Following are the important reasons for the emergence of cost differences which give rise to or form the basis of international trade:

(1) Provision of special facilities by Nature such as:

(a) Specific climate and nature of soil may favour cultivation of some crops like tea, rubber, jute, etc.

(b) There might be uneven distribution of mineral resources (e.g., petroleum in the Middle East countries, coals and iron only in some parts of the world and not in others.)

(c) Differences in land fertility due to factors like availability of water, nature of the soil (e.g., desert lands, black cotton soil, etc.), nature of rainfall, etc.

(2) Differences in human faculties may form the basis of international trade. The human faculties may differ from country to country because some races may have great physical and mental vitality (as for example people in cold region or European climate compared to tropical climate where due to extreme heat people mature early and die early and generally lack physical and mental vigour of people in cold climate).

Some people may by tradition or because of the impact of religion or circumstances be scientific and rational minded more than some other people or races. In some countries political and social structure is such that it promotes and encourages development of enterprise and spirit of adventure and risk-taking while in other countries the socio-political structure encourages indifference, lethargy, traditionalism and fatalism.

(3) Legacy of the past, especially in the intellectual field, plays a vital role. Some people have rich tradition in educational and scientific fields while other people lack such traditions or have traditions that hamper economic progress. In England past several generations have left great legacy in roads, railways, organisational abilities, entrepreneurial capabilities while in the case of some other countries (e.g., tribals in African countries) such traditions and such legacy may be lacking.

(4) Uneven distribution of population may also provide basis of comparative cost differences. In some countries labour may be plentiful while in some other countries labour may be relatively scarce and this may provide basis of comparative cost differences.

APPENDIX B

Bertil Ohlin's Criticism of the Classical School's Insistence on a Separate Theory of International Trade

Bertil Ohlin holds the view that there is, in fact, little difference between inter-regional trade and international trade. According to him, "International trade is but a special case of inter-local or inter-regional trade." He, therefore, maintains that there is no necessity or case to have a separate theory of international trade. Bertil Ohlin has put forward the following arguments to justify his view:

(1) According to Bertil Ohlin, it is not correct to say that labour and capital are perfectly mobile within a country but are perfectly immobile between or among countries. According to him, the fact is that even within a country, labour and capital are immobile to a certain extent. This is clear from the fact that wage rates differ not only in different parts of the same country but also within different firms in an industry even in the same area or region. This means that it is only a question of difference of degree of immobility of labour and capital within a country and between two or among many countries.

(2) Ohlin has also pointed out that labour and capital are not perfectly immobile between countries as the English Classical School assumed. For example, labour and capital moved relatively freely during the 19th and early part of the 20th century to help bring about economic development of countries like the United States, Australia, New Zealand, Canada, etc. Even at present labour has been moving fairly easily among the countries of the European Economic Community as also capital in response to changes even in the short-term rates of interest. Also, vast amount of capital has been flowing from developed to developing countries in Asia, Africa and Latin America, both on private account and through international monetary institutions, to help the developing countries to bring about their rapid economic development

(3) In both inter-regional (i.e., internal or domestic trade), and international trade, space factor is important and if there is any difference that is only a difference of degree. In both the cases, it is observed that goods move from regions where they are in plentiful to regions where they are relatively scarce. In both the cases, transport costs are involved, though their relative importance may differ in degree. In the case of both inter-regional and international trade, the main motive in trading transactions is the same, namely, maximisation of profits.

(4) As regards the existence of different currency systems through which international trade has to be carried on, according to Bertil Ohlin, since rate of conversion of one currency into another is based generally on their respective purchasing power, and since one currency is convertible into another, existence of different currency systems may be raising some problems regarding conversion of one currency into another. But that cannot be a reason to justify a totally separate theory of international trade.

(5) According to Ohlin, according to the theory of comparative cost advantage, countries specialise in the production of those commodities in which the country has a relatively greater advantage. Ohlin maintains that this principle applies not just to international trade but it also applies to internal or domestic trade.

All trade, internal or international is based on the basic principle of division of labour or specialisation, which means that there is no fundamental differences between internal and international trade; and, therefore, there is no necessity of a separate theory of internal trade.

Elaborating this point, Bertil Ohlin writes: "Regions and nations specialise and trade with each other for the same reasons that individuals specialise and trade. Some are better fitted by temperament for one work rather than another; one is better gardener, the other a better teacher, while the third proves an excellent doctor. The gardener would prove a poor teacher and teacher a poor doctor and so on. Thus, the gain from specialisation is clear. Even if every individual were equally alike in ability it would pay to specialise. This basic or fundamental principle which applies to all spheres of human activity and to all walks of life, applies exactly in the same way to the sphere of international trade. And, therefore, Ohlin writes that special formulation of the principle of comparative cost or advantage in the case of international trade is unnecessary. Bertil Ohlin concludes: "As nations are certainly the most significant of all regions... theory of international trade represents the chief application of the general theory of inter-regional trade." Ohlin, therefore, holds the view that international trade is a special case of inter-local or inter-regional trade and, therefore, there is no need of a separate theory of international trade as was thought by the classical school. According to Ohlin, prices of internationally traded goods are determined in the same way as prices of goods traded inter-regionally. The basic determinant of prices of goods traded inter-regionally is the general equilibrium of demand and supply of goods and the same principle of equilibrium is applicable in the case of internationally traded goods without substantial or basic changes.

Differences in currency system, in languages, habits and tastes and commercial policies are all differences of degree and not of kind and, therefore, they do not fundamentally affect exports and imports of goods among countries and international flow of goods. On these grounds, Bertil Ohlin opines that there is no need for a separate theory of international trade.

Criticism of Bertil Ohlin's View

Many economists do not agree with the above view of Bertil Ohlin that there is no basic difference between inter-regional (i.e., domestic or internal) trade and international trade. According to critics, there are sharp differences between the two.

Each country has its own national currency and people can buy and sell goods and services in the country without any hindrance in so far as the national currency is concerned.

In the case of international trade, payments have to be made for imported goods in foreign currencies. Often it is difficult to obtain some foreign currencies because those countries do not find any need to purchase goods from the country concerned. Such currencies are called hard currencies. In the case of such hard currencies the problem is how to acquire them while in the case of soft currencies while they are easily available in plenty, they are generally not convertible into hard currencies. In respect of different currencies, problems arise because of frequently fluctuating rates of exchange with disturbing effects on export earnings and prices of imported goods with vast implications for the entire economy of the country. In respect of different foreign currencies, problems arise because of the policy of devaluation or appreciation and above all the problem of attaining the position of equilibrium in the balance of payments of the country. These are all complicated problems which do not find place in domestic or internal or inter-regional trade but predominate the sphere of international trade. And, therefore, the critics of Bertil Ohlin maintain that the problems of international trade are basically different from those of domestic or internal or inter-regional trade and, therefore, should be dealt with separately.

Also in the case of international trade problems arise due to tariffs, import duties, export subsidies by some countries, and dumping, etc. But such problems do not arise in the case of domestic or internal trade. In order to deal successfully with these problems created by such trade barriers, international institutions like the World Bank, the International Monetary Fund, GATT, the UNCTAD, etc. have been established and have been functioning. Their concern is to try to remove such barriers to international trade. These bodies or institutions have hardly anything to do directly with internal or domestic trade. The problems and policies of these international institutions have to be and must be studied separately as part of international trade theory and policies.

More importantly, international trade is trade among politically sovereign nations which evolve, adopt and follow international trade policies with necessary changes in them from time to time. These policies create various problems of adjustment on the domestic as well as on the international front so as to attain both internal and external balance. All these considerations need a separate study of international trade.

On account of the above reasons, Prof. C.P. Kindleberger has observed: "International trade is treated as a distinct subject because of tradition, because of the urgent and important problems presented by international economic questions in the world, because it follows different laws from domestic trade, and because its study illustrates and enriches our understanding of economics as a whole."

And, therefore, it may be concluded that both on theoretical as also on practical grounds there is a necessity of a separate theory and study of international trade.

CHAPTER

4 HABERLER'S OPPORTUNITY COST THEORY OF INTERNATIONAL TRADE

Structure:

4.1 Introduction

4.2 Statement of Haberler's Theory of Opportunity Cost

4.3 Critical Assessment of Haberler's Opportunity Cost Theory

4.1 INTRODUCTION

Ricardo's comparative cost theory of international trade had many shortcomings. Of them, one important defect to Ricardo's theory was that his theory was based on the labour theory value. Thus, Ricardo's theory of international trade assumed that labour is the only factor of production, that all labour units are homogenous, and that value of a commodity is determined by the amount of labour embodied in the commodity.

As has already been pointed out, all the assumptions of Ricardian theory were unrealistic. Thus, labour is not the only factor of production; but labour produces goods in combination with other factors of production like land and capital; it is not true that all labour is homogeneous; in fact efficiency of labour differs from worker to worker; this means that one worker cannot take the place of any other worker and act as a perfect substitute for any other worker. In fact, labour comes to be divided into non-competing groups; and lastly, labour can be used in different proportions in combination with capital to produce the same amount of goods; in fact to a great extent labour and capital can act as substitutes for each other. Prof. Haberler's opportunity cost theory of international trade makes an attempt to overcome the shortcomings of the Ricardian theory of international trade.

4.2 STATEMENT OF HABERLER'S THEORY OF OPPORTUNITY COST

The opportunity cost theory of Haberler states that if a given amount of factors of production (say a given combination of land, labour and capital) can produce either 1 unit of commodity X or 1 unit of commodity Y, then the opportunity cost of 1 unit of commodity X is the sacrifice of 1 unit of commodity Y which could have been produced by the same combination of factors of production. Thus, the rate of exchange between commodities is expressed in terms of the opportunity forgone of producing with the same combination of factors or units of another commodity.[1]

The production possibility curve or substitution curve or transformation curve shows the various alternative combinations of commodities that can be produced in a country by fully utilising its factors of production under the given technological conditions. The slope of the production possibility curve or substitution curve or transformation curve shows the amount of one commodity, the production of which must be foregone in order to get an additional unit of another commodity. The slope of the production possibility curve or transformation or substitution curve indicates the marginal rate of transformation or substitution.

The slope of the production or substitution curve would be different under different cost conditions, namely, constant returns, increasing returns and decreasing returns. This means in order to get one unit of commodity X, the amount of commodity Y to be given up in exchange remains the same throughout, or the amount of commodity Y to be given up for getting one unit of commodity X would go on decreasing, if the law of increasing returns is operating in the production of commodity Y; and more of the commodity Y will have to be given up to get one unit of commodity X, if in the country producing commodity Y the law of diminishing returns is operating. This means the slope of the production possibility curve or of substitution or transformation curve would determine the basis of gains from international trade between any two trading countries.

1. The opportunity cost concept is also expressed in terms of 'Substitution Curve', or in terms of 'Samuelson's Production Possibility Curve' or what Lemer calls 'Production Indifference Curve' or "Transformation Curve."

(Haberler while stating his opportunity cost theory of international trade has made practically the same assumptions that were made in the case of the Ricardian theory of comparative cost advantage –namely, existence of only two countries, only two commodities, perfect mobility of factors of production within a country and perfect immobility of factors between two countries, full employment of factors of production in the two countries, no change in technology and full freedom in the field of international trade without any trade or other barriers).

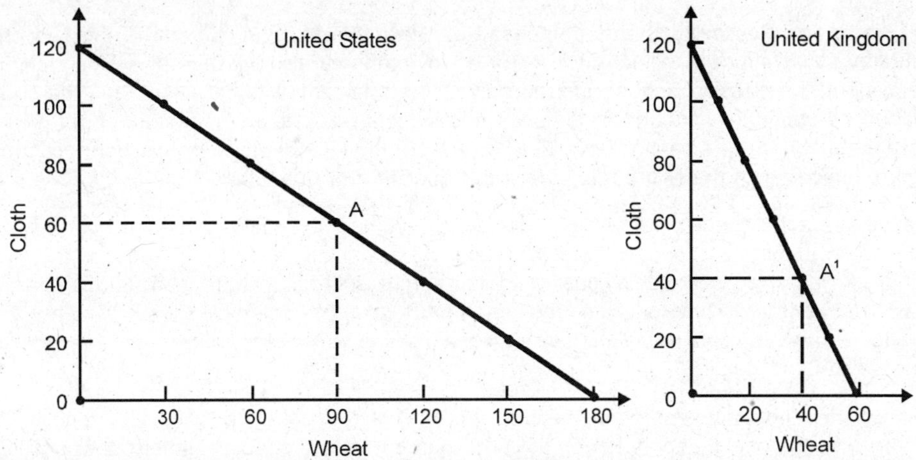

Fig. 4.1 The Production Possibility Frontiers of the United States and the United Kingdom. The U.S. and U.K. production frontiers are obtained by plotting the values. The frontiers are downward, or negatively sloped, indicating that as each nation produces more wheat, it must give up some cloth. Straight-line production possibility frontiers reflect constant opportunity costs.

4.3 CRITICAL ASSESSMENT OF HABERLER'S OPPORTUNITY COST THEORY

It would be observed that Haberler's theory of opportunity cost has made practically all the assumptions which Ricardo's theory of comparative cost advantage has made. And, therefore, all the criticism that is made against the Ricardian theory also applies to Haberler's opportunity cost theory. Is not Ricardian illustration that X number of mandays can produce in England either 200 units of cloth or 200 units of wheat in Australia either 80 units of cloth or 160 units of wheat indirectly expressing production possibilities or substitution or transformation possibilities? Only the language is different.

The only superiority of Haberler's theory is that along with labour, he has taken into consideration other factors of production, namely, capital. Also instead of only assuming law of constant returns, Haberler has introduced the operation of the law of increasing returns and decreasing returns.

The opportunity cost theory of Haberler is superior to the classical theory of comparative cost advantage, because Haberler's theory has dispensed with the unrealistic assumption of labour theory of value as also the classical assumption of constant returns. The opportunity cost theory has analysed pre-trade and post-trade conditions under constant as well as increasing and decreasing opportunity cost. This proves the superiority of the opportunity cost theory as an analytical tool in the field of international trade.

Samuelson commenting on the opportunity cost theory writes: "... the opportunity cost approach is more fertile because it can be readily extended into a general equilibrium system."

APPENDIX

Haberler's Opportunity Cost Doctrine of International Trade

Haberler's opportunity cost doctrine of international trade shows how much of one commodity will have to be sacrificed in order to get one additional unit of another commodity.

This point can be made clear by considering the possibility of producing both the commodities which a country is capable of producing.

The 'Production Possibility Curve' demonstrates the different combinations of the two commodities which a country can produce with the given factor endowment, as also with the given technology. While by factor endowment, the classical school referred only to the total labour force available in the country, in the case of Haberler's opportunity cost doctrine, factor endowment refers to all the factors of production (namely, land, labour, capital and organisation) available in the country. Technology in this connection means the input-output coefficients of the two commodities assumed in the illustration.

Because the factor endowment of the countries is assumed to remain unchanged and full employment is assumed it follows that in respect of the two commodities, namely, X and Y, increase in the production of the commodity X can take place only by sacrificing some units of the commodity Y. The ratio of the quantity of Y to be sacrificed in order to have a given increase in production of commodity X is known as 'The Marginal Rate of Product Transformation' (MRPT). (It also means that the MRPT is the ratio of the marginal costs of the two commodities X and Y).

The production possibility curve may take the slope of a (i) straight line, or (ii) be concave to the origin, or (iii) be convex to the origin, depending on whether the country is producing under condition of (i) constant costs, (ii) increasing costs, or (iii) decreasing costs.

The three situations in respect of the two commodities, namely, bread and cloth have been shown in the following graphs.

If a country can produce both the commodities, namely, Bread and Cloth, under conditions of constant costs, the country can produce one additional unit of bread by sacrificing one unit of cloth, through all the possible range of production and this is true of production of additional unit of bread also (see Fig. 4.2).

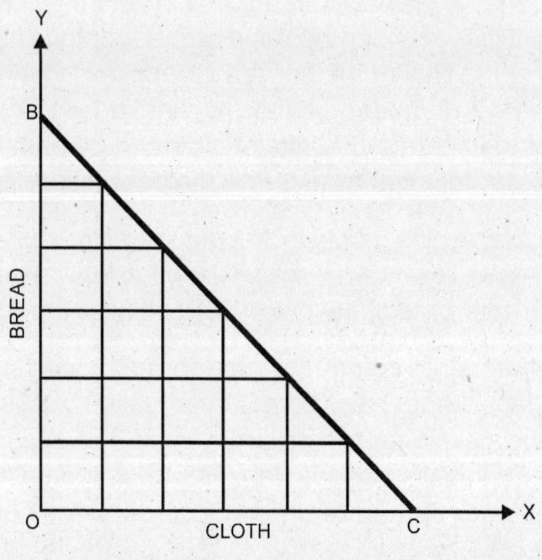

Fig. 4. 2 Production Possibility Curve Under Constant Costs

Production Possibility Curves or Opportunity Cost Curves

From Fig. 4.3 it would be clear that the country can produce additional units of Bread only by sacrificing increasing quantities of Cloth for every additional unit of Bread.

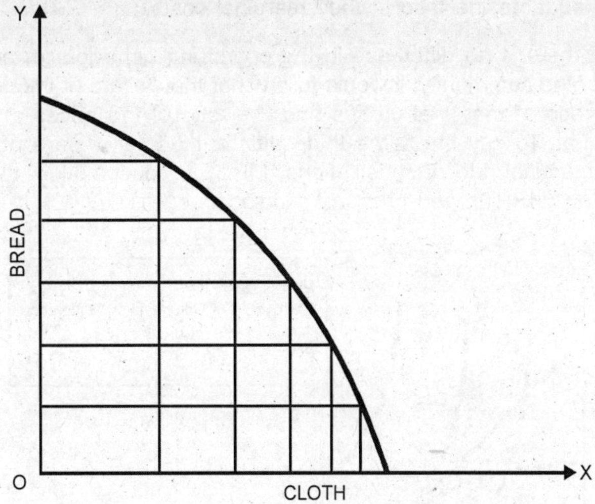

Fig. 4.3 Production Possibility Curve Under Increasing Costs

From Fig. 4.4, it would appear that for the production of every additional unit of Bread, the country has to sacrifice decreasing quantities of cloth.

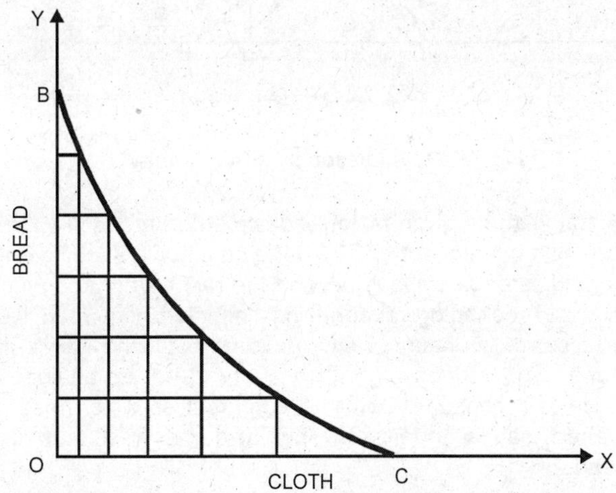

Fig. 4.4 Production Possibility Curve Under Decreasing Costs

Production and Consumption Decision by a Country When No International Trade Takes Place: Economic Autarky

If due to any reason a country is not taking part in international trade, the country in question (not engaged in international trade) will produce the two commodities, namely, Bread and Cloth, in such a combination that the total welfare of the community will be maximised. It is well-known that a consumer obtains maximum satisfaction from two commodities if the ratio of marginal utilities of the two commodities is equal to the ratio of their prices.

In the same way, a producer maximises his profit when the ratio of the prices of products (under competitive conditions) is equal to the ratio of their marginal costs.

If it is assumed that there is no difference in the optimising behaviour of an individual consumer and that of the producer and of the community; it would follow that the welfare of the community or country would be maximised when the ratio of marginal utilities and the ratio of the prices of products and the ratio of marginal costs are all equal. To say the same thing differently, total welfare of the community would be maximised by equalising marginal rate of substitutions (MRS) in consumption, the marginal rate of product transformation in production (MRPT), and prices of products.

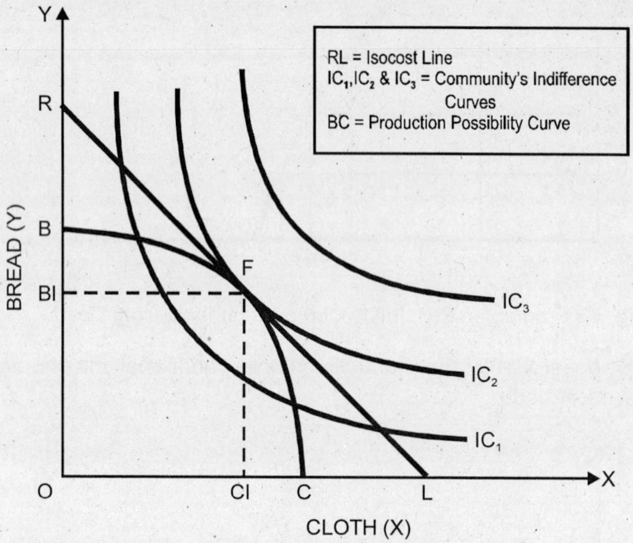

Fig. 4.5 Optimisation by a Community

It is clear from Fig. 4.5 that with the given factor endowment of a country, the highest conceivable level of satisfaction will be attainable by a country at point F on the community's Indifference Curve IC_2. It should be clear that a higher community indifference curve is beyond the reach of the community so long as the factor endowment of the community and technological conditions remain unchanged (as has been assumed). At point F, the community produces and consumes OC_1 units of cloth and OB_1 units of bread. This level of combination of production and consumption of cloth and bread will be attained in a condition when the community decides to produce and consume both the commodities which means production of both the commodities, namely, cloth and bread is undertaken only for domestic consumption and the country does not enter into international trade.

Three Cost Conditions and International Trade

It would be instructive to analyse the three cost situations and the theory of international trade. Attempt will be made first to examine the theory of international trade when a country is producing two commodities under conditions of constant costs (which means when MRTP is constant).

After that will be examined the theory of international trade when the opportunity cost is increasing (which means when the production possibility curve is concave to the origin).

The case of decreasing opportunity cost (when the production possibility curve is convex to the origin) is excluded from the analysis due to the fact of its logical inconsistency.

Production Possibility Under Conditions of Constant Opportunity Cost

Let us assume only two countries and only two commodities (namely, England and Australia and cloth and bread).

Table 4.1 describes the conditions of constant opportunity cost or in other terms, constant proportionality of output to input in the case of both the countries, namely, England and Australia over the entire range of desired production.

Table 4.1

	Input Units		*Output Units*	
	England		*Australia*	
	Bread	*Cloth*	*Bread*	*Cloth*
50	150	150	50	75
40	120	120	40	60
30	90	90	30	45
20	60	60	20	30
10	30	30	10	15

The above figures in Table 4.1 are expressed graphically in Fig. 4.6 and Fig. 4.7.

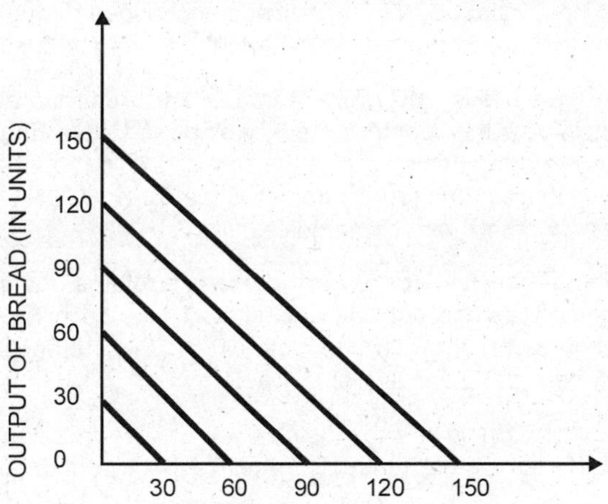

Fig. 4.6 Production Posibility Curves

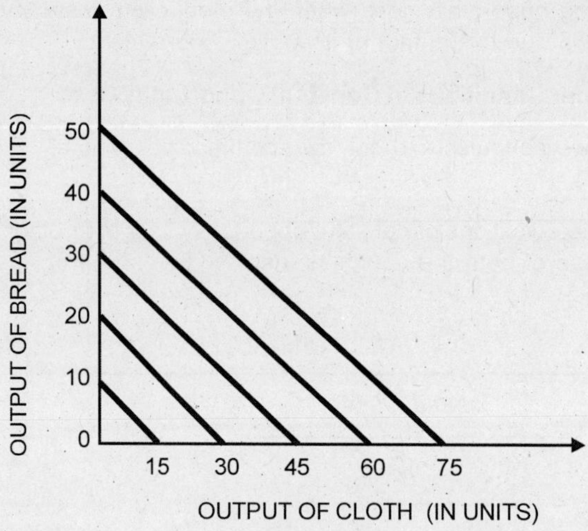

AUSTRALIA

Fig. 4.7

If the assumption of constant cost (which also means constant or proportionate returns) is made, as indicated in Fig. 4.6 and Fig. 4.7 the production possibility curve will be a straight line.

For the purpose of illustration, let us assume two countries, England and Australia and two commodities bread and cloth.

Table 4.1 shows a constant proportionality of output and input throughout the production process in the case of both countries England and Australia.

Figures in Table 4.1 have been expressed diagramatically in Fig. 4.6 and Fig. 4.7. In these two diagrams, the various production possibility curves indicate the different levels of output at different levels of input. In Fig. 4.6 and Fig. 4.7, because the input-output coefficient remains unchanged throughout the production process, it will be observed that in both the cases production possibility curves are linear or straight lines.

Assuming that England possesses 100 units of inputs and Australia also possesses 100 units of inputs and that all those inputs in both the countries are fully employed, then England can produce either 150 units of bread or 150 units of cloth or a combination of the two in certain proportions. In the case of Australia, if 100 units of inputs are fully employed, the country can produce either 50 units of bread or 75 units of cloth or an appropriate combination of both these commodities.

In the case of a condition of constant costs or proportionate returns, there will be optimum production possibility curves for both commodities and both the countries. These optimum production possibility curves demonstrate the possible combinations of bread and cloth which England and Australia can produce under the assumption of full employment of all the available inputs.

It is obvious that domestically, England and Australia will choose that combination of bread and cloth where their production possibility curves are tangent to their respective community indifference curves.

Refer to Fig. 4.8 and Fig. 4.9

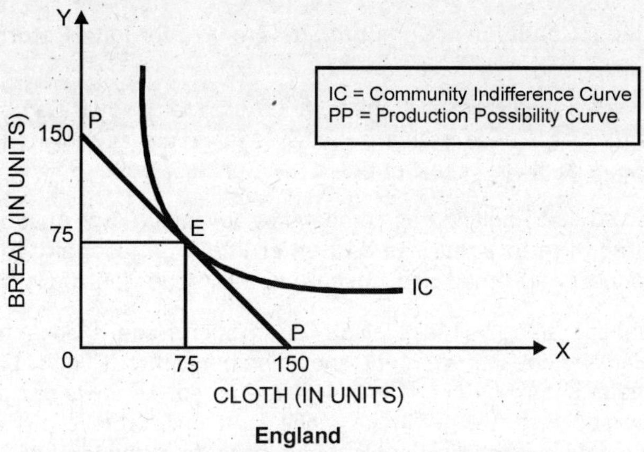

Fig. 4.8 Domestic Equilibrium of Producing in England at Constant Costs or Proportionate Returns

It would be observed that given full employment of all the available inputs and given constant costs or proportionate returns (i.e., equal returns to scale), England would be producing 75 units of bread and 75 units of cloth. This is indicated by Point E in Fig. 4.8.

If due to any reason demand for cloth increases (which means if England's community indifference curve touches at some other point the production possibility curve), then England will produce more units of cloth and proportionately less units of bread. But given the community's consumption function and full employment of all the available inputs, any movement away from point E will mean lower level of satisfaction for the community in England.

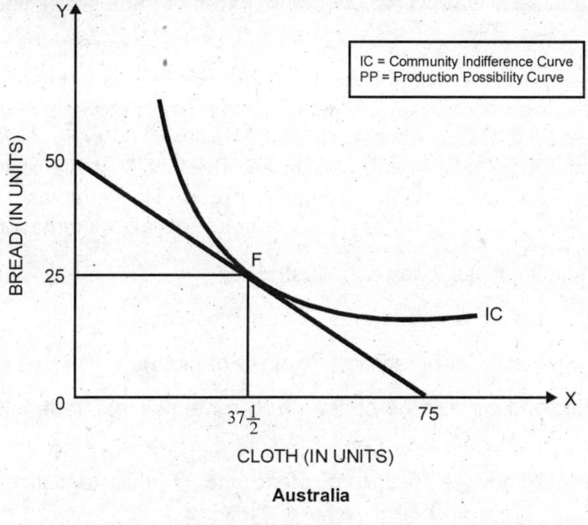

Fig. 4.9 Domestic Equilibrium of Production in Australia at Constant Costs or Proportionate Returns

By the same logic, in the case of Australia, with full employment of all the available resources, and with constant cost or proportionate returns or equal returns to scale, and given the production possibility curve and community's consumption function, the point of intersection F will be the point of equilibrium where

Australia will be producing 25 units of bread and $37\frac{1}{2}$ units of cloth. Any other point away from point F would mean lesser satisfaction for the community in Australia. (See Fig. 4.9).

Nature of International Trade Under Condition of Constant Costs (or Proportional Returns or Equal Returns to Scale)

As already noted domestic exchange ratios in England and Australia are indicated by the slopes of their respective production possibility curves. These exchange rates of ratios are as follows–In England 1 unit of bread: 1 unit of cloth; in the case of Australia, 1 unit of bread : $1\frac{1}{2}$ units of cloth.

From Table 4.1, it is observed that England has comparative advantage over Australia in the production of bread. This means if countries are to specialise and enter into international trade, England should specialise completely in the production of bread and Australia in the production of cloth.

It is observed that international trade will take place only if such trade is advantageous to both the countries. This means that for England, the terms of trade should be better than 1 unit of bread : 1 unit of cloth; and for Australia, the terms of trade should be better than 1 unit of bread: $1\frac{1}{2}$ units of cloth. This means that if England specialises only in bread, it should get in exchange for 1 unit of bread at least something more than 1 unit of cloth. If Australia is to specialise only in cloth and wants to exchange it for English bread, then Australia will have to give for 1 unit of bread, something less than $1\frac{1}{2}$ units of cloth.

Since for 1 unit of bread, England wants from Australia at least a little over 1 unit of cloth, and since Australia is prepared to give in exchange of 1 unit of bread from England anything up to $1\frac{1}{2}$ units of cloth, international trade is possible between England and Australia and that would be advantageous to both the participating countries. Naturally, England would want the terms of trade between bread and cloth that prevail in Australia and Australia would prefer most the terms of trade that prevail in England.

The actual terms of trade would lie between 1 unit of bread: 1 unit of cloth and 1 unit of bread: $1\frac{1}{2}$ units of cloth, depending upon reciprocal demand (i.e., England's elasticity of demand for Australian cloth *vis-à-vis* Australian elasticity of demand for English bread).

Let us suppose that on the basis of reciprocal demand, terms of trade get settled at 1 unit of bread: 1.2 units of cloth.

Let us also assume that when international trade was not taking place between England and Australia, Australia in its domestic equilibrium position was producing 50 units of bread and 75 units of cloth (satisfying domestic requirements of bread and cloth). After Australia specialises in cloth, Australia will produce only 150 units of cloth and no bread. Out of this quantity, let us assume that Australia consumes 75 units of cloth and exchanges the remaining 75 units of cloth for English bread. This enables Australia to obtain from England 62.5 units of bread. It can be seen that Australia is better off after international trade took place.

(Comparative positions would be as follows in Australia:

Before international trade–50 units of bread and 75 units of cloth

After international trade–62.5 units of bread and 75 units of cloth).

It will also be seen that England will also be better off after international trade than when she tried to be self-sufficient.

(England before international trade — 75 units of bread and 75 units of cloth).

England after international trade — 87.5 units of bread and 75 units of cloth. Thus, through specialisation and international trade, England's position is better than when she tried to be self-sufficient.

Increasing Opportunity Cost (i.e., Decreasing Returns) and Production Possibility Curve

So far the analysis assumed the condition of constant costs or proportionate returns. But it is quite possible that under certain circumstances, output may not increase proportionately with every increase in the dose of input used. It is possible that production will increase at a decreasing rate. Due to the operation of the law of diminishing returns, cost of production may go on increasing at an increasing rate. This means, in other terms, the marginal cost of production would go on increasing with the production of an additional unit of a commodity. Because of this condition, production possibility curve will become concave to the origin.

Taking the illustration of two commodities, namely, bread and cloth and measuring units of bread along OY-axis and units of cloth along OX-axis, it will be observed in Fig. 4.10 that if all the available resources of a country are employed for the production of bread, then OM quantity of bread can be produced. But if on the other hand, all the resources of the community are employed for the production of cloth, then ON quantity of cloth on OX-axis can be produced. It will be observed from Fig. 4.10, that the production possibility curve MN is concave to the origin indicating that as additional units of bread are produced, the opportunity cost in terms of bread will go on increasing.

Thus, it will be observed that when the production possibility curve is concave to the origin, it indicates the condition of increasing opportunity cost (or in other terms, condition of decreasing returns).

This means production of every additional unit of bread would involve increasing opportunity cost in terms of cloth; and production of every additional unit of cloth would involve increasing opportunity cost in terms of bread.

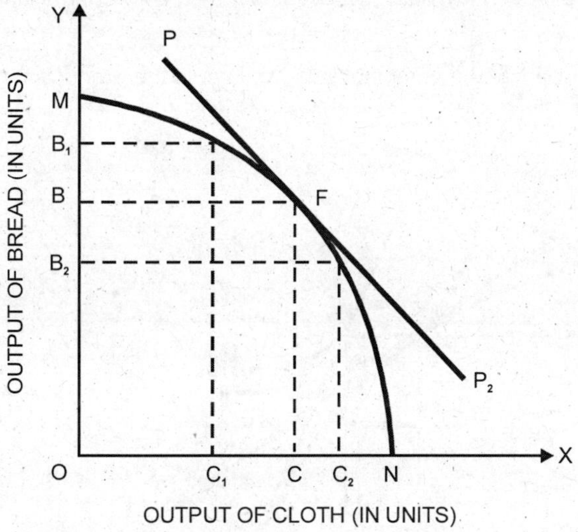

Fig. 4.10 Domestic Equilibrium of Production Under Condition of Increasing Costs (i.e. Decreasing Returns)

Fig. 4.10 shows the case of increasing cost condition and the limiting points of the production possibility curve are M and N which cannot be joined by a straight line.

From Fig. 4.10, it becomes clear that an additional unit of cloth can be produced only increasingly foregoing or sacrificing units of bread. In other terms, the opportunity cost of producing of an additional unit of cloth goes on increasing in terms of bread as we move along the production possibility curve.

But the movement along the MN curve may be in either direction. For example, in Fig. 4.10, if the initial equilibrium point is F, this would indicate that at the equilibrium point OB units of bread and OC units of cloth will be produced.

If the quantity of bread is to be increased from OB to OB_1, then the output of cloth will decline from OC to OC_1. It can be observed that increase in the quantity of production of bread, namely, BB_1 is less than the decrease in the quantity of cloth produced which is CC_1.

Also, if the output of cloth is to be increased from OC to OC_2, it will be observed that production of bread will decrease from OB to OB_2. It can be observed that in this case, increase in the production of cloth (indicated by CC_2) is less than the decrease in the quantity of bread produced (indicated by BB). Thus for every increase in the production of bread or cloth, the opportunity cost in terms of the other commodity to be sacrificed will go on increasing.

What will be the level of domestic production of bread and cloth, if the country wants to produce both the commodities and does not want to enter into international trade? As at this stage there is absence of price indicator, the above question cannot be answered. This means the question can be answered only by introducing the price-line which is indicated by PP_1 in Fig. 4.10. The tangency of this price-line PP_1 to the production possibility curve MN at point F will determine the equilibrium output of bread and cloth in the case of the country. The equilibrium output would be OB bread and OC cloth. In other terms, in the absence of international trade, the country will produce that combination of the two commodities, namely, bread and cloth, at which MRTP (i.e., Marginal Rate of Product Transformation) would equal the ratio of prices of products.

International Trade Under Condition of Increasing Costs

Let us now take into consideration the possibility of entering into international trade by England and Australia. If specialization is resorted to by both the countries, then only international trade will benefit both the countries.

Let us suppose that Australia has the comparative advantage in the production of cloth and that the new terms of trade established under international trade happen to shift the price-line from its original position of PP_1 to P_2P_3 (See Fig. 4.11).

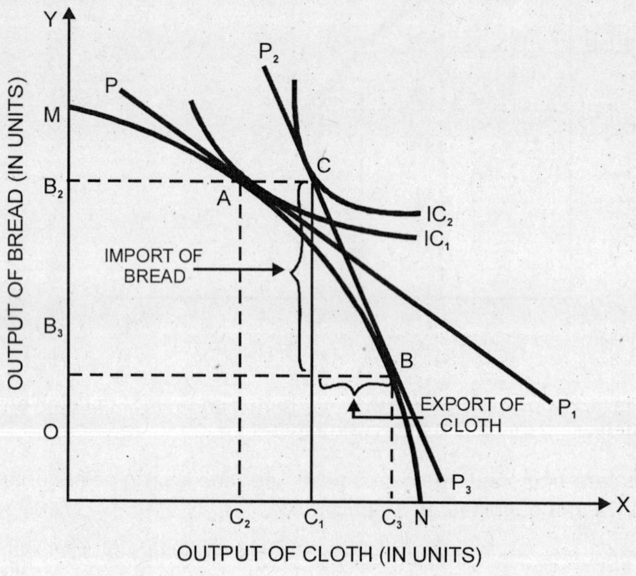

Fig. 4.11 Gains from International Trade under Condition of Increasing Costs

From Fig. 4.11, it is clear that at the original equilibrium point A, the country was getting the optimum combination of the two commodities of OC_2 units of cloth and OB_2 units of bread and also the community was maximising its level of satisfaction along the community indifference curve IC_1.

With the specialisation in production taking place, Australia now produces OC_3 units of cloth and OB_3 units of bread and optimises the use of its resources at point B where the new price-line cuts the production possibility curve.

However, the domestic demand for bread continues to be OB_2. Thus Australia would export cloth quantity which is indicated by C_1C_3 to England; in return, Australia would import from England bread quantity which is shown by B_2B_3.

Thus, specialisation and international trade would make Australia better off and the community is placed at higher indifference curve IC_2, Point C is the community's new equilibrium position which it attains in correspondence with the new product price-ratio (indicated by P_2P_3 in the Fig. 4.11).

It is also clear from Fig. 4.11 that Australia saves C_1C_2 units of cloth in this process of specialisation and international trade. At the price ratio indicated by P_2P_3, Australia can consume more of both the commodities, namely, bread and cloth. This would mean that by specialisation and by entering into international trade, the country is enabled to attain a higher level of satisfaction and at the same time make the optimum use of the community's resources.

Partial Specialisation

If it is a case of constant returns or proportional returns, there would be complete specialisation by both the countries and international trade would take place on the basis of complete specialisation by the two participating countries.

But in the case of increasing opportunity cost (i.e., decreasing returns), the above statement regarding complete specialisation is not true. (See Fig. 4.11). Under conditions of increasing opportunity costs or decreasing returns, the country would continue to devote some part of its resources to domestic production of imported commodity. This would mean that some producers would still be competing with imports of the commodity in question, because their relative costs are no longer higher than the international exchange ratio. This would explain why complete specialisation in the production of cloth by Australia has not been shown in Fig. 4.11. As is clear from Fig. 4.11, Australia produces larger quantity of cloth due to comparative cost advantage and yet Australia would produce some units of bread (OB_3) domestically and import some units of bread in order to meet domestic demand fully for it.

Proportional Cost Structures

If it so happens that the cost structure in the case of both the countries is proportionate, then it is obvious that no foreign trade between the two countries can take place. The cost structure is considered as proportional if the superiority of one country over the other country is the same in respect of both the commodities.

For example, let us assume that with given resources fully employed, the position is as follows:

England: Either 200 units of bread or 100 units of cloth;

Australia: Either 100 units of bread or 50 units of cloth.

From the above figures, it follows that for one unit of bread, England wants at least a little more than ½ unit of cloth from Australia. But by sacrificing ½ unit of cloth, Australia herself can produce 1 unit of bread and, therefore, Australia would not offer anything more than ½ unit of cloth for 1 unit of English bread. And, therefore, under conditions of proportionate cost structure in both the countries, international trade will take place.

If the factor endowments in both England and Australia are such that cost structures of England and Australia are proportional, it then follows that the slope of their production possibility curves will also be identical. The only difference will be that the production possibility curve of Australia will be at half the distance in relation to the production possibility curve of England. But the opportunity cost ratio of internal (domestic) exchange for both England and Australia will be identical. In such a case, no exchange of goods will take place between England and Australia.

Fig. 4.12 describes the situation when the distance between the two production possibility curves, namely, MN of England and MN of Australia is the same throughout.

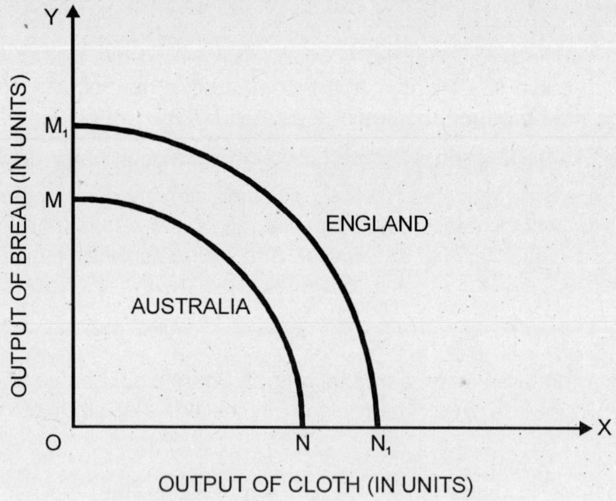

Fig. 4.12 Proportionate Cost Structures

Multi-country and Multi-commodity Model

The classical school analysed the problem of international trade in terms of two countries and two commodities.

In the real world, there are many countries and many commodities. How in such a case different countries specialise would be seen from the following illustrative Table 4.2. (Money wages are assumed to be the same in all the countries).

Table 4.2

Product	*Country*			
	I	*II*	*III*	*IV*
A	100	120	140	90
B	100	175	110	125
C	100	60	150	75
D	100	75	50	85

From Table 4.2, it will be observed that each of the countries will specialise in the production of one commodity and exchange that for commodities produced by other countries.

From Table 4.2, it can be seen that country-I specialises in the production of commodity-B; country-II will specialise in the production of commodity-C; country-III will specialise in the production of commodity D; and country-IV will specialise in the production of commodity-A. It is by comparing comparative cost advantage that the above specialisation by various countries will take place and through their export, the countries will import commodities which the other countries produce by specialising in their production.

CHAPTER

5 HECKSCHER-OHLIN THEORY OF INTERNATIONAL TRADE

Structure:

5.1 Introduction

5.2 Assumptions of Heckscher-Ohlin Theory of International Trade

5.3 Heckscher-Ohlin Theory of International Trade Explained

5.4 Heckscher-Ohlin Theory Compared to the Classical Theory of International Trade

5.5 Criticism of Heckscher-Ohlin Theory of International Trade

5.6 International Trade and Factor Prices

5.7 Criticism of Samuelson's Theory of Factor Price Equalisation

5.8 The Leontief Paradox: (Empirical Evidence)

5.9 Criticism of Leontief Paradox

5.1 INTRODUCTION

The classical theory of international trade was based on differences in productivity of labour. As already noted, the classical theory suffered from a number of limitations. And therefore, in recent years, the traditional theory of comparative cost advantage has come to be replaced by what has come to be known as the Heckscher-Ohlin theory (H-O theory) of international trade. (This theory is also often referred to as 'Factor-Price Equalisation Theory of International Trade').[1]

The H-O theory makes an attempt to go deeply in the causes that lead to differences in comparative cost advantage due to which international trade between any two countries takes place.

Bertil Ohlin (a student of Heckscher) argued that international trade is only a special case of inter-regional trade. According to him, instead of analysing the phenomenon of international trade separately from that of inter-regional (i.e., internal or domestic) trade, it would be better to consider differences in the cost of production of two commodities as these costs determine factor incomes and the pattern of demand for goods produced in two countries. Thus, Bertil Ohlin presents the interdependence of prices of goods (depending on their cost of production), factor prices, the incomes of factors of production which assures income to the owners of capital and labour, demand for products and supply of factors of production.

Bertil Ohlin argued that the general theory of price is a 'one-market theory', and concentrates its attention only on 'time' element. According to Ohlin, the traditional approach to international trade ignored 'the space factor', which according to Ohlin, is an important element in trade mainly because movement of goods and of actors of production is constrained by the space factor. This according to Ohlin, necessitates consideration of the determination of values in several markets simultaneously. This, in other terms, means that unlike conventional 'one-market theory', Ohlin has advocated the theory of international trade involving multi-market theory of value.

The Heckscher-Ohlin theory is based on the premise that international trade between two countries takes place because different countries have different factor endowments. Some countries have relative to labour more capital and some other countries have relatively abundant supply of labour. The H-O theory of international trade maintains that a country which has relatively abundant capital would specialise in and export capital-intensive goods a country with relatively abundant supply of labour would specialise in and export labour-intensive goods.

---

1. Much before the publication of Bertil Ohlin's book, Eli Heckscher had written an article in 1919 explaining effects of international trade on distribution of income between land, capital and labour. Heckscher first attempted to explain the reasons for differences in comparative costs among different countries. He stated that, "If two countries have the same relative scarcity of factors of production, the relative factor prices in both the countries will also be identical and, therefore, foreign trade between them will be impossible."

   Heckscher, therefore, summarised the necessary conditions for initiating international trade as follows: (i) Different relative scarcity (i.e., different relative prices of factors of production) in participating countries, and (ii) different proportions between factors of production used in different commodities. He assumed that these proportions remain unchanged.

   Eli Heckscher emphasised the relative scarcity of factors of production which leads to differences in relative factor prices and, hence, to differences in comparative costs which is the main cause of international trade. On the other hand, Bertil Ohlin focussed his attention on a multi-market theory of value.

   The Heckscher-Ohlin theory of international trade has combined these two elements.

5.2 ASSUMPTIONS OF HECKSCHER-OHLIN THEORY OF INTERNATIONAL TRADE

The Heckscher-Ohlin theory of international trade is based on two-factor, two-country, two-commodity model. The H-O theory is based on the following assumptions:

(1) There is full employment of resources in both the countries participating in international trade.

(2) Factors of production are perfectly mobile within the country but they are perfectly immobile between the two countries.

(3) The relative endowments of the two factors, namely, capital and labour are disproportionate in the two countries; one country having relatively more capital and the other country relatively more labour.

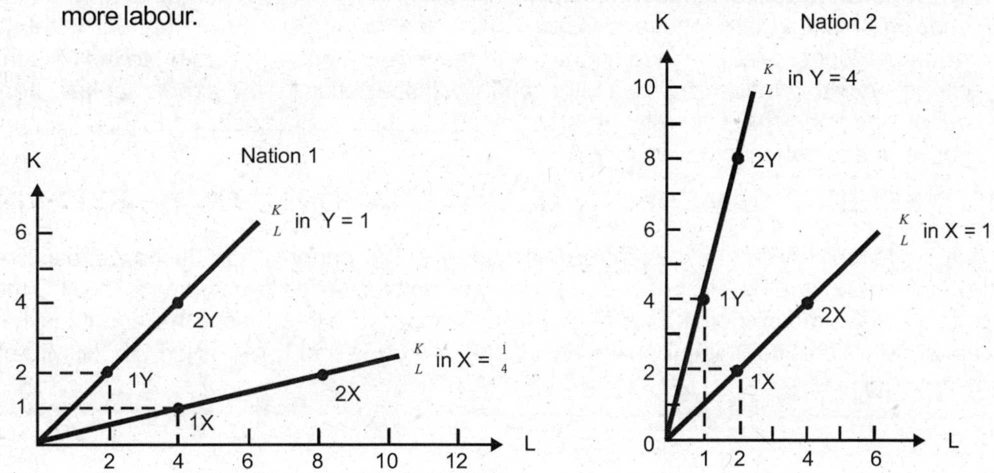

Fig. 5.1. Factor Intensities for Commodities X and Y in Nations 1 and 2. In Nation 1, the capital-labour ratio (K/L) equals 1 for commodity Y and K/L = ¼ for commodity X. These are given by the slope of the ray from the origin for each commodity in Nation 1. Thus, commodity Y is the K-intensive commodity in Nation 1. In Nation 2, K/L = 4 for Y and K/L = 1 for X. Thus, commodity Y is the K-intensive commodity, and commodity X is the L-intensive commodity in both nations. Nations 2 uses a higher K/L than Nation 1 in the production of both commodities because the relative price of capital (r/w) is lower in Nation 2. If r/w declined, producers would substitute K for L in the production of both commodities to minimize their costs of production. As a result, K/L would rise for both commodities.

(4) The two commodities involved show different factor-intensities. Thus, production function is such that whereas one commodity is capital-intensive, the other commodity is labour-intensive. But the H-O Theory assumes that the production function for each commodity are the same in both the countries, though production function for different commodities are different.

Thus, if we assume two countries – A and B and two commodities, namely, steel and cloth, the H.O. theory assumes that production of steel in both the countries – A and B would require (let us suppose) 3 units of capital and 1 unit of labour, whereas in both the countries – A and B production of cloth would require 1 unit of capital and 3 units of labour. Thus, while production functions of steel and cloth are different, these production functions for steel and cloth are the same in both the countries – A and B.

(5) Technology of producing the two commodities in the two countries remains unchanged.

(6) Prices of the two commodities are determined solely by factor prices. This means transport costs are completely ignored.

(7) All production functions are linear. This, in other terms means that they operate in both the countries and in the case of both the commodities the law of constant returns or constant costs or constant returns to scale, the same quantity of additional input producing every time the same quantity of output. There is no scope for the substitution of one factor for the other (i.e., substitution of capital for labour or of labour for capital).

(8) Demand functions (i.e., consumer's preferences) for the two commodities in both the countries remains identical.

The most important assumption of the Heckscher-Ohlin theory is related to different factor endowments (i.e., of capital and labour) in the two countries. Thus, country-A is relatively richer in respect of capital and country-B in respect of labour. According to the H-O theory country-A with relative abundance of capital will specialise in and export capital-intensive goods and country-B with relative abundance of labour, will specialise in labour-intensive goods and export them to country-A.

5.3 HECKSCHER-OHLIN THEORY OF INTERNATIONAL TRADE EXPLAINED

According to the H-O theory, then main determinant of the pattern of production, specialisation and trade between countries is "the relative availability of factor supplies." According to the H-O theory, "Some countries have much capital; others have much labour. The theory says that countries that are rich in capital will export capital-intensive goods and countries that have much labour will export labour-intensive goods."

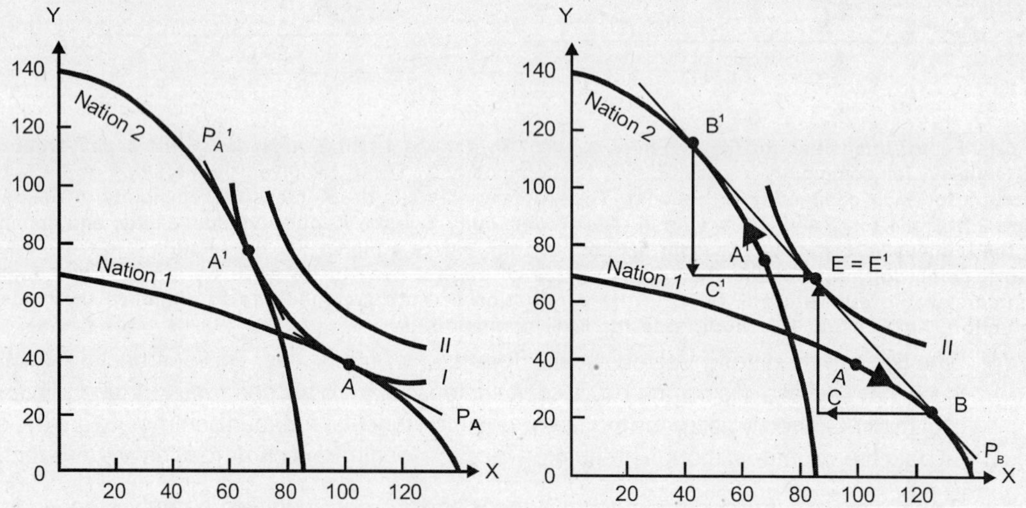

Fig. 5.2. The Heckscher-Ohlin Model. Indifference curve I is common to both nations because of the assumption of equal tastes. Indifference curve I is tangent to the production frontier of Nation 1 at point A and tangent to the production frontier of Nation 2 at A'. This defines the no-trade equilibrium-relative commodity price of P*A* in Nation 1 and P*A'* in Nation 2 (see the left panel). Since P*A* < P*A'*, Nation 1 has a comparative advantage in commodity X and Nation 2 in commodity Y. With trade (see the right panel) Nation 1 produces at point B and by exchanging X for Y reaches point E in consumption (see trade triangle BCE). Nation 2 produces at *B'* and by exchanging Y for X reaches point *E'* (which coincides with *E*). Both nations gain from trade because they consumer on higher indifference curve II.

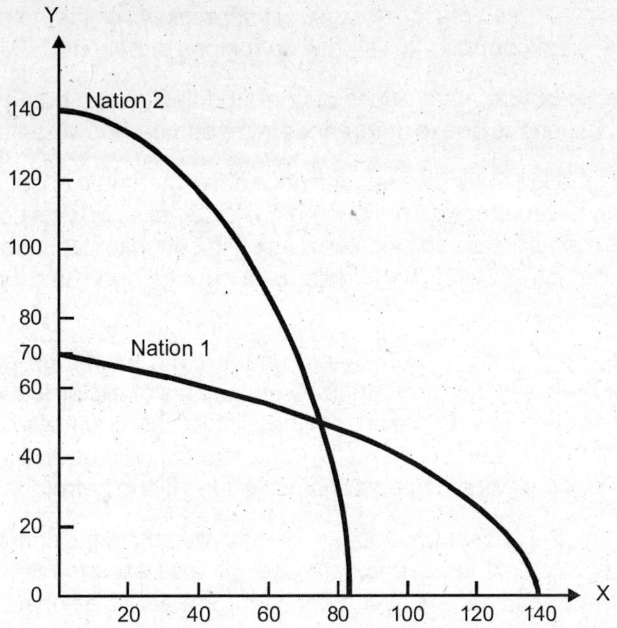

Fig. 5.3. The Shape of the Production Frontiers of Nation 1 and Nation 2. The production frontier of Nation 1 is flatter and wider than the production frontier of Nation 2. Indicating that Nation 1 can produce relatively more of commodity X than Nation 2. The reason for this is that Nation 1 is the *L*-abundant nation and commodity X is the *L*-intensive commodity.

According to the H-O theory, the immediate cause of international trade is the difference in relative commodity prices which is caused by differences in relative demand and supply of factor (i.e., factor prices) consequent on differences in factor endowments between two countries. Thus, the H-O theory maintains that basically the relative scarcity of factor shortages of supply in relation to demand is essential for trade between two countries. It means commodities which use large quantities of scarce factor are imported, because their prices, if domestically produced, would be higher than if they are imported: and commodities using relatively abundant factor are exported, because their domestic prices are low and their prices in foreign markets are high. Thus, if capital is relatively abundant and, therefore, relatively cheaper in country A and the same is true of labour in country B, then country A will specialise in and export goods which are capital-intensive and country B will specialise in and export goods which are labour-intensive.

The H-O theory has explained the theory of international trade both in terms of factor abundance or scarcity in physical terms as also in terms of factor prices because of abundance or scarcity.

Summary of Bertil Ohlin's Theory of International Trade

Bertil Ohlin's theory of international trade may be summarised as follows:

(1) Inter-regional trade and international trade are both two types of the same species; there is only a difference of degree between the two and this means that there is no fundamental difference between the two. (For example, the reasons for which western region of India purchases jute manufacture from the eastern region of India is also the reason why India purchases fine steel from England or West Germany or crude oil from the Middle East countries).

(2) The fundamental or basic reason or cause of inter-regional or international trade is the difference in relative prices of commodities in the two regions or nations.

(3) These differences in relative prices of commodities in two regions of the same country or between two nations is due to differences in resource-endowments or factors of production.

(4) The rate of exchange translates relative price differences into absolute price differences. This would determine what regions or countries will specialise in what commodities (e.g., eastern region in jute manufacture and western region in cotton textile, and similarly India in textiles and jute manufactures and the Middle East countries in the production of crude oil and petroleum products).

(5) At what rate of exchange the two commodities will exchange either in inter-regional or international trade will be determined by elasticities of reciprocal demand and supply (i.e. India's degree of urgency for crude from the Middle East countries compared to the degree of urgency of Middle Eastern demand for Indian textile will determine the rate of exchange at which cotton textiles will exchange against crude oil and petroleum products).

Thus, inter-regional and international trade both belong to the same species; this means the principles that explains inter-regional trade will also explain international trade. This also means that there is no necessity or reason for formulating a separate theory of international trade, according to Bertil Ohlin.

Movements of Commodities and Factors of Production

The classical theory of international trade (of Adam Smith, Ricardo and J.S. Mill) assumed that factors of production were mobile within a country, but perfectly immobile within countries.

Bertil Ohlin pointed out the unsatisfactory nature of this assumption. He pointed out that factors of production have also restricted mobility even within a country and at the same time there was never absolute immobility of factors of production between any two countries or among countries. For example, in the case of India, because of differences of languages, climate, of food habits, etc. movement of factors of production is limited between different regions of India. For this reason a person from Maharashtra does not want to leave Maharashtra and go to Assam or West Bengal (due to differences of climate, language, and psychological factors regarding cultural readjustment, attachment to one's village or region, sense of security at home, satisfaction of cultural needs, etc.). For the same reason an Indian would be reluctant to move to Australia or New Zealand or Kenya, even though there may be no restrictions on movement of factors of production from one region to another in India.

5.4 HECKSCHER-OHLIN THEORY COMPARED TO THE CLASSICAL THEORY OF INTERNATIONAL TRADE

It is generally claimed that the Heckscher-Ohlin or the modern theory of international trade is superior to the classical theory of international trade on the following grounds:

(1) The H-O theory goes to the very root of all trades and, therefore, comes to the conclusion that international trade is only a special case of inter-regional or internal or domestic trade. Both inter-regional and international trade basically belong to the same species.

(The fact that international trade is not fundamentally different from inter-regional or domestic trade can be proved by a few illustrative examples. Before 1st April 1935, Burma was a part of India and other regions of India used to get teak-wood and kerosene from Burma region and sent to Burma manufactured goods like cloth, sugar, metal goods, etc. After 1st April 1935 Burma was separated from India and overnight what was till then inter-regional or domestic trade became international trade. And, yet, what India imports from Burma and what it exports to Burma remain practically the same as before. Similarly, trade with Sind and Western Punjab (which after 15th August 1947 became part of Pakistan) was inter-regional trade; but after 15th August 1947 became international trade, though the composition of imports and exports of the two countries to and from each other practically continued to be the same for quite some time. This shows that there is no fundamental difference between inter-regional and international trade, that both belong to the same species and, therefore, there is no necessity of a separate theory of international trade as was thought by the classical school. All trade-inter-regional or international is due to differences in factor endowments of different regions and countries resulting in differences in factor prices).

(2) The H-O theory has avoided the serious shortcoming of labour theory of value on which the classical theory of international theory of trade was based and it has made an attempt to bring the theory within the broad framework of the general equilibrium theory of value.

(3) The H-O theory has made the difference in factor endowments of different countries the basis of international trade, whereas the classical theory takes no note at all of differences in factor endowments in different countries.

(4) Whereas the classical or the Ricardian theory of international trade speaks in terms of relative prices of goods only, the H-O theory is more realistic because it analyses in terms of differences in relative prices of factors of production (namely, labour and capital) which in turn influence relative prices of commodities. And, therefore, the H-O theory is more realistic because it is the relative prices of factors of production that explain differences in relative prices of commodities on the basis of which international trade takes place.

(5) The H-O theory is also more realistic than the classical theory because the former theory takes into account differences in productivity of both labour and capital, whereas the classical theory considers differing productivity of labour only in the two trading countries.

(6) As already noted, the chief merit of the H-O theory is that whereas the classical theory emphasised differences in the quality of labour in different countries, the H-O theory explains the basis of international trade in terms of differences in factor endowments of different countries. The H-O theory is, therefore, more realistic than the classical theory which, if not wrong, is certainly, an inadequate explanation of the basis of international trade.

(7) Whereas the classical theory assumes or takes for granted difference in comparative advantage, the H-O theory explains why different countries enjoy comparative advantage in the production of certain commodities and relative disadvantage in the production of some other commodities.

5.5 CRITICISM OF HECKSCHER-OHLIN THEORY OF INTERNATIONAL TRADE

Following are the main points of criticism of the H-O theory:

(1) Bertil Ohlin tried to answer the criticism of his model based on two countries, two commodities and two factors of production (namely, labour and capital) stating that his model could be extended to many regions or countries, many commodities and many factors of production.

But Bertil Ohlin's unrealistic assumption regarding perfect competition and full employment, the available resources in the countries make his theory unrealistic.

(2) An important point of criticism of Heckscher-Ohlin's theory is that essentially the theory is static in nature. The theory has taken for granted production conditions at any given point of time as also production function of commodities. The theory fails to give any idea about how the economy would be affected, if production conditions change (as in real world they are bound to change).

(3) Ohlin has assumed homogeneous nature of the factors of production. This is an unrealistic assumption. Labour varies from the point of view of skills both within a country and between any two countries; also capital goods can take different forms with different degrees of efficiency and productivity.

(4) Bertil Ohlin has taken for granted some production functions for commodities he has taken for his illustration. But one can easily imagine how production function can differ in the case of the same commodity. For example, in the case of production of cloth, it can be produced with simple tools and much labour (as in the case of handlooms) or by using automatic and sophisticated machines combined with a very small number of workers. Changes in production function in the case of different commodities being possible, international trade may not be strictly according to given factor endowments as indicated by Bertil Ohlin.

(5) Another assumption of Ohlin is that relative factor prices would be exactly reflecting the position regarding relative factor endowments in a country. Thus, if in the United States, there is abundance of capital but relative scarcity of labour, Ohlin assumed that relatively rate of interest in the United States would be low and wage rates high. But Bertil Ohlin did not take into account the demand factor — namely, demand for capital and labour in the United States (as also in other countries), in determining relative factor prices. For example, though relatively abundant, capital is also in great demand in the United States. The position regarding factor prices would be that in the United States rate of interest would be high. (Prof. Leontief in his empirical study later showed that the United States even with relatively high wage rates exported labour-intensive goods and imported capital-intensive goods, though the United States is a country relatively rich in capital and has relative scarcity of labour).

(6) Wijanholds has been critical of Ohlin's theory which hold the view that "commodity prices are determined by the factor prices which in turn determine costs." He holds the view that prices of commodities are determined by utility which consumers get from the consumption of commodities and then these consumer-determined prices of commodities are reflected by factor prices and cost of production. Wijanholds, therefore, holds the view that Ohlin, instead of starting from prices of factors of production should have started with prices of commodities.

(7) Prof. Haberler has maintained that Ohlin's theory is rather vague. He writes: "With many factors of production, some of which are qualitatively incommensurable as between different countries, and with dissimilar production functions in different countries, no sweeping *a priori* generalisation concerning the composition of trade is possible."

The H-O theory of international trade can also be criticised on the same ground as the Ricardian theory for making highly unrealistic assumptions such as perfect mobility of factors within a country, but perfect immobility between countries, assumption of free trade, of full employment of resources, absence of transport costs, operation of the law of constant returns, no technological changes, etc.

And yet the H-O theory is supposed to be an improvement over the classical theory as it attempts to explain international trade in terms of factor endowments of different countries.

5.6 INTERNATIONAL TRADE AND FACTOR PRICES

Introduction

According to the Heckscher-Ohlin theory of international trade, relative prices of traded goods differ in two countries before international trade takes place. Assuming that transport costs are absent, when international trade takes place, relative commodity prices in the two trading countries get equalised.

But since it is assumed that factors of production are perfectly immobile between the two trading countries, will the prices of the factors of production get equalised as a consequence of international trade between the two countries?

Much controversy has arisen among economists over the question of international trade and factor price equalisation.

Heckscher in his article, 'The Effect of Foreign Trade and Distribution of Income' (published in 1919) had suggested that if it is assumed that techniques of production and production functions of the two commodities in the two trading countries (i.e., the proportion in which factors of production are combined to produce the two commodities in the two countries) remain unchanged, then international trade would lead to factor price equalisation without the factors of production moving from one country to the other. But Heckscher was of the opinion that production techniques and production functions in the two trading countries are not likely to be similar or remain unchanged, and therefore, as a result of international trade whereby commodities move from one country to the other but not factors of production, complete factor price equalisation is not likely to take place.

Bertil Ohlin's view was that international trade would lead to only partial price equalisation and complete factor price equalisation would result only if factors of production were free to move from one country to another without hindrance of any type.

Factor Price Equalisation Theory

Prof. Samuelson tried to show that free commodity trade under specific conditions will lead to complete equalisation of factor prices.

Samuelson makes highly restrictive and unrealistic following assumptions to prove his theory of complete factor price equalisation. Some of the assumptions made by Samuelson are : Only two countries, America and Britain; only two commodities, America producing food and Britain cloth; only two factors of production, namely, land and labour; production function in the case of both the commodities is homogeneous and the law of constant returns is in operation; factors of production are subject to the law of diminishing marginal productivity; factor-intensities are different for each commodity (i.e., food is relatively land-intensive and cloth relatively labour-intensive); no technological changes take place within the two countries; land and labour inputs are qualitatively identical in the two countries; there is free trade between America and Britain; there are no transport costs; quality of factors in both the countries are supposed to be constant; and both countries can produce both the commodities, namely, food and cloth with the factors of production land and labour.

The factor price equalisation theory can be proved by an illustration on the basis of Samuelson's assumptions.

Let us suppose, to begin with, that wage rate in America is higher than the wage rate in Britain. Because cost of production is determined exclusively by factor prices, the cost of production of labour-intensive cloth in Britain would be lower than in America where wage rate is higher than in Britain. This will result in increase in demand for British cloth, in America. Due to increase in American demand for British cloth production of cloth in Britain will go up raising wage rate in Britain relative to rent from land. The same reasoning will apply to production of food in America — relatively low price of land-intensive food from America will push up British demand for American food which in turn will push up rent from land in America. Thus, movement of cloth from Britain to America and of food from America to England will go on until wage rate in America and Britain as also rent from land in America and England are equalised.

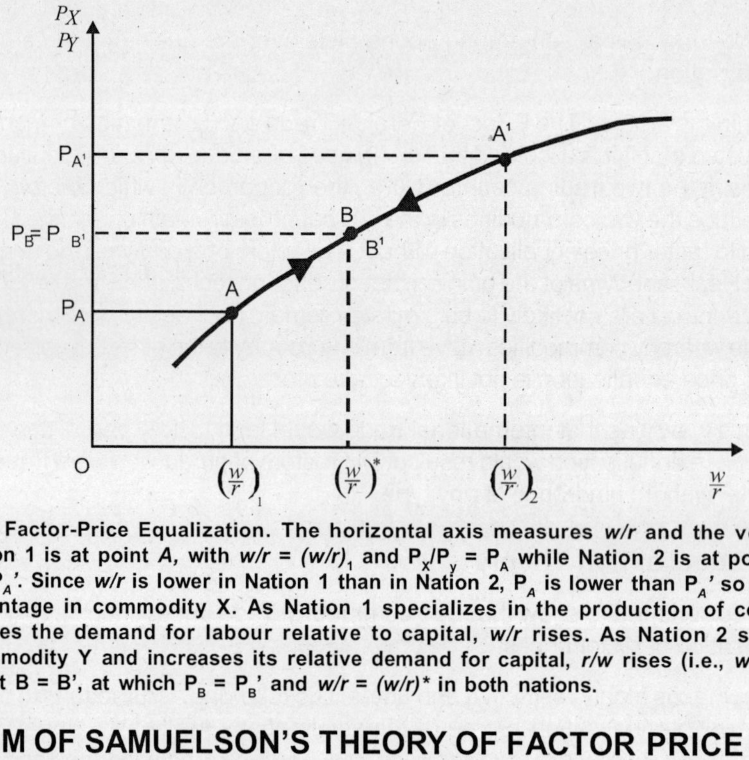

Fig. 5.4. Relative Factor-Price Equalization. The horizontal axis measures *w/r* and the vertical axis P_x/P_y. Before trade, Nation 1 is at point *A*, with *w/r* = $(w/r)_1$ and $P_x/P_y = P_A$ while Nation 2 is at point *A'*, with *w/r* = $(w/r)_2$ and $P_x/P_Y = P_A'$. Since *w/r* is lower in Nation 1 than in Nation 2, P_A is lower than P_A' so that Nation 1 has comparative advantage in commodity X. As Nation 1 specializes in the production of commodity X with trade and increases the demand for labour relative to capital, *w/r* rises. As Nation 2 specializes in the production of commodity Y and increases its relative demand for capital, *r/w* rises (i.e., *w/r* falls). This will continue until point B = B', at which $P_B = P_B'$ and *w/r* = $(w/r)^*$ in both nations.

5.7 CRITICISM OF SAMUELSON'S THEORY OF FACTOR PRICE EQUALISATION

Economists like Ellsworth, Meade and many others have criticised Samuelson's theory of factor price equalisation on the following grounds:

(1) According to Meade, production functions are never indentical. Even if resources are similar in America and Britain, they would not produce the same commodity in both the countries because of differences in physical, climatic, social and environmental reasons.

(2) Assumption regarding transport costs in international movement of goods is highly unrealistic. There being heavy transport costs, even with similar resources and production function, price of foodgrains will be higher in Britain than in America and price of British cloth will be higher in America than in Britain. Consequently, marginal product of labour and hence wage rates in America and Britain will be different — wage rate in Britain will be lower than wage rate in America and due to similar reason land rent will be lower in America than in Britain.

(3) Samuelson has made the assumption of constant returns to scale. Meade has pointed out that if Britain enjoys more economies of scale in the manufacture of cloth than America, marginal productivity of labour will be higher in Britain than in America. Under such circumstances though price of British cloth may be the same in America and Britain, wage rates in the two countries would be different.

(4) Factor price equalisation theory of Samuelson is a completely static theory. "It only studies some characteristics of a given equilibrium situation at a given point of time. It says only what the effects of trade will be with a given technique, with given factor endowments and so on. But the real world is not in a static equilibrium position forever; all sorts of changes occur."

(5) It is pointed out by economists like Kindleberger, Myrdal and many others that in the real world where Samuelson's most assumptions do not hold good, there has been taking place increasing inequalities in factor prices (i.e., factor incomes) rather than their showing tendency towards equality or towards factor price equalisation. According to Myrdal, there is taking place a cumulative process whereby factor prices appear to be continually widening. Myrdal writes "... trade between developed and less developed countries widens the gap in living standards (and in factor prices such as wages) rather than narrowing it, and it is evident after centuries of trade that there are still poor as well as rich countries."

Concluding Remarks

According to Kindleberger, though the assumptions for full factor price equalisation do not prevail anywhere in the world, " ... the analysis is nonetheless relevant among broadly similar countries, as in the European Common Market, and it focusses attention on significant consequences of trade. Trade tends to raise the price of abundant factor, and where trade is based on differences in factor endowments, this repercussion of trade on factor prices is vastly important politically as well as economically."

Samuelson's theory of factor price equalisation is based on a number of highly unrealistic assumptions, and, therefore, the theory is of little practical use. What we find in the real world is that there are a large number of countries and thousands of commodities that are internationally traded. Production functions are continually changing and technological advances are taking place at present at a breakneck pace. What is noticed during the post-World War II period and especially during 1970s and 1980s is that even developed countries of the West and the United States are suffering from certain amount of unemployment of labour force and have come to adopt various tariff and other policies of protection not only with respect to developing countries but even among themselves — for example, the United States imposing trade restrictions on certain imports from Japan and European Economic Community. And, therefore, we notice no strong trends towards factor price equalisation as a consequence of international trade. No wonder Sir Roy Harrod regarded Samuelson's theory as a curiosity and Kindleberger thought it as generally not true.

5.8 THE LEONTIEF PARADOX: (EMPIRICAL EVIDENCE)

According to the Heckscher-Ohlin theory of international trade, a country with relative abundance of capital would be specialising in and exporting capital-intensive goods and that country would be importing goods which are relatively more labour-intensive from the country where relative to capital labour is in abundance.

But Leontief, through his empirical study, arrived at the paradoxical conclusion that the United States (which possesses relatively large amount of capital and relatively small amount of labour in relation to rest of the world), in fact happened to export labour-intensive goods and import capital-intensive goods. This finding has come to be known as 'The Leontief Paradox.'

With a view to test the Heckscher-Ohlin theory according to which the United States should export capital-intensive goods and import labour-intensive goods (which in effect would mean that the United States would be exporting part of capital which is relatively abundant there and importing 'labour' which is relatively a scarce factor in that country, though capital and labour would be exported and imported respectively in the form of commodities).

Prof. Leontief, by using 1947 input-output tables of the United States economy, and classifying 200 groups of industries into 50 sectors of which 38 sectors traded their goods directly in the international market and taking only two factors of production, namely, capital and labour into consideration, arrived at the paradoxical conclusion that the United States, in fact, imported capital-intensive goods and export labour-intensive goods. Prof. Leontief wrote: "America's participation in the international division of labour is based on its specialisation in labour-intensive rather than capital-intensive lines of production. In other words, the country resorts to foreign trade in order to economise in its capital and dispose of its surplus labour, rather than *vice versa.*" Thus, the finding of Leontief was contrary to the Heckscher-Ohlin theory. This finding of Leontief which has come to be known as "The Leontief Paradox',not surprised many economists but also Leontief himself.

5.9 CRITICISM OF LEONTIEF PARADOX

The Leontief Paradox has been criticised on statistical and methodological grounds. Following are some of the main points of criticism:

(1) B.C. Swerling in his article 'Capital Shortage and Labour Surplus in the United States, has maintained that 1947 (the year selected by Leontief to calculate input-output tables of selected industries) was not a typical year for testing the Heckscher-Ohlin theory of international trade. According to Prof. Swerling, this is because the industrial disorganisation caused by the World War II (1939-45) had not been corrected in the economies of different countries of the world by the year 1947. And therefore, the Leontief"s results were biased.

Prof. Swerling was also critical of Leontief for including certain industries with low capital-labour ratios as that resulted in biased results. (By way of rejoinder, Leontief again conducted his tests with much wider coverage of industries which only confirmed the Leontief Paradox).

(2) Romney Robinson is critical of Leontief on the following ground: According to him, the demand conditions within a country may favour consumption of a commodity that the country may produce with a relative abundant factor of production (i.e., the United States' demand for capital-intensive goods may be strong); and, therefore, the United States may not export capital-intensive goods. Also, the United States may import capital-intensive goods from

abroad, if its level of income rises and if income-elasticity of demand in the United States for capital-intensive goods is high. In the same way a country with relative abundance of labour may export capital-intensive goods, if income-elasticity of demand in the country is strongly in favour of labour-intensive commodities.

(3) According to Travis, tariff policies adopted by different countries often distorted the pattern of international trade. And therefore, according to him, Leontief's findings were seriously affected by tariff policies of the United States and its trading partners. The weakness of Leontief's methodology was that he did not take into consideration the effects of tariff policies of different countries on the pattern and composition of exports and imports of internationally trading countries.

(4) Buchanan was critical of Leontief on the ground that Leontief only took into consideration two factors of production, namely, capital and labour. Leontief did not take into consideration the important role which national resources of countries play in determining the pattern of international trade.

(5) Prof. Ellsworth was critical of Leontief of the following ground: According to him, capital-intensity of goods imported by the United States is irrelevant. What Leontief should have done is to compare capital-intensity of goods exported by the United States with capital-intensity of goods imported by the United States. Leontief should have analysed and made an attempt to find out whether goods imported by the United States from abroad were capital-intensive or labour-intensive in the countries where those goods were produced. Ellsworth's criticism is based on the existence of different production functions among different countries. The criticism against Leontief was that he wrongly assumed identical production functions among different countries. But this assumption is not valid and this cuts the ground under the Leontief Paradox.

(6) Leontief himself has provided an explanation of the Leontief Paradox according to which with relative abundance of capital and relative scarcity of labour, the United States exported labour-intensive goods thus disproving the Heckscher-Ohlin theory of international trade.

Leontief maintained that labour in the United States is more efficient and produced as much as three times of what labour produced abroad in countries where there was relative abundance of labour. This higher productivity and efficiency of American labour is due to superior organisation, better entrepreneurship, more favourable environment and technical skills acquired rather than due to the use of larger amount of capital per worker in the United States. This, in fact, makes the United States a relatively more labour abundant country, contrary to the assumption that the United States is a relatively labour scarce country.

Concluding Remarks

In spite of the above criticism of the Leontief Paradox, Lenotief retested his findings using average composition of the exports and imports of the United States and enlarging the group of studied industries to 192 sectors. This study which Leontief carried out with reference to the year 1951 confirmed his earlier finding that the imports of the United States were relatively more capital-intensive relative to the exports of the United States. Using input-output tables for the year 1958, Prof. R.E. Baldwin arrived at the same conclusion as that of Leontief's study conducted in 1951. On this account, the Leontief Paradox continues to hold the ground in the United States.

5.10 THE LEONTIEF PARADOX AND EXPERIENCE OF OTHER COUNTRIES

Tatemoto and Ichimura analysing Japan's pattern of trade with the rest of the world confirmed the Leontief Paradox. Japan though relatively labour-abundant and capital-scare country, imported labour-intensive commodities and exported capital-intensive commodities like motor-cars, cameras, T.V. sets, computers, watches and so on while importing labour-intensive commodities like industrial raw materials, iron-ore, wood and wood-pulp etc. These findings were opposed to the Heckscher-Ohlin theory and in confirmation of the Leontief Paradox. The authors attributed this to the fact that Japan's 75 per cent of trade is with developing and underdeveloped countries which are relatively capital-deficient.

But their findings in relation to Japan's trade with the United States confirmed the Heckscher-Ohlin theory.

Prof. Stopler and Roskamp studying international trade of East Germany arrived at the same conclusion that was in conformity with the Heckscher-Ohlin theory.

Wahl's findings regarding Canada's trade with the United States did not confirm the Heckscher-Ohlin theory; on the other hand, the study confirmed the Lenotief Paradox.

Prof. Bhardwaj's study of India's international trade with the rest of world found that India's exports were labour-intensive relative to her imports. This finding is in line with the Heckscher-Ohlin theory. But in another study concerning India's trade with the United States, the author found that India's exports to the United States were capital-intensive. This finding refuted the Heckscher-Ohlin theory and confirmed the Leontief Paradox.

5.11 THE LEONTIEF PARADOX AND THE HECKSCHER-OHLIN THEORY — ATTEMPT AT RECONCILIATION

A number of economists have made an attempt to reconcile the Leontief Paradox with the Heckscher-Ohlin theory of international trade.

Leontief himself explained the paradox bringing about reconciliation between his paradox and the Heckscher-Ohlin theory. This he did in terms of 'Productivity of Labour in the United States.' He argued that the United States is, in fact, a relatively labour-abundant country, because though relatively scarce in the quantitative sense, the American labour is much more efficient and productive than labour in labour-abundant countries like India and China, not to speak of labour in African countries. This means that the United States is, in fact, a labour-abundant country. He attributed higher productivity of the American labour to better organisation and entrepreneurship rather than the use of more capital per worker.

Prof. Leontief failed to include in his analysis the significance of human capital. A number of economists studied the relationship between investment in human capital and the United States' trade composition. Baldwin has noted that by using human capital rather than physical capital, the United States exported more human capital-intensive commodities than the country imported labour-intensive commodities. There is no doubt that the United States has relatively abundant human capital (i.e., labour on which huge amounts have been invested to impart to them various types of skills of very high quality).

The third point to be noted is that Leontief neglected the important part played by natural resources in the United States, in relation to its international trade. Vanek in his article on 'The Natural Resources Content of United States' Foreign Trade' pointed out that the United States is relatively short of several natural resources. Natural resources and capital are complementary as capital is necessary to export natural resources. The author pointed out that though the United States is relatively capital-abundant, the United States imports are relatively capital-intensive because capital requires larger amounts of scarce natural resources for efficient production. The United States, according to the author, therefore, imports natural resources like minerals having high capital-labour ratio and exports farm produce having relatively low capital-labour ratios.

Fourthly, Travis's and Baldwin's studies have demonstrated that trade barriers and commercial policies adopted by different countries provide evidence for the Leontief Paradox. For example, the United States imposes heavy duties on imports of labour-intensive commodities from abroad in addition to erecting some non-tariff barriers against their imports. But these studies did not provide broad and adequate statistical material to support Leontief Paradox.

Fifthly, Leontief has not taken into account the impact of consumption pattern on the United States' exports and imports. Several studies have shown that with rise in the level of income, demand for labour-intensive commodities increases. Brown's study has demonstrated that the United States' consumption pattern has been moving in favour of labour-intensive commodities rather than capital-intensive commodities. This would mean that more and more capital-intensive goods no longer form part of consumption pattern of the people in the United States. And, therefore, more and more labour-intensive goods from abroad are being imported by the United States. This result goes against the Leontief Paradox.

Sixthly and lastly, the Leontief Paradox, like the Heckscher-Ohlin theory, has not taken into consideration the impact of technological changes on international trading pattern. Raymond Vernon in his article on 'International Investment and International Trade in the Product Cycle' (1966) has shown that the United States has a comparative advantage in new products which that country introduces into world trade because of their advanced R & D and continuous application of industrial technology, irrespective of the fact whether the new commodity is capital-intensive or labour-intensive. When a commodity is new in the United States, though it is labour-intensive, the United States would find it easy to export such a commodity. But when in course of time, the new commodity becomes a standard commodity produced in a number of countries the United States would lose the early advantage and begin to import such a commodity from countries with relative labour abundance. There is no doubt that R & D and technological advances play a crucial role in determining the pattern of international trade. For example, we find at present a labour-abundant country like Japan, because of technological excellence and its continual updating has been exporting to capital-rich United States capital-intensive articles like motor-cars, motor-cycles, cameras, electronic goods, electrical goods, etc. and though Japan has labour-abundance, it has been importing labour-intensive raw materials from developing countries to be converted into highly sophisticated articles mentioned above and export them. Both the Heckscher-Ohlin theory as also the Leontief Paradox failed to take note of the effects of changing technology on the pattern of international trade.

CHAPTER

6 GAINS FROM TRADE

Structure:

6.1 Gains from Trade

6.2 Factors Determining Gains from International Trade

Introduction

Just as domestic or internal trade benefits both sellers and buyers, in the same way, international trade, as shown below, benefits all the countries participating in international trading transactions.

6.1 GAINS FROM TRADE

The idea of gains from trade can be traced back to the Ricardian model itself. To Ricardo, "the extension of foreign trade... will very powerfully contribute to increase the mass of commodities, and therefore, the sum of enjoyments".[1] In modern terminology this implies that trade is a positive sum game.

Since Ricardo's writing of the *Principles of Political Economy and Taxation (1817)*, however, the terms like the mass of commodities and sum of enjoyments have been refined by successive generation of economists. Today we express gains from trade in terms of increase in country's real income and so on. What constitutes the gains from trading according to these modern theoretical developments is exactly the subject matter of this chapter.

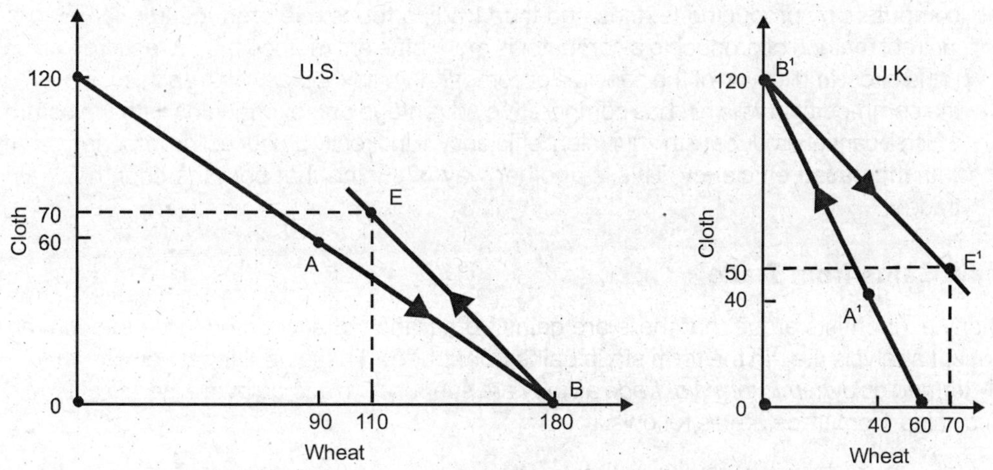

Fig. 6.1. The Gains from Trade. In the absence of trade, the United States produces and consumes at *A*, and the United Kingdom at *A'*. With trade, the United States specializes in the production of wheat and produces at *B*, while the United Kingdom specializes in the production of cloth and produces at *B'*. By exchanging 70W for 70C with the United Kingdom, the United States ends up consuming at *E* (and gains 20W and 10C), while the United Kingdom ends up consuming at *E'* (and gains 30W and 10C).

---

1. As quoted in Meier Gerald M., (1980), *"International Economics –The Theory of Policy"*, Oxford University Press, p. 57.

Static Gains from Trade

By the term static we mean gain at the given point of time or simply one time gain. The major contribution to this notion has been that by Paul Samuelson through two articles. One was published in 1939[2] and the other in 1962.[3] Kemp (1962)[4] also contributed to the initial development of the idea. Rather he extended the analysis of Samuelson's 1939 article. The propositions put forward are summarised in point one and two below:

(1) Trade enhances the range of choice and also entails increased consumption of both the importable and exportable goods. This means a country engaging in trade has consumption possibilities frontier beyond its production possibilities frontier. This not only holds for a small country case but also for a large country case.[5] This implies that existence of perfect competition is not a necessary condition for gains from trade to accrue. Rather as pointed out by Bhagwati (1968)[6] the proposition that the opportunity to trade is superior to autarky situation applies regardless of the institutional situation; in particular it even applies to a planned economy.

(2) We can also think of the gains from trade in terms of indirect method of production. For example, India could produce computers itself, but trade with USA allows it to produce computers by producing textiles and then trading the textile products for computers. This indirect method of producing a computer is more efficient method than direct production. This is the direct implication of the principle of comparative advantage. With each country producing the commodity in which it has comparative advantage and exchanging with the commodity, which it cannot produce with equivalent efficiency, it indirectly produces the imported commodity with increased efficiency. This is another way of seeing that both the countries gain from trade.

Dynamic Gains from Trade[7]

Many economists argue that there are gains from trade not accounted for in the conventional cost-benefit analysis (i.e., in the term static gains from trade). These additional gains from trade can be aptly termed as *dynamic terms of trade* as they are supposed to accrue over a period of time. These dynamic gains from trade are as follows:

(1) *Economies of Scale:* Protected markets provide opportunity to earn super normal profits which leads to proliferation of firms in the narrow domestic markets. This in turn makes the scale of production of each firm inefficient. Opportunity to trade allows a country to overcome these diseconomies of scale imposed by small size of its protected internal markets.

---

2. "The Gains from International Trade", *Canadian Journal of Economics and Political Science* 5, pp. 195-205.
3. "The Gains from International Trade Once Again", *Economic Journal,* 72: pp. 820-829.
4. "The Gains from International Trade", *Economic Journal,* pp. 803, 819.
5. This requires application of an optimal tariff. However, this is a slightly advanced point. Interested readers may consult Chapter 2 of Handbook of International Economics, Vol. I, Edited by R. W. Jones and P. B. Kenen, Elsevier Science Publishers B.V., 1984.
6. As quoted in Jones & Kenen (1984), p. 71, *op. cit.*
7. This section draws heavily on Krugman Paul and Obstfed Maurice (2000), *International Economics,* 5th Ed., Addison Wesley Longman, pp. 219-221.

(2) *Learning and Innovation:* By providing entrepreneurs with an incentive to explore new ways to export or compete with imports, free trade offers more opportunities for learning and innovation than are provided by a system of "managed" trade, where the government dictates the pattern of imports and exports. With freer trade in an increasingly techno savvy world, technological diffusion and adaptation, the transfer of skills, and know-how, contribute to accelerating the country's learning rate.

(3) *Economic growth:* International Trade transforms production functions and induces outward shift in the production frontier. This implies stimulus to economic growth and hence leading to economic development. This is supposed to happen through following channels emphasized by growing theoretical and empirical literature in the area:[8]

Government policy: Trade openness may create incentives for policy makers to pursue virtuous macroeconomic policies, either because of threat of capital flight or because of international agreements, implicit or explicit, that act as a check on policy.

Open economies are less likely to have tradable goods prices that diverge substantially from the world prices. Secondly, as they are also expected to specialize according to their comparative advantage, the effect of non-tradable goods on deviations from purchasing power parity will be eventually eliminated. Hence, we can expect lower price distortion in open economies and price distortions have been shown to adversely affect factor accumulation and growth.

Trade liberalisation may simply allow domestic agents to import capital goods that were previously unavailable or available only at prohibitive prices, thus removing structural constraints on investment. This would have a positive effect on growth.

Technological transmissions: If knowledge spillovers are a driving force for sustained, long run growth, and open economies are more exposed to a world wide stock of productivity-enhancing knowledge, then trade openness can affect growth and convergence through technology transmissions.

Trade, Growth and Poverty

The post 1980 period has seen a number of globalizers including India. Does their economic performance reflect gains from globalizing? The following are the facts about these globalizers, which are documented by David Dollar and Aart Kraay.*

Globalizers have experienced a significantly higher growth rate in real per capita GDP as compared to non-globalizers.

They have also seen reduction in poverty in post-globalisation period.

They don't record any systematic increase in inequality.

On an international level the gap between the rich nations and the poor nations has narrowed.

* David Dollar and Aart Kraay (2001a), "Growth is Good for the Poor", World Bank Policy Research Department Working Paper No. 2587 (Washington).

— (2001b), "Trade, Growth and Poverty", World Bank Policy Research Department Working Paper No. 2615 (Washington).

8. Wacziarg Romain (2001), "Measuring the Dynamic Gains from Trade", *The World Bank Economic Review,* Vol. 15, No. 3, pp. 393-429.

6.2 FACTORS DETERMINING GAINS FROM INTERNATIONAL TRADE

Following factors determine how gains from international trade will be shared by participating countries:

(1) *Differences in Cost Ratios or Relative Cost Advantage:* As Prof. Harrod has pointed out "A country gains by foreign trade, if and when, the traders find that there exists abroad a ratio of prices very different from that to which they are accustomed to at home. They buy what to them seems cheap and sell what to them seems dear. The bigger the gap between what to them seems low profits and high profits, and more important the article affected, greater will be the gain from trade."[9]

If Australia has a comparative advantage over England in the production of wheat and if England has comparative advantage in the production of cloth both Australia and England will gain from specialisation and international trade. The size of the gain from international trade will depend upon cost of production of each commodity in both the countries. If due to increase in the efficiency of labour, cost of production of wheat declines in Australia, England will gain more from international trade. Opposite will take place in case efficiency of English labour goes up and cost of production of cloth declines, Australia will have greater gain than before from international trade. Thus, greater the comparative cost differences or greater the relative cost advantage, larger the gains from international trade.

The point can be illustrated with some illustrations.

Let us assume that the original position was as follows:

X number of mandays produce in —

England 200 units of cloth or 200 units of wheat;

Australia 80 units of cloth or 160 units of wheat.

If due to increased efficiency of labour in Australia in the production of wheat, let us assume that the new situation is as follows:

X number of mandays produce in Australia either 80 units of cloth or 240 units of wheat.

If all the other conditions remain the same, in the new situation, Australia will be in a position to offer England not upto 2 units of wheat for one unit of cloth, but upto a maximum of 3 units of wheat for one unit of English cloth. England will, therefore, benefit because of increased efficiency of Australian labour in the production of wheat.

If on the other hand, because of improvement in the efficiency of labour in England in the production of cloth, let us assume that

X number of mandays can produce in England –

Either 400 units of cloth (not 200 units as before) or

200 units of wheat, whereas in Australia

X number of mandays produce, as in the original illustration, either 80 units of cloth or 160 units of wheat.

This means now England, due to increased efficiency of labour in the production of cloth, will be willing to offer not as before anything upto 1 unit of cloth for 1 unit of wheat, but anything

9. R. F. Harrod, *International Economics,* p. 34.

up to the maximum of 2 units of cloth for 1 unit for wheat from Australia. This means, other conditions remaining the same, this increased labour efficiency in the production of cloth will be more beneficial to Australia.

(2) *Reciprocal Demand or Relative Elasticities of Demand for Each Other's Commodities:* Within the lower and upper limits fixed by comparative cost advantage, the actual terms of trade will be determined by relative elasticities of demand for each other's commodity. If for example, England wants Australian wheat more urgently (i.e., if the demand is more inelastic) than Australian demand for English cloth, gains from international trade would be more in favour of Australia, though both the countries would be gaining from international trade.

(3) *Size of Participating Countries:* What is the relationship between size of a country and gains from international trade?

One argument is that a small country gains more from international trade than a large country. A small country does not normally possess diverse types of productive resources; also the size of the domestic market is small or limited. And therefore, by specialising on the basis of its advantageous resources and by exchanging its goods against goods produced in other countries, the small country can thus get commodities it cannot produce because of its small size and lack of different varieties of resources.

If both the trading countries are small and both specialise and enter into international trade, gains from international trade would be relatively smaller as both the small countries have relatively small exportable surplus.

If one of the trading countries is large and the other small, exportable surplus with the large country would be fairly large; but the exportable surplus with the small country would be relatively small. While the small country can exchange all the exportable surplus in exchange for goods in which the large country has specialised, the large country would not be in a position to exchange all its exportable surplus and while the gains from international trade in the case of small country would be substantial, for the larger country gains would be limited.

If however, both the internationally trading countries are large, both with large exportable surplus of commodities in which they have specialised, both the large countries would be reaping substantial gains from international trade.

(4) *Level of Income in a Country and Gains from International Trade:* The level of income of people in a country has great influence on sharing gains from international trade.

If, for example, exports of a country are in great demand because level of income of people in the importing country is fairly high, such goods will be in a position to command higher price and income level of people in the country exporting those goods will rise. This will mean higher wages in export industries. The rising income of people in export industries will also mean increasing demand for other domestic goods whose prices will also go up and therefore, level of income of people producing those goods would also rise.

On the other hand, if in a country, demand for imported goods from the other country is relatively small or elastic (i.e., imported goods are not urgently wanted) people in the importing country will be getting imported goods at relatively lower price; income of the people producing such goods will be lower. This will also mean lower demand for other domestically produced goods while they will be paying high prices for imported goods (assuming that demand for such goods is inelastic in the importing country).

CHAPTER 7

TERMS OF TRADE

Structure:

7.1 INTRODUCTION

After countries decide to take advantage of international division of labour and specialization and enter into international trading transactions, the most important question that arises is: How are the terms of trade (i.e., how much of one country's commodity is going to be exchanged against how much of the other country's commodity) becomes an important matter. One reason for this is that though both the trading countries gain from international trade, it is the determination of terms of trade that decides how the total gains from international trade will be shared between the two trading partners. Hence the importance of terms of trade and of the study of factors that influence and determine the terms of trade.

7.2 COMMODITY TERMS OF TRADE, FACTOR TERMS OF TRADE, INCOME TERMS OF TRADE AND UTILITY TERMS OF TRADE

Terms of trade are interpreted in different ways by different economists:

(1) *Commodity Terms of Trade:* Commodity terms of trade refer to the ratio of prices of exported goods to the prices of imported goods. If, for example, prices of exported goods decline or prices of exported goods rise relatively more slowly than prices of imported goods, it is said that commodity terms of trade have become unfavourable. This would mean that in order to maintain favourable terms of trade it is necessary to regulate prices of exported goods and those of imported goods (by tariffs, etc.).

But the concept of commodity terms of trade does not throw light on the capacity to import on the part of the country; this is because capacity to import depends not only on terms of trade but also on volume of exports.

(2) *Factor Terms of Trade:* The concept of 'Factor Terms of Trade' explains gains from international trade in terms of sacrifice of factors of production in the production of exported goods. The concept refers to the ratio of factors of production employed in the production of one unit of exported goods to the amount of imports made by the exporting country by exporting that one unit.

It is possible that prices of exported goods are declining because productivity of factors of production employed in the production of exported goods is increasing and, therefore, to produce one unit of exported goods, a smaller amount of factors of production than before is required. This means that it might happen by sacrificing a smaller amount of factors of production, the country would be able to get the same amount or even larger amount of imported goods. In this case there is improvement in factor terms of trade. It is likely that commodity terms of trade and factor terms of trade may change in the opposite direction; this is because prices of exported goods may decline without decline in the prices of imported goods, thus making commodity terms of trade unfavourable. But if at the same time there is increase in productivity of factors of production employed in the production of export industries at a rate faster than decline in the prices of exported goods, the amount of imports that would be secured for per unit of factors of production would increase so that factor terms of trade would improve.

(3) *Income Terms of Trade:* And, therefore, with a view to explain a country's capacity to import by exporting goods, the concept of income terms of trade was devised. 'Income Terms of

Trade' represents the ratio of export prices to import prices multiplied by the index of volume of exports.

It should be clear that commodity terms of trade may become unfavourable even as income terms of trade are improving. This is because, if prices of exported goods decline without corresponding decline in prices of imported goods, it would mean that commodity terms of trade are deteriorating; but it may also happen that the volume of export may increase at a rate faster than declined in prices of exported goods. For example, if prices of exported goods decline by, say, 5 per cent, and even if volume of exports of the country increases by more than 5 per cent, the export earnings would increase, increasing capacity to import. This means even as commodity terms of trade have deteriorated, income terms of trade have improved.

(4) *Utility Terms of Trade:* Like 'Factor Terms of Trade', there can also be 'Utility Terms of Trade.' Utility terms of trade explain the gains from international trade with reference to utility or satisfaction by the consumption of internationally traded goods. If, for example, utility of imported goods increases with sacrifice of utility involved in making exported goods remaining constant, it can be said that there is improvement in utility terms to trade. This is because by sacrificing the same amount of utility, the country is securing a larger amount of utility in terms of imported goods.

But it may be noted that utility terms of trade are not of much practical use, because it is impossible to accurately measure utility sacrificed and utility obtained in exchange through international trading transactions. And, therefore, though theoretically utility terms of trade are of significance, for policy purposes the concept is not of any use. This explains why the concepts of commodity terms of trade, income terms of trade and factor terms of trade are used while formulating international trade policies and not utility terms of trade.

It should be clear that while commenting on changes in terms of trade, it is necessary to specify which terms of trade we have in view, because there are different policy implications in the case of different concepts of terms of trade.

7.3 FACTORS INFLUENCING TERMS OF TRADE

Following are the important factors that influence terms of trade:

(1) *Cost Differences or Relative Cost Advantage:* How comparative cost differences or relative cost advantage influences terms of trade can be illustrated with an example (already analysed earlier).

Let us assume that X number of mandays produce:

In England either 200 units of cloth or 200 units of wheat; and

In Australia either 80 units of cloth or 160 units of wheat.

This means by sacrificing 1 unit of cloth, England can produce 1 unit of wheat in its own country. If England specialises in the production of cloth, it follows that in exchange of her 1 unit of cloth, England must get at least something more than 1 unit of wheat. This is the lower limit of terms of trade from England's point of view.

If we consider the figures for Australia, it will be observed that Australia can herself produce 1 unit of cloth by sacrificing 2 units of wheat. This means in exchange of 1 unit of English cloth, Australia will be prepared to give anything upto 2 units of wheat.

Thus, England for 1 unit of her cloth wants from Australia at least a little more than 1 unit of wheat, while Australia for 1 unit of English cloth is prepared to give anything upto 2 units of wheat. Thus, relative cost differences in England and Australia in respect of cloth and wheat determine the lowermost and uppermost limits of terms of trade between English cloth and Australian wheat.

(2) *Reciprocal Demand:* Between the above lowermost and uppermost limits, the actual terms of trade between English cloth and Australian wheat will be determined by 'reciprocal demand' (i.e., elasticity of demand for each other's commodity).

To revert back to the above illustration, if England's demand for Australian wheat is relatively more urgent and pressing (i.e. more inelastic) than the Australian demand for English cloth, then between the above two limits, the actual terms of trade will move more in favour of Australia than England. Australia will be giving for 1 unit of cloth from England above 1 unit of wheat but far less than the maximum of 2 units of wheat. Thus, the terms of trade will be determined in such a way that they ate far more favourable to Australia which will be gaining more from international trading transaction than England.

On the other hand, if due to any reason, Australian demand for English cloth is much more urgent and pressing (i.e., inelastic), than England's demand for Australian wheat, then the actual terms of trade will move more in favour of England (which though prepared to accept just a little over 1 unit of wheat for 1 unit of cloth), will be in a position to extract from Australia anything up to 2 units of wheat for her 1 unit of cloth. In this case, though both England and Australia will be gaining from international trading transaction, the share of England in the total gain will be more than that of Australia.

(3) *Changes in Tastes and Fashions:* Changes in tastes and fashions also influence terms of trade. Suppose, tastes of Australian people change and they prefer to have much more clothing than before due to change in tastes or fashion, this would mean that the Australian demand for English cloth has become relatively more urgent. This will turn the terms of trade more in favour of England which for 1 unit of cloth will be getting in return something nearer to 2 units of Australian wheat.

(4) *Technological Changes:* If due to technological advances (e.g., better seeds, better chemical fertilisers, etc.), Australia can produce wheat more efficiently so that the new position in Australia is: X number of mandays can produce either 80 units of cloth or 240 units of wheat (and not just 160 units of wheat as before), it would mean that with this technological advance in the production of wheat in Australia, for 1 unit of English cloth, Australia can now offer the maximum of anything upto 3 units of wheat (and not 2 units of wheat as before).

If on the other hand, because of technological progress in England, X number of mandays begin to produce 400 units of cloth (and not just 200 units as before) or 200 units of wheat, it would mean that England is prepared to accept anything above 1/2 unit of wheat (and not anything above 1 unit of wheat as before).

Thus, technological changes in England and Australia would change the lowermost and the uppermost limits of terms of trade between English cloth and Australian wheat. The actual terms of trade between these two lowermost and uppermost limits would be determined by relative elasticity of demand for each other's goods (i.e., how urgent Australian demand for English cloth is compared to the urgency of English demand for Australian wheat).

(5) *Capital Inflows and Outflows:* When a country borrows from abroad, especially from hard currency countries, this results in increase in demand for goods of creditor countries and pushes up their prices. This results in influencing the terms of trade. Also, when the time for the repayment of the loan comes, the required foreign currencies must be obtained anyhow to pay the loan back to the creditor country. This may require selling domestically produced goods rather cheaply to get the required hard currency. This may also result in making terms of trade less favourable for the debtor country.

(6) *Balance of Payments Position:* If a country has been facing continually adverse balance of trade and payments, the country will have either to devalue its currency or follow the policy of deflation to correct the adverse balance of trade and payments position. This would make the terms of trade go against the country facing continually adverse balance of trade and payments position.

(7) *Tariffs:* Imposition of tariffs can influence terms of trade. This can be shown with the usual illustration of English cloth and Australian wheat. If England imposes tariff duties on Australian wheat exports to England, and if Australian demand for English cloth is inelastic compared to the English demand for Australian wheat, the burden of tariff will have to be borne by Australian exporters of wheat which in other terms means that per unit of cloth exported, England will be getting more units of Australian wheat than before when tariff duties were not imposed.

For example, after independence, India had the monopoly of jute manufactures which were in great demand in the United States (to store agricultural produce). India doubled export duty on jute manufactures; the American demand for jute manufactures being inelastic, the American importers were made to pay twice the price (in terms of dollars) per ton of jute manufacturers exported to America. This, in effect, meant that per ton of jute manufactures exported to America, India started securing twice the quantity of American goods than before. Thus, the export duty turned the terms of trade more in favour of India than of America.

Concluding Remarks

In the real world, there are not just two countries and two commodities. And therefore, with the lowermost and uppermost limits of terms of trade determined by comparative cost differences, it is the degree of elasticity of demand for different commodities that determines the actual terms of trade at which exchanges take place. And elasticity of demand for commodity, as is well-known, is influenced by factors like tastes and fashions, available substitutes, whether a commodity has single or multiple uses, whether use of a commodity can be postponed or not, and so on.

7.4 TERMS OF TRADE AND ECONOMIC WELFARE

It is with the help of real per capita income that economic welfare of people in a country is measured.

It is generally believed that changes in terms of trade (i.e., the rate at which 1 unit of exported commodity of a country is exchanged for how many units of a commodity imported from another country) has significant impact on the welfare of the people in a country.

With improvement in terms of trade (i.e., greater increase in the prices of exported commodities relative to increases in the prices of imported goods, with foreign exchange rate remaining the same as before), if the volume of export remains the same or increases, that increases the volume of goods available for people in the country.

It has, therefore, favourable effect on the welfare of the people in the country (i.e., there is relative increase in the total welfare of people in the country). On the other hand, deterioration in terms of trade (other things remaining the same) has unfavourable impact on the total welfare of people in the country.

While thinking of commodity terms of trade, one has to be careful in calculating their impact on the welfare of the community.

For example; if there is an increase of 10 per cent in the productive efficiency in country A, that may result either in 10 per cent increase in total output or total output remaining the same in saving of productive resources needed to produce 10 per cent output.

It is possible that increased efficiency reduces cost of production and, therefore, prices of exported commodity. If so, it is possible that the terms of trade will decline. But this does not mean that the country is worse off than before. If cost of production declines by 10 per cent due to increase in efficiency, and if the terms of trade declines by say 5 per cent only, the volume of exports remaining the same, it would mean that the country is in fact well off than before, in spite of decline in its terms of trade. This means that deterioration in terms of trade does not necessarily mean that the country against which the terms of trade have deteriorated is worse off than before.

Changes in Terms of Trade and Economic Welfare

Changes in the terms of trade in respect of country A may be the result of operation of external factors or internal factors. Suppose terms of trade improve in respect of country A because demand in country B for country A's commodity has declined due to some or the other factor. Under such circumstances, country A will benefit because a given quantity of export of A's commodity will hereafter exchange for a larger quantity of commodity of country B. Thus, favourable changes in terms of trade because of external factors will increase welfare of people in country A.

But there can be an exception. If improvement in terms of trade in favour of country A results at the same time in substantial decrease in export of that commodity from country A resulting in unemployment in that export industry of country A, welfare of people in country A will be adversely affected, even if the terms of trade have moved in favour of country A. Thus, the conclusion is that if other things remain the same, improvement in terms of trade in favour of country A due to external factors will have favourable impact on the welfare of people in country A.

If on other hand, due to external factors like decrease in demand for A's commodity in country B, or increase in supply of similar commodity in country B, result in making terms of trade unfavourable to country A, other conditions remaining the same, such deterioration in terms of trade against country A will have unfavourable impact on the welfare of people in country A.

Changes in terms of trade of country A can also be brought about due to internal factors operating in country A. If cost of production of a certain commodity rises in country A because of internal factors, and if price of exportable commodity rises, the following effects are likely to result.

If demand in country B for country A's commodity is rigid (i.e., inelastic), then the same quantity as before of A's commodity will be bought by country B. This in effect means that the same quantity of A's export will bring in exchange larger imports from country B than before. This will have a favourable impact on the welfare of people in country A.

But if on the other hand, rising cost of production and rising price of the commodity produced in country A led to substantial decline in demand for it in country B because demand for the commodity is elastic, it will lead to an increase in unemployment in that industry in country A. This will produce adverse effect on the welfare of people in country A.

If due to technological changes in country A, cost of production gets reduced but prices of export commodities are not reduced to the same extent due to inelastic demand for it in country B, this would mean that by using fewer domestic resources, country A is in a position to get the same quantity of imports from country B. This will naturally have a favourable impact on the welfare of people in country A.

Concluding Remarks

Thus, the relationship between changes in terms of trade and their impact on the welfare of people is rather complex and no direct and straightforward answer can be given in this regard. Prof. Haberler has summed up the relationship between the terms of trade and welfare of the people as follows: "The knowledge that the terms of trade for a country or group of countries have changed in a certain way over a certain period of time is of precious little importance unless it is combined with other types of information."

7.5 CAN A COUNTRY IMPROVE ITS TERMS OF TRADE?

A country can influence terms of trade in its favour, only if the country can successfully influence the prices of its exports and imports. For example, if country A contributes a significant portion of commodity in the world market, it will be in a position to influence prices of its exports in its favour. India was in a position to do that for some decades in respect of her jute manufactures.

If there are only a few countries supplying a substantial portion of a commodity in the world market, they can join hands in a consortium and secure a near-monopoly position in respect of that commodity and thus be in a position to influence the price of that commodity and thus make the terms of trade more favourable to the group of countries in the consortium. The Middle Eastern petroleum producing countries adopted this strategy in the mid-1970s by forming Organisation of Petroleum Exporting Countries (OPEC) and successfully raising the price of crude by about ten times the original price (from an average of 3 US dollars per barrel to US dollars 30 per barrel).

A country can influence the price of an imported commodity in its favour, either by finding a substitute for the formerly imported commodity, or imposing import duties and make the trading partner bear the entire burden of the tax or substantial part of it by reducing the price of that commodity, provided the demand for that commodity is fairly elastic.

The terms of trade have their own natural tendency to find their own level at which the terms of trade get fixed and change with fundamental changes in the economies of trading countries.

This means any attempt to artificially alter favourably the terms of trade by imposing export or import duties or by fixing quotas, etc. will not be effective in the long run as such measures are bound in the long run to bring retaliation or even otherwise being about reduction in the volume of world trade with unfavourable consequences on the welfare of the peoples of the world.

7.6 TERMS OF TRADE AND DEVELOPING COUNTRIES

Developing countries depend mainly on exports of primary products (i.e., agricultural commodities, industrial raw materials like skin and hides, iron ore and other raw materials, wood and wood pulp, etc.) to earn foreign exchange with which to import capital goods and other essential industrial raw materials needed to successfully execute their plans of rapid industrialisation which objective most developing countries have accepted to successfully deal with the problems of vast unemployment and mass poverty.

Observation of trends in terms of trade during the post-World War period makes it clear that the terms of trade have been continuously moving against primary or agricultural products which happen to be the main export items and source of foreign exchange earnings of developing countries. In fact, Raul Prebisch had demonstrated that terms of trade have a secular tendency to move against primary products (i.e., against developing countries) and in favour of manufactured and capital goods (which means in favour of industrialised or developed countries). Prebisch has tried to prove his thesis with reference to the exports of the United Kingdom between 1870 and 1940. There is ground to believe and adequate proof to show that the above trend has continued to this day.

Raul Prebisch has advanced two reasons for the above state of affairs. One is that there had been taking place technological progress in developed countries and the fruits of this progress have not been passed on to developing countries. Secondly, industrialised countries have had monopolistic control over production of industrial goods so that they could manipulate their prices in their favour and against the interest of developing countries.

There are a number of reasons responsible for terms of trade moving against exporters of primary commodities (i.e., against developing countries):

(1) Developed countries are also agriculturally developed countries. Not only they are self-sufficient in agricultural commodities, but they have vast surplus agricultural stocks available for export to different countries in Asia and Africa. Vast quantities of food grains, cotton and oil-seeds sold in India during 1950s and 1960s under PL 480 programme is proof enough of this. Accumulation of vast dairy stocks in the European Economic Community countries and their anxiety as to how to get rid of those stocks provides proof of the developed state of the agricultural sector in developed countries.

(2) As the level of income rises in developed countries, their demand for foodgrains does not rise to the same extent. After a limit demand in developed countries for agricultural commodities remains more or less stable or even declines creating growingly unfavourable effect on developing countries where agricultural sector is the predominant sector and often the only sector.

(3) There has been taking place technological progress in developed countries at a very rapid pace, especially during the post-World War II period. One consequence of this has been that synthetic substances like plastics, artificial rubber, man-made fiber, metallic silos for storing foodgrains (instead of jute bags) are being made use of to an increasing extent. The consequence is that demand for primary products like natural rubber, cotton, jute manufactures, etc. has not been rising significantly. Also, the above development has been forcing the terms of trade to move more and more against primary goods producing developing countries. Another consequence of the use of substitutes is that more and more synthetic substances are being used for manufacturing goods instead of natural products. For example, the amount of steel used per motor-car has gone down by about 50 per cent and substitutes like durable plastic and unbreakable artificial glass are being used to a greater extent. This would mean that demand for iron ore from India for the manufacture of steel to be used for the manufacture of motor-cars would decline or would be demanded at a lower price, thus making terms of trade much more unfavourable to India.

(4) Industrialised countries have been trying to trade more and more among themselves. For example, the European Economic Community was formed so that mutual economic cooperation among the twelve member-countries goes on increasing. If necessary, the EEC will not mind putting restrictions on imports from developing countries, to promote trade among themselves. This is also responsible for slow increase of exports from developing countries and for terms of trade moving against them.

(5) Even as some of the developing countries have launched programmes of rapid industrialisation, developed countries have been adopting protectionist policies especially against manufactured goods being exported from developing countries. This is forcing terms of trade against them.[1]

7.7 POSSIBLE EFFECTS OF ADVERSE TERMS OF TRADE ON DEVELOPING COUNTRIES

The fact that during the post-World War II period, terms of trade are continuously deteriorating against primary products which means against developing countries has been producing various adverse effects on developing countries and on the pace of their economic development which has been their main objective after they became independent after the end of World War II (1939-45).

1. Prof. Haberler does not agree with the Raul Prebisch's thesis of secular tendency of terms of trade moving against primary products and in favour of manufactured goods.

According to Haberler, this thesis is essentially based on commodity terms of trade of the United Kingdom and without careful verification. The United Kingdom's experience cannot be taken as representative of terms of trade of all the other manufacturing countries.

Secondly, the commodity terms of trade did not make any allowance for improvement in quality of industrial products. For example, motor-cars or motor – cycles imported then from developed countries during 1940s and 1950s by developing countries are not the same as those imported during 1980s. The quality of presently manufactured goods from developed countries is vastly superior to quality of goods imported during earlier decades. The same holds good in respect of many other industrial products imported from developed countries by developing countries during recent decades.

Thirdly, the Prebisch's thesis does not make allowance for new products being exported by developed countries [e.g., automatic watches, tape-recorders, calculators, detergents, new medicines, computers and so on.]

Haberler and H.G. Johnson have not accepted the Prebisch thesis. Haberler even maintained that terms of trade are not a proper guide to understand the gains from international trade and economic growth in developing countries.

Following are the main adverse effects of deteriorating terms of trade on developing countries:

(1) In commodity terms of trade, a unit of exported commodity from developing country is getting in exchange less and less in terms of manufactured goods from developed countries.

(2) Developing countries are finding it very difficult to push their exports to the level that would enable them to earn adequate foreign currencies to meet their demand for essential capital goods, spares, industrial raw materials, foreigners' service and technical know-how. And therefore almost all the developing countries have been facing balance of payments problems with a big and widening gap between their export earnings and import bills.

(3) Difficult balance of payments position of developing countries has been continuously forcing developing countries to borrow from developed countries and from the World Bank and other international financial institutions. Also, what is noticed in recent years is that the terms and conditions on which foreign loans are being made available to developing countries are becoming harder and harder. For example, sometimes developing countries are asked to devalue their currencies (as was done in the case in India in 1966); developing counties are asked to depend more and more on loans from commercial banks in developed countries. This means paying higher rate of interest on foreign loans. Also, while granting loans, the World Bank, the I.M.F. and the creditor countries are often found dictating economic policies of debtor countries. They are, for example, asked to adopt more and more liberal policies in the case of imports from developed countries and give up protectionist policies. This is bound to have adverse effects on industries in developing policies. Increasing foreign debts are making developing countries more and more politically and economically dependent on developed countries.

(4) The amounts of foreign debt of developing countries from developed countries and international monetary and financial institutions have been continually increasing as also the servicing charges on foreign debts. Extremely difficult foreign exchange position has arisen in the case of some of the Latin American countries like Brazil and Mexico in whose case almost the entire export earning of those countries are inadequate for servicing charges on foreign debts. These countries requested that some part of their foreign debt should be written off, the remaining part should be rescheduled in regard to repayment and the rate of interest reduced. But the developed creditor countries are not prepared to agree to any of the above proposals and naturally this has been posing an extremely difficult and complex problem for those Latin American countries.

In the case of India also, the balance of payments position has been deteriorating and foreign debt and servicing charges have been continuously mounting. For example, in 1980 India's foreign debt amounted to 1920 crores of US dollars and annual servicing charges took away nearly 7.7 per cent of that year's export earnings of the country; in 1986, foreign debt of India rose to 4000 crores of US dollars and servicing charges on foreign debt took away a little more than a quarter of India's export earnings of that year. There appears to be no sign of improvement in this regard in India. In fact things appear to be getting worse year after year, especially in recent years of drought, foreign loans were being raised to meet even current needs (like import of foodgrains and edible oil), though foreign loans should be strictly for productive purposes, creating productive assets in the economy so that production, exports and export earnings would go on increasing out of which repayment of foreign debts can be arranged without unbearable burden on the Indian economy.

ANNEXURE 1

Marshall-Edgeworth Offer Curves

Dr. Alfred Marshall and Prof. Edgeworth further extended J.S. Mill's theory of 'Reciprocal Demand', with the help of 'Offer Curves.'

The Offer Curve may be defined as "a curve on which any point indicates what one country is prepared to offer in exchange for the commodity produced by other country."

For the purpose of illustration, let us assume two countries, namely, England and Germany. Let us also assume only two commodities designated as M and N.

It is first necessary to find out the Domestic Price Lines of both England and Germany.

England

Assuming England were to devote all her productive resources to the production of commodity M, England can then produce the maximum of that commodity indicated in Fig. 7.1 by OM.

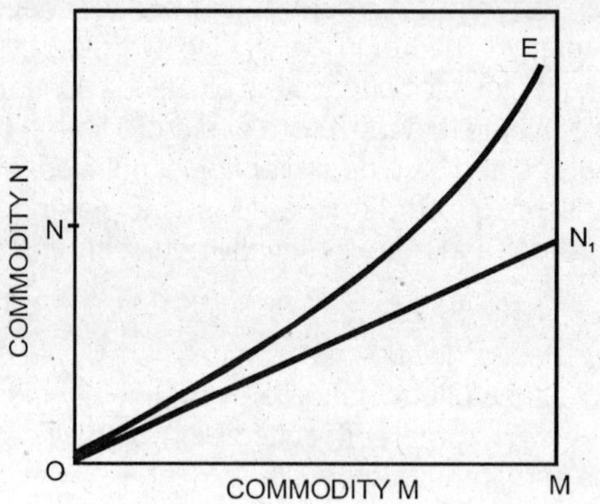

Fig. 7.1 Offer Curve of England

If, on the other hand, England were to use all her resources for the production of commodity N, England then can produce the maximum of product N denoted in Fig. 7.1 by ON which is equal to MN_1. When O and N_1 are joined, the line ON_1 shows the (England's) domestic exchange ratio (which is OM: MN_1).

If trade is to take place between England and Germany, it is obvious that the offer curve of England should never be below ON_1. Because, if that happens, that would mean that for getting less quantity ON_1 of the commodity N from Germany, England will be giving in return OM. Obviously, such a situation will not be in the interest of England. Thus, it follows that England should get more than ON_1 of the commodity N from Germany for OM of her (England's) commodity M. This alone would ensure that England gains from specialisation and international trade with Germany. Thus, it follows that the offer curve of England must be somewhere above ON_1. For example, as shown in Fig. 7.1, England's offer curve can be OE.

Germany

If the offer curve of Germany is to be shown on a graph, that offer curve will be represented by the curve OG in Fig. 7.2.

It should be noted that England's offer curve rises upward at a relatively faster rate indicating that for every additional unit of commodity N from Germany, England will be prepared to offer decreasing quantities of commodity M. Same is the case with Germany.

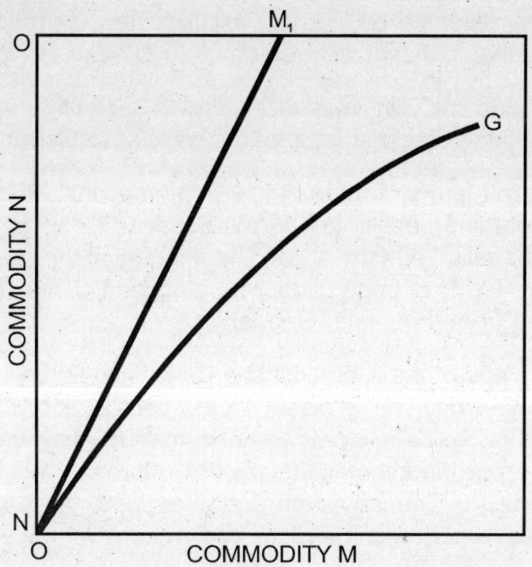

Fig. 7.2 Offer Curve of Germany

If the two offer curves ON_1 of England and OG of Germany are considered simultaneously, the point of intersection of the two curves will be the point that will determine the terms of trade between England's commodity M and German's commodity N.

Dr. Alfred Marshall's illustration is in terms of two countries, England and Germany. Exports of both England and Germany are expressed in terms of 'Bales.' Each bale containing the same amount of labour represents a country's exports. The explanation of terms of trade in terms of offer curves is explained with the help of Fig. 7.2.

In Fig. 7.3, OY-axis measures the German bales and it represents the total of England's demand for bales of Germany or total of the Germany's supply of bales to England.

In the same way, in Fig. 7.3, OX-axis measures the total demand of Germany for England's Bales or total supply of bales from England to Germany.

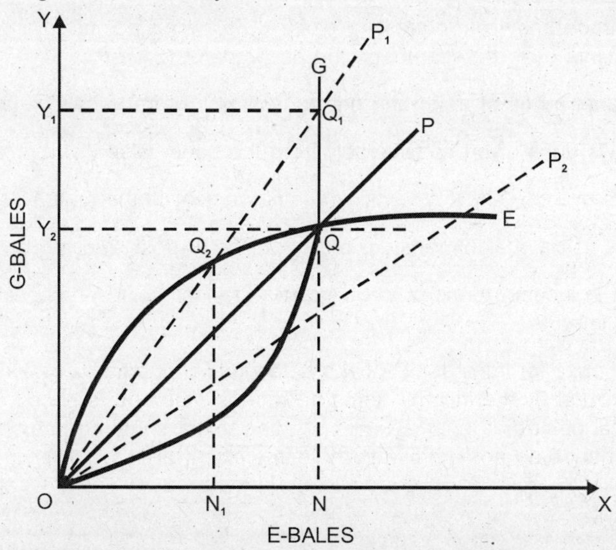

Fig. 7.3 Offer Curves and Terms of Trade

Germany's offer curve is represented by OG. OG explains how Germany is prepared to offer her bales at different terms of trade. OG curve is drawn with reference to OY-axis in Fig. 7.3.

In Fig. 7.3, OE is the offer curve of England. OE is drawn in relation to the OX-axis and different points on OE curve denote how many bales England is prepared to offer to Germany at different terms of trade.

Let us assume OP_1 to be the terms of trade. It is the international 'Price Ratio.' The international Price Ratio cannot be a vertical straight line parallel to OY-axis because it is so, the international trade between England and Germany will not benefit Germany at all. The international price-line will be completely in favour of England. In the same way, the terms of trade cannot be a horizontal straight line parallel to OX-axis as that will mean no benefit to England from trade with Germany.

This would mean that the slope of the international price-line would be closer to the vertical line or to the horizontal line. If the international price-line is closer to the vertical line, the terms of trade would favour England; and if the international price-line is closer to horizontal line, terms of trade would favour Germany. It may also be stated that whenever, the international price-line turns in a clock-wise manner, terms of trade become more and more favourable to Germany; if on the other hand, the international price-line rotates in an anti-clock way, the terms of trade would become more and more favourable to England.

At OP_1 price-line, the terms of trade are favourable to England. The reciprocal demand situation is such that England will be experiencing a trade deficit. For example, at OP_1 terms to trade, exports from Germany would be OY_1 while German imports from England would be ON_1. To express the same thing in other way, at OP_1 price-line, England's exports would be ON_1 while her (England's) imports from Germany would be OY_1. With a view to overcome the trade deficit, England would offer better terms of trade to Germany. This would mean that the price-line will start rotating in a clock-wise manner.

Let us assume that the international price-line is OP_2. Clearly this would favour Germany. But at this point, Germany would experience trade deficit. Germany would then offer better terms of trade to England. The international price-line would then rotate in an anti-clockwise manner.

Finally, equilibrium in the balance of trade between England and Germany would be achieved at OP price-line where there will be equilibrium in the reciprocal demand condition and England's and Germany's exports will pay for each other's imports.

India's Terms of Trade

India's terms of trade show an interesting picture. Following points emerge after the analysis of the terms of trade movements over the years (see the accompanying chart):

The gross barter terms of trade and net barter terms of trade have a fair correlation.

Both the series don't divert considerably from the base value (100).

Income terms of trade show a significant improvement in the post 1991 period.

Income terms of trade significantly diverge from both gross and net barter terms of trade.

Improvement in income terms of trade reveals the increasing purchasing power of our exports in terms of our imports.

Though, terms of trade for India don't show a deterioration in terms of gross as well as net barter terms of trade, the picture painted by the income terms of trade is much more encouraging. The movement only highlights the theoretical point that income terms of trade might show an improvement even though gross and net barter terms of trade do not improve to the same extent or in fact even deteriorate.

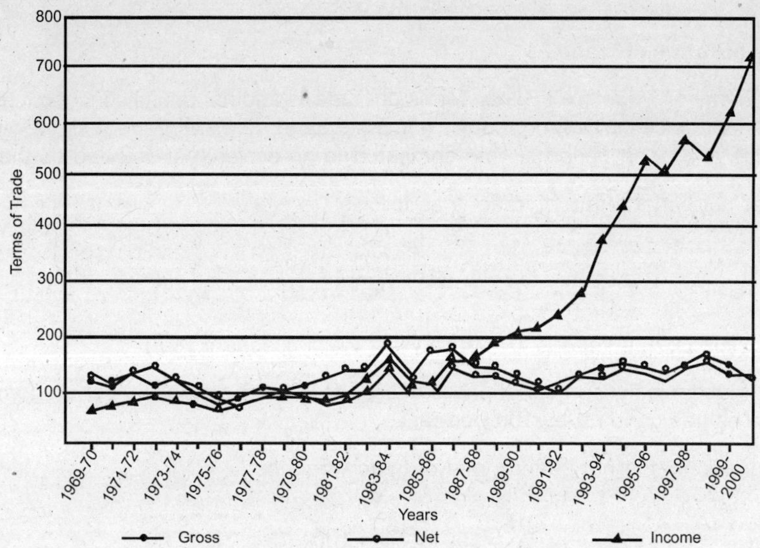

Fig. 7.4 Movements in India's Terms of Trade

ANNEXURE 2

Advanced Analysis of Terms of Trade

1. *Net Barter Terms of Trade*: 'Net Barter Terms of Trade' is another useful concept. It refers to the ratio of export price and import price indices, or in other terms net barter terms of trade refer to "the ratio of export prices to import prices at a given period of time compared to an earlier year selected as the base year."

The formula for net barter terms of trade is as follows:

$$\frac{Px}{Pm} \times 100 \text{ or } \frac{Px1}{Pm1} : \frac{Px0}{Pm0}$$

(P = price; x = exports; m = imports; 0 = base year, 1 = subsequent year)

Let us assume that the index number of prices of exports has gone up by 50 per cent whereas the index number of import prices has gone up by 100 per cent.

Under such conditions, the net barter terms of trade would be:

$$\frac{Px}{Pm} \times 100 \text{ or } \frac{150}{200} \times 100 = 75$$

This means the net barter terms of trade has declined to 75. Any decline below 100 is taken as unfavourable with reference to the base year.

But let us assume that the index of export prices has doubled whereas the index of import prices has gone up by only 50 per cent; then the position will be as follows:

$$\frac{Px}{Pm} \times 100 \text{ or } \frac{200}{150} \times 100 = 133.3$$

Any rise over 100 is taken as favourable, and net barter terms of trade are said to have improved with reference to the base year.

But the concept of 'Net Barter Terms of Trade,' though useful in some sense, by itself it does not tell very much.

For example, granting that adopting the above principle, we find that compared to the base year, the net barter terms of trade have become favourable (say it has risen to 133.30). But what exactly does this favourable net barter terms of trade indicate? Does it show that a country's exports and imports have exactly balanced? Or that the same amount of exports is getting in exchange more imports? Or that less amount of exports (compared to that of the base year) get more imports in return? Does it show that a country's exports exceed her imports and the surplus is invested abroad?

The fact that there is improvement (with reference to the base year) in net barter terms of trade does not provide an answer to any one of the above questions. (It only shows that a unit of exports is getting in exchange more units of imports as compared to the position in the selected base year).

It was with a view to overcome the above deficiencies of 'Net Barter Terms of Trade' that Prof. Taussig devised the concept of 'Gross Barter Terms of Trade'.

2. *Gross Barter Terms of Trade:* According to Prof. Taussig, 'Gross Barter Terms of Trade' refer to the total quantities of exports and imports of a country exchanged for each other (i.e. total exports of a country in return for total imports of the country) at a particular point of time or in a particular year as compared to some selected base year's total exports and total imports of that country.

The formula to calculate 'Gross Barter Terms of Trade' is as follows:

$$\frac{Qx}{Qm} \times 100 \text{ or } \frac{Qx1}{Qm1} : \frac{Qx0}{Qx0}$$

It should be noted that total quantity of exports and total quantity of imports of a country are also expressed in terms of index number (and not in terms of tonnes of steel, bales of cotton and so on).

The total quantity of exports of a country is calculated by dividing the value of exports (Px × Qx) by index number of prices (Px). Similarly total quantity of imports by a country is calculated.

The superiority of 'Gross Barter Terms of Trade' as propounded by Prof. Taussig over 'Net Barter Terms of Trade' can be explained as follows:

Let us take the case of India as an example. Let us suppose that the net barter terms of trade have become unfavourable to India from 100 to 75, but at the same time India's balance of payments has balanced. This would imply that the gross barter terms of trade have improved from 100 to 133.3. This is unfavourable from the point of view of India because India in exchange of a larger quantity of exports is getting the same quantity of imports as in the selected base year.

To express the same thing differently, for larger quantity of exports, India is getting in exchange the same volume of imports as in the base year; or to put it in a still different way, for same volume of exports, India in exchange is getting a smaller volume of imports as compared to the position in the base year.

If on the other hand, India's balance of payments was in equilibrium position (i.e., total value of India's exports is exactly equal to total value of India's imports) and the net barter terms of trade have become favourable from 100 in the base year to 133.3 in the current year, then this would mean that the gross barter terms of trade have declined from 100 to 75. This would mean that a smaller quantity of total exports from India would be in a position to get in exchange the same quantity of imports as in the base year. This is a favourable position for India, because India would be in a position to get greater quantity of imports in exchange of the same quantity of her exports as in the base year.

Criticism of Commodity Terms of Trade

Following are the points of criticism of the concept of commodity terms of trade:

(1) It should be noted that net and gross barter terms of trade are of significance, only if during the two periods under consideration, balance of payments of a country balances. Otherwise, the mere fact that net or gross barter terms of trade have become favourable has little significance. They become significant only when in the base year and subsequent year selected for calculation, balance of payments of a country balances.

(2) Commodity terms of trade (net as also gross) explain only the relative changes in prices of exports of a country and prices of its imports. They fail to take into account continual changes in quality of goods that are taking place, especially rapid changes that are taking place during post-World War II period.

(3) Another serious defect of commodity terms of trade (both net and gross) is that it fails to take into account changes in productivity due to improvement in technology. For example, due to relatively rapid technological progress in a country, productive efficiency may rise and prices of exportable goods may decline bringing about decline in commodity terms of trade. But this does not necessarily mean that the country is worse off compared to what it was in the base year. True, a given volume of exports now brings in exchange smaller volume of imports than in the base year. But it must be noted that the given volume of export uses smaller amount of productive resources of the community than in the base year.

To conclude, commodity terms of trade (both, net and gross) are significant only if balance of payments of a country balances in the base year in the subsequent year and the base year and subsequent year are close enough as not to allow any significant changes in technological efficiency and productivity.

(3) *Income Terms of Trade:* The concept of net barter terms of trade was improved upon by Prof. Dorrance in his article on 'The Income Terms of Trade' (1948) by formulating the concept of 'the Income Terms of Trade.'

The income terms of trade takes into account the volume of exports of a country and its export prices and import prices. This concept shows a country's changing import capacity in relation to changes in its exports. Thus, the income terms of trade index is the net barter term of trade of a country multiplied by its export volume index.

If there is a rise in the index of income terms of trade, it would imply that a country can import more goods in exchange for its exports. It is possible that a country's income terms of trade might improve and yet its commodity terms of trade might deteriorate. If import prices are assumed to be constant, and if export prices decline, there will be an increase in the sales and value of exports. Thus, though the income terms of trade have improved, the commodity terms of trade might have at the same time deteriorated.

Income terms of trade denote the capacity of a country to import. A country's capacity to import may increase, if other things remaining the same, prices of exports rise or prices of imports decline or volume of the country's exports increases.

From the above, it should be clear that the concept of income terms of trade is of much practical utility, especially for developing countries which have a limited capacity to import, while there is an urgent need for them to import more of capital goods, spares and essential industrial raw materials.

Criticism of 'Income Terms of Trade'

It may be pointed out that the index of income terms of trade fails to measure accurately gains or losses from international trade. When it is found that the capacity of a country to import has increased, it also means that the country is exporting more than before. Also, the index of income terms of trade is related to the export-based capacity of a country to import. The concept is not based on the total capacity of a country to import which depends upon not only the country's exports which also include the country's foreign exchange receipts. Thus, it is possible that the index of income terms of trade of a country has deteriorated but at the same time the country's foreign exchange receipts have gone up which would mean that the country's capacity to import has actually gone up, though the index of income terms of trade has deteriorated. This explains why the concept of commodity terms of trade is preferred to the income terms of trade for measuring gains to a country from international trade.

(4) *Single Factoral Terms of Trade:* Productivity changes in a country's export industries are not taken into account by the concept of commodity terms of trade.

Prof. Viner has developed the concept of a single factor terms of trade. This concept takes into consideration changes in the domestic export industries.

The single factoral terms of trade is calculated by multiplying the commodity terms of trade index by an index of productivity changes in the country's export industries.

The concept show that a country's factoral terms of trade improve as productivity rises in the country's export industries. It is possible that if the productivity of a country's export industries rises, its factoral terms of trade may improve, even though the country's commodity terms of trade may deteriorate. To give an example, the prices of country's exports may decline relative to its import prices as a consequence of improvement in the productivity of the country's export industries. The commodity terms of trade may deteriorate, but the country's factoral terms of trade would show an improvement.

Criticism

The single factoral terms of trade suffers from certain limitations. In the first place, it is difficult to get the necessary data to measure accurately productivity index. Secondly, this concept does not take into account the potential domestic cost of production of import industries in the other country.

With a view to overcome these limitations of single factoral terms of trade, Prof. Viner formulated the double factoral terms of trade.

(5) *Double Factoral Terms of Trade:* Prof. Viner's concept of the factoral terms of trade takes into consideration changes in productivity both in the domestic export industries and the foreign country's export sector.

The double factoral terms of trade is helpful in measuring the change in the rate of exchange of country as a consequence of the change in the productivity efficiency of domestic factors of production engaged in export industries and that of foreign country's factors of production manufacturing exports of that country.

Thus, a rise in the index of double factoral terms of trade of a country would mean that the productivity efficiency of the factors of production producing a country's exports has increased relatively to the factors producing imports in the other country (or in other terms in foreign country's export sector).

Limitations

It is obvious that it is not possible to measure accurately the index of double factoral terms of trade of a country. This is because it involves measuring and comparing productivity changes in the export sectors of the participating countries.

Also, the significant thing is the quantity of commodities that can be imported with a given quantity of exports of a country and not so much the quantity of productive factors required in a foreign country to produce former country's imports.

Prof. Kindleberger writes: "The single factoral terms of trade is a much more relevant concept than the double factoral. We are interested in what our factor can earn in goods, not what our factor services command in the services of foreign factors."

(6) *Real Cost Terms of Trade:* Viner developed real cost terms of trade index to measure the real gain from international trade.

The real cost terms of trade index in calculated by "multiplying the single factoral terms of trade with the reciprocal of an index of the amount of disutility per unit of productive resources used in producing export commodities."

If there is a favourable real cost terms of trade index, it shows that the amount of imports received is greater in terms of the real cost involved in producing export commodities.

But the real cost terms of trade index fails to measure the real cost involved in the form of goods produced for export which could be used for domestic consumption to pay for imports.

With a view to rectify the above deficiency, Prof. Viner developed the concept of 'utility terms of trade index.'

(7) *Utility Terms of Trade:* Utility terms of trade index makes an attempt to measure "changes in the disutility of producing a unit of exports and changes in the relative satisfactions yielded by imports and the domestic products foregone as the result of export production."

The utility terms of trade index is calculated by "multiplying the real cost of terms of trade index with an index of the relative average utility of imports and of domestic commodities foregone."

But the real terms of trade index and utility terms of trade index are considered as elusive concepts, because these concepts involve the measurement of disutility in terms of pain and sacrifice. It is obvious that it is not possible to accurately or even approximately measure disutility (or utility) in accurate and concrete terms.

Concluding Remarks

All this means that the concepts of single factoral terms of trade index, double factoral terms of trade index as also the concepts of real cost terms of trade index and utility terms of trade index are of little practical use. They are only of academic and theoretical interest. This explains why the concepts of the commodity terms of trade and income terms of trade are generally used in measuring gains from international trade.

CHAPTER

8 FREE TRADE: CASE FOR AND AGAINST

Structure:

8.1 Meaning of Free Trade

8.2 Case for Free Trade (or Advantages Claimed for Free Trade)

8.3 Arguments or Case Against Free Trade

8.1 MEANING OF FREE TRADE

Prof. Jagdish Bhagwati has defined free trade policy as "absence of tariffs, quotas, exchange restrictions, taxes and subsidies on production, factor use and consumption."[1]

According to Prof. R.G. Lipsey "a world of Free trade would be one with no tariffs and no restrictions of any kind on importing and exporting. In such a world, a country would import all those commodities that it would buy from abroad at a delivered price lower than the cost of producing them at home."

Thus, the policy of free trade among countries of the world implies complete freedom of international trade without any kind of restrictions, direct or indirect, on movement of goods and services among the trading countries. Under free trade policy, restrictions such as import duties, restrictions on exports through taxes and other measures, quota fixation and export subsidies and exchange controls do not exist and there is free movement of goods and services, including capital movements from country to country, each country trying to sell its goods to a country which would give the exporting country the highest price for its exports and purchase goods and services from that country which would supply goods and services the country intends to import at the minimum price.

But some exceptions may be noted. Government of a country may levy a small duty on the import of some goods for the purpose of raising revenue and not with the objective of providing protection to home industries through such import duties from the competition of similar foreign goods. For example, if government of a country imposes a levy of, say 5 per cent per unit of an imported commodity, when the comparative cost advantage in the country exporting that commodity is, say 10 or even 15 per cent, such an import duty will not hamper international trade in that commodity which, in spite of the levy of import duty on that commodity, will continue to be imported as before which means that such an imposition of import duty will not be contrary to free trade. But if the relative cost advantage in the case of production of a commodity in country A is 15 per cent compared to its cost of production in country B, and if country B imposes an import duty of 15 per cent per unit of that commodity or even at a higher rate, the idea in the case of such imposition of import duty being to grant protection to that particular industry in country B against competition from country A, in such a case imposition of the import duty would be contrary to the principle of free trade. Only if a country imposes an import duty at a rate lower than the country imposing such an import duty is at a rate lower than the lowest cost of advantage enjoyed by a foreign country, it cannot be said that the country imposing such an import duty is violating the principle of free trade. Thus, even during the heydays of free trade (i.e., from 1846 when the Corn Laws were abolished in England to the beginning of World War I in 1914), many countries imposed import duties at fairly low rates, the aim being to raise revenue for the state and not to grant protection to domestic industries against foreign competition. Such imposition of import duties for purely revenue purpose did not mean violation of the principle of free trade.

In brief, by the principle of free trade is meant that a country is free to purchase any commodity it wants from any country from where that commodity is available at the lowest price and sell its commodities in any country where it can get the highest price for the exported commodities — all such trading transactions taking place without the governments of either country placing any direct or indirect hindrances in bringing about such international trading transactions.

---

1. Bhagwati J., (Ed.), *International Trade*, (1986), p.10.

8.2 CASE FOR FREE TRADE (OR ADVANTAGES CLAIMED FOR FREE TRADE)

Classical economists like Adam Smith and David Ricardo were generally in favour of free trade policy. Many modern economists like G. A. Haberler and others have made out a case in favour of the principle of free trade among the nations of the world on the following grounds:

(1) *Free Trade Results in Maximisation of World Output:* According to the principle of comparative cost advantage, every country would specialise in the production of that commodity for which it is best suited or in other terms, in the production of which it has comparatively the greatest advantage or the least disadvantage. Therefore, different countries would practise the principle of division of labour or specialisation on international plane producing and exporting those goods for which they are comparatively best suited and in return importing those goods for which they are relatively less or least suited. This means due to international specialisation consequent on the adoption of the principle of free trade, resources of the world would be put to the maximum use resulting in maximum world output which would be to the advantage of all the participating trading countries of the world.

(2) *Free Trade Ensures Optimum Utilisation of World's Productive Resources:* Under the regime of free trade, each country specialises in the production of those commodities for which it is best suited. Naturally, international division of labour or specialisation consequent on the adoption of free trade results in the optimal or most efficient use of production resources of the world.

(3) *Free Trade Ensures Optimisation of Consumption of Peoples in the World:* The principle of free trade among the countries of the world would result in international division of labour and in putting the world's resources to the maximum possible use in other terms enabling them to produce those goods for which they have the greatest comparative cost advantage (or the least comparative disadvantage). This would result in optimum production of goods, thus enabling optimum level of consumption to the peoples of the world. Each country would purchase foreign goods and services at the cheapest possible prices which would enable people to raise to the maximum their standard of living.

(4) *Free Trade Would Result in Widening of Markets:* As the principle of free trade means absence of all types of restrictions on international movements of goods and service, that would result in widening of markets for different commodities and services. In effect, markets for different commodities would be world markets. Also, because of keen competition to capture as wide a part of international market as possible, there would result improvement in quality of goods and services which would also be available to consumers all over the world at the lowest possible prices.

(5) *Free Trade Would Prevent Emergence of Monopolies:* Because of the regime of free trade, each country would be specialising in the production of a few commodities and services according to the principle of comparative cost advantage. Due to prevailing competition among the countries of the world, each industrial unit would try to be of the optimum size and produce and sell goods at the lowest possible price. And, therefore, the principle of free trade and open international competition would prevent emergence of private monopolies with power to manipulate output and prices of goods to the detriment of public good and welfare.

(6) *Free Trade is the Most Efficient Tool of Economic Development of Developing Countries:* It is claimed that adoption of the principle of free trade is the most favourable policy for rapid economic development of backward countries. The policy of free trade would enable developing countries into import capital goods and essential raw materials, technological know-how and managerial and organisational skills and knowledge from the best available sources and at the lowest possible rates and prices. Naturally, this would help the process of rapid economic development of backward countries as they would be free to import these developmental goods without any hindrance.

(7) *Free Trade Helps Development of Citizen's Qualities:* According to Prof. Haberler, adoption of the principle of free trade by nations would result in exposure of domestic producers to international competition which they would be required to face without any direct or indirect support from the government. Naturally, this exposure to international competition would help development of qualities like competitiveness, efficiency, obsession for excellence, inventiveness, acquisition of various types of industrial skills and organisational and managerial abilities. These are all desirable qualities in the modern world and time, if a country is to succeed in this highly competitive world of the present times.

8.3 ARGUMENTS OR CASE AGAINST FREE TRADE

The policy of free trade came to be practically abandoned after the Great Depression (1929-33), both on theoretical and practical grounds of which the following are the important ones:

(1) The various advantages of free trade were claimed on the basis of a number of assumptions such as perfect mobility of factors of production within a country, working of price mechanism under conditions of perfect competition and so on. But these assumptions proved to be mostly invalid. Not only there did not exist perfect competition but in fact there emerged monopolies and oligopolies.

Under such circumstances benefits claimed from adoption of the principle of free trade or policy just could not be enjoyed. Advantages claimed on behalf of free trade proved to be only theoretical advantages with very little practical use or benefit.

(2) It came to be observed that under the regime of free trade, countries came to specialise only in some industries, neglecting development of some other industries or sectors of the economy. Thus, predominantly agricultural countries remained only agricultural countries as they were supposed to specialise only in that sector because of abundance of land and labour. Also, on the basis of international division of labour or specialisation, some countries specialised only in some industries and neglected some other industries, depending upon the principle of comparative cost advantage. Naturally, free trade resulted in lop-sided development of economies of many countries, especially in the 19th century. For example, India become mainly an agricultural country supplying industrial raw materials like cotton, jute, iron ore, leather and other minerals to England and had to go without those industries for which she had enough raw materials. Such lop-sided economic development has many undesirable socio-economic and political as also cultural consequences such as dependence on other countries even for vital goods, absence of abilities needed to establish and manage large-scale industries, continuance of old and traditional value-system, absence of industrial culture with its discipline, hard work, incentiveness and so on.

(3) As under the regime of free trade there was *laissez faire* policy and the state did not impose any restrictions on international movements of goods among nations, many harmful commodities came to be imported by unscrupulous merchants in a number of countries. This had extremely harmful effects on the health and welfare of the community. In order to prevent such harmful effects on the health and welfare of the community, at some stage the State had to step in and impose restrictions on the import of harmful commodities. This was one of the reasons why many countries came to give up free trade policy.

(4) The policy of free trade also resulted in some other undesirable consequences. For example, countries with similar factor-endowments or with better factor-endowments resorted to cut-throat competition to capture as large a portion of world market as possible. Often this cut-throat competition resulted in the adoption of dumping of goods in foreign countries at prices often below even the cost of production. Once as a consequence of this dumping policy, the potential or actual rivals were driven out of their industries, the country previously dumping goods would raise prices to a very high level by taking advantage of absence of rivals and make good the previous losses on account of dumping and later retain the market conquered by dumping in the first instance. Japan for example, followed this policy *vis-a-vis* India in respect of textiles. Naturally, such a dumping policy would have continued to destroy a number of industries if the affected country were to continue with free trade policy. Naturally, such dumping policy resulted in abandonment of the policy of free trade by the affected countries. They resorted to high tariffs to protect their industries against dumping.

(5) According to Prof. Haberler, the policy of free trade (which also means in effect the policy of *laissez faire* on the part of the state) may lead to the emergence of international as also national monopolies. While international monopolies would hamper the development of domestic industries for which resources may be available in the country, both types of monopolies would definitely result in reduction of community's welfare.

(6) Prof. Haberler's view that policy of free trade would help rapid economic development of backward countries cannot be accepted.

Countries of Western Europe had an early start in the sphere of industrialisation and they have accumulated vast managerial and organisational skills and technical ability and have developed infrastructural facilities to build up highly developed industrial structure in their countries. It also needs to be noted that presently industrially advanced and developed countries have also highly developed agriculture. Under such circumstances, adoption of the policy of free trade would just not allow development of industries in developing countries, though they may possess vast industrial potentialities. Thus, by taking advantage of their strong industrial position (and, therefore, also of vast military strength), Western countries built their empires in Asia and Africa in the 17th and 18th centuries. The policy of free trade that was forced on India by the British rulers came to reduce countries like India to the position of suppliers of industrial raw materials to Western highly industrialised countries. Even at present, taking advantage of their strong economic position, the developed countries are making terms of trade more and more adverse against developing countries. No wonder, India's share in world exports has declined from 1.05 per cent in 1960-61 to a mere 04.4 per cent in 1986-87.

Under such circumstances, it follows that developing countries like India can develop their industries, agriculture and economy only by adopting a judicious policy of protection to industries.

CHAPTER

9 TARIFFS AND IMPORT QUOTAS

Structure:

Definition

Tariff refers to duties or taxes imposed by the government on commodities which are imported into a country from abroad. Tariff it thus synonymous with import duties (also known as custom duties).

9.1 TYPES OF TARIFFS

The following four types of tariff are generally imposed depending upon objectives and circumstances:

(1) *Ad Valorem:* The *ad valorem* import duty is possibly the most common tariff or imported duty. *Ad valorem* import duty is imposed as a percentage of the value of the imported commodity. *Ad valorem* import duty is fixed percentage of the c.i.f. (cost of production, insurance and freight) value of the imported commodity. Let us suppose the *ad valorem* import duty is levied at 50 per cent. It would mean that on an imported watch valued at Rs. 1,000, import duty of Rs. 500, would be levied, and on an imported watch valued at Rs. 10, 000, import duty of Rs. 5,000 would be levied. *Ad valorem* import duty appears reasonable as it is imposed on the basis of value of the imported commodity — higher the value of the imported commodity, more would be the amount of import duty than import duty paid by an imported commodity of lower value.

(2) *Specific Import Duty:* Specific import duty is imposed by the government on the basis of number of units imported-duty on the basis of number of watches imported, on cloth per meter, on fertiliser per ton, on petroleum per litre and so on.

(3) *Compound Import Duty:* Compound import duty on an imported commodity represents a combination of *ad valorem* import duty and specific import duty. In the case of compound import duty, a specific duty is imposed on each unit of the commodity plus a percentage of *ad valorem* duty also.

(4) *Sliding Scale Import Duty:* Sliding scale import duty is imposed on *ad valorem* basis or on specific basis. Generally, sliding scale import duty is levied on a specific basis — for example, no import duty is imposed on one watch brought into the country by an Indian tourist coming from abroad; Rs. 50 per watch on imported watches numbering between 50 and 100; Rs. 100 per watch on imported watches numbering between 101 to 200 and so on.

9.2 TARIFF AND ITS EFFECTS

Effects of a tariff can be analysed from two points of view: (i) Effects of tariff from the point of view of a particular commodity or market. This approach to tariff is known as 'Partial Equilibrium Approach'; and (ii) Effects of a tariff may be analysed from the standpoint of the nation's economy as a whole. This approach to tariff is known as "The General Equilibrium Approach.' It should be clear that there is not only a contradiction between the two approaches but in fact they help to understand each other in a better way.

It is convenient to begin with 'Partial Equilibrium Approach' to tariff. Charles Kindleberger has made an attempt to analyse 8 effects of tariff: (1) Protective Effect; (2) Consumption Effect; (3) Revenue Effect; (4) Redistribution Effect; (5) Terms of Trade Effect; (6) Competitive Effect; (7) Income Effect; and (8) Balance of Payments Effect.

It should be obvious that it is the price that is first affected by a tariff and therefore, it may be said that all the above eight effects of a tariff are the result or consequence of 'Price Effect' of a tariff.

An attempt is made to analyse the above eight effects of a tariff not necessarily in the above order.

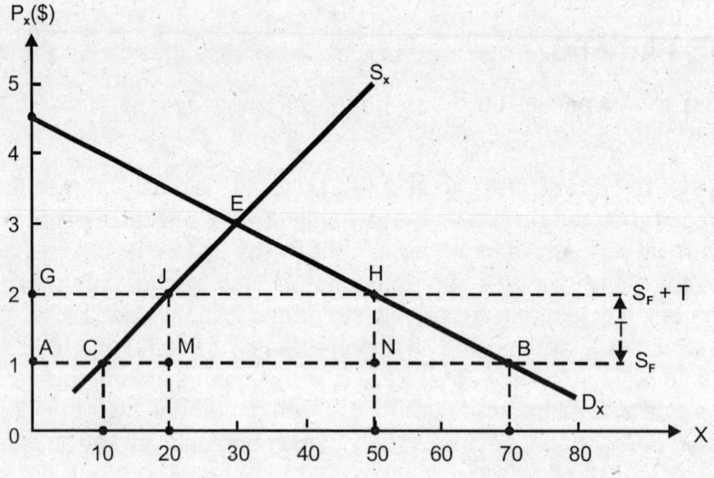

Fig 9.1. Partial Equilibrium Effects of a Tariff. *DX* and *SX* represent Nation 2's demand and supply curves of commodity X. At the free trade price of *PX* = $1, Nation 2 consumes 70X *(AB)*, of which 10X *(AC)* is produced domestically and 60X *(CB)* is imported. With a 100 per cent import tariff on commodity X, *PX* rises to $2 for individuals in Nation 2. At *PX* = $2 consumers 50X *(GH)*, of which 20X *(GJ)* is produced domestically and 30S *(JH)* is imported. Thus, the consumption effect of the tariff is (–) 20X *(BN)*; the production effect is 10X *(CM)*; the trade effect equals (–) 30X *(BN + CM)*; and the revenue effect is $30 *(MJHN)*.

Elastic *DX* and *SX* are in Nation 2, the greater is the trade effect of the tariff (i.e., the greater is the reduction in Nation 2's imports of commodity X) and the smaller is the revenue effect of the tariff.

(1) *Tariff and Price Effect:* If a tariff is imposed on an imported commodity, the price of the commodity will rise, if the demand for the commodity is inelastic in the importing country; if on the other hand, demand for the imported commodity is highly elastic, the price of the commodity will not rise and the import duty will be paid by the exporting country. If the position is in-between, the price of the commodity in the importing country will not rise by the full amount of the tax but only partly, thus part of the tariff burden falling on the country importing the commodity and partly falling on the exporting country, the proportions depending on the degree of elasticity of demand for the commodity.

(2) *Tariff and Protective Effect:* If the idea behind imposing a tariff is to protect and promote the competing domestic industry, logically it should mean that the revenue from such a tariff should be nil or insignificant, if the competing domestic industry is to be fully protected from foreign goods. The substitution of domestic product for foreign goods is called 'the import-substitution effect of a tariff.'

(3) *Tariff and Consumption Effect:* In this case, the idea behind imposing a tariff is to reduce consumption of goods that were hereto being imported. Such a tariff will reduce net satisfaction of domestic consumers.

(4) *Tariff and Revenue Effect:* In this case, the idea is to raise revenue for the state. In this case the rate of tariff is likely to be much lower than cost differentials or relative cost advantage in the production of the commodity. Practically the same amount will continue to be imported and a relatively low rate of import duty (say around 5 to 10 per cent) will help raise revenue for the state.

(5) *Tariff and Terms of Trade Effect:* If the supply of a commodity is perfectly inelastic in the exporting country and demand for it fairly elastic in the importing country, the entire burden of the tariff will be borne by the exporting country, while the importing country will receive substantial amount of revenue. This in effect will mean that after imposing the tariff, terms of trade would move in favour of the country imposing the tariff.

(6) *Tariff and Competitive Effect:* As in the case of infant industry argument, in this case of tariff imposed for increasing competitive power of the competing domestic goods, such a tariff can and does improve competitive strength of domestic goods. But there is the possibility that under such protective tariff, the infant industry may remain infant for long and may not be in a position to face foreign competition for that length of time. Also, tariff imposed to limit foreign competition may result in the emergence of domestic monopolies and inefficient industries. Prof. Kindlberger writes: "... the competitive effect of tariff is really anti-competitive; competition is stimulated by tariff removal."

(7) *Tariff and Income Effect:* The main objective of imposing a tariff on imported goods is to cut down quantity of goods imported by raising their prices in the domestic market. This stimulates import-substitution industries in the country. Expansion of these industries will mean more employment to people and increasing opportunities of earning income. When this additional income is spent on various consumer goods, demand for them will increase and so would their production and employment in those industries with newly employed workers getting income. "Under conditions of less than full employment, this (i.e., import duties) will raise money and real income and employment."

But if there is already full employment in the country imposing the tariff, effects of such a tariff will be different. "With full employment in the country imposing a tariff, it can raise money income through inflation, leaving real income worsened by the altered allocation for the resources. But with idle resources, it would be true that the tariff would raise domestic income."

But there is a limit and if a tariff is raised beyond a limit, the exporting country might take counter-measures with adverse effects on the exports of the country first imposing the tariff. Thus would mean unemployment and lowering of incomes in export industries. If this adverse effect far exceeds the favourable effects through development of import-substitution industries, the net result of imposing a high tariff may well be reduction in net income of the people and lowering of their standard of living.

(8) *Tariff and Balance of Payments Effect:* When a country finds that year after year the total value of its import of goods and services far exceeds the total value of its export of goods and services, it is said that the country is facing the problem of imbalance (i.e., deficit) in its balance of payments position. For some time, the situation of such deficits may be met by drawing foreign currencies from the reserves built up during the past years or by borrowing from abroad and paying for the excess of imports over exports. But this cannot go on forever as soon the reserves will dry up and time for the payment of debts raised abroad will arrive.

Generally, therefore, a country finding itself in the above position would impose tariffs on selective basis to cut down its imports. Such a tariff reduces the country's spending on goods and services available from abroad and tends to bring stability of equilibrium in the balance of payments position (wherein exports of goods and services of a country earn enough foreign currencies to pay for all the imports of goods and services).

Tariff and its Effects Under Conditions of General Equilibrium

As Prof. Kindleberger has pointed out, when a country imposes a tariff, practically every sector of the economy would be affected in one way or the other, until a new equilibrium position is reached. Thus, a tariff is "... likely to alter trade, prices, output and consumption, and to reallocate resources, changes in factor proportions, redistribute income, change employment and alter the balance of payments.[1]

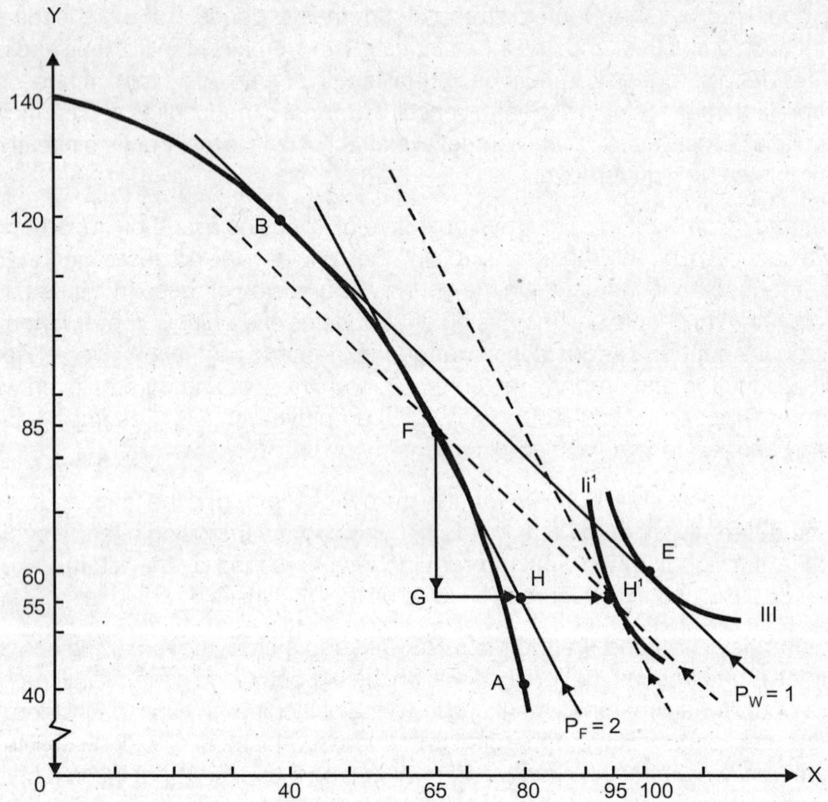

Fig. 9.2. General Equilibrium Effects of a Tariff in a Small Country. At $P_X/P_Y = 1$ on the world market, the small nation produces at point B and consumes at point E (as in the right panel of Figure). With a 100 per cent *ad valorem* tariff on imports of commodity X, $P_X/P_Y = 2$ for individuals in the nation, production takes place at point *F*, and the nation exports 30Y *(FG)* for 30X, of which 15X *(HH')* is collected by the government as a tariff. Since we assume that the government redistributes the tariff revenue in full to its citizens, consumption with the tariff takes place on indifference curve II' at point *H'*, where the two dashed lines cross. Thus, free trade consumption and welfare (point *E*) are superior to consumption and welfare with the tariff (point *H'*).

1. Charles Kindleberger, *op.cit.*, p. 107.

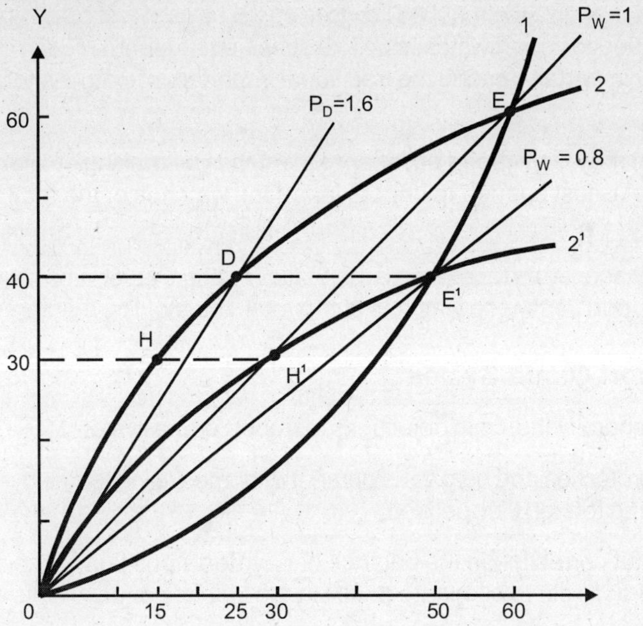

Fig. 9.3. General Equilibrium Effects of a Tariff in a Large Country. Free trade offer curves 1 and 2 define equilibrium point *E* and P_X/P_Y = 1 in both nations. A 100 per cent *ad valorem* import tariff on commodity X by Nation 2 rotates its offer curve to 2', defining the new equilibrium point *E'*. At point *E'* the volume of trade is less than under free trade and P_X/P_Y = 0.8. This means that Nations 2's terms of trade improved to P_X/P_Y = 1.25. The change in Nation 2's welfare depends on the net effect from the higher terms of trade but lower volume of trade. However, since the government collects half of the imports of commodity X as tariff, P_X/P_Y for individuals in Nation 2 rises from P_X/P_Y = 1 under free trade to P_X/P_Y = *PD* = 1.6 with the tariff.

9.3 IMPORT QUOTA SYSTEM

Definition

Import quota system is often practised as an alternative to the device of imposing import duties or tariffs.

By an import quota system is meant permitting import of a fixed quantity of commodity in volume or value during a specified period of time, generally one year. To give an example, Government of India may permit import of watches from Japan either specifying the number of watches, say one million watches per year, or specifying the value of watches to be imported from Japan (say Rs. 25 crores per year).

Methods of Fixing Import Quotas

The import quota fixation policy may be implemented in one of the following ways which can be illustrated, assuming that Government of India has decided to import watches from Japan of the total value of Rs. 25 crores per year.

(1) Government may give import licence to import Japanese watches valued at Rs. 25 crores per year to the highest bidder in an open market or by calling for tenders, the highest bidder getting the necessary import licence.

(2) Government may give the required licences on the basis of first come firstserved, each importer being permitted to import watches up to a specified amount, all such import licences given to one or many importers among the traditional importers of watches totalling Rs. 25 crores per year.

(3) Government may limit import of Japanese watches by making available to importers foreign currency that is just enough to import Japanese watches of the total value of Rs. 25 crores per year.

(4) Government agency as for example the State Trading Corporation may be given the required licence to import Japanese watches of the total value of Rs. 25 crores per year.

Objectives of Import Quota System

Following are generally the main objectives of import quota system:

(1) To provide protection and help development of domestic industries by restraining imports and thus restricting foreign competition;

(2) To bring about correction in the balance of payments position of the country (i.e., to reduce deficit and if possible to eliminate deficit in the balance of payments of the country);

(3) To make rational use of foreign currencies earned by exporting goods and services, especially as developing countries find it very difficult to earn sufficient foreign currencies to meet import bill fully;

(4) To influence pattern of living of people especially of the elite classes in developing countries by reducing imports of luxury and semi-luxury goods and services;

(5) To make use of import quota system as a retaliatory measure and, therefore, to extract concessions in regard to a country's exports to foreign countries.

Types of Import Quotas

Following are the important types of Import Quota Systems:

(1) Bilateral Quota Agreement: Under this system, for example, India can negotiate with each country separately and fix import quotas, as for example, watches worth Rs. 25 crores per year from Japan; dairy products worth Rs. 5 crores from Australia; small machine tools worth Rs. 100 crore from Czecoslovakia; one thousand bales of long staple cotton from Egypt; one thousand tones of metallurgical coal from England, and so on. Prof. G. Haberler calls these 'Agreed Quotas.'

(2) Unilateral Quota Fixation: Under this system, import quota of a particular commodity from a particular country is fixed by law or decree by the importing country without any negotiation or agreement with the other country or countries.

These unilaterally fixed import quotas may be broadly of two types: (a) Global, and (b) Allocated. Under the Global Quota System, the full amount of the quota fixed may be imported by the quota-fixing country from any one country. Under the Allocated Quota System, the full amount of the quota fixed is allocated or distributed among several countries.

(3) *Tariff Quota Fixation System:* Under this system a pre-determined quantity of a commodity is permitted to be imported either free (i.e., without paying any import duty) or on payment of import duty that is relatively low. But import of the commodity beyond such a fixed quota is charged a relatively high import duty.

(4) *'Mixing' Quota System:* Under this system, the quota-fixing country insists that domestic producer of a certain specified commodity compulsorily use imported raw material in a certain fixed proportion along with domestically produced raw material while producing the commodity.

Implementing the Quota System

After import quotas of concerned commodities are fixed in one of the above methods, the concerned government department or authority issues import licences to import specified quantities or fixed quotas of commodities to be imported in whose cases quotas have been fixed.

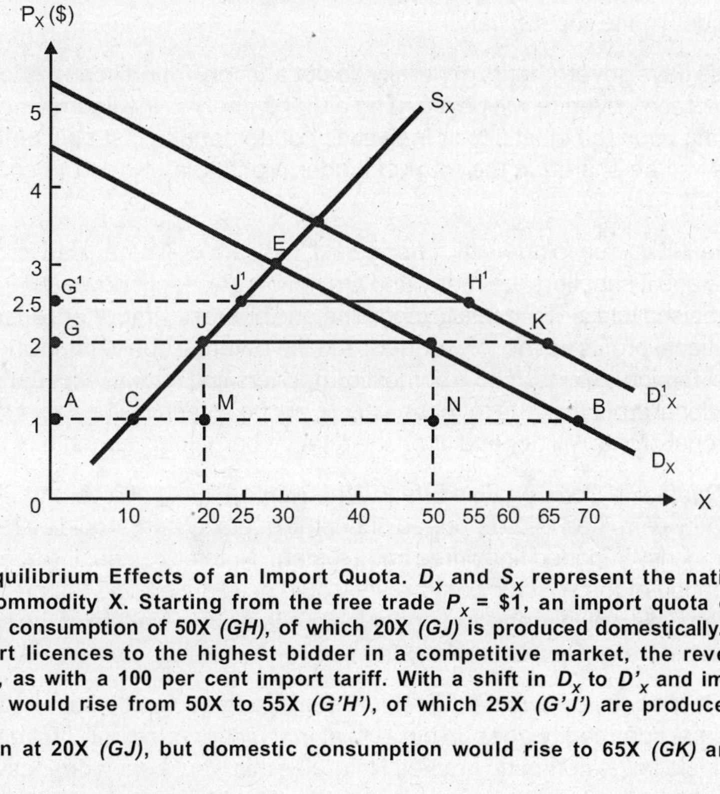

Fig. 9.4. Partial Equilibrium Effects of an Import Quota. D_X and S_X represent the nation's demand and supply curves of commodity X. Starting from the free trade P_X = \$1, an import quota of 30X *(JH)* would result in P_X = \$2 and consumption of 50X *(GH)*, of which 20X *(GJ)* is produced domestically. If the government auctioned off import licences to the highest bidder in a competitive market, the revenue effect would also be \$30 *(JHNM)*, as with a 100 per cent import tariff. With a shift in D_X to D'_X and import quota of 30X *(J'H')*, consumption would rise from 50X to 55X *(G'H')*, of which 25X *(G'J')* are produced domestically.

Domestic production at 20X *(GJ)*, but domestic consumption would rise to 65X *(GK)* and imports to 45X *(JK)*.

Effects of Import Quota Fixation

The effects of import quota fixation may be analysed under the following headings:

(1) *Import Quota and its Price Effects:* The basic or the main objective of the policy of fixing an import quota of a commodity is to put a limit on the imported quantity of the commodity and to ensure that it is less than what the imported quantity of that commodity would have been under free trade. Naturally, when the import quota of a commodity is fixed so that less is imported than before when there was free trade, it will tend to raise the price of the commodity.

By how much the price of the commodity will rise will depend upon the quantity of the quota fixed and the nature of demand for it. For example, if the demand for the commodity is highly inelastic and quota fixed is practically half of what used to be imported before under free trade, price of the commodity will rise considerably than if the demand were elastic and quota fixed was of considerable amount (i.e., only slightly less than what was imported before the quota came to be fixed).

(2) *Import Quota and its Revenue Effect:* Estimating the revenue effect of fixing an import quota of a commodity appears to be a relatively complicated task. For example, if the government auctions the necessary import licences and gives them to the highest bidders, government will get her revenue and its amount will depend upon what the bidders think its price will be in the domestic market after the import quota is fixed. If the bidders expect the price to rise considerably because of highly inelastic demand for the commodity and the low quota fixed, the auction will give substantial revenue to the state than if the demand were elastic and import quota quite substantial.

But these days governments generally do not auction import licences to the highest bidder. In such a case, revenue will be accruing either entirely to the licence-holder or the exporter depending upon the elasticity or inelasticity of demand and supply of the commodity. The revenue will be shared in the form of higher profits than when the commodity was freely imported.

Revenue will accrue to domestic importers, if they are well organised forming a monopolistic combine and if suppliers are many and are not organised. If, however, foreign exporters are well organised into a monopolistic combine and domestic importers are not organised at all, the additional profits will go to exporters and the revenue due to imposing the quota will be in favour of foreign exports. If both domestic importers and foreign exporters are well organised, the additional profit (i.e., the revenue effect), will be shared by the two and the relative shares in additional profits will depend upon the relative bargaining strength of the two parties.

(3) *Import Quota and Consumption Effect:* When import quota of a commodity is fixed, naturally the quantity permitted to be imported under the quota system would be lower than quantity of that commodity imported under free trade system. Naturally, under the quota system, domestic consumption of the specific commodity would be reduced and the price of the commodity would rise. This would mean that under the quota system welfare of the community would be less than before under free trade system.

(4) *Import Quota and Its Protective Effect:* When import quota of a commodity is fixed, not only price of that commodity goes up but also at that higher price only limited amount of it would be available in the domestic market. Naturally, this would have protective effect as it would afford an opportunity for domestic industry to develop as it comes to be protected to some extent from foreign competition.

(5) *Import Quota and its Terms of Trade Effect:* Whether fixing of an import quota will make terms of trade in greater favour or against the country imposing the quota will depend upon a number of factors. If for example, the supply of the commodity is inelastic and importers constitute a monopoly, the new terms of trade would be more favourable than before to the country imposing the import quota. If on the other hand, supply of the commodity is elastic and suppliers have formed a monopolistic combine, the new terms of trade would be more in

favour of the exporting country. On the whole, it has been the general and historical observation that in the real world where there are many suppliers of a commodity, terms of trade generally become more favourable than before to the country imposing an import quota for a commodity.

(6) *Import Quota and its Redistributive Effect:* When an import quota of a commodity is fixed, there is inevitably some redistributive effect. The price of the concerned commodity rises and this results in higher profits for the domestic sellers and domestic manufacturers of that commodity and diminution of the welfare of consumers. This fixation of import quota makes consumers lose and their loss becomes the gain of domestic producers.

(7) *Import Quota and its Balance of Payments Effect:* The import quota fixation, by reducing the quantity of the import of the concerned commodity, produces favourable impact on balance of payments position of the country adopting the import quota fixation policy. In fact, one of the important objectives of import quota fixation is to improve balance of trade and balance of payments position of the country. Further, when import quota of a commodity is fixed, portion of the national income hereto spent on larger quantity of the imported commodity remains in the country. This may push saving and investment which in turn may help push up exports of the country. This in turn not only helps earn more foreign exchange but also further improves balance of payments of the country adopting import quota fixation policy.

9.4 IMPORT QUOTAS AND TARIFFS : A COMPARISON

Since import quota fixation policy and tariffs (i.e., import duties) aim to achieve practically the same objectives (such as cutting down imports, improving terms of trade, providing protection to domestic industries, etc.), it would be instructive to compare and contrast the import quota fixation policy with tariff policy bringing out the strong and weak points of both in a comparative way.

Import quota as also import duty cause reduction in imports of the concerned commodity, bring about increase in the price of the imported commodity which in turn leads to the development of import-substitution industry and increase in the domestic production of the concerned commodity.

Though both operate in the same direction, there are certain important differences in the operation of the policy of import quota fixation and the policy of imposing import duty.

In this connection the following points may be noted:

(1) The policy of import quota fixation brings speedier and also definite quantitative results in respect of the imported commodity compared to the effects of tariff or import duty policy.

(2) While tariff eventually influences price of the concerned imported commodity, one cannot be definite as to the exact quantity of the commodity imported; on the other hand, import quota fixation has direct and immediate effect on the quantity of import of the concerned commodity. This means unlike import quota fixation policy, tariff policy does not directly control the quantity of the imported commodity.

(3) Import quota fixation policy fixes the maximum quota of a commodity that is to be imported. If the quota fixed is much below what used to be imported before and if domestic production does not increase in response to quota fixation, that will result in steep rise in the price of the concerned commodity.

Tariff policy on the other hand, might work slightly differently. If there is an initial decrease in the quantity imported because of the tariff imposed, and if prices of imported commodity declines, quantity of imported commodity may increase; or if demand increases that would also result in increase in the quantity of the commodity imported.

(4) Import quota is generally fixed by an executive decree of the government; it is, therefore, often arbitrary and is liable to be altered by another order under pressure, domestic or foreign. On the other hand, tariff duty is imposed after passing due legislation which is debated in the legislature; legislative changes cannot be brought about often and certainly not in an arbitrary way as can be done in the case of import quota fixation.

(5) It may be noted that import quota fixation is more discriminatory than import duties. Import quota fixed in the case of a commodity may vary from country to country due to political or other reasons. Such discrimination while fixing import quota of a commodity is likely to result in some international bitterness between the country imposing the import quota and the country or countries which entertain the feeling that they are discriminated against as compared to some other favoured countries. Quota fixation is not based on any single scientific principle and can, therefore, be highly discriminatory, political factor playing a notable role in such discrimination.

In the case of import duties or tariff, there is less scope for discrimination from country to country. It generally operates on the general plane and without discrimination. Also, under tariff policy, forces of demand and supply, which means the market mechanism operates freely once the import duties are imposed.

(6) Imposition of an import duty benefits the government as it brings revenue to the government. In the case of import quota fixation, unless the necessary import licence is auctioned in the open market and is granted to the highest bidder, gains of import quota fixation would go to the licence-holder in the country, or to foreign suppliers depending upon elasticity of demand and supply of the commodity concerned.

(7) It may be noted that fixation for an import quota in the case of commodity by eliminating foreign competition is more likely to result in a monopoly which generally is not possible in the case of a tariff or import duty on a commodity. This means import quota policy may prove harmful especially from the consumers' point of view than import duty or tariff.

It may be concluded that whether the government should adopt the policy of import quota fixation or imposing import duty will depend upon a number of factors operating in the country and the objectives aimed at and the efficiency of either will depend upon the efficiency with which both are implemented.

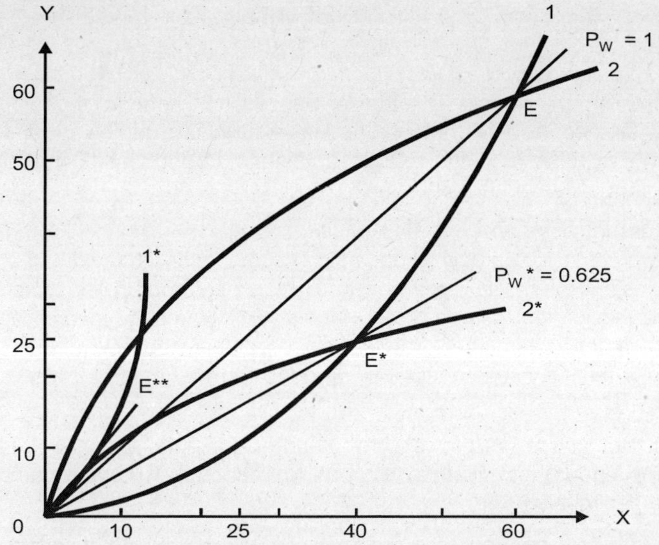

Fig. 9.5. The Optimum Tariff and Retaliation. Offer curves 1 and 2 define free trade equilibrium point *E* and P_X/P_Y = 1, as in Figure. If the optimum tariff for Nation 2 rotates its offer curve to 2*, Nation 2's terms of trade improve to $P_X/P_Y = 1/P^*_w = 1/0.625 = 1.6$. At equilibrium point *E*. However, since Nation 1's welfare is reduced, it is likely to retaliate with an optimum tariff of its own, shown by offer curve 1* and equilibrium at point *E*. Nation 2 may then itself retaliate so that in the end both nations are likely to lose all or most of the benefits from trade.**

ANNEXURE A

The Stopler-Samuelson Theorem : Effects of Tariff on Income Distribution

In what has come to be known as The Stopler-Samuleson Theorem, the two economists have tried to show in their article published in 1941 that in a general equilibrium framework and under certain restrictive assumptions, "a tariff can raise both the relative and absolute income of the relatively scarce factor of production and lower that of the abundant factor."

(The restrictive assumptions are: only two trading countries — though the analysis is confined to only one country — only two commodities (say wheat and watches), only two factors of production, namely, labour and capital, law of constant returns to scale in operation, supply of both the factors is limited and both the factors are fully employed, perfect competition in factor and commodity markets, production of watches is relatively more capital-intensive and that of wheat more labour-intensive, labour is an abundant factor of production and capital a relatively scarce factor of production, and terms of trade between the two countries remain unchanged).

With these assumptions, let us assume that country A exports a certain quantity of wheat (which is relatively more labour-intensive) and in return imports from country B certain number of watches (watches being relatively more capital-intensive).

Let us assume that both the countries are, to being with producing a certain quantity of wheat and a certain number of watches. Let us now assume that country A imposes a tariff on import of watches from country B. Watches being relatively more capital-intensive, there will be an increase in demand for capital in country A. As perfect mobility of factors is assumed, both more capital and labour will move into watch industry from the production of wheat. But as watches are relatively more capital-intensive, in country A that is imposing the tariff, the demand for capital would be more than demand for labour. This will tend to raise price of capital (i.e., rate of interest). This will lead to increasing substitution of labour for capital in country A. As increasing quantity of labour is used in the production of watches, its marginal productivity will decline and marginal productivity of capital will go up. The result will be that real wages will decline and real return on capital will rise in country A that is imposing the tariff on the impose of watches from control B. Thus, imposition of a tariff will result in country A reallocation of factors of production resulting in declining wages to labour which is an abundant factor of production and increasing rewards to capital which is relatively scarce factor of production in country A.

The Stopler-Samuleson theorem provides some insight into the effect of a tariff on income distribution among people in a country.

Thus, one implication of the above theorem is that it cannot be said that if a country adopts the principle of free trade, all sections of the community will be benefited. The above theorem shows that by imposing a tariff, it is possible to provide benefits to one section of the community at the expense of the other sections. We have plenty of historical evidence to show that certain sections of the community demand tariff to protect or even to raise their level of income often at the cost of other sections of the community. Thus, to quote Bo Sodersten "a tariff lowers the national income but benefits the country's scarce factor of production." (But the argument cannot be used in favour of raising wages in a country where labour is a relatively scarce factor because full employment is assumed. This would suggest that real wages of labour should be increased by other measures such as fiscal and monetary measures).

Lancester had criticised the Stopler-Samuelson theorem. According to him, the theorem has not taken into account consumption pattern of people in the country imposing a tariff. It is possible that people give higher priority in their consumption pattern to labour-intensive goods so that comparative cost difference would necessitate its import. In such circumstances, imposition of a tariff would benefit not the relatively scarce factor in a country but the relatively abundant factor, namely, labour, Lancester writes: "... protection will raise the real wages of labour, if, and only if, the country imports the labour-intensive goods."

According to J. Bhagwati, "Protection (prohibitive or otherwise) will raise, reduce or leave unchanged the real wage of the factor intensively employed in the production of a good according as protection raises, lowers or leaves unchanged the internal relative price of that good."

ANNEXURE B

Optimum Tariff

Before the concept of 'Optimum Tariff' is explained, it is necessary to understand two other related concepts, namely, 'Consumption Cost of Tariff' and 'Production Cost of Tariff.'

Consumption Cost of Tariff and Production Cost of Tariff

Under the regime of free trade, different trading countries practise international division of labour and specialisation and this results in the most efficient use of their productive resources.

When a country imposes a tariff on imports from a foreign country, that generally raises prices of imported goods. Thus, when prices of imported goods rise, there is generally certain amount of decline in their consumption of those foreign commodities on which tariff is imposed. This may be regarded as 'Consumption Cost of Tariff.'

When tariff is imposed on imported goods, there would be higher prices of imported goods and decline in their amounts consumed in the country imposing the tariff. This might encourage domestic producers to produce import-substitutes. Though the domestic producers would be less efficient and their cost of production of import-substitute goods would be higher, they can afford to produce those goods (i.e., impost-substitutes) as some degree of protection through tariff on imported goods is provided to domestic producers. Thus, tariff provides protection to relatively inefficient domestic producers of import-substitutes. They would attract more resources from industries where factors of production could have been utilised more efficiently. As a consequence of import duties or tariff, there is thus a certain amount of decline in total production due to inefficient use of productive resources. This indicates 'Production Cost of Tariff.'

Thus, wherever import duties or tariff is imposed, there would be some consumption cost of tariff and production cost of tariff.

The optimum tariff is that which maximises the real welfare of the people in the country that imposes the tariff. This means in other terms, that tariff which takes the community to its highest indifference curve thereby maximising real income and level of satisfaction in the optimum tariff.

It may be pointed out that such optimum tariff results when gains resulting from improved terms of trade consequent on the imposition of the tariff, are larger than production and consumption cost of tariff.

The optimum tariff may be said to be in operation when the following conditions are satisfied: (a) The country that imposes the tariff has a substantial volume of international trade in relation to its national income. This is so because, in that case improved terms of trade would be applicable to a larger portion of national income and, therefore, that will increase real income by a large amount. (b) When the foreign country's offer is less elastic; this is because of foreign country's demand and supply are highly responsive to changes in relative prices, that country's offer curve would be more elastic and, therefore, there would not be much improvement in terms of trade in favour of the country imposing the tariff. In the extreme case of perfectly elastic offer curve of the foreign country, the optimum tariff would be zero. (c) The optimum tariff is applicable only if the distribution of income in their tariff imposing country remains unchanged. This would not take place automatically because imposition of a tariff does result in change in distribution of income among people of the country imposing the tariff. This would mean that tariff to be optimum, the country imposing the tariff must have some policy (say, monetary or fiscal) through which those whose incomes have declined due to the imposition of the tariff are duly compensated so that distribution of income in their country imposing the tariff remains the same as before that tariff was imposed.

ANNEXURE C

Effective and Nominal (Actual) Rate of Protection

Prof. Johnson and Cordon and many other economists have made a distinction between 'Effective rate of protection' and 'Nominal or actual rate of protection.'

On the basis of these concepts, they have argued that in many cases effective rate of imports by developing countries could be much higher than the nominal or actual rate of duties.

This implies that in view of higher effective rate of protection, the developing countries which want to increase exports to developed countries would require much more competitive advantage than what is apparently suggested. When the domestic import-competing industry uses inputs subject to a different nominal tariff rate than that on the final commodity, there is a difference between effective and nominal rate of tariff. It may be said that the effective rate of tariff measures the actual rate of protection that the nominal rate of protection offered to the import-competing industry.

SECTION II

INTERNATIONAL FINANCE

CHAPTER 10

BALANCE OF TRADE AND BALANCE OF PAYMENTS

Structure:

10.1 Introduction

10.2 Balance of Trade

10.3 Balance of Payments

10.4 Balance of Payments on Current Account and Balance of Payments on Capital Account

10.5 Balance of Payments

10.1 INTRODUCTION

'Balance of Trade' and 'Balance of Payments' are two very important concepts in the field of international trade. And, therefore, proper understanding and appreciation of these two concepts is essential to understand some of the basic problems in the field of international trade and the manner in which attempts are being made and should be made to solve them.

10.2 BALANCE OF TRADE

We have already observed that countries trade with one another and exchange commodities for commodities.

'Balance of Trade' refers to the total value of a country's exports of commodities and total value of imports of commodities. Only export and import of commodities are included in the statement of balance of trade of a country. Movement of goods (i.e., exports and imports of commodities) is also known as 'visible trade', because the movement of commodities between countries can be seen by eyes and felt by hands and can be verified physically by custom authorities of a country.

During a given period (generally one year is taken as the basis for calculation in this matter), total value of exports of commodities of a country and total value of imports of commodities by that country might be exactly equal. In this case, it is said that the balance of trade of that country has balanced. But generally such a balance in the balance of trade of a country is a rare thing. This means balance trade of a country rarely balances.

When the total value of commodity exports of a country exceeds the total value of commodity imports of that country, it is said that the country has a 'favourable' balance of trade. If, on the other hand, total value of commodity exports of a country is less than the total value of commodity imports of that country, that country is said to have an 'unfavourable' balance of trade.[1]

It should be noted that balance of trade of a country need not necessarily balance every year. This means the total value of commodity exports and total value of the country's commodity imports over a period of one year need not be equal to each other. If a country's total value of commodity imports exceeds the total value of the country's total value of commodity exports over the course of

---

1. The terms 'unfavourable balance of trade' and favourable balance of trade are the legacy of Mercantilism which flourished in Europe roughly from 15th to 18th century. Money in the form of precious metal (gold and silver, especially gold) was just being introduced in West European countries. And, therefore, gold came to occupy an important place in the money-economy which was just emerging in West European countries. If gold is such a valuable metal that it would command any commodity, then how should countries not possessing gold mines acquire gold? The stock of gold which a country came to possess came to represent the economic as well as political strength of the country.

   The method advocated by the Mercantilists to acquire gold was as follows: A country should export maximum amount of commodities and import as small amount of commodities as possible. If for example, country A exported to country B commodities worth Rs. 500 crores and imported commodities from country B of the total value of Rs. 400 crores only in that year, country B will have to pay to country A the difference of Rs. 100 crores in gold. Then A should be getting gold out of international trading transactions and B would be losing gold — the most precious metal sought in those centuries by most European countries. Since A by exporting goods worth Rs. 500 crores and cutting down imports to Rs. 400 crores succeeded in acquiring gold worth Rs. 100 crores from country B, A's balance of trade was called 'favourable' and B lost gold worth Rs. 100 crores and therefore B's balance of trade came to be called 'unfavourable' balance of trade. Mercantilism gradually disappeared after the publication of Adam Smith's Wealth of Nations in 1766, but the term 'favourable' and 'unfavourable' balance of trade once introduced by Mercantilists continue to be used even to this day.

one year, it should not or need not cause grave concern because there are other ways, as we shall see, of making payments for excess value of the country's commodity imports over the total value of commodity exports.

The following Table 10.1 gives the balance of trade position of India in recent years.

Table 10.1

Position Regarding Balance of Trade of India

(Rs. in Crores)

Year	*Exports**	*Imports*	*Trade Balance*
1949-50	485	617	–132
1950-51	606	608	–2
1960-61	642	1,122	–480
1970-71	1,535	1,634	–99
1980-81	6,711	12,549	–5,838
1990-91	32,553	43,198	–10,645
2000-01	2,03,571	2,30,873	–27,308

* Including re-exports.

Source: Statistical Outline of India 1988-89, Tata Services Ltd. Table 96, p. 9.

From Table 10.1, it is observed that since 1980-82, India has been experiencing adverse or unfavourable balance of trade. In fact, if we consider the period 1950-51 onwards, except during the year 1972-73 and 1976-77 when India's balance of trade was favourable to the extent of Rs. 103.4 crores and Rs. 68.9 crores, respectively during the rest of the years, India's balance of trade throughout has been adverse or unfavourable. The adverse balance of trade which amounted to Rs. 480 crores in 1960-61 rose to Rs. 6,624 crores in 1987-88.

As stated already, 'adverse' or 'unfavourable' balance of trade need not be a matter of undue concern, if the country has at the same time at its disposal other methods of making payments for the excess of commodity imports over commodity exports.

That brings us to the consideration of the concept of 'Balance of Payments.'

10.3 BALANCE OF PAYMENTS

Just as India (or for that matter any other country) exports commodities and imports commodities (which are visible items of the country's exports and imports), India also sells or exports various services like shipping, insurance, tourism, educational and technical services, etc., which are called 'invisible' items of exports. India naturally receives annually payments not only for her commodity exports but also for exports of the above-mentioned exports of invisible items.

In the same way, just as India has to make payments for commodity imports (i.e., for visible exports), she also imports or purchases various types of services from other countries such as services of foreign shipping companies to bring goods home from abroad, of foreign insurance companies, educational facilities in foreign universities, for Indian tourists who avail of foreigners' hotel and tourist services for which India has to make payments.

Thus, compared to the concept of 'Balance of Trade', 'Balance of Payments' is a more comprehensive concept. The concept of balance of payments includes not only payments to be made and received for commodity imports and commodity exports, respectively, but also includes payments which a country has to make to other countries and which that country receives from other countries for various invisible items of imports and exports, respectively. Invisible items of export of a country and imports by the country include items like: shipping, banking, insurance, tourism, royalty payments and other fees, payment of interest on foreign debts, etc. Thus, India has to make payments to other countries not only for commodity imports but also for the import of above services rendered to her by other countries. In the same way, India receives payments not only for export of commodities but also for export of various invisible items which other countries purchase from India.

Thus, balance of payments statement includes all the payments which a country has to receive for exporting visible and invisible items and which the country has to pay for importing all the visible and invisible items.

As we have already seen, balance of trade of a country need not balance. This is because even if there is unfavourable or adverse balance of trade, the gap can be filled by the surplus of value of invisible exports over value of import of invisible items.

But when it is the question of balance of payments (namely, total payments which a country has to receive for exports of visible and invisible items, and which the country has to make for imports of visible and invisible items), it needs to be noted that these total payments to be made and received must balance each other.

If debit items (i.e., payments to be made to other countries) in the balance of payments go on exceeding credit items or payments to be received by the country (i.e., if balance of payments of a country does not balance year after year). It becomes a matter of grave concern and step will have to be taken to see that in the long run all the payments to be made to other countries and all the payments to be received from other countries are made to balance.

If in a particular year, total payments to be received on account of visible and invisible exports are less than total payments to be made on account of visible and invisible imports, the gap can be filled by using foreign exchange reserves built during the past years, or by raising loans from abroad and utilising them for filling the gap. But this cannot go on forever, because sooner or later the foreign exchange reserve is bound to get exhausted and time will come when foreign debts will have to be repaid. And, therefore, how balance of payments of a country is made to balance or what steps are taken to establish equilibrium in the balance of payments position of a country or should be taken is an important topic that will be discussed at length at the proper place in later chapters.

10.4 BALANCE OF PAYMENTS ON CURRENT ACCOUNT AND BALANCE OF PAYMENTS ON CAPITAL ACCOUNT

Distinction is made between 'Balance of Payments on Current Account' and 'Balance of Payments on Capital Account.'

'Balance of payments on current account' refers to payments to and by a country for currently purchased or sold goods and services; it also includes interest paid to and by the country on debts as also donations and gifts made to other countries or received from other countries.

Balance of payments on capital account, on the other hand, refers to payments to and by a country of debts and such other long-term claims on each other.

It would be seen that balance of payment on current account influences the level of income of the people in the concerned country directly and almost immediately. Thus, when India imports goods and services from foreign countries and pays for them, that money could have been used to purchase Indian goods and services but it flows out of the country and to that extent reduces the level of income of people in India.

On the other hand, when India sells her commodities and services to foreign countries, the producers of those goods and services get income and that pushes up the level of income of people in India. Thus, balance of payments on current account has a direct impact on the level of income of people in a country. (Balance of payments on current account is also known as balance of payments on trading account).

On the other hand, 'balance of payments on capital account' does not have such a direct and immediate impact on the current level of income of the people in a country; but it influences the volume of assets which a country holds and that will have effect on the level of income of people in a country in the long run.

10.5 BALANCE OF PAYMENTS

Balance of Payments is the statement of what we owe to the rest of the world and what the rest of the world owes to us. Such a systematic record of a country's economic transactions with the rest of the world generally forms the part of its National Accounts. Most of these transactions are between residents and the non-residents. However, before we understand the precise structure of the balance of payments, a couple of terms have to be clearly defined. One is that of *economic transaction* and the other is that of the *resident.*

I. Preliminary Definitions

Economic Transaction: By economic transaction we mean transfer of economic value from one economic agent (i.e., individual, firm, government and so on) to another. The following basic types of economic transactions can be identified[2]:

(1) Purchase or sale of goods or services with financial *quid pro quo* – cash or a promise to pay. One real and one financial transfer.

(2) Purchase or sale of goods or services in return for goods or services or a barter transaction. Two real transfers.

(3) An exchange of financial items, e.g., purchase of foreign securities with payment in cash or by a cheque drawn on a foreign deposit. Two financial transfers.

(4) A unilateral gift in kind. One real transfer.

(5) A unilateral financial gift. One financial transfer.

The above transactions are fairly obvious. They only become relevant to the BOP because they take place between a resident and a non-resident and therefore can be characterised as international transactions.

---

2 . Apte, P. G., (1998), *International Financial Management,* Tata McGraw-Hill Publishing Company, New Delhi, p. 58.

Other than the above transactions BOP account also records imputed transactions. For example, suppose there are retained earnings attributable to non-resident equity holders in a country. This transaction will be recorded as payment of income to foreign investors and simultaneously as reinvestment of that income by foreign investor in the same enterprise.

Resident: According to the IMF Manual, all persons, whether nationals or non-nationals, whose general centre of interest is considered to rest in an economy with some degree of permanence are treated as residents of that economy. Centre of interest implies that these persons are expected to consume goods and services, contribute in production, or engage in other economic activities in the territory of a given economy on other than a temporary basis. Permanence is recognised if the stay is for one year. Thus, all persons staying in the territory of an economy for 12 months or more are considered as residents and those staying for less than 12 months are regarded as non-residents.

Of course there are exceptions to this rule. Tourists, troops stationed abroad, members of diplomatic and consular missions, students and patients are considered as residents of their own country and hence are exception to the 12-month rule. International institutions like the IMF, FAO, WHO, UNICEF are regarded as residents of the international area and hence cannot be deemed as citizens of the country where they are located.

II. Accounting Principles underlying the Balance of Payments

The BOP is maintained on a standard double-entry accounting system. It implies that every debit given to the account will have an equal and corresponding credit. Hence in strictly accounting sense the BOP account will always balance.

The question that becomes pertinent is what constitutes a debit entry and a credit entry. The following rules should be remembered as generally accepted principles to classify an entry into debit or credit:

(1) All transactions that give rise to a receipt are recorded as credit while the actual receipt is recorded as debit.

(2) All transactions which gives rise to payment are recorded as debit and actual payments as credit.

The above rules imply that an increase in foreign assets (or a decrease in foreign liabilities) is recorded as a debit entry. Whereas a reduction in foreign assets (or an increase in foreign liabilities) is recorded as a credit entry. Thus, a transaction which results in an increase in demand for foreign exchange is to be recorded as a debit entry while a transaction which results in an increase in the supply of foreign exchange is to be recorded as credit entry.

Structure of the BOP: The Balance of Payments has two parts: **the Current Account and the Capital Account.** Current account is a record of exchange of goods and services and unilateral transfers. Ready-made garments exported from India or Computers imported from the USA are examples of current account transactions. On the other hand, capital account is a record of transactions representing foreign assets and liabilities. Examples of capital account transactions include investment in real estate, equities, and bonds.

These preliminary definitions will help to clarify further aspects of the accounting principles underlying the BOP. The original entries of transactions in goods and services, income from foreign investments and unilateral transfers are made in the current account. The reverse entry will depend

Table 10.2

India's Balance of Payments (Performa)

(In Crores)

	Year
1. Imports (c.i.f.)	
2. Exports (F.o.b.)	
3. Trade Balance (2-1)	
4. Invisibles	
(a) Receipts	
(b) Payments	
(Of which: Interest & Service payments on Loans and Credits)	
(c) Net	
5. Current Account (Net)	
6. Capital Account	
I. Foreign Investments	
(a) Inflow	
(b) Outflow	
(c) Net	
II. Loan	
(i) External Assistance	
(a) Inflow	
(b) Outflow	
(c) Net	
(ii) Commercial Borrowings	
(a) Inflow	
(b) Outflow	
(c) Net	
III. Banking	
(a) Receipts	
(b) Payments	
(c) Net	
IV. Rupee Debt Service	
V. Other Capital	
(a) Receipts	
(b) Payments	
(c) Net	
VI. Errors & Omissions	
7. Total Capital (I... VI)	
8. Overall Balance (5 + 7)	
9. Monetary Movement	
(a) IMF Transactions	
(i) Purchases I	
(ii) Repurchases	
(iii) Net	
(b) Increase (-) decrease (-) in Reserves	
10. Total (a + b)	

upon whether the second aspect of the transaction happens to be a financial or a real flow. If it is a financial flow the entry goes to the capital flow and if it happens to be a real flow the entry goes in the current account. For example, if a firm in India exports some commodities to Country A, then the initial entry is a credit to the current account (why?). Now if the receipts are in the form of foreign exchange, i.e., a financial flow, the reverse entry is recorded in the capital account. However, if the receipt is in the form of goods, i.e., a real flow, the reverse entry goes as debit entry to the current account.

If transaction itself is of financial nature, for example, a loan given or an investment made, then the entry is made in the capital account. An increase in the financial assets or a decrease in liabilities means an outflow of capital and therefore will be treated as a debit entry and *vice versa.* The process of reverse entry essentially remains the same as described above.

Content of the Current and the Capital Account: The following table gives the Indian format of the BOP. It displays all the items that are grouped under Current and the Capital account.

Before we discuss the above format in detail, the idea of Deficit or Surplus has to be made clear. Deficit in the BOP means excess of our liability to the world over what the world owes us. Given this surplus would mean excess of what the world owes to us over our liability to the world. In this way we can define deficit on the Current Account implying excess of current payments over the current revenue and similarly for the Capital Account. (How can we define surplus on Current Account and the Capital Account?)

The Reserve Bank of India adopted the above format recently. In the earlier format amounts against each entry used to be displayed as debit, credit and net of the two. Hence, surplus or deficit could be identified item-wise. However, this net balance in autonomous transactions is no longer recorded separately in the format. Yet comparable accommodating transactions can be conveniently spotted in the new format. (See the Box below for the definition of the autonomous and accommodating transactions).

If the value of the accommodating transactions turn out to be positive, it means that there is deficit in the BOP, which is financed by these accommodating transactions. Thus, in the new format if we wish to calculate deficit in the BOP, we will have to identify the accommodating transactions. The autonomous transactions and the accommodating transactions in the balance of payments of India are given in the following table. Note the sign associated with the numbers and try to understand their significance.

Table 10.3

India's Balance of Payments (2000-2001)

Items	*US $ Million*
Autonomous Transactions	
1. Net Merchandise (Trade Balance)	– 14,370
2. Net Invisibles	11,791
3. Net Capital Transactions	8,409
4. Errors & Omissions	–588
5. Total Deficit (–)/ Surplus (+) = (1 + 2 + 3 + 4)	–5,242
Financed By (Accommodating Transactions)	
6. External Assistance	427
7. Drawing from IMF	–26
8. Allocation of SDRs	
9. Decline in Reserves (+)/ Increase (–)	–5,830
10. Total (6 + 7 + 8 + 9)*	5,429

Source: Economic Survey 2001-2002.

* Difference between item 5 and item 10 is because of rounding off errors.

Autonomous Transactions: Transactions undertaken independently of other transactions on the balance of payments or for their own sake are called autonomous transactions. They are result of voluntary action. For example, exports, imports, unilateral transfers, etc. These transactions are influenced by factors like prices, incomes and interest rates in two countries.

Accommodating Transactions: Accommodating transactions are undertaken to compensate the imbalances in the autonomous transactions. Hence these transactions are not independent transactions. For example if a country imports more than what it exports, then it will have to pay for the excess imports by resorting to the foreign aid or by using the accumulated foreign exchange reserves. Therefore, all such transactions in foreign aid or foreign exchange reserves are accommodating transactions as they are undertaken to accommodate the deficit or surplus in autonomous transactions.

Source: Agarwala S.K. (2000)[3], p. 281 & Sodersten Bo & Reed Geoffrey (1994), p. 505[4].

Items in the Current Account

Merchandise: These are nothing but the imports and exports. Note that in the above format that Exports minus Import (X – M) is termed as Trade Balance. This difference is also called as Net Exports. Exports are valued at free on board (f.o.b.) prices. This price includes carriage only from the supplier's premises to the port from which the goods are supposed to be dispatched. Imports are valued at 'cost, insurance and freight' price. This price covers the ex-warehouse price to which the cost of delivery to the docks, dock dues, carriage and insurance as far as the port to which the goods are to be consigned, are to be added. It excludes the cost of delivery from the docks to the purchaser's premises. Trade in merchandise is sometimes called trade in visibles. This brings us to the next point, i.e., invisibles.

3. Agarwala S. K. (2000), *"National Income Accounting"*, Book Land Publishing Co., Third Ed.
4. Sodersten Bo & Geoffrey Reed (1994), *"International Economics"*, Macmillan, Third Ed.

Invisibles: Trade in invisibles include services (non-factor services, travel, insurance, etc.), investment and transfer payments. Miscellaneous receipts, comprise receipt and payment for professional services, royalties, management fees, subscription fees and so on. Out of this, software service exports, i.e., a type of professional service, has been a major contributor to the buoyancy of the receipts on the invisibles account in the recent period. Transfer payments include official as well as private transfer payments.

Items in the Capital Account

- Foreign Investment includes the Foreign Direct investment as well as the investments of the Foreign Institutional Investors, investment in Euro equities and others.
- External Assistance in the form of loans, official as well as private, is included in the capital account.
- IMF includes purchases and repurchases from under the various facilities provided by the Fund.

Disequilibrium in the Balance of Payments and Methods to correct them — Appendix of Chapter 7 and Chapter 12 from the original text can be merged with this chapter or can be grouped as a separate chapter.

Concluding Remarks

We have analysed the concepts of 'Balance of Trade', 'Balance of Payments on Current Account' and 'Balance of Payments on Capital Account.'

We have already noted that it is not necessary that balance of trade of a country should balance. This means it is not necessary that every year total value of commodity exports of a country should equal total value of commodity imports of the country. Even if the total value of commodity imports of a country goes on exceeding the total value of commodity exports of the country, this should not be a matter of grave concern.

Similarly, when we consider 'Balance of Payments on Current Account' (i.e., total value of exports of commodities and services and total value of commodity and services imports), it is again not necessary that the credits and debits should exactly balance each other every year.

But when we consider all the three together, namely, balance of trade, balance of payments on current account and balance of payments on capital account, the situation is radically different. If the total debts which a country incurs because of commodity imports, of various services and on account of debt repayment and servicing charges on debts raised in foreign countries, go on exceeding the total of all the credits on account of the country's exports of commodities, of services and repayment of loans, etc. for some years, the gap may be filled by using its stock of gold, or reserve of foreign currencies built over past years or by additional borrowing from foreign countries.

But clearly there is a limit to the use of stock of gold, reserves of foreign currencies and borrowing from abroad to fill the gap appearing in the balance of payments of a country year after year.

This would mean that if we take into consideration the overall picture of balance of payments in all its aspects, a country cannot go on facing deficits year after year. Measures will have to be taken to correct such imbalance in the overall balance of payments position of a country.

What measures or policy is or should be adopted under such circumstances to successfully meet the situation will be considered at length in later chapters.

ANNEXURE

Different Types of Balance of Payments Disequilibrium

Following are the main types of balance of payments disequilibrium:

(1) *Temporary Disequilibrium:* Temporary disequilibrium in balance of payments of a country may occur because of the operation of some temporary factor which is not likely to repeat itself regularly (e.g., locusts destroying crops completely in a country, an earth-quake affecting some vital industries, prolonged strike, as for example the prolonged textile strike in Mumbai some years ago, drought over wide areas of the country, a short war (as between India and Pakistan in 1962, 1965 and 1971) etc., Most of the above causes are not likely to persist year after year adversely affecting production and exports of a country causing recurrent disequilibrium in the country's balance of payments.

(2) *Cyclical Balance of Payments Disequilibrium:* This refers to a situation when a deficit or surplus in balance of payments position of a country renews itself in a cyclical manner. Cyclical disequilibrium in balance of payments is said to occur when a deficit and a surplus take place in an alternative way. Thus, the situation of favourable or surplus balance of payments is followed next year by a deficit or unfavourable balance of payments position in the concerned country. Cyclical disequilibrium in balance of payments is closely associated with business or trade cycles which occur fairly regularly.

(3) *Structural Disequilibrium in Balance of Payments:* This type of disequilibrium refers to situation when there take place structural changes in the economy of a country. These structural changes may be due to changes in tastes of the people or changes in technology or changes in fashions of people preferring foreign goods to domestic goods and services. These structural changes may result in a deficit or surplus in balance of payments of a country.

Some examples of structural disequilibrium in the balance of payments of a country may be given to illustrate the point.

A decline in foreign demand for Indian tea because of changes in tastes of foreigners would affect production of tea, investment in tea plantation, production of related commodities and investment in those industries. Resources employed in tea and related industries will have to be shifted to production of goods for which demand has gone up because of changes in tastes of foreigners. If exports of Indian tea decline and her imports remain the same as before, there will be disequilibrium in the balance of payments of the country.

Structural change may also occur on the supply side. New oil fields may be found (as in the case of Bombay High) leading to development of petro-chemical industries with vast implications for export and import trade of India with significant effect of balance of payments position of the country.

(4) *Fundamental Disequilibrium:* Fundamental disequilibrium in balance of payments of a country is said to occur when there is a persistent deficit (or surplus) in the balance of payments of a country. This fundamental disequilibrium may occur because of radical changes in the economic structure of a country greatly influencing its exports and imports, totally changing composition of both; or it may occur because of radical structural changes in other countries or due to changes in monetary and fiscal policies of a country either in the country or in other countries (e.g., formation of European Economic Community adopting a common tariff in case of goods imported from India).

Continual deficits in balance of payments of a country would mean that the concerned country is continually losing gold or is facing a continual decline in her foreign exchange reserve built over past years or continual borrowing from abroad to fill the deficit. Thus, outwardly the balance of payments would be shown as balancing for accounting purposes, but in fact there is fundamental disequilibrium the symptom of which would be declining stock of gold or foreign exchange reserve or mounting borrowings abroad. Or the country may devalue its currency or adopt deflationary policy in which case fundamental disequilibrium in the balance of payments would appear in the form of declining prices, rising level of unemployment and declining level of income of people in the country facing fundamental disequilibrium in its balance of payments position.

(5) *Secular Disequilibrium:* Secular disequilibrium in balance of payments of a country may occur because a country's economy is moving from lower level or stage of development to a higher or next stage in the process of her development due to planned efforts at economic development. This economic development or transition from lower stage to the next stage of development may occur because of rise in the rate of capital formation, advancement in technological field, increase in population of a country, discovery of new sources of supply of vital metal or crude oil as in the case of North Sea off the coast of England. It may be said that disequilibrium (deficits) in the balance of payments position of India that is taking place year after year is a secular type of disequilibrium and so also in the case of Japan and West Germany which are having continual surplus in their balance of payments during the last two decades or so.

An important cause of secular disequilibrium may be substantial and regular increase in population of a country as in the case of India. Around 1.5 crores of persons are being added annually to the total population of India which has already crossed in 85 crore mark. Such rapid and substantial increase in a country's population means that increasing proportion of domestic production would be consumed domestically and to that extent less would be available for export. Also, increase in population of a country might also lead to continual increase in imports of some vital commodities (e.g., as in the case of edible oil the annual imports costing around Rs. 1,000 crores) for which domestic demand is inelastic. This would result in secular disequilibrium (deficits) in balance of payments of a country like India.

In the case of West Germany and Japan, due to rapid advancement in the field of technology, those countries have been continually having substantial surpluses in their balance of payments and, therefore, are having secular disequilibrium in their balance of payments position.

Concluding Remarks

The above types of balance of payments disequilibrium do not constitute water-tight and completely exclusive types, each type totally independent of other types and with absolutely no relation with other types.

This means when in a country disequilibrium in her balance of payments occurs, that may be due to one or many types of causes operating at one and the same time. For example, appearance of a disequilibrium in the balance of payments position of a country may be due to concurrent operation of temporary causes mixed with structural changes in the economy or with cyclical causes as also operation of some fundamental causes of such disequilibrium. This means that it is not possible to put a particular disequilibrium in the balance of payments of a country exclusively in just one or any other class.

CHAPTER

11 MEASURES TO CORRECT BALANCE OF PAYMENTS DISEQUILIBRIUM

Structure:

11.1 INTRODUCTION

The problem of disequilibrium (especially due to deficits) in balance of payments position is being faced by both developed and developing countries. For example, at present the United States has been facing annually an enormous deficit of a few billion dollars in her balance of payments. But the United States' problem has arisen due to its military and such other commitments all over the world from political considerations and its internal monetary and fiscal policies. West Germany and Japan are having annual surplus in their balance of payments and this has been causing a lot of concern in countries like the United States which are insisting on revaluation of mark and yen and are also threatening stiff trade measures especially against Japan. But the problem of balance of payments in developed countries does not become a matter of as grave a concern as it does in the case of developing countries. The developing countries are finding it very difficult to push up their exports and cut down their imports needed to accelerate growth rate of their economies. The consequence is that the developing countries like India are continually facing deficits in their balance of payments year after year since independence and these deficits are being financed by falling back on foreign exchange reserves (which are in most cases very slender or do not exist at all) and mostly by borrowing from other countries or from the World Bank and the international monetary institutions. Obviously, this cannot go on forever and developing countries like India will have to take appropriate measures to overcome or correct deficits in their balance of payments position.

Following are the important measures which are generally suggested and followed to correct disequilibrium in balance of payments position (especially and mostly deficits) in the case of developing countries.

11.2 EXPORT PROMOTION

The main reason for deficit in balance of payments especially of developing countries like India is that the total value of country's exports of goods and services is less than the total value of imports of goods and services by the country. The final remedy, therefore, in removing deficits in a country's balance of payments is to take steps to promote and increase and see that total value of country's export of goods and services is equal to the total value of its import of goods and services. And therefore export promotion assumes great importance as a measure to fill up deficits in balance of payments of developing countries like India.

Export promotion to the maximum possible extent requires the following measures, especially by developing countries:

(1) There should be comprehensive commodity surveys of developed countries to find out potential export markets from the point of view of developing countries like India.

(2) With these comprehensive commodity surveys as background, production of commodities with export potentialities should be developed to the maximum possible extent.

(3) Emphasis should be on promoting exports of non-traditional goods and items in addition to efforts to promote export of traditional goods and services for which, however, there will be clear limits with the changing pattern of production and consumption. Myrdal has observed that "they (developing countries) should rather take a good look at the competition of these exports and at their prospects in the world market and then make up their minds about which export they should try to increase and which exports they should rather leave alone or reduce.

They should seek out for themselves the dynamic commodities with rising demand trends and try to get away from those with doubtful future."

(4) Attainment of production targets set in sectors with increasing potentialities is an essential condition, if exports are to be promoted to the maximum possible extent.

(5) Steps should be taken to restrain domestic consumption of goods which have increasing export potential in developed as also in developing countries. The idea is to create maximum export surplus.

(6) For promoting exports, maintenance of price stability is an essential condition. This is because unless the goods are competitive in foreign markets, their export cannot generally be promoted.

(7) Special steps should be taken for modernization of export-oriented industries. In the case of India, this step was neglected for long in respect of textile industry with adverse effects on its exports until modernisation got under way. The same is true in respect of India's jute industry.

(8) Successful efforts must be made to get timely imports of essential raw material and capital goods necessary to accelerate growth-rate of export-oriented industries.

(9) If there are any domestic restrictions that hamper exports, they should be removed. Taxes on export goods should be reduced and if possible removed depending upon the degree of competition domestic goods are likely to face in foreign markets.

(10) In the case of developing countries, there is an urgent need for providing transport facilities as also export-credit, insurance etc. The Import-Export Bank of India has been doing commendable work in the sphere of export promotion by providing credit facilities to Indian exporters. Credit facilities are also being provided to exporters by the Reserve Bank of India, the State Bank of India and Refinance Corporation. There is also functioning in India 'Export Credit and Guarantee Corporation.' The Corporation insures all export risks; it furnishes guarantees to banks on behalf of Indian exporters who have availed from those banks credit facilities; the Corporation also provides supplementary credit for promoting exports of Indian goods. Indian railways have been providing preferential and cheaper transport facilities for goods exported by Indian exporters.

(11) Tax concessions should be offered to exports using imported raw materials, spare parts and machinery etc. for manufacturing exportable goods.

(12) Quality control is an absolutely essential step for promoting exporters of goods. Consumers in foreign countries, especially in developed countries, are extremely quality conscious. Many Indian exporters have been giving in recent years warranty period guarantee from 1 to 5 years in the case of their goods to foreign customers. There should be compulsory inspection of quality of export items. Indian producers will have to be particularly more quality conscious. At present Export Inspection Council has been performing the function of inspection of quality of goods to be exported. Much more needs to be done in this respect in India. It is only recently that Indian producers have realised the importance of quality and many industrial establishments have set up their 'Quality Circles' at every stage from beginning to the end product ready for export. India needs to take note of the fact that many developed countries, and especially Japan, are in the export market with goods of excellent quality and with competitive prices on the basis of which the Japanese car industry has made substantial inroads in the car-market of the United States.

(13) For the promotion of exports a number of steps need to be taken such as : establishment of commercial intelligence service and collection and distribution, comprehensive commercial intelligence from foreign countries, dissemination of commercial information among Indian businessmen and industrialists, especially exporters, establishment of an institution to represent and protect interests of Indian exporters in foreign countries and branches of such an institution in all important international trading centres, participation in international exhibitions and trade fairs (which India has been doing regularly in recent years), commercial publicity abroad making foreigners aware of Indian goods, establishing export promotion councils (in the case of important Indian goods with export potentialities).

(14) Countries like India should conclude bilateral trade agreements with developed as also developing countries to promote exports. (Since independence India has entered into several such bilateral trade agreements with a number of countries, especially of the Eastern block).

(15) There should be cooperative and joint action or programme by developing countries to promote their exports (as for example, is contemplated in the case of jute manufacture, tea, etc.). This is necessary because most of the developing countries export to developed countries also similar type of goods resulting in destructive mutual competition among developing countries to capture foreign markets. The only way exports of developing countries to developed countries can increase is if their bargaining position or strength improves and that is possible only if they come together and chalk out and execute joint action in the sphere of exports to developed countries.

Concluding Remarks

Developing countries need to promote their exports to an increasing extent, especially because terms of trade are continually moving against them and a unit of exported item is buying less and less of an imported commodity. India has all the greater need to promote her exports as her share in world exports has been diminishing as is indicated by the fact that India's share in world exports which was 1.05 in 1960-61 went down in 1970-71 to 0.65 per cent, and to 0.44 per cent in 1986-87.

Exports must not be viewed separately but must become part of general production process. Developing countries must concentrate on non-traditional items and on export of new products (as India, for example has been doing in respect of ready-made garments and jewellery). Also developing countries must trade more and more among themselves as there is great scope for such trade and they must act jointly through commodity agreements among themselves while trading with developed countries.

11.3 REDUCTION OF IMPORTS AND PROMOTION OF IMPORT SUBSTITUTION

Here reduction of imports to the minimum and attempts to substitute imports by domestic production wherever possible will be discussed as a method of removing disequilibrium or deficits in balance of payments, especially in the case of developing countries like India.

When we talk of cutting down imports or of promotion of import-substitution, it should be obvious that the government is going to exercise substantial control over import and export trade of a country.

The strategy to remove disequilibrium in balance of payments is to cut down or, if possible, to eliminate import of luxury and semi-luxury goods as also of as many consumer goods as possible, especially of low priority. It is possible to direct investment in industries that would be producing goods that would be substitutes for imports of such goods and services. This is easily possible in a developing country like India where technology is fairly well developed to produce most of the consumer goods, not only for domestic markets but also for exports especially to developing countries, thus removing substantial deficits in balance of payments. Thus, the strategy of import substitution is desirable both for the purpose of achieving self-sufficiency in essential goods and services and also to save foreign exchange by substituting domestic production for imports which absorb a substantial amount of foreign exchange.

But import-substitution strategy to remove or lessen deficits in balance of payments has a number of limitations.

The import-substitution industries, instead of helping to save foreign exchange, might actually result in using more foreign exchange. Developing countries are in great need of imports of essential raw materials, capital equipment and spare parts and technological know-how. And, therefore, the immediate effects of attempting to develop import-substitution industries in a developing country like India would be increasing pressure on the country's foreign exchange and, therefore, on balance of payments position. Such an attempt would also mean diversion of domestic resources towards import-substitution industries, possible neglect of export-oriented industries and, therefore, decline in export and in export earnings with consequent increase in deficit in balance of payments. This was, for example, what happened in some of the Latin American countries and to some extent even in India for a considerable period of time.

If import-substitution is indiscriminately adopted, the high wall of protection to domestic industries by cutting down competition from abroad might lead to rising cost of production and prices and deteriorating quality of goods and services, not only of those produced in protected industries but in other industries also adversely affecting the country's exports and export earnings.

Concluding Remarks

While adopting the policy of import-substitution, a number of considerations or precautions will have to be taken into account.

In the case of vital goods and industries like defence goods, life-saving drugs, heavy engineering machinery, heavy chemicals, etc., it is both economically and especially politically dangerous to depend exclusively on their imports (as India has learnt this lesson to its cost). And, therefore, in the case of above basic, heavy and defence industries, countries like India will have to develop them, whatever the cost in terms of initial import bill to get necessary capital goods and technology to establish and develop those industries. But once these industries are developed, their imports will decline and that will mean saving of foreign exchange that would have been annually spent on them. Thus, India's becoming self-sufficient in respect of machinery and spares necessary for industries like textile, jute, sugar, cement, paper and printing and life-saving drugs, etc. has been resulting in considerable annual saving of foreign exchange which otherwise would have been spent on their imports annually.

On the other hand, these industries have developed in India to such an extent that their products are bring exported in recent years earning foreign currencies resulting in the reduction in deficit in India's balance of payments.

In regard to import-substitution policy in respect of consumer goods, it should be planned carefully taking into consideration available domestic resources and cost and savings in foreign exchange by starting and developing such consumer goods industries.

It should be noted that there is no basic conflict between export promotion and import-substitution. In the long-run both the strategies are supplementary and complementary to each other. And therefore, a country like India, while concentrating on the strategy of export promotion, should also have a carefully planned import-substitution policy by taking into account the availability of foreign exchange, domestic resources as also short-term and long-term effects of development of import-substitution industries.

11.4 DEFLATION

Deficit in balance of payments is only a symptom. One basic cause of such deficit is purchasing more foreign goods and services relative to foreigners' purchasing the deficit country's goods and services. Naturally, the basic solution to the problem of limiting or eliminating such deficits lies in cutting down domestic demand for foreign goods and services and persuading foreigners to purchase more of goods and services produced in the deficit country.

Deflation is a means of cutting down imports and bringing about increase in exports of a country. This point can be illustrated by taking an Indian illustration. If India begins to face recurring deficits in her balance of payments, with a view to adopt deflationary policy, the Reserve Bank of India should raise the Bank Rate; this will result in rise in interest rates charged by commercial banks to its customers. Rise in the market rates of interest would bring reduction in the level of investment, decline in incomes of the people, less demand for domestic goods and services and, therefore, decline in prices of domestic goods and services.

Decline in the level of income of people in India following deflationary policy would also result in cutting down of imports on the one hand; and decline in prices of domestically produced goods and services would result in increase in the country's exports. Thus, decline in volume of imports and increase in volume of exports would help remove deficits in balance of payments of the country.

But the policy of deflation to fill up deficits in balance of payments is generally opposed on the following grounds. As we have seen, rise in Bank Rate and market rates of interest, and decline in investment all result in rise in the level of unemployment and decline in level of income of people. All these are opposed by trade unions of workers and the other affected sections of the community, and if the country is already suffering from substantial unemployment as in the case of India, the policy of deflation to fill up deficits in balance of payments of a country like India will not find favour either with the people or the democratic government which is sensitive to people's wishes and opinions.

11.5 'DEVALUATION' (OR DEPRECIATION)

Technical meanings of Devaluation and Depreciation: Technical meaning of 'Devaluation' can be made clear by an example. When two countries, say America and England, are on the gold standard, let us assume that 1 English pound is convertible into X quantity of gold of specified quality in the Bank of England and in America the same quantity of gold of specified fineness is convertible into 5 dollars in the Federal Reserve System. The rate of exchange in the above case would be 1 English pound = 5 American dollars.

Now let us assume that with this rate of exchange, England, due to some reason or other, begins to face recurring deficits in her balance of payments. With a view to correct such deficits, England may resort to what is technically known as 'devaluation.' England would reduce gold content of her pound, say to half of X quantity of gold per one unit of pound, while in America the rate of conversion of gold into dollar and dollar into gold remains the same as before, namely, X quantity of gold of specified fineness = 5 dollars. Under such circumstances, the new rate of exchange between English pound and American dollar would be 1 English pound = $2\frac{1}{2}$ American dollars. This means English pound has become cheaper in terms of American dollar or to look at it differently the American dollar has become dearer in terms of pound. This would also mean that English goods and services have become cheaper for Americans and American goods and services have become dearer for English customers. This would push up English exports and reduce her imports from America, and thus, devaluation would help reduce and possibly eliminate deficits in England's balance of payments position. Thus, technically speaking 'devaluation' takes place when countries are on the gold standard.

Technical meaning of 'Depreciation': If England and America have adopted inconvertible paper currency standard and if the rate of exchange between English pound and American dollar is allowed to freely fluctuate according to market forces of demand and supply, in that case deficit in England's balance of payments position (which means relatively less American demand for English pound compared to English demand for American dollars) would automatically result in more English pounds being offered for a unit of American dollar. Market forces of demand and supply would automatically make English pound cheaper and American dollar dearer. Technically this automatic cheapening of English pound in terms of American dollar is known as 'depreciation.'

But as we have seen, in recent times, rates of exchange in the case of inconvertible paper currency standard are not allowed to freely fluctuate according to market forces of demand and supply. Rates of exchange are bring managed so that fluctuations in them are avoided. And, therefore, in the case of recurrent deficits in England's balance of payments, Government of Great Britain cheapens English pound, say from 1 pound = 5 dollars to one pound = 3 dollars or if necessary 1 pound = 1 dollar. Technically this is known as 'depreciation.'

Though technically the meanings for devaluation and depreciation are different, at present the two terms are used as synonymous or interchangeable. Thus, though India has adopted inconvertible paper currency standard, Indian rupee was said to have been 'devalued' in 1966 and 1971. It may be noted that what is common to both is that in both the cases English pound has been made cheaper in terms of American dollar.

Devaluation (Depreciation) and Balance of Payments

Following are the conditions that must exist, if devaluation (depreciation) is to succeed in removing deficits in balance of payments position of a country:

(1) *Elasticity of Demand:* Success of devaluation in bridging the gap between the total value of exports of goods and services of a country like India and the total value of imports of goods and services by the country, will depend upon elasticity of demand for imports and exports. For example, devaluation will mean high prices of foreign goods for Indians. But if the Indian demand for, say American goods, is inelastic (i.e., the same quantity of American goods and services is going to be imported by India) the total value of Indian imports from America will rise. Also, if American demand for Indian goods is also inelastic (i.e., Americans buy the same quantity as before, though Indian goods and services are cheaper for them), Indian

exports will not increase and will not earn more dollars; on the other hand, the same quantity exports by India will earn less amount of dollars than before. Thus, if demand for imports and exports is inelastic, devaluation will not fill up the deficit but on the other hand, will increase deficit in the balance of payments of India. This also means that only if the Indian demand for American goods and services is elastic and American demand for Indian goods and services is elastic (i.e., American purchasing substantially more because Indian goods and services are cheaper because of devaluation of the Indian rupee), will devaluation of Indian rupee succeed in reducing and possibly eliminating deficit in India's balance of payments position.

(2) *Cost-Price Structure:* Devaluation (depreciation) measure will succeed in reducing or eliminating deficit in balance of payments, provided there is no change as a result or devaluation in cost of production and prices of commodities in the country that is devaluating its currency. This means devaluation will succeed only if domestic purchasing power of the national currency remains the same as before devaluation.

But there is possibility that in the case of a developing country like India, domestic cost and price structure may not remain the same as before devaluation. This may happen due to the following reasons: (a) As devaluation is going to reduce imports, merchants and speculators are likely to raise their prices; if these imports serve as inputs for domestic industries, then cost of production and prices are bound to rise in the country devaluing the currency. (b) If imports form a substantial part of consumption pattern of people in the country devaluing its currency, rise in the cost of living due to rise in prices of imported goods may result in demand for higher wages and that may push up domestic cost of production and prices of goods. (c) If imports constitute essential inputs for domestic industries, rise in price of imported goods and services will push up cost of production and prices. If this happens, then favourable effect of devaluation or cheapening of the national currency will be neutralised by rising prices of domestic goods and services.

(3) *Cooperation of Internationally Trading Partners:* If devaluation (depreciation) of a country's currency is to succeed in its objective of reducing and possibly eliminating deficit in balance of payments of the country, that country's trading partner must cooperate in this process. If, for example, India devalues her rupee, say *vis-a-vis* Japanese yen, that would mean that Japan will be buying more from India whereas Japan's exports to India would be reduced. This decline of Japan's exports to India may cause problems for Japanese industries such as increase in unemployment in her export industries. It is therefore possible that Japan may take some retaliatory steps and in its turn devalue her currency or provide subsidy to her exportable goods, or Japan may put tariff barriers to cut down her imports from India. If this happens, India's devaluation of her rupee *vis-a-vis* Japanese yen will not be in a position to realise the objective of reducing and if possible eliminating deficit in her balance of payments *vis-a-vis* Japan.

11.6 COMMERCIAL POLICY

Commercial policy of a country can be an effective measure under certain circumstances of correcting disequilibrium in balance of payments of a country.

Commercial policy (which includes matters like import policy, prohibiting certain imports, imposing import duties on some commodities, quota-fixation, payment of subsidy to exports, etc.) is a very important subject and therefore it is discussed in a separate chapter.

CHAPTER

12 GOLD STANDARD

Structure:

2.1 INTRODUCTION

Though the gold standard is at present only of historical significance, it would be useful to study the various aspects of gold standard for two main reasons, namely, under the gold standard the country's problem regarding balance of payments used to be solved almost automatically without state intervention, and secondly, the gold standard has left its impact even on the present day currency system and rates of exchange at least to some extent.

The gold standard was in operation for about 125 years in most of the countries engaged in international trade. After 1870 most of the countries adopted gold standard because there was a strong belief that currency of a country should be based on a commodity like gold which should be valuable in itself. The years 1870 to 1914 might be referred to as 'the Golden Age of Gold Standard.' The gold standard was suspended during the period of World War I (1914-18) but came to be resumed during post-World War I period. But by then the economic and political conditions had so changed that countries after countries started abandoning the gold standard. Thus, England abandoned the gold standard in 1931, the United States in 1934, and finally France in 1936 which for all practical purposes heralded the end of the gold standard.

In this chapter an attempt is made to define gold standard, describe its different forms or varieties, how the problem of balance of payments of countries on the gold standard were automatically solved, rules of the gold standard, merits and defects of that standard and finally why gold standard came to be abandoned during 1930s.

As stated earlier, though the gold standard is now only of historical significance, it has left its impact on the present day currency standards in different countries of the world and hence the significance of the study of the gold standard.

12.2 DEFINITION OF GOLD STANDARD

When the value of a country's currency is fixed in terms of gold, the currency is said to be on the gold standard. According to Colborn, when the main currency unit of a country is legally convertible into gold of given quantity and quality and *vice versa*, the country is said to be on the gold standard.

Thus, under the gold standard (Rupee of India, British Pound, US Dollar, Japanese Yen, etc.) the standard unit was either made of gold of stated quantity and fineness, or value of the basic unit of currency was fixed in terms of gold of stated quantity and quality, and the government was legally bound to convert currency into gold and gold into currency at the specified rate without any limit when people wanted such conversion; and there were absolutely no restrictions on export and import of gold. When these conditions are fulfilled in a country that country was said to be on the gold standard.

12.3 TYPES OF GOLD STANDARD

Following are the main types of gold standard:

(1) *Gold Coin or Currency Standard:* Before the World War I, many countries in the world had adopted the gold coin or gold currency standard.

The main features of this type of gold standard were as follows:

(i) The main or basic coin of a country consisted of or was made up of gold of a given quantity and specified quality or fineness.

(ii) Such gold coins were unlimited legal tender in the country.

(iii) All the bank created money (i.e., bank money or credit money) was convertible into gold coins at the central bank of the country.

(iv) There was free minting of gold coins at the government mints (that is people could take gold and get that minted into golden coins which was legal tender) or take golden coins and get in return gold bullion at the officially declared rate.

(v) There were no restrictions on free export and import of gold from one country to another which were on the gold standard.

(2) Gold Bullion Standard: After World War I (1914-18) many countries came to adopt the gold bullion standard. The main reason was that handling of golden coins was found inconvenient, especially when making large payments (as for example when purchasing a car or a house). And, therefore, gold bullion standard came to be adopted.

The main features of the gold bullion standard were as follows:

(i) The basic coin of a country was linked to gold of specific quantity and fineness.

(ii) Gold coins were not in use or in circulation (as in the case of gold coin or currency standard), but the currency of the country was convertible at the officially specified rate into gold bullion or bars at the central bank to any extent; and similarly gold bullion (i.e., uncoined gold) or bars into currency at the central bank to any extent (which as already noted, currency not being made of gold).

(iii) Gold bullion bars were sold or bought by the central bank of the country without any limit at the officially specified rate in terms of basic coin.

(iv) There were no restrictions on export and import of gold.

(v) Since not all people would come at one and the same time to the central bank of a country to convert currency or coins into gold bullion, gold bullion was kept as reserve in the central bank of the country and it informed only relatively small proportion of the total currency that was in circulation in the country.

(3) Gold Exchange Standard: It was found that poor countries like India could not afford to keep bullion in an idle form as was required in the case of gold bullion standard. And, therefore, 'Gold Exchange Standard' came to be adopted by India from 1898.

Under the gold exchange standard, there were no gold coins or gold currency into circulation in the country; also the national currency was not convertible into gold bullion at the central bank of the country.

But the national currency of a country was linked to gold in an indirect manner. Thus, Indian rupee was convertible into British pound at the central bank of the country and British pound was convertible into given quantity of gold of specified quality at the Bank of England. In this way, the Indian rupee was indirectly linked to gold through the British pound.

Whatever the type of the gold standard, the essence of gold standard is that a nation's currency or coins are linked to gold at legally specified rate and the national currency is either directly or indirectly convertible into a given quantity of gold of specified fineness and further there is no prohibition or restriction of any kind on export and import of gold from one country to another which are on gold standard.

The gold standard had two aspects — internal and external. Internal aspect of gold standard would mean that quantity of money in circulation in a country had some correspondence with the stock of gold with the central bank of the country; and international aspect of gold standard meant that any importer wanting to make payments in gold for his imports of commodities was in a position to get legally stipulated quantity of gold of specified fineness in return of domestic currency at the central bank of the country.

12.4 FUNCTIONING OF GOLD STANDARD

The following account of functioning of the gold standard will explain how disequilibrium in balance of payments between internationally trading countries was automatically removed and equilibrium in balance of payments automatically established.

This can best be illustrated by taking the realistic example of Great Britain and the United States, both of which were on the gold standard before World War I.

How the Rate of Exchange between British Pound and American Dollar got fixed

Assuming that both England and America were on the gold standard, if in England one pound could be legally exchanged against X quantity of gold of specified fineness and if in America X quantity of gold of the same fineness could be exchanged against 5 dollars, the rate of exchange between English pound and American dollar would automatically get established at the rate of 1 pound is equal to 5 dollars. This is the mint parity of exchange rate between English pound and American dollar. One advantage of gold standard was that the rate of exchange got automatically established.

Any Englishman wanting to purchase American goods would go to foreign exchange bank or dealer or Bank of England, exchange 1 British pound for 5 US dollars and purchase or import American goods and at the same would happen in America. Americans wanting to purchase English goods would go to the Federal Reserve System or foreign exchange dealer, exchange 5 US dollars for 1 British pound and purchase or import British goods.

Now suppose that due to increased efficiency and productivity of American labour and, therefore, lower prices of American goods, or due to change in tastes of English people who begin to prefer American goods than before, but American purchases of British goods did not increase but remained the same as before.

This would mean that the demand for American dollars by the British went up whereas American demand for the British pound was the same as before.

The foreign exchange dealers would find that there was greater demand for American dollars in return of British pound whereas the American demand for British pound was the same as before. The foreign exchange operators or banks in England would feel the pressure of demand on American dollars and stock of dollars would be getting smaller and smaller because of increase in demand on them, whereas the British pound stock would be gradually increasing. If this persisted for long, the foreign exchange operators or banks in England would find that at the rate of 1 British pound equal to 5 US dollars, the stock of dollars would soon get exhausted and stock of British pound go on mounting so that a time would come when no dollars would be left in their stock to exchange against British pound.

Experiencing increasing demand for dollars (because of increase in English demand for and decreasing stock of dollars because the American demand for English goods was the same as before), the foreign exchange banks would begin to give less dollars for one pound. They would start giving for 1 pound 4.9 dollars, and if still there continued increasing pressure on dollars by British importers of American goods, they would start giving for 1 pound 4.8 dollars.

But the British importers would not accept for 1 pound less than 4.8 dollars which they would accept because the cost of converting 1 pound into gold, shipping charges and insurance, etc. would come to around 20 cents. If the exchange banks begin to offer less than 4.8 dollars per 1 pound because of increasing demand for dollars and its decreasing stock, the British importers would prefer to convert 1 pound into X quantity of gold, ship that gold to America and get that X quantity of gold converted into 5 dollars at the Federal Reserve System. From England's point of view 4.8 dollars per 1 pound becomes the gold export unit.

On the other hand, if British labour becomes relatively more efficient and productive and if prices of British goods decline, or if due to change in tastes and fashions, American demand for British goods increase whereas the British demand for American goods remains the same as before, there would develop demand pressure on pound and the rate of exchange would move against American dollars, say 1 pound would be equal to 5.1 dollars and then 5.2 dollars for 1 pound. But American importers of British goods would not pay more than 5.2 dollars for 1 pound as the cost of shipping gold, insurance, etc. would be about 20 cents. The American imports of British goods would prefer to convert 5 dollars into X quantity of gold at the Federal Reserve System, ship that gold to England and for X quantity of gold secure 1 pound at the Bank of England. From the British point of view 5.2 dollars per 1 pound would mean gold import point (and from the American point of view gold export point).

Thus, the rate of exchange between British pound and American dollars fluctuated between 1 pound equal to 4.8 dollars and 1 pound equal to 5.2 dollars. The rate of exchange would not move beyond 4.8 dollars and 5.2 dollars per pound. This was because there was alternative and more advantageous method of making payments for imports available to British and American importers of each other's goods. The second advantage that was claimed for the gold standard was that there could not be violent fluctuations in the rate of exchange when countries are on the gold standard. The fluctuations would be within extremely narrow limits of range. And this was advantageous from the point of view of international or world trade.

12.5 HOW DISEQUILIBRIUM IN BALANCE OF PAYMENTS IS AUTOMATICALLY REMOVED

If the total value of what England exports (both visible and invisible items) to America is exactly equal to the total value of what England imports (visible and invisible items) from America, this will mean that supply of American dollars (due to British exports) is exactly equal to the demand for dollars (due to British imports from America). If supply of dollars and demand for dollars is exactly equal, it would mean that from England's point of view (or from American point of view also) the balance of payments has exactly balanced.

Now let us assume that the balance of payments of England is in disequilibrium. This disequilibrium might be caused because of lowering of American prices due to increased efficiency and productivity of American labour compared to English labour, due to rapid technological advance in America or might be because Englishmen developed preference for American goods while prices of English goods and American tastes for English goods remain the same as before.

This would mean that whereas England's demand for dollars has been increasing, the supply of dollars has not been increasing to the same extent. This would mean increasing demand or pressure on dollars by offering pounds. The foreign exchange banks, finding that dollars are in increasing demand whereas their supply has remained the same as before, would reduce the rate of exchange by offering for 1 pound only 4.9 dollars, then 4.8 dollars and the rate of exchange would tend to go down even further depending upon increase in English imports from America *vis-à-vis* American demand for English goods. When the rate of exchange for 1 pound goes down below 4.8 per pound, the British imports would prefer to take their pounds to the Bank of England, get their pounds converted into gold at the rate of X quantity of gold per pound, ship that gold to America, take that to the Federal Reserve System and convert that gold into dollars at the rate of 5 dollars for X quantity of gold. Thus, because of disequilibrium in England's Balance of payments, gold would begin to flow out of England.

Since England was on the gold standard in which system quantity of money is directly linked to the stock of gold with the Bank of England because of the legal obligation of convertibility of English currency into gold at the specified rate, England because of the increasing loss of gold to America would be forced to bring about contraction in the quantity of money in circulation in England. This would be done by raising the Bank Rate and by selling securities in the open market, forcing the policy of credit contraction on commercial banks in England raising rate of interest charged by them to commercial and business community and to the general public.

As a consequence of rise in the rate of interest in England, there will be decline in the level of investment. The consequence of this decline in investment would be increase in unemployment, lower level of income of people in England, lower demand for goods and lower prices of goods in England.

As a consequence of lower income, English demand for American goods would decline; also due to lower prices in England, consumers in America would be purchasing more of English goods and less of American goods; also lower prices in England would push England's exports to America.

Thus, because of initial increase in England's demand for American goods and services and consequent disequilibrium in England's balance of payments position, England will have to pay for it in terms of more unemployment in the country and lower level of income of the people in England.

Exactly the opposite trends would come into operation in America. As quantity of money bears direct relation to stock of gold with the Federal Reserve System (i.e., the central bank of the United States of America), as gold begins to flow into America, the central bank in America will reduce the bank rate and also begin to purchase securities in the open market paying for them in cash. This will improve cash position of commercial banks and their credit creation in America and lower rate of interest there.

As a consequence of lower rate of interest in America, level of investment will rise. The high level of investment in America would mean higher level of income for the people in America, higher demand for goods in domestic markets in America and rising prices there. As a consequence, both lower prices of goods in England and higher prices of goods in America, American exports will decline and import of goods from England would go up. These movements in England and America would go on until the initial disequilibrium in the balance of payments (i.e., deficit in the balance of payments of England and surplus in that of America) get removed.

12.6 RULES OF THE GOLD STANDARD

If the gold standard were to function smoothly and automatically establishing equilibrium in balance of payments position of trading countries on the gold standard, then those countries were expected to observe certain rules of the gold standard which were as follows:

(1) Countries on the gold standard must maintain 'direct' link between quantity of money in circulation and stock of gold with the central banks of the concerned countries to enable, if necessary, conversion of currency into gold of stated quantity and specified fineness, and *vice versa.*

(2) Countries on the gold standard must have fairly elastic economies. For example, the country losing gold must be ready to face a certain amount of unemployment and reduction in wage rates which must not be resisted by strong trade unions in gold losing countries. The economies must be flexible and effects of gold outflow and gold inflow must get reflected in the level of employment, price level, wage rates, etc. in respective countries.

(3) Gold outflow and inflow from country to country on the gold standard must not take place for speculative purpose.

(4) Demand for commodities in each country for goods and services of the other country must be fairly elastic (i.e., responsive to price changes taking place in both the countries).

(5) Gold parities (i.e., rate at which currency of a country is converted into gold at the mint or central bank of the country for example 1 pound into X quantity of gold of specified fineness and X quantity of gold of the same fineness into 5 American dollars) must be held at a stable level. Mint parity of rate of exchange of gold into currency and currency into gold must be held at a stable level.

Gold standard will operate smoothly and automatically removing disequilibrium in the balance of payments in America and England (i.e., in countries on the gold standard), if rules of the gold standard are observed by both the countries in cooperation with each other. Thus, England for its deficit in her balance of payments must be prepared to face certain amount of decline in level of income of her people and a certain amount of unemployment in the country and America must be prepared to face rising price level and decline in her exports to England. Thus, both the countries must come forward some steps and be ready for a certain amount of sacrifice on their part, if gold standard is to function smoothly and automatically to remove disequilibrium in balance of payments of trading countries and establish equilibrium in their balance of payments position.

12.7 ADVANTAGES OF GOLD STANDARD

Following are the main advantages of gold standard:

(1) There is stability in the rates of exchange between the currencies of countries on the gold standards, fluctuations in rates of exchange (1 pound being equal to 5 dollars fluctuating up to 4.8 dollars and rising up to 5.2 dollars only).

(2) Stability in rates of exchange between currencies on gold standard encourages smooth flow and, therefore, increase in the volume of international trade.

(3) The most important advantage is that disequilibrium in balance of payments of countries on gold standard gets automatically corrected without any direct intervention by the State which is not required to take steps like imposing tariff barriers, import duties or export subsidies and so on, thus ensuring freedom of trade.

12.8 DISADVANTAGES OF GOLD STANDARD

Gold standard has the following disadvantages:

(1) Gold exporting countries have to follow a policy of bringing but contraction in the quantity of money in circulation with the public and deflation policy with consequent price decline and rise in the level of unemployment. There is no guarantee that countries with gold inflow would expand their money supply, create inflationary tends in their economy and be ready to face decline in their exports. This is exactly what America did during the inter-War period. Though vast quantities of gold flowed into America, that country did not bring about due expansion in its money supply fearing inflation and decline in her exports.

(2) Another defect of gold standard is that inflationary and deflationary trends in one country on the gold standard are almost automatically transferred to all the other countries on the gold standard.

(3) Gold standard gives more importance to exchange rate stability than price stability in a country. A country on gold standard will not be in a position to adopt price stabilisation policy which domestically has many advantages. Thus, under gold standard reconciling the two objectives of exchange rate stability and domestic price stability becomes practically impossible.

(4) After the Great Depression (1929-33), the main objective of economic policy in most European countries was to bring about full employment of labour force in the country. The nationalist forces went on becoming stronger and stronger emphasing independent domestic economic policies to achieve the objective of full employment rather than international cooperation as under gold standard which meant sacrificing certain domestic economic interest for the sake of international economic cooperation.

(5) Under gold standard considerable amount of gold lies idle with the central banks of countries. This is waste of a valuable resource that can be put to productive uses.

(6) If all or most of the countries of the world happen to be on gold standard, world stock of gold would be extremely unevenly distributed among the countries with the consequence that while in some countries there will be powerful inflationary trends in operation, in other countries there will be equally strong deflationary tends. Thus, under gold standard, there would be neither stable world economy nor will there be stability in domestic economies of the countries on the gold standard.

(7) Gold standard assumes *laissez faire* policy (i.e., policy of non-intervention by the State in the economic activities of the people). But in modern times, it is impossible to conceive of *laissez faire* policy on the part of any modern government, including those of West European countries including England which was once the strongest advocate of the policy of *laissez faire*.

12.9 WHY GOLD STANDARD FUNCTIONED SMOOTHLY DURING THE 19TH CENTURY

The reasons for the fairly successful functioning of gold standard during the 19th century must be sought in the then economic environment.

The first reason was that during the 19th century, countries of West Europe were progressing economically at fairly the same rate and adjustments needed in balance of payments position were only of marginal nature.

Secondly, the economies of countries on the gold standard were then fairly flexible. For example, a certain amount of unemployment in a country was accepted as a matter of course.

Thirdly, there was a yet strong sentiment in favour of *laissez faire* policy and as economic problems were relatively less complex, interference by the state in the economic affairs of the people was strongly resented.

Due to the above factors, gold standard functioned fairly successfully during the 19th century.

12.10 WHY GOLD STANDARD CAME TO BE ABANDONED DURING INTER-WAR PERIOD AND AFTER

It might be broadly said that decline in gold standard began after the end of World War I. This was because economic and political environment that was emerging after the end of World War I was almost fundamentally different from the 19th century world.

During the period of World War I and later on, fundamental changes took place in the sphere of international trade. Industries in America made tremendous progress and gold flowed into America from West European countries. But America adopted the policy of building up stock of gold, instead of allowing stock of money in circulation in America to grow with it, allow inflationary pressures to emerge and bring about decline in her exports. America was not prepared to take those steps. It meant that America failed to observe the rules of the gold standard.

When after 1920 countries like England and America brought back gold standard, they adopted the old rates of exchange (i.e., one pound equal to five dollars). But during the war period, economic conditions had so changed as also the volume and pattern of international trade that pre-war parity rates of exchange based on gold standard were not tenable and were bound to result in continual disequilibrium in the balance of payments position of countries like England. Thus, when England readopted gold standard in 1925 at the old parity rate of exchange, level of income of the people and price level in the country could just not support the pre-War foreign exchange rate which England had adopted in 1925.

With the outflow and inflow of gold, different countries did not follow the rules of the gold standard, allowing quantity of gold with the central banks to influence quantity of money in circulation. This was because countries were not prepared to face inflationary or deflationary trends in their economies with their unfavourable impact on domestic economies.

After the Great Depression of 1929-33 much emphasis came to be placed on domestic or internal economic policies by most European countries. They started following protectionist policies; even America started following protectionist policy. This meant that America was not prepared to accept imports of European goods for its exports to those countries which were forced to make payment in gold. But the stock of gold with them was limited. In this changed economic environment with emphasis on domestic economic policies and protectionist trend, gold standard was found to fail as in fact it did during 1930s.

The basic tenet of the gold standard is that export of goods would be paid by import of goods and only the marginal difference between values of export and imports would be met by payment of gold. But the protectionist policies adopted by most countries after the Great Depression made such adjustments impossible as export of goods and services were not allowed to be paid for by import of goods and services.

Another very important reason for the breakdown and eventual abandonment of the gold standard was that after the end of World War I economies of West European countries had ceased to be flexible as before. England had relatively small reserves of gold and, therefore, to maintain balance of payments in equilibrium position it was essential under gold standard that England should reduce the quantity of money or currency in circulation with the public, raise the rate of interest, reduce cost of production by reducing wage rates and reduce prices to promote exports. But trade unions had by then become very powerful and they would not allow reduction in wage-rates while the monopolists would not allow reduction in prices of goods. Thus, rigidity in economic system had become the important features of economies after the end of World War I. No wonder, in the changed environment, economic and political, gold standard just could not function and had to be abandoned.

Theoretical death-blow to gold standard was delivered by J.M. Keynes in his book *"The General Theory"* published in 1936. Keynes emphasised that quantity of money in circulation with the public should be decided by the requirements to carry out smoothly trading transactions in the country and monetary policy should aim at providing full employment and continually raising standard of living of the people in the country. The quantity of money and monetary policy should be so manipulated as to attain the above objectives. J.M. Keynes emphasised that the quantity of money in circulation with the public should not be allowed to be determined by the accidental find of gold in some places in the world. Gold production in the world was increasing roughly at an annual rate of one per cent while as international trading transactions among more than 150 countries were increasing annually by many times the rate of increase in gold annually. Under such circumstances, gold could not be and should not be the arbiter of international trading problems among nations of the world.

The fact is that economic institutions (like gold standard) found suitable during the 19th century could not function smoothly and successfully during the 20th century. No wonder, the gold standard came to be finally abandoned during 1930s after which there never has been any talk of reviving the gold standard in the international trade sphere.

13

CHAPTER

PURCHASING POWER PARITY THEORY

Structure:

13.1 INTRODUCTION

If there is no common commodity like gold (into which different currencies are convertible at legally specified rates) to determine the rate of exchange between currencies of any two countries, then how is the rate of exchange between any two inconvertible paper currencies determined? After the countries left the gold standard during the period of World War I (1914-18) exchange rates among different inconvertible paper currencies of different countries started fluctuating very widely and, therefore, the problem of why these wide fluctuations in rates of exchange were taking place and what exactly determines rate of exchange between any two inconvertible paper currencies assumed great significance. Answer to this question was provided by Gustav Cassel in 1920 by formulating the 'Purchasing Power Parity' theory (PPP theory). The PPP theory became popular during those days when gold standard came to be suspended and later abandoned during 1930s. Even at present, there are economists who believe that the core of the PPP theory is broadly true or has the core of truth in it.

13.2 PURCHASING POWER PARITY THEORY EXPLAINED

The PPP theory maintains that "... the equilibrium rate of exchange between two inconvertible paper currencies comes to be determined by equality of their purchasing power." For example, if we take into account India and the United States (US), Indians want American dollars because they want to purchase American goods and what amount of goods dollars will purchase in America will depend upon the price level in that country. Similarly, the American people want Indian rupees because with Indian rupees they want to purchase Indian goods and how such of Indian goods the Indian rupee can purchase will depend upon price level in India. And, therefore, it was stated by Cassel that equilibrium rate of exchange between American dollar and the Indian rupee will be determined by equality of their purchasing power. In other terms, this would also mean that equilibrium rate of exchange between dollar and rupee will be determined by relative price levels in America and India.

The PPP theory can be illustrated by an example.

Let us suppose that a bale of cotton is sold in America for 20 dollars and in India for Rs. 100. This would mean that 20 American dollars would be equal to Rs. 100 or 1 dollar would be equal to Rs. 5 (which also means that one Indian rupee would be equal to 20 cents as 100 cents make one dollar). This equilibrium rate of exchange between dollar and rupee would be arrived at by comparing their purchasing power in America and India, respectively.

Let us see what will happen if the rate of exchange between dollar and rupee moves away from the equilibrium rate of 1 dollar is equal to Rs. 5.

Let us assume that the rate of exchange between dollar and rupee becomes 1 dollar = Rs. 10. Americans would rush to convert 20 dollars into Rs. 200, purchase 2 bales of cotton for Rs. 200 (as one bale of cotton is priced in India at Rs. 100); ship them to America and sell the two bales of cotton in America at the rate of 20 dollars per bale and thus get 40 dollars for two bales, thus making a profit of 100 per cent. The Americans would again convert those 40 dollars into Rs. 400, purchase 4 bales of cotton in India, ship those 4 bales to America and sell those 4 bales for 80 dollars thus again making a profit of 100 per cent. This would mean that there would be increasing demand in America for Indian rupees and naturally less and less Indian rupees would be given in exchange of 1 dollar. This would go on until the equilibrium rate 1 dollar = Rs. 5 is established.

If, on the other hand, instead of 1 dollar = Rs. 5, the rate of exchange, let us assume, becomes 1 dollar = Rs. 3. In that case, Indian importers would rush to convert their Rs. 3 into 1 dollar or Rs. 30

into 10 dollars, purchase one bale of cotton for 10 dollars and sell that in India for Rs. 100, thus making an enormous profit. This will go on and will result in increasing demand for dollars and, therefore, more and more Rs. will be presented demanding dollars at the rate of Rs.3 = 1 dollar. This would increase demand for dollars and, therefore, sellers of dollars finding that demand for dollars is increasing will demand more Rs. per dollar and this will go on until the equilibrium rate of 1 dollar = Rs. 5 is established. Thus, the PPP theory maintained that no other rate of exchange than 1 dollar = Rs. 5 will be stable or equilibrium rate of exchange.

Thus, according to the PPP theory, exchange rate between inconvertible paper currencies of any two countries is determined at a point where there is equality between the respective purchasing powers of the two currencies.

It should be clear that this purchasing power parity is a moving point (and not a fixed point as in the case of gold standard). Thus, every change in price level of a country or price levels of any two countries would change the equilibrium or long-term rate of exchange.

This can be illustrated with an example. We begin with the equilibrium exchange rate of 1 dollar = Rs. 5 say in 1960 when the index number of prices in both the countries was 100. Suppose in 1989, Indian price index is 600 and the American price index is 300. The new rate of exchange in 1989 would be the old exchange rate multiplied by the quotient of price changes during the intervening period.

(Price quotient is arrived at by comparing price changes in India and America. If, as we have noted, Indian price index has moved to 600 and American price index to 300, the price quotient will be 300/600, if we want to know the rate of exchange of dollar and the quotient will be 600/300 if we want to know the exchange rate of Rs. in terms of dollars).

$$\text{Thus, 1 dollar in 1989} = \frac{600}{300} \times 5$$

$$= \text{Rs. } 10$$

If we want to know the rate of exchange of Indian rupee, then

Re. 1 = 300/600 × 20 = 20/2 = 10 cents.

This will be the new rate of exchange between dollar and rupee.

(What happens in actual fact is that the equilibrium rate of exchange will be modified to some extent by cost of transporting goods, banking and insurance charges. These costs of transport, banking and insurance are the limits within which equilibrium rate of exchange will fluctuate. But these limits are not as definite as the gold export point and gold import point in the case of currencies of countries on the gold standard).

13.3 CRITICISM OF THE PURCHASING POWER PARITY THEORY

The Purchasing Power Parity theory is criticised on the following grounds:

(1) While calculating price levels in two countries, the use of index number may pose many problems and difficulties such as choice of the base year, commodities to be included, weightage to be given to different commodities when formulating index number etc. The concerned two countries (in our illustration) while constructing their index numbers may not use the same type of commodities. All this means that the index numbers with all their

deficiencies and defects can only serve as a rough guide for measuring price levels and, therefore, fail in correctly measuring purchasing power parity of the currencies of the two countries with inconvertible paper currencies.

(2) The PPP theory maintained that purchasing power parity between currencies of any two countries is determined by comparing the general price levels in those countries. But it is obvious that general price level may be made up of prices of internally or domestically traded goods plus prices of internationally traded goods or only prices of internationally traded goods.

If the price index is calculated on the basis of only internationally traded goods, the prices of such goods would tend towards equality, even allowing for cost of transport, insurance, tariffs, etc. But according to J.M. Keynes, "...confined to internationally traded commodities, the purchasing power parity becomes an empty truism."

If, on the other hand, for purposes of calculating index number, if prices of both internationally traded goods and domestically traded goods are both taken into account, it is possible that prices of internally or domestically, traded goods might be moving in opposite direction of the prices internationally traded goods. This would mean that the prevailing exchange rate may not conform to parties of purchasing powers of concerned currencies.

Also, if index number is calculated on the basis of not only internationally traded goods but includes also prices of internally traded goods, it is possible that people in two countries may be spending their incomes differently. This means the basis for accurate comparison of price levels and, therefore, for comparing purchasing powers of two paper currencies is lacking.

(3) The PPP theory takes into account demand for currencies for purchasing only goods. But Indians may want American dollars for investment purposes in America and similarly Americans may want Indian rupees for investment purposes in India. Demand for currencies arising out of capital movements from one country to another is totally neglected by the PPP theory. This is a serious defect of that theory. The PPP theory is thus based on zero capital movements between countries.

(4) The PPP theory does not explain how in the initial stages or period or at the start, the rate of exchange comes to be fixed at all. Subsequent price changes and changes in index numbers may explain changes in exchange rates. But how does the rate of exchange gets fixed in the first instance when for example trade between any two countries has just begun? The PPP theory has no answer to this question.

Also, the PPP theory has assumed that there is equilibrium in balance of payments position in the base year in the case of two trading countries. But it is very difficult to find the base or initial year when balance of payments is in balance and when the stable exchange rate is established denoting the initial equilibrium position.

(5) In addition to purchasing commodities, foreign currencies are also needed for payment of shipping charges, banking transactions, for capital movement, payment of interest and installments of capital borrowed, payment of royalties and consultation fees, etc. Demand for foreign currencies arises not just for importing commodities but also for above purposes. The PPP theory takes into account only demand for currencies arising out of commodities to be imported, neglecting the influence on exchange rate of demand arising out of above types of transactions (i.e., various services).

(6) The PPP theory maintained that in the case of inconvertible paper currency, it is the price level in trading countries that would determine the rate of exchange. But it is equally possible that it is the exchange rates that might determine the price level.

For example, suppose that the equilibrium or long-term rate of exchange between Indian rupee and American dollar is Re. 1 = 20 cents. Let us suppose due to factors such as capital movements, etc. the rate of exchange becomes Re. 1 = 25 cents. If this rate holds the ground for some time, now that more American cents are available for 1 Indian rupee, Indian demand for American goods would increase and this might push up the prices of American goods. Also, since the Indian rupee now costs not 20 cents but 25 cents, it would mean that Indian goods have become costlier for Americans and, therefore, American demand for Indian goods decreases and, therefore, prices of Indian goods decline. This means instead of price levels in America and India determining the rate of exchange between Indian rupee and American dollar, it is the rate of exchange which might come to influence and determine the price levels in India and America (so that the new rate of Re. 1= 25 American cents might get stabilised and become the new equilibrium rate of exchange).

(7) The PPP theory is based on the assumption that governments follow *laissez faire* policy and there is free trade. But the assumption is not realistic. After World War I, governments have been imposing various restrictions on international trade and capital movements even in countries like America. Thus, tariffs, quota-fixation, export subsidies etc., have become quite common these days even in capitalist countries. All these are bound to have great influence on foreign exchange rates and, therefore, it cannot be said that foreign exchange rates are determined only by their purchasing power and price levels in the respective trading countries.

(8) The PPP theory has neglected changes in demand and supply conditions of commodities and their impact on foreign exchange rates. For example, if formerly Indians getting 20 cents per Re. 1 were satisfied with purchasing an American commodity priced at say 20 cents, it is possible that Indians' preference for American goods (i.e., Indian demand for American goods) has gone up steeply and Indians are prepared to pay 25 cents for one unit of that commodity. This would push up demand for American dollars and the rate of exchange instead of Re. 1 = 20 cents might become Re. 1= 15 cents due to Indians' increases in demand for American goods.

And, therefore, as J.M. Keynes has pointed out the PPP theory has totally neglected or not taken into consideration at all elasticities of reciprocal demand. If, for example, American demand for Indian goods increases steeply, Americans, instead of insisting on 20 cents to get on Indian rupee, may be ready to accept just 15 cents for one Indian rupee which means pay more than before in terms of dollars for Indian goods.

(9) As Prof. Ragnar Nurkse has pointed out, the PPP theory assumes that demand is a function of price only. But aggregate income and changes in it due to changes in the rate of saving and investment and their impact on aggregate income and expenditure of the community would have their impact on demand and on the rate of exchange between any two inconvertible paper currencies.

Concluding Remarks

Foreign currencies are wanted because foreign goods and services are wanted and what one unit of a currency can purchase of foreign goods and services will depend upon the price levels in respective countries. And, therefore, there is no doubt that price levels in different countries have powerful influence (if not the only influence) on determining rates of exchange. This becomes particularly obvious when inflation is raging in different countries at different rates. Also, in the long run, it is the relative price levels that greatly influence exchange rates. Relative price levels may not be the only factor determining rates of exchange (which can be manipulated by monetary authorities in different countries as was done by Japan during 1920s), but the fact remains that it is the relative price levels that exert great influence on the rates of exchange between inconvertible paper currencies of different countries.

13.4 WHY FOREIGN EXCHANGE RATES FLUCTUATE?

We have already seen that under gold standard, rate of exchange fluctuates within only narrow limits of gold export and gold import points. If the rate of exchange goes above or below these narrowly defined limits, there is available an alternative mode of making payments for exports by converting currencies into gold at a specified rate with the central banks and shipping gold to exporting countries, and making payments for exports in the national currency of the exporters.

But the case is different in the case of inconvertible paper currency standard. Though even here the rate of exchange can be legally fixed and attempts made by the government through various devices to stabilise the rate of exchange, such artificially fixed rate of exchange would produce results in other spheres of national economy. If in the case of inconvertible paper currency standard, government does not interfere, there would be no upper and lower limit between which rate of exchange would fluctuate.

It would be instructive to know the factors that influence rate of exchange between two inconvertible currencies and the factors that bring about wide fluctuations in rate of exchange in the case of inconvertible currency standard.

The rate of exchange between two inconvertible paper currency standard, say the Indian rupee and American dollar would depend on Indian demand for dollars as compared to American demand for Indian rupees. This American demand for Indian rupees and Indian demand for American dollars would arise for the following main reasons:

(1) International Trading Transactions: The most important reason why foreign currency is wanted is for importing goods and services. Thus, Indians, want dollars to purchase American goods and services and Americans want Indian rupees to purchase Indian goods and services. If value of Indian imports from America is equal to value of American imports from India, this item of international trading transactions will not produce any change in the rate of exchange between dollar and rupee. But if Indian demand for American goods and service increases while American demand for Indian goods and services remains the same as before, this would mean that demand for dollars has gone up and exchange rate will move in favour of dollar and against rupee. Dollar will appreciate and one dollar would now be available not for Rs. 5, but for Rs. 6 or even more rupees, the present rate (as in August 1989) having gone above Rs. 18 per dollar (and the black market rate around Rs. 17 for one American dollar, depending upon degree of increase in Indian demand for American goods).

If on the other hand, American demand for Indian goods and services increases due to any of the reasons such as change in tastes and fashions, etc. there will be increase in American demand for Indian rupees and the Indian rupee will appreciate and the rate of exchange will move in favour of Indian rupee depending upon the degree of increase in American demand for Indian goods and services, while Indian demand for American goods and services remains the same as before. Thus, reciprocal demand for each other's goods and services and changes therein would determine the rate of exchange and bring about changes in rate of exchange because of changes in mutual demand for each other's commodities and services.

(2) *Changes in Price Levels:* Relative price changes will influence exchange rates. If for example, price level in India rises relatively more than price level in America, this will mean that Indian goods will be dearer than before compared to American goods for Indians. There will thus be less exports of Indian goods and more imports of American goods and services. This will mean more pressure on dollar and less pressure on Indian Rupee. This will make Indian rupee cheaper than before in terms of dollars. This will mean that exchange rate would move against Indian rupee and in favour of American dollar.

(3) *Capital Movements:* If there is no government intervention through exchange controls etc. capital movements have great influence of determining rate of exchange. Capital movements may take place for short period to take advantage of differentials in short-term rates of interest (hot money), or capital movements for long-term investment purposes. If, for example, American short-term or long-term loans or both begin to flow into India, it will mean greater increase in demand for Indian rupees (and as demand for dollars is assumed to remain the same as before), the rate of exchange will move against dollars. When Americans begin to send back their capital invested in India to America, there will be increase in demand for dollar and the rate of exchange will move against Indian rupees, more rupees being offered per one dollar.

(4) *Speculative Activities:* Speculative activities play an important role to bring about fluctuation in the rate of exchange, if it is free to fluctuate. If, for example, if speculators think that in the near future dollar is going to appreciate in terms of Indian rupee, they will go on purchasing dollars at once in exchange for rupees with a view to sell them in future at appreciated rate. This will bring about immediate pressure on dollars which will begin to appreciate in terms of rupees. If later on dollar does appreciate in terms of Indian rupee, the speculators who had purchased dollars at a lower rate of exchange will begin to sell dollars for Indian rupees at higher rate in terms of rupees. This will mean increase in demand for Indian rupees and increase in the supply of dollars. This would push down the rate of exchange against dollar in terms of rupee. Thus, speculative activities play an important role in bringing about wide fluctuations in rate of exchange between inconvertible paper currencies.

(5) *Monetary Policy:* Monetary policy plays an important role exerting influence on rate of exchange. For example, suppose that Indian government resorts to deficit financing to an increasing extent year after year by printing increasing number of currency notes, this would mean great increase in money supply and demand for goods and services and this would push up price level in India. This will mean diminishing purchasing power of Indian rupee. American importers of Indian goods and services will reduce their imports of Indian goods and services because of rise in prices of Indian goods and services. On the other hand, since prices of goods and services are the same as before, here will be increase in Indian demand for American goods and services. Thus while American demand for Indian goods and services (and, therefore, for Indian rupees) will decrease, Indian demand for American goods and services (and, therefore, for American dollars) will increase. The consequence of the expansionist monetary policy of the government of India would be that the rate of exchange will move against Indian rupee making it cheaper in terms of American dollars.

On the other hand, if Indian government adopts contractionist monetary policy and the American government expansionist monetary policy, the opposite trends will come into operation and the rate of exchange will move against American dollar which would become relatively cheaper in terms of Indian rupees.

(6) *Influence of Stock Exchange Activities:* How the stock exchanges in a country function has great influence on foreign exchange rates. If for example, stock exchanges in India are more successful in selling equity, debentures and other types of securities to Americans, this would mean more supply of dollars and increase in American demand for Indian rupees. This would, therefore, raise exchange rate in favour of Indian rupee. If, on the other hand, stock exchanges operating in India or in America are successful in selling increasing number of shares and stocks of companies floated in America to people in India, this would mean that Indian demand for dollars has gone up and supply of Indian rupee has increased. The exchange rate, therefore, will move in favour of American dollar making it dearer in terms of Indian rupees.

(7) *Structural Changes in the Economy:* Technological changes bring about structural changes in the economy, in efficiency and productivity of labour, reduction in cost of production and prices, appearance of new products, etc. If structural changes in America are more pronounced than in India, that might result in increasing Indian demand for American goods and services and, therefore, increasing Indian demand for American goods and services and, therefore, increasing demand for American dollars. This would change foreign exchange rate in favour of dollar and against the Indian rupee.

(8) *Political Conditions:* Political conditions greatly influence foreign exchange rates. For example, if Government of India is strong in ensuring peaceful conditions in future on which economic progress of the country depends, more Americans would be interested in investing in India and visiting India as tourists. This would mean supply of more dollars and increasing demand for Indian rupees. This would push exchange rate in favour of Indian rupee. If on the other hand, political conditions in a country are disturbed with the threat of political revolution taking place at any time in future, not only Americans will not invest in such a country but even Indian investments will try to move out of such a country. This would change exchange rate against domestic currency and in favour of foreign currency like the American dollar.

13.5 BALANCE OF PAYMENTS THEORY OF FOREIGN EXCHANGE RATES

Under the conditions of free exchange rate system (i.e., when there is inconvertible paper currency standard and there is no direct or indirect intervention of the government in foreign exchange market), according to the Balance of Payments Theory of Exchange Rates, rate of exchange of currency of one country (say India) into currency of any other country, depends upon its balance of payments position.

India's demand for American dollars arises out of Indian demand for American goods and services and Indian capital seeking investment in America. This Indian demand for American dollars also represents the supply side of Indian rupees paid by Indian importers of American goods and services and Indian investors seeking dollars for Indian rupees for investment in America.

The supply of American dollars is represented by American demand for Indian goods and services and Americans seeking to invest their capital in India. This also represents American demand for Indian rupees.

When India's balance of payments exactly balance or is in equilibrium position, with neither deficit or surplus in the balance of payments, the rate of exchange established under such conditions is the equilibrium rate of exchange. If India has surplus in her balance of payments (that means when American demand for Indian rupees is more than Indian demand for American dollars, which means more Indian rupees are demanded than are supplied), the rate of exchange will move away from the equilibrium rate of exchange in favour of Indian rupee, Indian rupee becoming dearer in terms of American dollar. If on the other hand, India faces a deficit in her balance of payments (which means the total value of India's exports to America of goods and services is less than the total value of India's imports of goods and services from America, which also means Indian demand for American dollars is more than the supply of dollars or which also means the supply of Indian rupees is more than American demand for Indian rupees), the rate of exchange will move against Indian rupee compared to the equilibrium rate of exchange, Indian rupee compared to the equilibrium rate of exchange, Indian rupee becoming cheaper in terms of dollar than before. Thus, this theory holds the view that exchange rate between two inconvertible paper currencies is determined at that level where the demand for foreign currency is equal to the supply of that foreign currency. Thus, if we look at it from the American side, equilibrium exchange rate between American dollar and Indian rupee will be determined when there is equilibrium and Indian demand for American dollars is equal to American supply of dollars; or considering from the Indian point of view, supply of Indian rupees (i.e., demand for American dollars) is equal to American demand for Indian rupees (i.e., supply of American dollars in exchange for Indian goods).

When exchange rate between, say Indian rupee and American dollar declines below the equilibrium rate of exchange in a situation of India facing deficit in her balance of payments, Indian exports to America will rise and imports from America will decline and deficit in balance of payments will be eliminated and equilibrium rate of exchange will be established.

If on the other hand, India has a surplus in her balance of payments *vis-a-vis* America, exchange rate will rise above the equilibrium rate of exchange. This will result in decrease in India's exports and increase in imports from America and the rate of exchange between American dollar and Indian rupee will move towards equilibrium rate of exchange.

It may be said by way of summary that at any point of time, rate of exchange between any two inconvertible paper currencies will be determined by demand for and supply of foreign currency. Any change in the condition of demand or of supply reflects itself in a change in the exchange rate and at the ruling rate the balance of payments balances from day-to-day or from moment to moment.

It may be further stated that the American demand for Indian goods and services (i.e., supply of dollars) and Indian demand for American goods and services (i.e., Indian demand for dollars) will depend upon reciprocal elasticities of demand for each others' goods and services and strength of mutual desire to invest in each others' country.

13.6 CRITICISM OF THE BALANCE OF PAYMENTS THEORY OF FOREIGN EXCHANGE RATES

Following are the main points of criticism against the Balance of Payments Theory of Foreign Exchange Rates:

(1) The main defect of this theory is that the theory is based on the unrealistic assumption of the existence of free trade. In the real world, almost as a rule governments have been intervening in the sphere of international trade, have been imposing restrictions on imports, have been

giving export subsidies and have been practising on an extensive scale exchange controls to avoid, or if possible, eliminate disequilibrium or deficit in balance of payments of the country.

(2) Another serious defect of this theory is that the theory assumes that balance of payments is an independent phenomenon and that it determines exchange rate. This is patently untrue. It is equally true to say that it is the exchange rate that may establish balance in the balance of payments. In fact each depends on the other and both are closely interdependent. It will be as much true to say that it is the rate of exchange that determines balance of payments as it is to say that it is balance of payments that determines rate of exchange.

(3) The theory neglects the role of domestic price level changes on the rate of exchange and on balance of payments. These changes in domestic price level may take place due to domestic monetary and fiscal policies and independently of the ruling rate of exchange and of balance of payments position of a country. These domestic price changes would greatly influence exchange rates and balance of payments position of a country. The impact of domestic price changes on exchange rates (through changes in foreign demand for domestic goods and services) and on the balance of payments of a country has been completely neglected by this theory.

(4) The theory states that there is an equilibrium exchange rate when balance of payments is in an equilibrium position. This is just a truism and does not reveal anything new or anything substantial. The fact in the real world is that the ruling foreign exchange rate may not be the one prevailing under conditions when balance of payments is in equilibrium position. In fact, there is continually either deficit or surplus in balance of payments and equilibrium position in balance of payments position is more of an exception. The prevailing foreign exchange rate denotes and is influenced by either deficit or surplus in the balance of payments of a country.

Concluding Remarks

With all the above defects, the balance of payments theory of foreign exchange rates has the core of truth in it. This theory studies the problem of exchange rate fixation in the framework of general equilibrium and in terms of demand for and supply of foreign currencies.

For example, if we assume two countries B and A (B representing the rest of the world), it is obvious that though at any particular time the balance of payments position of country A may not be in equilibrium position, however, the tendency will be to move in the direction of equilibrium and the tendency on the part of country A will be to see that its credits and debits on account of international trading transactions are equal to each other. Country A cannot go on facing continual deficits in its balance of payments position. It will have to take steps to see that its credits and debits arising out of International trading transactions balance each other.

What about countries like Japan which have been having continual surplus in their balance of payments, say *vis-a-vis* the United States of America? Well, if Japan experiences continual surplus in its balance of payments, it means that some other country (in this case the United States) has been having continual deficits in its balance of payments position. The United States, the deficit country will have to take steps, sooner or later, to see that its credits and debits on account of international trading transactions balance each other. The United States has already started imposing restrictions on imports from Japan.

On account of this, the balance of payments theory of foreign exchange rate is regarded as superior to the purchasing power parity theory of foreign exchange rates.

CHAPTER 14

FOREIGN EXCHANGE RATES POLICY

Structure:

14.1 INTRODUCTION

Maintenance of stable rate of foreign exchange has always been considered a desirable objective of foreign exchange rate policy as that provides encouragement to international trade. With the experience during 1930s after the abandonment of gold standard and when rates of foreign exchange were experiencing wide fluctuations, it was seen that such frequent and uncertain fluctuations adversely affected international trade and balance of payments position of trading countries.

And, therefore, when after the World War II (1939-45), the International Monetary Fund (IMF) came to be established, though it was not possible to re-establish gold standard with its stable foreign exchanges rates, one of the objectives of the IMF was and has been to establish and maintain fairly stable rates of foreign exchange among paper currencies of different countries of the world. Under the IMF Charter, every member country was required to fix the par value of its currency in terms to gold or American dollar and make an effort to maintain that parity or foreign exchange rate in conformity with the declared parity. This automatically helped to establish stable exchange rates among various currencies. This IMF-inspired system came to be known as 'the pegged exchange rate system.' The IMF system at the same time allowed some marginal changes in rates of foreign exchange, if balance of payments position of some countries found alteration in pegged rate of exchange necessary.

But due to various reasons, a number of countries found it difficult to maintain the system of pegged exchange rates prescribed under the IMF system. A number of countries altered their rates of exchange without reference to the IMF and without the IMF consent. For example, around 22 countries followed the policy of devaluation of their currencies (i.e., the policy of cheapening their currencies in terms of American dollar) in 1949. This left many policy-makers and economists wondering whether it is worthwhile pursuing the objective of stable foreign exchange rate policy. This raises the question of merits and demerits of stable or pegged versus fluctuating foreign exchange rates.

14.2 FIXED (PEGGED) OR STABLE FOREIGN EXCHANGE RATES: ARGUMENTS IN FAVOUR AND AGAINST

Introduction: Under the system of fixed (or pegged) foreign exchange rate system, all transactions relating to foreign currency exchanges take place at the exchange rates determined by the government. Government may fix exchange rates by legislation or by direct intervention in foreign exchange market, if necessary by buying and selling foreign currencies with a view to maintain fixed exchange rates.

Arguments in Favour of Fixed or Stable Foreign Exchange Rates

Following advantages are claimed for fixed or stable foreign exchange rates:

(1) Fixed or stable exchange rates encourage and promote international trade by making prices of internationally traded goods stable and predictable. Fixed or stable exchange rates help to promote international trade.

(2) Fixed or stable exchange rates by promoting international trade encourage international division of labour and specialisation with all-round increase in world productivity and production in which all trading countries have their share. This leads to promotion of welfare of world community. As Prof. H.G. Johnson had pointed out "The case for fixed rates is part of a more general argument for national economic policies conducive to international economic integration."

(3) Fixed or stable exchange rates encourage and bring about long-term capital outflows and inflows in a smooth way as there is no uncertainty or undue risk-taking that would have resulted if exchange rates were fluctuating.

(4) In the case of fixed or stable exchange rates there is no question or problem arising out of appreciation or depreciation of foreign currencies. Stable exchange rates, for example, remove fears that if a large amount of foreign currency is held in reserve, it might depreciate and result in losses. This also means that it creates great confidence among citizens in the nation's currency.

(5) In the case of fixed or stable exchange rates, there is hardly any scope for speculation and speculative activities which can have extremely disturbing effects on the economy.

(6) One great advantage of fixed or stable exchange rates is that such a policy imposes discipline on the monetary authority of the concerned country. Government will be compelled to avoid both inflation and deflation as such a development might result in disequilibrium in the balance of payments position of the country.

Case or Arguments Against Fixed (pegged) or Stable Foreign Exchange Rate Policy

Following arguments are put forward against the policy of fixed or stable foreign exchange rates policy:

(1) Fixed or stable foreign exchange rate policy means abandonment of independent domestic economic policy aiming at objectives like full employment, price stability etc. Policy of exchange rate stability would necessarily be at the cost of independent domestic economic policy with various objectives in the national interest. For example, if India's balance of payments position shows a continual deficit, it will be forced to reduce domestic price level with increase in unemployment, all with a view to correct adverse balance of payments arising due to the policy of fixed or pegged or stable foreign exchange rate. If on the other hand, India's balance of payments shows a continual surplus, domestically she will have to follow the policy of raising domestic price level to cut down her exports. This would impose heavy cost in terms of nation's welfare.

(2) The policy of fixed or stable exchange rates will carry economic disturbances in one country to other countries. For example, if due to technological reasons there is increase in labour efficiency and productivity and therefore lower prices in America, that would mean import of cheap American goods adversely affecting competing Indian industries. Thus, deflationary trends in America would result in deflationary trends coming into operation in India. Similarly, under the fixed or stable exchange rate policy, inflationary trends in foreign countries would result in inflationary trends coming into operation in India. Thus, under the policy of fixed or stable exchange rates, a country cannot keep itself protected or immune from economic disturbances taking place in India's trading partners.

(3) A serious defect or shortcoming of fixed or stable exchange rate policy is that large resources of foreign currencies would be required to be maintained. Holding such large resources in the form of foreign exchange (especially resources like hard currencies like American dollar, West German mark and Japanese yen, etc.) would not always be possible because India's exports to hard currency areas may not be adequate to build such reserves after meeting

import bills from those countries. India, therefore, may be forced to borrow hard currencies to maintain their reserve stocks and continue with the policy of fixed exchange rates. This will ultimately upset India's balance of payments position and India might be forced to devaluate her currency with all its adverse effects on the country's economy.

(4) The policy of fixed or stable exchange rates requires extremely complicated exchange control mechanism and bureaucratic administration. This might result in corruption and misallocation of the country's foreign exchange resources.

(5) Fixed or stable exchange rate policy cannot be pursued for long period of time. Technological developments are taking place in different countries at different pace with differing effects on efficiency, productivity, cost of production and price levels. There are bound to be changes in price levels in different degrees in different countries creating balance of payments problems for countries following fixed or stable exchange rate policy. The changing international economic environment would make pursuit of fixed or stable exchange rate policy practically impossible in the long run. This means fixed exchange rate policy can be followed only for a short duration of time and not for longer period.

14.3 FLEXIBLE OR FLUCTUATING FOREIGN EXCHANGE RATES POLICY: ARGUMENTS FOR AND AGAINST

Introduction: In contrast to fixed or stable exchange rate policy which requires government intervention or regulation in foreign exchange market, flexible or fluctuating exchange rates come to be determined by market forces of demand and supply for and of foreign currencies. For example, Indian demand for American goods and services will mean supply of Indian rupees and demand for American dollars; and American demand for Indian goods and services would mean supply of American dollars and demand for Indian rupees. The relative strength of these reciprocal demand and supply of each other's currencies (i.e., market forces) will come to determine from time to time rate of exchange between American dollar and the Indian rupee or any two inconvertible paper currencies. Government or monetary authority does not and is not supposed to intervene or interfere or regulate in any way, directly or indirectly activities in foreign exchange market. From this it follows that if there is larger supply of Indian rupees compared to American demand for them, Indian rupee will depreciate which means it will become cheap in terms of American dollar and exchange rate will move against the Indian rupee (which means more Indian rupees will have to be offered for one American dollar). If, on the other hand, American demand for Indian rupees goes up, it will mean supply of more dollars and increasing demand for Indian rupee. This would result in rate of exchange moving against American dollar and in favour of Indian rupee (which would mean less and less Indian rupees will be offered per one American dollar). The first is called depreciation of the Indian rupee and the second appreciation of the Indian rupee.

Thus, market forces of demand for and supply of foreign exchange or currencies will so adjust the rate of exchange from time to time that equilibrium in balance of payments will be automatically established without any government intervention. Market forces will automatically equate demand for and supply of dollars as also of Indian rupees. Thus, equilibrium in balance of payments of India *vis-a-vis* America will be established automatically by market forces of demand and supply and without any state or government intervention or regulation.

In the following paras, an attempt is made to examine the case for and against flexible or fluctuating exchange rate policy.

Arguments in Favour of Flexible (or Fluctuating) Exchange Rate Policy

The following arguments are put forward in favour of flexible (i.e., fluctuating) exchange rates:

(1) Flexible exchange rate policy is quite simple in its operations and is the most natural. The prevailing rate of exchange appreciates or depreciates automatically equating demand for and supply of foreign currencies. This means the system will not result either in a deficit or surplus (i.e., disequilibrium either in the form of deficit or surplus) in balance of payments of a country.

(2) Another great advantage of this system is that it is not necessary to bring about changes in income of the people and prices of commodities and services for restoring equilibrium in balance of payments of a country.

(3) Third advantage of this system is that under it movements in exchange rates are smooth and without heavy jerks as compared with adjustments required in the case of fixed exchange rates policy. In flexible exchange rate policy there is no accumulation of pressures on balance of payments position of a country as in the case of fixed or stable exchange rate policy when various serious corrective measures become necessary to establish equilibrium in the balance of payments of a country. If any sign of disequilibrium in balance of payments position of a country makes its appearance, there is automatic appreciation or depreciation of the concerned national currency and automatically the country begins to move towards equilibrium position in this balance of payments.

(4) Under flexible exchange rate system, a country is free to follow its own autonomous economic policy or domestic economic policy committed to maintain full employment and rapid economic growth. A country is not required to sacrifice its independent domestic economic policy to attain external balance (i.e., equilibrium in her balance of payments position). It is the exchange rate that will get adjusted and brought in line or in conformity with independent domestic economic policy. Domestic economic policy will not have to be adjusted to exchange rate policy, as it happens in the case of fixed exchange rate policy. As Prof. H.G. Johnson has pointed, "The fundamental argument for flexible exchange rates is that they allow country's autonomy with respect to use of monetary, fiscal and other policy instruments, by automatically ensuring the preservation of external equilibrium."

(5) In the case of this system, since disequilibrium in balance of payments is automatically removed or corrected, there is no necessity of gold movements or flow of capital out of a country.

(6) Another great advantage of this system is that there is no necessity of building or stocking of reserves of foreign currencies as is required in the case of fixed exchange rate policy.

A deficit country will simply allow its currency to depreciate (i.e., become cheaper *vis-a-vis* another foreign currency in question), instead of government intervening and supply foreign currency from its built-up reserves which poor countries like India are either not in a position to do or will find it very costly to do. Holding idle foreign exchange or currency reserves amounts to waste of valuable resource which could have been put to productive uses. This is not necessary in the case of flexible foreign exchange rate policy while building up of foreign exchange reserve is a must in the case of fixed exchange rate policy.

(7) E. Shomen has pointed out in his book *'Flexible Exchange Rates'* that the system of flexible exchange rates would automatically solve the problems of international liquidity (of which much is talked about at present). He has pointed out that shortage of international liquidity was the outcome of fixed (i.e., pegged) exchange rate policy and intervention of monetary authority to peg down or peg up exchange rates, instead of allowing them to take their own course depending upon market forces of demand for and supply of foreign currencies. He has pointed out that under the system of flexible exchange rates, speculators in foreign exchange market would supply foreign currencies to meet private liquidity needs whereas traders, bankers and governments will continue to hold liquid assets in the form of gold or foreign exchange as working reserves and not for the maintenance of fixed exchange rates.

(8) Another advantage of flexible or fluctuating exchange rate policy is that institutions like the International Monetary Fund are no longer necessary as short-term lending and borrowing of foreign currencies to correct disequilibrium in balance of payments would not be required at all.

(9) Under this system, complicated and extensive trade restrictions and regulations and foreign exchange controls will not be required. There will be no necessity to establish a body to exercise exchange controls and trade regulations providing opportunities for corruption to bureaucrats and politicians.

(10) Another great advantage of the flexible or fluctuating exchange rate policy is that there will not be required competitive exchange rate depreciation and tariff wars between countries, nor would there be the necessity of forming customs union and 'currency areas' (such as Sterling Area, Dollar Area and so on) as these are consequences of the fixed exchange rates policy.

Arguments Against Flexible (Floating) Exchange Rates System

Following arguments are put forward against flexible or fluctuating exchange rates policy:

(1) It is argued that as in the case of commodities, market forces or market mechanism may fail to establish exchange rates that would lead to the establishment of equilibrium in balance of payment position of a country. Market forces of demand and supply of foreign currencies may not always give correct signals and this may lead to misallocation of productive resources in a country.

(2) It is impossible to have in practice (if not in principle) freely fluctuating exchange rates or flexible exchange rates. Government may not directly intervene in foreign exchange market with exchange controls and regulations; but monetary and fiscal policies of the government will always have great impact on foreign exchange rates. For example, if excise duties are raised in country A, cost of production and, therefore, prices of commodities in that country will rise leading to fall in their exports. This would mean less demand for domestic currency of country A to that extent and rate of exchange would move against that currency. Similarly, government borrowing abroad or government investments abroad will have great impact on the so-called flexible exchange rates. It thus means that it is difficult to define strictly what is freely fluctuating or flexible exchange rate policy supposed to determine by the market forces of demand and supply, without government intervention.

(3) One serious argument against this system of flexible exchange rate policy is that frequent (or even day-to-day) variations in exchange rates would create risks, breed uncertainty and greatly

impede international trade transactions and capital movements. For example, suppose an Indian importer orders American goods when the rate of exchange is Re. 1 = 10 cents, hoping that the American goods would be sold in India for Re. 1 per unit plus his reasonable profit. But if by the time the ordered American goods arrive the rate of exchange has moved to Re. 1= 5 cents, he will have to pay Rs. 2 per unit of the American commodity and he may find that he is unable to sell that American commodity in the Indian market for Rs. 2 per unit plus his reasonable profit margin. The same would be the difficulty experienced by American importers of Indian goods. And, therefore, flexible exchange rate policy by enhancing risks in international trade would hamper smooth flow of international trade which will come to be characterised by great uncertainty and risk which might reduce total volume of international trade with adverse effects on welfare of peoples of the world.

(4) Flexible exchange rates will have much more damaging effects on long-term foreign investments or capital movements from one country to another. Let us suppose that an Indian invests Rs. 10 lakhs in America when the rate of exchange was Re. 1 = 10 cents. Naturally, the shares or bonds held in America will be in terms of American dollars. When after 10 years, the Indian investor wants to get back his investment of Rs. 10 lakhs, and if at that time the rate of exchange is Re. 1 = 20 cents, by disposing of his shares and bonds in American dollars and converting dollars into Indian rupees, he will find that he will get not Rs. 10 lakhs but only Rs. 5 lakhs. This means the system of flexible exchange rate will make smooth inflow and outflow of capital or capital movements from country to country a risky affair adversely affecting capital movements among countries.

(5) Another serious defect of flexible exchange rates policy is that it provides great scope to speculation. Speculation will bring about greater and artificial changes in exchange rates. Thus, speculation has de-establishing effects on international trade and, therefore, on the nation's economy and welfare. Thus, it is often said that speculators see a decline in the exchange rate as a signal for further decline, and that their action (i.e., selling foreign currency before further decline in exchange rate) will cause the movement in the exchange rate to be larger than it would have been in the absence of speculation. Such speculation made for pure gain in the shortest possible time will further increase risks and uncertainties in the sphere of international trade and that might tend to reduce volume of international trade and, therefore, the total welfare of the community.

(6) For the above reason of increasing risk associated with flexible exchange rates from the point of view of international trade, for countries like England, Japan, South Korea, Hong Kong, Taiwan and Singapore which greatly depend for their prosperity and progress on international trade, flexible exchange rates would pose perpetual problems and the future of those economies would be characterised by great uncertainty.

(7) Another defect of flexible exchange rate policy is its generally inflationary bias. Thus, if due to any reason, currency of a country depreciates, that would result in greater imports by the countries whose currency has depreciated. This would push up prices of imported goods. These imported goods may be inputs of other domestic industries and, therefore, rise in prices of imported goods would mean rise in price level of many domestically produced goods and, therefore, in the general price level in the country. This would mean rise in cost of living, demand for higher wages and salaries all of which will intensify inflationary pressures in the economy. Once the vicious circle of inflation starts, it would become difficult to check it and

break the vicious circle. Because even if the currency due to some reason begins to appreciate, wages and prices generally being sticky will not decline.

(8) The most serve criticism against flexible or fluctuating exchange rates policy is that the system deprives the world economy of a stable medium of exchange, of a stable unit of account, a stable store of value and a stable standard of deferred payments. This would bring about fragmentation of world economy, divided markets, less international specialisation with adverse effects on world trade and welfare of peoples of the world.

14.4 FOREIGN EXCHANGE RATES SYSTEM IN PRACTICE AT PRESENT

Prior to World War I (1914-18) almost all major national currencies were on the gold standard and, therefore, they adopted what might be said to be the system of fixed foreign exchange rate system based on the international gold standard.

During the period of World War I most of the countries left the gold standard and introduced 'Exchange Controls.' Most nations returned to the gold standard with stable rates of exchange during 1920s.

But most of the countries left gold standard during 1930s — England in 1931, the United States in 1934 and finally France in 1936.

During the period of World War II (1939-45) almost all the countries involved in the war directly or indirectly introduced and practised a rigorous system of 'Exchange Controls,' the idea being that all the available foreign exchange or currencies should be used for the successful prosecution of the war.

Adjustable Pegging System of Foreign Exchange Rates

Under the Bretton Woods Agreement, the International Monetary Fund (the IMF) came to be established in 1946. As per the IMF direction and agreement, exchange rates between currencies of member countries of the IMF came to be pegged theoretically in terms of gold or US dollar (at 35 US dollars per ounce of gold). Thus, exchange rates of member-countries came to be pegged to a fixed exchange rate but with permissible changes in the exchange rate within a band or range of 1 per cent above or 1 per cent below the par value of their currencies informed to the IMF at the time of acceptance of the membership of the IMF. But movement of exchange rate beyond the narrow band of 1 per cent above or below the pegged rate of exchange was to be effective only after convincing the IMF that the country concerned was facing 'fundamental disequilibrium' in its balance of payments position. The member-countries of the IMF were forbidden to impose restrictions on imports or introduce exchange controls, except for a transitional period. The member-countries were allowed to hold their reserves partly in dollars and British pounds. The function of these reserves was to meet temporary deficits in balance of payments, without at the same time changing exchange rates.

Criticism of the IMF Standard

Following are the points of criticism against the IMF standard:

(1) The IMF did not give any precise definition of 'Fundamental Disequilibrium' (which would allow changes in exchange rate within the stated narrow band). By 'Fundamental Disequilibrium' was meant persistent and chronic deficit that could be corrected ultimately only by devaluation of the nation's currency.

(2) The general tendency among deficit countries and surplus countries was their reluctance to change exchange rate for fear of harming national interests.

(3) Since the American dollar was a very strong currency, there was increasing tendency among member countries to build reserves of US dollars which were for long convertible into gold at the rate of 35 dollars per ounce of gold. This brought tremendous pressure on US dollars (which ultimately was forced in 1971 to stop conversion of dollars into gold at the Federal Reserve System).

(4) The IMF system as it operated during 1960s led to establishing speculation in foreign exchange markets in different countries.

(5) The IMF insisted on expenditure-reducing policies for correcting disequilibrium in balance of payments and this was not welcome to many countries which after World War II had come to undertake expanding welfare expenditure in their budgets.

The consequence of all the above defects was that the IMF standard collapsed in 1971 when US dollar (which was convertible into gold at the rate of 35 dollars per ounce of gold) was declared as inconvertible into gold at the Federal Reserve System.

Managed Floating

Between 15th August 1971 and Smithsonian Agreement on 18th December 1971, the United States, Japan and a large number of European countries (in all about 41 countries) abandoned the fixed exchange rate system (i.e., the IMF standard).

The Group of Ten (which are highly industrialised countries) brought about the Smithsonian Agreement on 18th December 1971. They agreed to adopt a new system of exchange rate with 'wider bands.' As a first step, the United States devalued her dollar by 8 per cent, Japan her yen by 17 per cent, and West Germany her mark by 14 per cent. The Smithsonian Agreement on December 1971 widened the margin of fluctuating exchange rates to 2.25 per cent above or below the new parities announced then. By agreement the 'Band' was further widened to 4.5 per cent.

Another significant development in the sphere of foreign exchange took place when the countries of the European Economic Community agreed to limit the fluctuations of their currencies relative to the currencies of each other to a smaller band. Though the EEC currencies were thus tied together permitting fluctuation within a narrow band, they could however fluctuate in relation to other currencies of non-EEC countries within the limits set by the band proposals (i.e., in a wider band).

The Smithsonian Agreement of December 1971 broke down following the devaluation of US dollar by the United States on 12th December 1973. By March 1973 a number of countries, namely, the United Kingdom, Canada, Japan, Switzerland, India and several others adopted the system of floating exchange rates. But the 'joint float' of the EEC countries continued even after 1973.

The European Monetary System (EMS) was formed in March 1979 creating the European Currency Unit (ECU) with a 'basket' of currencies as a unit of account consisting of the currencies of major European countries. The EMS limits the internal exchange rate fluctuation of member-countries to not more than 2.25 per cent of the 'initial rates' (only Italian Lira is permitted, if need arises, to fluctuate up to 6 per cent).

Meanwhile the Jamaica Agreement of 1976 formally adopted the system of floating exchange rates under the auspices of the IMF. The adoption of floating exchange rate was forced upon those countries by a number of factors such as short-term capital flight which the central banks could not stop as also prevalence of speculation in foreign exchange markets during period of adjustable pegs.

The 'Oil Crisis of 1973 and 1974' led to recession in industrialised countries of the world and as a consequence US dollar went on depreciating assuming such proportion by 1978 that the United States finally decided on a policy of massive government intervention with a view to prevent further decline in the value of US dollar and to head off a possible financial panic. By 1978, the system of floating exchange rate had come to stay.

By another amendment of IMF Charter in 1978, member-countries of the IMF are not expected to maintain and establish par value of their currencies in terms of gold or US dollar. This means the IMF has no control over exchange rate fluctuations and adjustment policies of member-countries. The IMF only lays down guidelines and performs the function of international supervision of exchange rate policies of member-countries.

But the system adopted by most countries since the second amendment of the IMF in 1978 is the system of 'managed floating.' The system as it operates is rarely without governmental intervention and, therefore, it has come to be called 'managed floating system.'

In the present-day world full of complexities, a system of 'clean float' (i.e., floating exchange rates without any government intervention but determined only by the market forces of demand and supply) is practically impossible. And, thus the system of managed foreign exchange rates is evolving wherein central banks of the countries try to control exchange fluctuations around some 'norms' adopted by them. For example, India has at present linked the exchange rate of its rupee to a basket of 7 or 8 important currencies (the names of which are not revealed).

15

CHAPTER

POLICY OF EXCHANGE CONTROL

Structure:

15.1 INTRODUCTION

After the final abandonment of the gold standard during 1930s, there came to be adopted in its place the system of inconvertible paper currency system with its freely fluctuating foreign exchange rates. Under this system, the rate of exchange between any two inconvertible paper currencies is left to be determined by the market forces of demand for foreign currency and supply of that foreign currency. But this system meant that there would be wide fluctuations in foreign exchange rates influenced by ever-changing market forces of demand and supply. Naturally, this situation invited state intervention in the determination of foreign exchange rates. Rise of Hitler's Nazi Germany in 1932 saw the rates of exchange entirely determined by the government completely suppressing the market forces of demand for and supply of foreign currencies. Naturally, this invited retaliation by other national governments where also governments started in intervening influencing or determining foreign exchange rates. During the period of World War II (1939-45) almost government of every country adopted extensively the practice of exchange control.

Even after the end of World War II in 1945, an attempt was made through international monetary institutions like the International Monetary Fund (the IMF) to lessen the role of governments in determining foreign exchange rates. But the exchange control policy continued in an open or concealed manner and has continued to do so till today so much so that exchange control has become a widely accepted policy and practice of practically every government including governments in democratic states. Naturally, this prevailing widespread phenomenon of exchange control requires to be studied in all its aspects.

15.2 DEFINITION AND MEANING OF EXCHANGE CONTROL

Prof. Haberler has defined Exchange Control as "...state regulation to exclude the free play of economic forces from the foreign exchange market."

According to Prof. Ellsworth, exchange control "...disregards market forces and substitutes for them the arbitrary decisions of governmental officials. Imports and other international payments are no longer determined solely by international price comparisons, but by consideration of national need as perceived by frequently misinformed bureaucrats. Not only is government intervention direct rather than indirect, but since the core of exchange control is a set of restrictions in international payments, convertibility is also sacrificed."[1]

Exchange control system when practised on a comprehensive scale involves extensive government control over all transactions involving converting domestic currency into any foreign currency. Domestic exporters are required legally to hand over to the government (generally to the central bank of the country through which exchange control operates) all their export earnings (which are obviously in foreign currencies) in exchange for which the exporters are paid in domestic currency. Similarly, all domestic importers wanting to import goods and services from any country have to apply to the central bank of the country for the necessary foreign currency which the government may or may not give taking into consideration various factors such as availability of foreign exchange, purpose for which particular foreign currency is wanted by the domestic importers, government's priorities in the matter of imports, the balance of payments position of the country and so on. If the domestic importer is permitted to have the necessary foreign exchange, it is made available to him by the central bank in exchange of domestic currency which the domestic importer has to pay to the central bank.

1. P.T. Ellsworth and J.K. Leith, *The International Economy* (1975), p. 375.

Thus, it is government (i.e., the central bank of the country which acts on the direction of the government of the country) which regulates the demand for and supply of foreign currencies, conversion being at rates determined by the government. This means that in the sphere of foreign currencies, the role of market forces of demand and supply is ruled out and in their place government control is substituted. Thus, it is the government which determines the priorities according to which foreign currencies will or will not be made available to domestic imports and if it is to be made available, in what quantities it is to be made available. Thus, the essence of exchange control policy is the substitution of government or state control and regulation in the sphere of conversion of one currency into another in place of freely operating market forces of demand and supply in the sphere of foreign currencies which in effect means in the sphere of international trade.

15.3 MAIN OBJECTIVES OF EXCHANGE CONTROL POLICY

The policy or system of foreign exchange control has come to be used extensively since the commencement of the World War II to attain various objectives. Exchange controls continue to be used at present, though priorities of objectives of exchange controls may have altered somewhat or even to a great extent and even new objectives may have been added.

Following are the main objectives of foreign exchange control policy or system:

(1) *Avoidance of Fluctuations in Exchange Rates:* This has been the earliest objective of exchange control. When during 1930s country after country left the gold standard and in its place adopted inconvertible appear currency standard, there started taking place day-to-day fluctuations in the rates of exchange between American dollar and British pound as also in the case of other currencies. It is obvious that such fluctuations taking place frequently are extremely disturbing to both import and export trade of the countries concerned causing disturbances in national economies.

    Government of England started intervening and practising exchange control through the establishment of 'Exchange Equalisation Fund.' This fund was used to ensure that exchange rate fluctuations were minimum and if possible eliminated. (More about the working of the Exchange Equalisation Fund later on when discussing 'Methods of Exchange Control').

(2) *Correcting Disequilibrium in Balance of Payments Position:* It is noticed that in the case of both developed and developing countries, balance of payments position has been in disequilibrium (which means mostly deficits in balance of payments).

    In the case of developing countries like India which have launched their programmes of rapid industrialisation, they are required to import capital goods in substantial quantities, spares and other essential industrial raw materials as also technological know-how. But their export earnings are mostly inadequate to meet fully their heavy import bills of above-mentioned goods and services without which programmes of rapid industrialisation cannot be successfully executed.

    And, therefore, countries with deficits in their balance of payments have been resorting to exchange control. They refuse foreign currencies (obtained through export earnings) for the import of luxury and semi-luxury goods and services which occupy lower position in their scale of preferences. Thus, through exchange control, an attempt is made to cut down the total value of imports and to see that just that much foreign exchange is made available to

Indian importers which would be equal to the country's export earnings. The idea is to cut down deficit in balance of payments to the minimum and if possible to eliminate such deficit.

(3) *Protection to Domestic Industries:* Exchange control policy is often being used to give protection to domestic industries, especially infant industries, against foreign competition. Exchange control authority (working in collaboration with customs authority) would either totally refuse or grant only pre-determined amount of foreign currency for importing foreign goods likely to compete with domestic industries that are to be protected and encouraged to develop. Thus, exchange control policy may aim at protecting and promoting selected domestic industries in the face of foreign competition, especially from industries in highly industrialised countries.

(4) *Checking Imports of Non-Essential Commodities:* Developing countries like India find it difficult to earn through their exports the necessary foreign currencies. And, therefore, with a view to see that the hard-earned foreign currencies are not wasted on imports of luxury and semi-luxury goods or on imports of harmful drugs etc. exchange control authority may not make available foreign currencies to import such goods and services. Licensing authority will issue licences only for the import of essential articles and services and the exchange control authority will make available the requisite foreign currencies only to those licence-holders to import essential commodities like capital goods, spares, essential industrial raw materials, etc.

(5) *Exchange Control to Facilitate Economic Planning Process:* Exchange control policy is an essential part of the national economic planning process. Economic planning in India fixes priorities as also sectoral and individual targets after great deal of deliberation and taking into consideration the needs of the people and of the country (e.g., defence of the country, etc.). A developing country like India requires vast imports of capital goods and sophisticated technological know-how for attaining the objectives of her Five Year Plans. It is here that the exchange control policy plays its vital role. From out of the available foreign exchange resources, the exchange control authority provides foreign currencies that would bring in necessary imports and facilitate the planning process and make effective implementation of Five Year Plans possible.

(6) *Tackling the Problem of Foreign Debt Repayment:* A developing country like India cannot earn all the foreign exchange that is required only through her exports which are limited because of the underdeveloped nature of the economy. Naturally, to speed up economic development, developing countries like India are required to raise foreign debts. These foreign debts help import of capital goods and sophisticated technological know-how necessary to speed up the process of rapid economic development. But to maintain the country's credit-worthiness in foreign money markets, principal and interest payments must be made on stated dates and different countries must be paid back their loans in their own national currencies (or in hard currencies like dollars, mark or yen, etc.). If the foreign debt must be paid on time, it becomes necessary to preserve and store foreign currencies and not fritter them away. In this, exchange control policy plays a vital role by building up reserves of foreign currencies so that foreign debts and servicing charges are paid regularly so that the country's credit-worthiness remains high and trustworthy.

(7) *Preventing Flight of Domestic Capital:* Exchange control comes to be often adopted by developed and especially developing countries (which are generally short of domestic capital) to prevent flight of capital to other countries and also preserve hard-earned foreign currencies preventing their investment abroad. For example, in India the Reserve Bank of India will not

allow any Indian exporter to invest earnings in foreign currencies abroad without the direct permission of the Reserve Bank or the government.

(8) *Means of Retaliation:* If any country is imposing arbitrary restrictions on exports of a country like India, India can take retaliatory action through exchange control so that no foreign currency is made available to Indian merchants to import goods from the offending country.

Also, the policy of exchange control can be adopted to extract concessions or more favourable terms of trade from other countries. The fear that a country can take retaliatory measures will keep the other trading countries on the right path and conduct international trading transactions in a proper way. Since in these days political considerations often incite some countries to take hostile action against some countries not in their political camp, the affected country has an effective weapon at its command in the shape of exchange control.

15.4 POLICY OF OVER-VALUATION OR UNDER-VALUATION OF NATIONAL CURRENCY

Introduction: It is observed that historically two main objectives of exchange control policy have been either 'over-valuation of the national currency,' or 'under-valuation of the national currency.' It would therefore be instructive to analyse the problems raised by over-valuation and under-valuation of a national currency.

The Policy of Over-valuation of National Currency

The historical experience shows that under certain circumstances, many countries through their exchange control policy keep their currencies over-valued. This means through exchange control, the value of the national currency is maintained at a higher level than what the exchange rate would have been if it had been determined by market forces of demand for and supply of that national currency. This is technically known as 'pegging up the rate of exchange.' Assume that if exchange rate between the Indian rupee and the American dollar, if left to market forces would have been Re. 1 = 10 cents. The Reserve Bank in case it decided to over-value the Indian currency, would through exchange control maintain the rate of the Indian rupee at 15 cents per one rupee.

Generally when a country is at war or in the process of rapid economic development, the government makes available to Indian importers not ten cents per one rupee but 15 cents per one rupee. This enables Indian importers to get foreign goods more cheaply. Thus, to get cheaply essential war materials as also essential capital goods for rapid economic development, a country under certain circumstances decides to over-value its currency. Thus, if the price of an American commodity is ten cents in the domestic market per unit, at the exchange rate of ten cents per one rupee, Indian importer would be getting for one rupee only one unit for that commodity; but when the Indian rupee is over-valued at 15 cents per one rupee, Indian importer would get $1^1/_2$ units of that commodity for one rupee. This process would help development of defence industries or help to bring rapid economic development through cheapening of essential imports of capital goods, spares and essential raw materials etc.

But the policy of over-valuation of national currency has to face some problems. The first problem is that since for one Indian rupee not 10 but 15 cents are being offered, there will be great demand for American dollars in exchange of Indian rupees. This means the country adopting the policy of over-valuation will have to have sufficiently large reserve of foreign currency in terms of which the national currency is over-valued. It is not possible that there would be indefinitely large quantity of the reserve of foreign currency. This means the policy of over-valuation of the national currency can essentially be a short-term measure or policy.

There is another serious difficulty. Since the Indian rupee (in our illustration) has been pegged up to 15 cents per one rupee (and not to ten cents which would have been the rate of exchange if market force were allowed to operate), it would be clear that while imports would become cheaper in Indian market, Indian exports would become dearer in American market, because instead of paying 10 cents to get one Indian rupee and getting one unit of a commodity in the Indian market, now the Americans will have to pay for that one Indian rupee not ten cents but 15 cents and get that one unit of the Indian commodity which he used to get for 10 cents before the Indian rupee was over-valued.

This means over-valuation of a national currency would result in substantial increase in imports and reduction of exports from the country which has decided to over-value its currency. And, therefore, it may be concluded that the policy of over-valuation can essentially be a short-term policy.

15.5 POLICY OF UNDER-VALUATION OF CURRENCY

Some countries, through exchange control policy purposely manipulate the exchange rate in such a way that their currency units come to be purposely under-valued which means in the case of such currency the rate of exchange would be lower than what market forces would have determined. Thus, to take an example, if free play of market forces of demand and supply would have meant the exchange rate of one Indian rupee equal to 10 American cents, through exchange control, the rate of exchange is maintained at a lower level than that, say one Indian rupee equal to 5 cents, though the market forces would have determined the rate at 10 cents per rupee. This is known as 'pegging down the currency.'

After such devaluation, Indian rupee is available at a relatively cheaper rate *vis-a-vis* American currency. This means Indian goods and services are available relatively cheaply to American importers of Indian goods. An Indian commodity priced at Re. one per unit is now available to American importer, not at 10 cents, but at 5 cents per unit of the commodity. At the same time, American goods and services priced in America at 10 cents per unit would now be available to Indian importers of American goods not at Re. 1, but at Rs. 2 per unit of the commodity. This means as a consequence of under-valuation of the Indian currency or for that matter any national currency, exports of such countries will rise while imports will decline. In the case of a small country such a policy may be tolerated by countries whose exports have suffered and whose markets are filled with cheap imported goods from the country which has under-valued its currency. But if a large country practises the policy of under-valuation of its currency, the affected countries are bound to take retaliatory measures such as prohibiting such cheap imports or imposing heavy import duties on them and so on.

15.6 METHODS OF EXCHANGE CONTROL

Broadly there can be said to be two types of exchange control:

(1) Direct methods of exchange control, and (2) Indirect methods of exchange control.

Direct Methods of Exchange Control

We shall first analyse the direct methods of exchange control.

Following are the important direct methods of exchange control generally adopted by governments:

(1) *State Intervention:* The government intervenes directly to manipulate exchange rate. For example, when the United States and England left the gold standard during 1930s and exchange rate between dollar and pound started fluctuating far too frequently disturbing export and import trade and, therefore, economies of both the countries, to avoid such frequent exchange rate fluctuations, England set up a fund known as 'Exchange Rate Equalisation Fund.'

If the American demand for English pound started going up and exchange rate started moving up in favour of English pound, the government would step in and release required additional English pounds out of the Exchange Rate Equalisation Fund in the foreign exchange market to meet the additional American demand for English pound. This would help avoid fluctuations in exchange rate. If on the other hand, British demand for American dollars went up relative to American demand for English pounds, this would push up exchange rate in favour of dollars, making them dearer in terms of English pounds. Under such circumstances, American dollars previously acquired by moving pounds from the Exchange Rate Equalisation Fund to acquire dollars would be released to the extent necessary, thus meeting increase in demand for dollars by increasing its supply and thus avoiding fluctuation in the rate of exchange between dollars and English pounds.

As we have already seen, there can be direct state intervention for pegging up the national currency (i.e., over-valuing the national currency) or for pegging down the national currency. As we have observed in the case of over-valuation of national currency, as the demand for English pound will go up, country like India will have to have very large reserves of English currency and this may not be possible for long. In the case of under-valuation of the Indian rupee, there will be increasing demand for Indian rupees which is under-valued in terms of English pound and India will have to be ready to supply increasing quantities of her rupees which can be done by printing more Indian currency notes. But as we have already seen, both pegging up a currency and pegging down a currency by direct state intervention can only be a short-term measure or policy.

(2) *Exchange Restrictions:* In the case of all domestic exporters, they will be legally required to deposit all their export-earnings (in foreign currencies) in return of Indian rupees with the central bank of the country; and all domestic exporters will be legally required to apply to the government for the required foreign currencies stating the purpose for which that is wanted (i.e., what they are going to import). Government will scrutinise all the applications of importers from India for foreign currencies, may or may not grant or may grant only a lesser amount of foreign currency as per the policy of the government in respect of imports from abroad (i.e., government's import policy).

With economic planning for rapid economic development of the country and rapid industrialisation of the country, a developing country like India would, as indicated in her Five Year Plans, fix priorities in respect of her imports (giving top priorities to items such as defence goods, capital equipment, spares, technological know-how and so on), fix quantities to be imported from different countries within the framework of Five Year Plan objectives and then the Reserve Bank would give in exchange of Indian rupees, the required quantities of foreign currencies needed to import articles as per plan priorities. In all this, the idea is to make the best use of hard currencies (i.e., of those currencies which are hard to get because those countries would not purchase Indian goods in sufficient quantities).

(3) *System of Multiple Exchange Rates:* This system was adopted extensively in Nazi Germany after 1932 when there were hundreds of different exchange rates *vis-a-vis* a single currency, say between German mark and American dollar. Under this system government fixes priorities of imports from the most urgently wanted goods to those that are low on the priority list. On the basis of these priorities, exchange rates would vary – one rate (say, more dollars for a unit of German mark in the case of most urgent goods) and another rate (say, a very small amount of dollars for a unit of mark in the case of goods which occupy low priority).

This system of multiple exchange rates was used to make the best use of foreign currencies earned through exports as also to establish equilibrium in balance of payments of the country.

But the system of multiple exchange rates is an extremely complicated one to operate smoothly; the system can be highly discriminatory giving enormous power to bureaucrats. As noted earlier Germany during 1930s and many Latin American countries during 1940s and 1950s adopted this system which at present appears to have been given up.

(4) *Blocked Accounts:* Germany adopted this system of 'Blocking of Accounts' (during 1930s and England during the period of World War II in the case of Commonwealth countries like India).

German imports of foreign goods owed huge amounts to foreign exporters of goods. The Nazi government did not permit payment of marks to foreign exporters but blocked their accounts or in other terms froze them. Sweden took retaliatory action by blocking payments by Swedish importers to German exporters. Later on Germany released some of these blocked accounts not at the prevailing rate of exchange but at a much lower rate to foreign exporters who therefore did not get their due payments for goods sold to Germany.

During the period of World War II (1939-45) India supplied huge quantities of goods and services of essential nature needed for the prosecution of war to England. England which was morally bound to make payments to India in English pounds did not make any payments to India then but showed the amounts as credit which England owed to India in the Bank of England. These came to be known as 'Sterling Balances.' England released these sterling balances in convenient installments to India after the end of the war and only as and when England was in a position to pay in terms of goods and services for which English pounds would be used by India.

But the system of blocking accounts is strictly illegal and greatly hampers free flow of international goods and services with adverse effects on welfare of peoples of the countries concerned.

(5) *Clearing Agreements:* By 'clearing agreement' is meant a system of exchange control whereby two trading countries agree to establish and open accounts in their respective central banks through which all payments for exports and imports are arranged.

This system is known as 'Bilateral Clearing Agreement.' When Germany blocked the accounts of Swedish exporters and in retaliation Sweden blocked accounts of German exporters Germany was forced to enter into bilateral clearing agreement with Sweden and payments due to German exporters and Swedish exporters were settled bilaterally between them on mutually agreed basis.

During World War II England made vast amount of purchase of foodgrains, defence goods and other services for the prosecution of the war against Germany. England did not make immediate payments of pounds to Indian exporters but credited the amount in favour of India and that came to be known as 'Sterling Balances,' the total sterling balance amounting (in terms of Indian rupees) to about Rs. 1,700 crores.

Since at the end of the war, British industries were completely destroyed and England had very little to export by way of machinery, etc., there were clearing agreements between England and India and England agreed to release sterling balances in installments as and when England built up her industries and was in a position to sell goods, because English pounds would be used by India only to buy English machinery and other essential goods from England. Also, only some part of English pounds released were allowed to be converted into dollars by India, because England herself wanted American dollars very badly to purchase goods from America to build her economy.

There is another sense in which the term 'Clearing Agreement' is interpreted. If there are two countries A and B, payments to exporters from importers of each other country are settled through central banks of respective countries and there are no direct payments to exporters of each country by importers of the other country. If there is a deficit in the balance of payments of country A, then country B lends to A amounts in its own currency up to a specified limit to the central bank of country A and *vice versa* in case there is deficit in balance of payments of country B.

(6) *Payments Agreement:* This is another form of bilateral agreement in respect of payments and receipts arising out of international trading transactions. The terms 'Payments Agreement' is higher than 'Clearing Agreement' as the former covers not only payments arising out of exports and imports of commodities but also payments arising between the two trading countries out of transactions in regard to various services such as tourism, shipping charges, debt servicing etc., items which are not included in the statement of balance of trade but are included in the statement of balance of payments.

Payments agreement is generally entered into by two countries in respect of payment of debt incurred by one country from the other. Payments agreement which is a bilateral agreement and provide part of repayment of debt in the form of export of goods from country A which may be the debtor country and that is to be adjusted towards payment of past debt and payments of interest. Or the country B which may be the creditor country imports certain articles from country A which is a debtor country, instead of B paying full value of imports from A, only part payment is made to country A and the balance is adjusted towards payment of debt due from country A to country B. Generally, in such Payments Agreements creditor countries do not put any restrictions on imports from the debtor country, though debtor country often puts restrictions on imports from creditor country so that the debtor country is in a position to pay back the debt in full through larger quantities of exports of their commodities.

Indirect Methods of Exchange Control

Following are the important indirect methods of exchange control generally resorted to even at present:

(1) *Quantitative Restrictions on Imports.* It so happens that various restrictions are imposed on import of goods and services from other countries. These restrictions may take the form of

heavy import duties, import quota fixation, complete prohibition, restrictive policies of state trading corporations, etc. The idea behind these quantitative restrictions on imports is to ease the position in respect of foreign currencies and help to move towards equilibrium position in respect of balance of payments.

(2) *Providing Export Bounties:* A number of countries provide export bounties or subsidies whereby a country sells its specified commodities at relatively lower and competitive prices in foreign markets, government making payment of bounty for every unit of the commodity exported. The idea behind export bounty is to push up exports and earn more foreign exchange by cheapening export goods to foreigners in their markets.

(3) *Changes in Interest Rates:* Very often an attempt is made to manipulate and raise the rate of interest in the country so that more funds from foreigners (in the form of foreign currencies) arrive in the country to take advantage of relatively higher interest rate. Also, because of higher rate of interest at home, domestic capital is also prevented from its flight to foreign countries for investment purposes. But there is a clear limit up to which domestic rate of interest can be raised to attract foreign capital in the form of foreign currencies and help ease foreign exchange position. This is because if the rate of interest is raised to an unreasonably high level, it is likely to produce adverse effects on investment and cost of production and prices adversely affecting both growth rate of the economy and exports from the country.

15.7 EXCHANGE CONTROL : ITS MERITS AND DEMERITS

The policy of exchange control in one form or another is being followed by many developed and developing countries at present, though their objectives may often be different. For example, developing countries like India have resolved to the policy of exchange control to secure essential capital goods, spares and essential raw material, etc. and high-level technology not available in the country. All these are essential for rapid industrialisation and economic development of the country.

On the other hand, developed countries are often required to adopt the policy of exchange control to strengthen their defence arrangements, to stop flight of capital abroad, to protect domestic industries from foreign competition, especially from labour-abundant countries, and to attain equilibrium in their balance of payments position.

There is no doubt that the policy of exchange control, if used judiciously and impartially, does help development of domestic industries and leads to efficient use of hard-earned foreign currencies by restricting imports of luxury and semi-luxury goods and services which developing countries like India can hardly afford. Exchange control policy sometimes helps to make terms of trade more favourable and fill up deficit in the country's balance of payments position. In a developing country like India the policy of exchange control becomes an inevitable and essential part of the general policy of economic planning for bringing about planned economic development. There is no doubt that judiciously used and efficiently administered exchange control policy has important merits and it can play a very useful role especially in developing countries like India.

While exchange controls–direct as also indirect–are being adopted since the abandonment of the gold standard during 1930s, the policy of exchange control, while it has above-mentioned merits, also suffers at the same time from some grave defects:

(1) Policy of exchange control generally results in contraction or reduction in the volume of international trade. When a country adopts exchange control policy and limits import of foreign

goods, it becomes logical and inevitable that the affected country or countries would also restrict their imports from the other country adopting exchange control policy. At present a large number of countries have come to adopt exchange control policy with adverse effects on international division for labour, specialisation and volume of international with adverse effects on welfare of peoples of the world.

(2) The policy of exchange control, by protecting domestic industries from foreign competition, is likely to breed inefficiency in protected industries with rising costs and falling exports and adverse effects on welfare of domestic consumers because of higher prices of goods of protected industries.

(3) Since the policy of exchange control has to be implemented by bureaucracy, the policy breeds red-tapism and corruption among those administering exchange controls, apart from engaging a large number of government servants for the purpose which means waste of so much of labour-force in the country.

(4) The policy of foreign exchange control, however strictly and efficiently enforced will carry an element of arbitrariness; also the policy is likely to create black market especially in the case of hard currencies. Exports come to be under-invoiced and the concealed amount comes to be deposited in foreign banks or comes to be invested abroad all by mutual and previous agreement between domestic exporter and foreign importer. The policy of exchange control thus results in loss of foreign currencies for the government which wants to use them for development purposes. Thus, the policy of exchange control meant to make the best use of foreign currencies, in fact, often results in substantial loss of foreign currencies to the country.

(5) The policy of exchange control lays down various criteria for releasing foreign exchange as per the priorities fixed by the government. But there is bound to be a great amount of arbitrariness in them favouring some and aversely affecting some others.

(6) When used to protect domestic industries from foreign competition, the policy of exchange control is likely to result in the creation of certain vested interests who would bring all sorts of pressures to protect their vested interests created by the policy of exchange control. This means domestic consumers have to pay higher prices for some domestically produced goods of inferior quality. All this is likely to have adverse effects on the pace and pattern of industrial development of the country which shuns foreign competition. India has gone through bitter experience of this kind for about 2 to 3 decades. This has adverse effects on the welfare of the community.

(7) And lastly, while the policy of exchange control protects some industries, it exposes other industries to foreign competition. This leads to unequal and unfair distribution of income among different sections of people in the community. Proprietors of protected industries make abnormal profits while those not enjoying protection through exchange control make relatively smaller profits or even face losses, if they are using as inputs the outputs of protected industries.

Taking into consideration all the serious defects of the policy of exchange control, the United Nation's agencies like the GATT have been advocating lessening and eventually eliminating exchange controls. But at this stage, it appears that no country, especially no developing country, would do away with exchange controls, each country following the policy of exchange control to attain its own desired objectives.

SECTION III

TRADE AND DEVELOPMENT

16

CHAPTER

COMMERCIAL POLICY AND ECONOMIC DEVELOPMENT OF LESS DEVELOPED COUNTRIES

Structure:

16.1 DEFINITION OF COMMERCIAL POLICY

Commercial policy may be defined as a policy that contributes (along with monetary and fiscal policies) to the economic development of less developed countries (LDCs) by (i) helping LDCs to have an increasing share in world trade; (ii) helping to raise the rate of capital formation in the country; (iii) promoting export trade of LDCs and helping them develop import-substitution industries and thus lessening their extreme dependence on developed countries in respect of essential goods such as capital equipment, spares, essential industrial raw materials and technological know-how; (vi) helping LDCs to establish equilibrium in their balance of payments position; (v) helping the LDCs to have more favourable terms of trade; and (vi) helping the LDCs to have increasing amounts of foreign currencies through trade and thus helping them to push up the rate of saving and investment in the country. In brief, the commercial policy of a country is concerned with export policy, import policy, foreign collaboration agreements and foreign capital, with problems of balance of payments and attaining the objective of having an increasing share in world trade and rapid industrialisation and economic development through foreign trade (of course, along with monetary and fiscal and other government policies).

Commercial policy, in one sense, concentrates on export policy and import policy and policy of protection to infant domestic industries against well-developed foreign industries in developed countries.

16.2 OBJECTIVES OF COMMERCIAL POLICY

The following are the objectives of commercial policy:

(1) *Making Terms of Trade Favourable:* If by commercial policy (i.e., through export duties and import duties) terms of trade (i.e., what a unit of exported commodity brings in exchange unit or units of imported commodity) can be made increasingly favourable (by raising prices of exportable goods in foreign markets and getting imported goods at lower prices), that would amount to increase in national income, resulting in pushing up the rate of saving and investment and thus accelerating growth-rate of the LDCs.

Limitations: Commercial policy will be successful in achieving the above objective provided the following conditions are fulfilled: (a) Improvement in terms of trade and rise in export earnings would lead to increase in domestic rate of saving and investment, if increased export earnings are not spent on importing non-essential consumption articles but are used for importing capital goods; (b) Tariffs can help improve terms of trade only if foreign demand for goods of the LDCs is inelastic. This would be possible only if the LDCs act in consortium and not compete among themselves to push their exports as LDCs are doing at present due to mutual political differences which are being exploited by developed countries. Tariff policy will succeed in making terms of trade more favourable only if the affected countries do not adopt retaliatory measures which they very likely will do by taking advantage of the absence of united action by the LDCs.

Thus, the terms of trade can be made increasingly favourable to LDCs, if they act together through commodity agreements and if foreign demand for their goods and services if fairly inelastic. This means price and income elasticities of foreign demand and domestic supply will act as an important limitation on using tariff policy to make terms of trade increasingly more favourable to LDCs.

(2) *Accelerating Rate of Saving and Investment:* Commercial policy can be used to push up rate of saving and investment. By imposing fiscal and physical restrictions on imports of consumption goods and instead stimulating import of capital goods, it is possible to push up rate of saving and investment and push up rate of growth of economies of the LDCs.

Limitations: The above development due to tariff policy will result provided the following conditions are satisfied: (a) when imports of foreign consumption goods are restricted through tariff policy, their place must be taken by expenditure on consumption goods domestically produced. As Prof. Nurkse has pointed out: "When the escape valve of consumable imports is shut off, the pressure of the steam in the system increases, demand becomes excessive in relation to domestic supply and tends to push up the level of prices." Once inflationary pressures gets generated, that would produce adverse effects on the rate of growth of the economies of the LDCs. (b) Decreasing imports of consumer goods must not result in increase in consumption of domestically produced consumption goods, because in that case factors of production formerly used for producing domestic capital goods would be diverted to increasing production of consumer goods. This would have adverse effect on the rate of investment and growth rate of the economies of the LDCs. This means if restricting imports of foreign consumption goods is not accompanied by similar restriction on production of domestic consumption goods, domestic resources would be used for producing consumption goods rather than capital goods with adverse effects on growth rate. (c) Import restrictions on foreign consumption goods must not divert domestic resources away from producing export goods and into the production of consumption goods because this will have adverse effects on export earnings essential for import of much needed capital goods, spares and essential industrial raw materials. (d) If policy of import restriction leads to increase in domestic cost of production and production of low quality export goods, that will have adverse effect on export earnings urgently needed for import of developmental goods from developed countries.

(3) *Attracting Foreign Capital*: If fairly high import duties are imposed by LDCs, foreign companies may directly invest their financial resources in LDCs to avoid heavy import duties and to take advantage of highly protected domestic markets in LDCs. For example, that is what has been happening in India when developed countries entered into collaboration agreement with Indian companies and set up their branches or subsidiaries in India (such collaboration agreements numbering above 2,000).

But for this policy to succeed, domestic market must be large enough because otherwise foreign companies will hesitate to invest in LDCs many of which have small domestic markets. Also, direct foreign investments must not be allowed in industries producing luxury and semi-luxury goods which are more profitable, but should be allowed only in capital goods producing industries.

(4) *Infant Industry Argument:* There are or may be some industries with potentialities which can be developed, if they are protected during the period of their infancy from highly developed competing similar industries in developed countries. Initially the cost of production in the case of such infant industries might rise due to absence or inadequacy of infrastructure facilities in LDCs, absence of skilled workers, etc. But if protection for reasonable period is granted to infant industries, these facilities may get removed, the infant industries may get developed and ultimately be in a position to stand on their own legs with enough competitive power to compete with foreign goods successfully in domestic and possibly even in foreign markets.

The future benefits of industrialisation would more than compensate sacrifices undergone by forgoing cheap foreign goods and paying relatively high prices for products of protected domestic infant industries. Generally the period between infancy and adulthood of industries means transition of an agricultural country or economy to an industrial country or economy.

Limitations: The infant industry argument suffers from the following limitations: (a) Prof. Nurkse has pointed out that mere protection to infant industries may not bring about their development, if the country has inadequate capital for investing and developing infant industries. Thus, lack of capital (i.e., saving because of low level of income) may impede development of infant industries in spite of protection; (b) Infant industry protection will not create necessary capital (i.e., savings) in LDCs; protection can only create an opportunity for investment in such industries by shutting off domestic markets for foreign goods; (c) Import-substitutes thus produced may be very costly adversely affecting rate of saving and investment which are already generally low in the LDCs; (d) For protection to succeed, infant industry must satisfy certain rigorous conditions. Infant industry must within reasonable time develop the necessary skills and be in a position to stand on its own feet ready to successfully face foreign competition; (e) Protection must be granted only for a reasonable period of time. What generally happens is that vested interests come to be created and political pressure is brought to continue the policy of protection of particular industries almost indefinitely. This means once protection is granted, it becomes difficult to withdraw it; (f) With the perpetuation of protective policy, infant industry may forever remain infant and may continue to be inefficient producing high-cost, low-quality goods, with adverse effects on the welfare of the people.

(5) *Promotion of External Economies:* Another argument is that commercial or tariff policy would result in development of a number of industries leading to reaping of external economies which in turn would push up further industrialisation in LDCs.

These external economies may be technological and monetary. External economies arise because of close inter-dependence among different industries in a country. Thus, technological external economies exist whenever the output of a firm depends not only on the factors of production utilised by this firm but also on the output and factor utilisation of another firm or group of firms.

According to Prof. Scitovsky, "Pecuniary external economies are invoked whenever the profits of one producer are affected by the action of other producers. He has explained that "with an expansion in the capacity of an industry as a result of investment, prices of its products would fall and the prices of the factors used by it could rise. The lower prices of products will benefit consumers and rising factor prices would increase level of income of their suppliers. These are the pecuniary external benefits of economies which may result by appropriate tariff or commercial policy in the case of LDCs."

Limitations: Scitovsky has pointed out that, "Only if expansion in industries were integrated and planned together, would the profitability of investment in each one of them be a reliable index of social desirability."

(6) *Commercial Policy and Factor Redistribution:* In LDCs like India, traditional type of agriculture is the predominant sector of the economy with extreme pressure of population and workforce on land so much so that the marginal product of agricultural labour is zero. This means even if some workers are removed from the agricultural sector in India, that will not have any adverse effect on the absolute or total output in that sector.

But the surplus removed from the agricultural sector will have to be provided productive employment opportunities. M. Manoilesco and also W.A. Lewis and Gunnar Myrdal have advocated protection for industry and development of industries with the help of protection in LDCs. Without tariff protection industries will not be in a position to develop in LDCs as they cannot compete with cheap imported goods from abroad. And, therefore, the argument is that with the help of protection (i.e., appropriate commercial policy), LDCs should develop industries so that they can absorb surplus labour from the agricultural sector which also will have to be modernised as an essential part of rapid economic development of LDCs. Modernisation of agriculture in LDCs would also mean mechanisation of agriculture and this would displace a substantial workforce in the agricultural sector. And, therefore, protection through commercial policy will result in factor reallocation between agricultural sector and industrial sector which compared to the agricultural sector has very large capacity to absorb labour force. This is because while the law of diminishing returns comes into operation relatively early in the agricultural sector, the law of increasing returns operates over a longer range in the case of industries which may not only provide employment to displaced labour from the agricultural sector but would also add substantially to the wealth of LDCs.

But while bringing about diversion of labour from agricultural sector to the industrial sector, it should be noted that this should not mean that LDCs can afford to neglect agricultural sector. LDCs should not think in terms of superiority of industry over agriculture. If LDCs are poor, this is not because of predominance of agricultural sector but because agriculture in those countries is still carried on in a traditional way with low productivity. Along with industrialisation, LDCs must also modernise their agriculture to increase their foodgrains production and for stopping food imports and also to provide increasing amounts of agricultural raw materials for their developing industries.

(7) *Commercial Policy and Balance of Payments of LDCs:* One of the main objectives of the commercial policy of LDCs is and should be to help them to prevent fundamental disequilibrium or recurring deficits in their balance of payments position, and thus help them to attain the objectives of their Five Year Plans which most of them have adopted as a means of rapid economic development.

In the case of LDCs total monetary value of imports of goods and service generally will go on exceeding the total monetary value of their exports of goods and services, thus creating recurring deficits in their balance of payments. This is due to continual increase in their imports and failure of their exports to rise proportionately.

With a view to develop infrastructure facilities like transport, power irrigation facilities, etc. LDCs are required to import capital equipment and technological services of experts in substantial quantities. This increases imports of LDCs substantially. Also, in the case of many LDCs rapidly increasing population necessitates increasing imports of food grains pushing up total value of imports. Thus, India since independence till the middle of 1970s was compelled to import on an average, 3 million tones of foodgrains every year and even at present annually has been importing edible oil worth around Rs. 1,000 crores. This creates deficits in the balance of payments of LDCs. This is still true of most LDCs.

A number of LDCs including India adopted the policy of developing import-substitution industries. To develop these industries like iron and steel, basic and heavy industries, heavy engineering and chemicals, etc., initially large imports of capital equipment becomes necessary. This is another reason of increasing the import bill of LDCs and increasing deficits in their balance of payment.

The LDCs have all become independent only after World War II. For their defence they are still required to import huge quantities of defence equipment and this only results in rising import bill and rising deficits in their balance of payments. Also most LDCs are required to make use of foreign shipping services to ship their imported goods and also make use of the insurance companies as also banking services of foreign countries.

All these factors raise import bills of most of LDCs to a very high level compared to their regular annual export earnings.

On the other side, exports of LDCs have not been rising adequately relative to rise in their imports. Exports of LDCs have not been rising as much as their imports because most of the LDCs have small export surplus; due to inflation in those countries their prices are high and generally quality comparatively low; developed countries which used to import some goods like raw rubber and leather have successfully found artificial substitutes for such natural raw material and to some extent the same is the case in respect of raw cotton and raw jute which are being replaced by artificial fibers. And therefore, even traditional exports from LDCs have been declining. There is also lack of aggressive marketing strategy on the part of most of the LDCs. Due to all these reasons most of the LDCs have been incurring recurring deficits in their balance of payments position.

Commercial policy, if properly evolved and effectively implemented, would to a great extent help LDCs to reduce imports and increase their exports and thus help to reduce, and if possible, eliminate deficits in their balance of payments position.

CHAPTER 17

FOREIGN CAPITAL AND DEVELOPING COUNTRIES

Structure:

17.1 Introduction

17.2 Different Types of Foreign Capital

17.3 Role and Advantages of Foreign Capital

17.4 Arguments Against Foreign Capital

17.5 How Much Foreign Capital (Aid) a Developing Country Needs or can Absorb for its Economic Development?

17.6 Problem of Tied and Untied Foreign Capital (Loans)

17.7 Trade Or Aid?

17.8 Multinational Corporations (MNCs) and Developing Countries Introduction

17.1 INTRODUCTION

The role which foreign capital can play in economic development of developing countries like India has often become a matter of controversy. And therefore, it would be instructive to critically examine various aspects of the role of foreign capital (erroneously called as foreign 'aid') in helping developing countries like India to bring about rapid economic development.

17.2 DIFFERENT TYPES OF FOREIGN CAPITAL

It must be made clear at the outset that the word 'aid' gives the impression that foreign capital that is coming to a developing country like India comes into the country by way of assistance without carrying any rate of interest or economic reward for the part it plays. The truth is far from that and the term 'aid' in foreign aid used in that sense (i.e., capital given free without charging any interest or given gratis) is wrong. Of the total foreign capital that has come to a country like India, only a small fraction has come as free grant or gift for relief for drought affected people, to run charitable hospitals, etc. It needs to be noted that most part of foreign capital from various countries and international agencies like the World Bank and International Monetary Fund carries substantial rate of interest, though some part of foreign capital is made available to developing countries at 'concessional' rate of interest.

Foreign capital can come to a developing country like India either as 'Private Capital' or as 'Public Capital.'

(A) Private Foreign Capital

Private foreign capital can come to India either as 'Direct Investment' or in the form of 'Indirect Investment.'

(1) *In the case of 'Direct Investment',* people in investing countries exercise almost complete control (legal and formal) over the assets created by private foreign capital investment. India may come to have a subsidiary of a major company with headquarter in a foreign country from where private foreign capital has come; the people in the investing country may have a majority share in the subsidiary company in India; or a private foreign company may have exclusive possession of shares of a company. There may be set up a corporation in a foreign country for operating subsidiary companies in India or for holding private assets in India. Such corporations or companies come to be known as 'Multinational Corporations' (MNCs). In all the above cases, the private foreign investors have either complete or subsidiary share in the management of companies in India in which private foreign capital has been invested.

(2) *Private Foreign Indirect Investments:* Private foreign capital may come to India in the form of 'Portfolio' investment.

This form of private foreign capital takes the form of or consists of mainly holding transferable shares or securities generally guaranteed by the Government of India. Holding of shares of companies in India by private foreign investors does not involve the right to control the company of which the shares or debentures are purchased by private foreign investors. The foreign shareholders are entitled to dividend only.

In recent years a new system has been emerging whereby foreign private nationals purchase securities floated by the World Banks or its affiliate meant for financing specific projects in developing countries like India.

(B) Public Foreign Capital

Public foreign capital may take the following forms: (i) Granting of bilateral loans say by the government of the United States or United Kingdom to Government of India in dollars or pounds at previously negotiated and agreed rate of interest and for the stated period of time. (ii) There may be bilateral 'Soft Loans', as for example sale of food grains to India by the United States under PL 480 programme. (iii) There may be multilateral loans such as loans to India by multinational bodies such as Aid India Club and its member-countries. In this category may also be included loans made to developing countries like India by various multinational or world agencies like the International Bank for Reconstruction and Development (i.e., the IBRD or the World Bank), International Finance Corporation (IFC), Special United Nations Fund for Economic Development (SUNFED), the United Nations Development Programme (UNDP) International Development Assistance (IDA), and the Asian Development Bank (ADB), etc.

17.3 ROLE AND ADVANTAGES OF FOREIGN CAPITAL

Following is the role or are advantages claimed for foreign capital (i.e., for private foreign capital as well as public foreign capital or capital made available from government to government). This may also be called the positive or constructive role of foreign capital. This matter is discussed mainly from the point of view of developing countries like India or the other less developed countries (i.e., LDCs).

(1) Rate of Saving and Investment: The LDCs like India are caught in a vicious circle of poverty. There is low per capita income and, therefore, low rate of saving and low rate of investment which again results in low per capita income. India, for example, on the eve of independence could save just about 5 per cent of her national income. With depreciation charges and growing population requiring increasing quantities of consumption goods, the level of saving then was hardly sufficient to bring about sustained and accelerated growth of the Indian economy, with all its vast natural and human resources. In one sense, economic development is the consequence of rate of investment which is dependent on rate of saving in the community.

Foreign capital that flows into India has helped to fill the gap between the rate of saving and the required rate of investment for sustained and accelerated growth of the economy. If India at present is in a position to save about 22 to 23 per cent of her national income and push up the rate of investment to around 20 per cent or more and could attain annual growth rate of 3.5 per cent over the planning period of the first three decades of planning and around 5 per cent growth rate during the period of Seventh Five Year Plan, a substantial credit for that must go to the flow of foreign capital which came to India in substantial quantities since independence.

(2) Filling up of Technological Gap: LDCs generally suffer from technological backwardness. This results in low labour efficiency, high cost of production and low level of production and low level of per capita income, apart from inability to use vast potential productive resources like sources of hydro-electricity, mineral and oil deposits, forest resources and so on. In fact, one main reason of mass poverty in India for centuries is the low level of technology prevailing in various sectors of the Indian economy.

Foreign capital helps to overcome technological backwardness of the LDCs. Along with financial capital, it also brings into LDCs high level technology, skilled labour, organisational ability, advanced production technology, new products and so on. Foreign capital with its sophisticated technology, for example, helped India to exploit vast natural resources like oil and natural gas, mineral deposits, etc., trained manpower in various and latest skill, introduced organisational and managerial ability. If India is fairly advanced in these technological and organisational fields at present, much credit goes to the role played by foreign capital and foreign technicians from various developed countries. (Like the United States, the United Kingdom, France, West Germany, the Soviet Union and other East European countries) during 1950s and also during the early part of 1970s. Today we hardly find any foreign technicians working in Indian factories wherein hundreds of them used to be found working during the early years of Indian planning.

(3) *Development of Infrastructure:* It is found that generally the LDCs lack social and economic infrastructure like railways, roads, electricity, canals, ports as also social infrastructural facilities like technical institutes, scientific laboratories, hospitals, research institutes and so on. Generally development of economic infrastructure requires huge investment and involves long gestation period. The LDCs are neither in a position to afford such heavy investment, nor afford to wait for long. And, therefore, LDCs will not be in a position to undertake development of such infrastructure without foreign capital and technical assistance. Thus, in the case of India, foreign capital and technical assistance which accompanied the former have played an important role in the development of infrastructure like roads, railways, power, ports, etc.

(4) *Development of Basic and Heavy Industries:* The LDCs are not in a position to invest on their own and establish and develop basic and heavy industries like iron and steel, heavy engineering, heavy chemicals, manufacture of locomotives, aircraft, steamships, fertilisers, etc. All these are essential for rapid economic development of the LDCs. As the rate of saving and investment is relatively low in LDCs, foreign capital helps development of the above-mentioned industries which provide foundation of industrial structure in the country. In India, foreign capital has greatly helped the development of above-mentioned industries, e.g., Rurakela, Bokharo, Durgapur iron works, railway locomotive factory, integral coach factory, oil and natural gas, fertiliser factories and so on. Their development in India would have been very slow or even impossible in some cases without foreign capital and technical assistance.

(5) *Undertaking Initial Risks:* The LDCs lack entrepreneurial skills as also ability to invest amount in projects like minerals and oil exploration, etc. where the element of risk and loss of capital are great. Private foreign capital invited by LDCs undertakes these initial risks and the projects if and when completed are handed over to local entrepreneurs or government who subsequently learn to undertake such risks when they come to possess enough capital funds for investment and acquire entrepreneurial skills because of their association with foreign entrepreneurs who accompany foreign capital to LDCs.

(6) *Providing Employment Opportunities:* As already pointed out, foreign capital brings about development of basic and heavy industries and of infrastructure which, in turn accelerate industrial growth-rate in the country. An important effect of this is the creation of increasing employment opportunities in the economy, especially in urban areas. The surplus labour force from rural areas that has migrated to industrial centres for employment helps to reduce pressure of population on agricultural land. In India, this pressure on agricultural land is excessive. Modernisation of agriculture brought about the introduction of agricultural machinery and chemical fertilisers produced with the help of foreign capital makes substantial agricultural labour-force redundant. Modern Industries with the aid of foreign capital will be in a position to absorb substantial part of displaced agricultural labour.

The above development due to foreign capital raises level of employment, of income and of consumption and hence leads to increasing welfare of the community. India, for centuries, has been suffering from vast amount of unemployment and mass poverty. Foreign capital by helping development will help solve, at least to some extent, India's problems of mass unemployment and age-old poverty.

(7) *Containing Inflationary Pressures:* In developing country, there generally exist dormant inflationary pressures. To accelerate growth-rate of the economy, more and more investment is undertaken and that immediately raises the level of income of people and they generally being poor or with inadequate income, a substantial part of their additional income comes to be spent on essential consumer goods the supply of which is generally inelastic in developing countries. Under such circumstances, foreign capital by helping to import and other essential consumer goods helps to restrain or contain inflationary pressures in LDCs. In the case of India, for example, imports of huge quantities of foodgrains under PL 480 during 1950s and 1960s helped to a considerable extent to restrain inflationary pressures in the economy.

(8) *Dealing with Balance of Payments Problem:* The LDCs or developing countries require for quite some time heavy import of capital goods, spares and other essential industrial raw materials as also import of essential consumer goods like foodgrains and edible oil to meet demand for them for their growing population. On the other hand, their exports are either stagnant or declining and terms of trade are moving against them. Consequently, the LDCs have been facing recurrent deficits in their balance of payments.

Under such circumstances, it is the flow of foreign capital that helps to fill the gap or deficit in the balance of payment of LDCs. When later on servicing charges on foreign loans are required to be paid, that again widens deficit in balance of payments of LDCs; and here again it is the flow of foreign capital that comes to the rescue of LDCs. When foreign capital helps development of industries and modernisation of agriculture, by cutting down imports and increasing exports, it would be possible for developing countries to build foreign exchange reserve out of which old foreign loans might be paid off and the country attains external balance which means the total value of their exports of goods and services if more or less equal to their import bill on account of import of goods and services.

(9) *Introduction of New Culture and Value-system:* Foreign capital through modernisation and industrialisation exposes people in LDCs to foreign influences and gradually introduces industrial or modern culture that is in consonance with modern times and basic to rapid economic development as for example emphasis on hard work, discipline, innovativeness, cooperative efforts and above all self-confidence. These facts of modern culture in place of traditional values are necessary, if the objective is to attain rapid economic development. (Whether the modern value-system is superior to old value-system and which of the two value-systems leads to greater human happiness is an irrelevant question in this connection as the basic objective is to bring about rapid economic development of the LDCs).

Concluding Remarks

From the above analysis it should be obvious that in the case of LDCs like India, foreign capital becomes essential to accelerate their economic development, because without that even with the best of national efforts, the LDCs would take very very long time to develop their economies and cost of such development in terms of human energy and sacrifice would be enormous. In this connection it needs to be brought to notice that most of the presently developed countries (excepting possibly the Soviet Union) brought about their economic development with the help of foreign capital.

17.4 ARGUMENTS AGAINST FOREIGN CAPITAL

A number of arguments are brought forward against the use of foreign capital, especially by the developing countries. The important arguments against foreign capital are as follows:

(1) *Foreign Capital Not a Sufficient Condition for Economic Development of LDCs:* Prof. Bauer is a critic of the role of foreign capital in developing countries. He has pointed out that a number of countries in Far East, South East Asia and West Africa brought about their economic development fairly rapidly without foreign capital or foreign aid. He, therefore, maintains that rapid economic development of a backward country can be brought about without foreign capital or aid. For, example, the Soviet Union brought about its economic development by its bootstraps.

Bauer has also rightly pointed out that "... if the main springs of development are present, material progress will occur even without foreign aid." This means foreign capital may promote economic development of LDCs; but it is not a sufficient condition for economic development of the LDCs. If a strong motive for material progress is lacking (as it is found lacking among the poorest sections in Indian society because they have got used to poverty with which they are associated for thousands of years and cannot even perceive in their imagination what better living means) no amount of foreign capital will help bring about economic development, leave aside rapid economic development of the LDCs.

(2) *Wasteful Use of Foreign Capital:* If foreign capital is available easily or is available at concessional rate of interest or free of any cost (i.e., without any interest), it is very likely to be misdirected towards the production of low priority goods or industries producing luxury and semi-luxury goods for the ruling and elite class. This would also mean that indigenous resources required to supplement foreign capital will also come to be misallocated. For example, in India a very large number of collaboration agreements with foreign companies providing their share of capital have been signed up to produce articles like toothpastes, toilet soaps, ceiling fans, refrigerators, cosmetics and so on. From the point of view of LDCs, this amounts to wasteful use not only of foreign capital but also of supplemental domestic resources.

(3) *Foreign Capital May not Bring Increase in Net Investment:* It is observed that most of the LDCs have adopted economic planning to bring about rapid industrialisation and economic development. They have put a number of restrictions on the inflow of foreign capital and on investment of domestic resources, especially in the private sector. This would mean that most industrial units may work below capacity and due to controls, outflow of foreign capital may actually exceed inflow of foreign capital. This may result in no net addition to foreign investment.

Also, if foreign capital is easily available, it may discourage government of LDCs from making efforts through taxation, etc., to raise domestic resources for investment. Thus, the result of inflow of foreign capital may actually result in decline in net total investment in the economy with adverse effects on growth-rate of the economy.

(4) *Possibility of Foreign Debt Trap:* If foreign aid is used to meet consumption needs of the community and not efficiently for creating productive assets, a country may be caught in foreign debt-trap and it will be very difficult to come out of the debt-trap. For example, Brazil and Mexico have been caught up in such a foreign debt-trap so much so that a substantial part of their national income and most of their export earnings are spent on merely servicing the foreign debts. In fact, those countries have to raise more foreign debts for servicing foreign debts already raised in the past. Some fear that India may also be caught up in such a foreign debt-trap. India's outstanding foreign debt in 1987-88 stood at Rs. 22,999 crores (i.e., this is the rupee equivalent of debts, raised in foreign currencies and India at present is spending around 15 to 16 per cent of her export earnings on the servicing of foreign debts (i.e., on payment of interest and part of the principal that is due). This would suggest the fear of India being caught up in foreign debt-trap is genuine according to some economists.

(5) *Foreign Capital and Balance of Payments Problem:* Instead of containing potential inflationary pressures in developing countries, foreign capital and investment may in fact reinforce inflationary pressures in the economies of LDCs. This is because it is found that generally the LDCs undertake ambitious industrial projects involving huge investments and with the aid of foreign capital takes place, level of income of the people newly employed rises immediately; but supply of essential goods etc. does not rise proportionately because supply of such essentials is inelastic. This reinforces inflationary pressures in the economy. This negates the possible favourable effects of foreign capital. What is more important is that rise in prices adversely affects exports of LDCs while foreign capital increases servicing charges. All this generally results in increasing deficits in balance of payments position of LDCs. Thus, foreign capital at least for many years in the initial stages creates problem of increasing deficits in balance of payments in the case of LDCs. This problem has become a major headache for many developing countries including India.

(6) *Adoption of Unsuitable Models of Growth:* It is observed that in the case of most of the LDCs including India, foreign capital is generally accompanied by foreign experts in various fields like engineering, economic planning and so on. Naturally, they try to introduce Western models of growth in LDCs as they are well acquainted with only those models (e.g., western system of education, medical system, economic planning, factory system and so on). These models are clearly unsuitable for LDCs in most cases and have been proved unworkable all this leading to waste of foreign capital. For example, in the case of India, a host of so-called economic and administrative experts used to visit India during 1950s and 1960s. They tried to mould models of Indian economic development according to their convictions and experience in their own countries where conditions were totally different from those in India. Naturally, those models were found mostly unsuitable for Indian conditions. All this resulted in great amount of waste of foreign and also domestic resources. (After 1970s visits of the so-called foreign experts have become very rare and Indian planners and administrators have been formulating their plans based on domestic socio-economic environment and this has led to greater success than when such plans and policies were formulated on Western or foreign models.)

(7) *Production of Low Priority Goods and Services:* It is argued in favour of foreign capital that it helps to bring in from foreign countries essential goods necessary for rapid economic development of the LDCs. But often the factors are otherwise.

From the Indian experience it is observed that foreign capital has often encouraged production of non-essential goods such as luxury and semi-luxury items of consumption for the elite classes.

(8) *Tied Foreign Capital:* Foreign capital generally insists on purchasing capital goods and essential raw material, etc. from specified suppliers from countries supplying foreign capital. By taking advantage of such clauses, the suppliers hike prices of goods and equipment supplied by them. Capital-receiving countries have no option but to pay such high prices. Often such goods supplied by producers are not of good quality and technology supplied by them is obsolete or otherwise unsuitable to LDCs receiving foreign capital.

(9) *Possible Adverse Effect on Domestic Rate of Saving:* Very often easy availability of foreign capital and production with its help of luxury and semi-luxury goods raises consumption level of foreign capital-receiving countries. This very often results in declining domestic rate of saving and investment. This means foreign capital often acts substitute for domestic capital.

(10) *Political Pressures:* Foreign capital, especially from foreign governments often brings in political pressures and attempts are made to drag in capital-receiving LDCs in their own camps, especially when the world atmosphere was full of cold war climate between the Western capitalist countries led by the United States and the communist block countries led by the Soviet Union. India has had experience of this type of political pressure from the American quarters to settle Kashmir problem at the time India was receiving foodgrains under PL 480 programme and later at the time of Chinese aggression in 1962.

Concluding Remarks

Foreign capital by accelerating rate of investment, production of capital goods and other essential raw materials would definitely help the process of rapid economic development of LDCs, provided due precautions are taken for proper use of foreign capital. It should be seen that it is invested in high priority industries, for development of appropriate infrastructure facilities, that it is not frittered away on the production of luxury and semi-luxury goods and that it does not discourage domestic rate of saving and investment. With adequate care and appropriately planned use, foreign capital can definitely help to accelerate growth-rate and help the process of rapid development of LDCs.

17.5 HOW MUCH FOREIGN CAPITAL (AID) A DEVELOPING COUNTRY NEEDS OR CAN ABSORB FOR ITS ECONOMIC DEVELOPMENT?

The following factors would generally determine the amount of foreign capital needed or can be profitably absorbed by a developing country like India for its economic development.

(1) The most important factor is the availability of surplus financial resources with the developed countries which they are in a position to lend to LDCs. The United States is one country that happens to have enough funds to spare for investment in foreign countries; the United Kingdom appears to be in the same category and now West Germany, France and Japan appears to have surplus financial resources which they can lend to LDCs. The OPEC had more than adequate funds at one time to invest in LDCs but they preferred to invest in developed countries notably in the United States and the United Kingdom. Countries like Canada and Australia appear to borrow from abroad for their own growth. International agencies like the World Bank,

the IMF and the Asian Development Bank, etc. have fairly large funds to lend; but there are so many borrowers, especially from among the LDCs that all their financial requirement cannot be met fully by these international financial institutions.

(2) *Absorptive Capacity of the LDCs:* How much foreign capital can be availed of even if substantial amount of foreign capital is available would depend upon the absorptive capacity of the LDCs. This absorptive capacity of the LDCs would depend upon availability of complementary domestic resources, availability of infrastructural facilities and the extent of their development (as for example in the case of roads, railways, power, shipping services and ports, accommodation, etc.) and such other overhead facilities, availability of domestic entrepreneurial talent and administrative personnel, availability of skilled manpower in LDCs and their geographical and occupational distribution, size of domestic markets and markets in adjoining countries etc.

(3) *Well-planned Projects:* As the World Bank pointed out in its fourth Annual Report, "The principal limitation upon Bank financing in the development fields has not been lack of money but lack of well-prepared and well-planned projects ready for immediate execution. This is an important limitation." And, therefore, capacity of a developing country to prepare and keep ready comprehensive project reports is an important factor determining how much foreign capital will flow into a developing country and how much foreign capital it can absorb at any given point of time. Many of the countries in Africa just do not have such project reports either in the industrial or agricultural sector or in other sectors of economy like transport, energy and so on; and, therefore, foreign investors find it very difficult to decide whether to invest or not in such countries.

(4) *Availability of Natural and Human Resources:* If LDCs have inadequately developed natural and human resources (as in the case of some of the most backward countries in Africa), that would impede inflow of foreign capital into such countries. This means the extent of availability of natural and human resources of the required types would determine how much foreign capital would flow into such countries.

(5) *Law and Order Situation:* One of the essential conditions for foreign capital to flow into a developing country is that foreign investors must be sure that they will be in a position to reap in future what they are going to sow at present. If a country is going to be rocked by frequent internal political revolutions (as in the case of some of the countries in South America and the Middle East), foreign investors, public or private, will shy away from such a country as also from a country where labour and capital are at constant war so that strikes and lockouts are the order of the day. Domestic peace is essential for economic prosperity and that means government and administrators must be efficient to enforce law and order, if foreign capital is to flow into a developing country. Also if the business-laws are extremely complicated and anti-foreign capital, or riddled with hundreds of clumsy clauses causing complications at the time foreigners want to invest in a developing country or at the time they want to repatriate their capital, there will be disenchantment among foreigners about investing their funds in such a country.

(6) *Capacity to Repay:* If a country is extremely poor with hardly any surplus over current consumption and, therefore, with hardly any surplus to export to earn foreign exchange, this will dissuade foreigners from investing in such a country.

But if a country can curtail consumption and build up surplus, it may inspire foreign investors to invest in such a country, even if her export earnings are presently low. For example, when the Soviet Union and some other East European countries gave loans to India, they were (and even at present they are) prepared to accept Indian rupees (which in effect means Indian goods) in repayment of their loans which were given in their national currencies. This means that India must possess surplus of tea, coffee, leather goods, textile and such other consumer goods which the Soviet Government is prepared to accept in return for their loans in Russian rubbles.

But most Western countries want their loans to be repaid in their own currencies. This would mean that the foreign-capital receiving country like India uses foreign loans efficiently, increases productivity and production and is in a position to build up export surplus and push up her export earnings consequent on the use of such foreign loans and be in a position to use that foreign exchange for payment of loans and interest on them. This means foreign loans should be so invested and used that they become self-liquidating. Broadly, it may be said that India in this respect has a remarkably good record as it has rarely defaulted either in payment of interest or repayment of foreign loans secured either from private sources or international financial institutions.

(7) *Motivation to Bring about Economic Development:* The fundamental condition for foreign capital to flow into a developing country is that people of the economically backward country must have strong convictions and determination to bring about rapid economic development and capacity to put forward sustained and disciplined efforts to bring about economic development of the country. If due to religious value-system or social structure of the society, people have no strong desire to bring about economic development of themselves and of their country, no foreign capital would flow into such a country. The character and the value-system of the people must be such as would make people pursue the goal of economic development, if foreign capital is to flow into the country. Thus, the totality of social, political, ethical and economic environment will determine how much foreign capital will flow into a developing country.

17.6 PROBLEM OF TIED AND UNTIED FOREIGN CAPITAL (LOANS)

It will be useful to make a distinction between 'Tied' foreign loans and 'Untied' foreign loans or capital.

Tied foreign loans may be tied to a project or to a source from which machinery, etc. is to be purchased. On the other hand, 'untied' foreign loans are general purpose loans and can be used at the discretion of the borrower country.

Tied Foreign Loans

The United States, the United Kingdom and West Germany generally provide tied loans. For example, the United States' loans are given on the condition that the loan-receiving country spends the loans on American goods and services only. This means loans from the United States are generally linked to US exports to loan-receiving country. If this rule is not obeyed, it generally results in discontinuance of the US capital or loans to developing countries.

Another form of tied foreign loan is to provide foreign capital or loans for projects proposed by the loan-giving country. This practice is followed generally by West Germany.

Tied foreign loan has certain disadvantages. The project to be aided may be occupying low priority in the loan-receiving country. Also, since tied loans generally insist on purchasing machinery and other equipment from the loan-giving country, this generally increases cost of the project as global tenders for the project cannot be invited. This tend to reduce the real value of the foreign loans. Further, in the case of tied loans, technology and capital equipment passed on the loan-receiving country may be of obsolete type and inappropriate and, therefore, not efficient. Projects selected by loan-giving countries generally are those with high import-content. The tied foreign loans may force a country to adopt capital-intensive projects which means opportunities for the employment of labour in a labour-surplus country like India are limited. Also, tied foreign loans may distort priorities in the loan-receiving country and, therefore, they lead to inefficient allocation of domestic resources needed to supplement foreign tied loans.

Tied-foreign loans or project-based foreign loans may have certain other disadvantages, The foreigners may see that there is substantial expenditure on spares and maintenance in future. It may also lead to inter-governmental bureaucratic wranglings and frictions over interpretations of clauses in the contract and in this lender countries are generally in a stronger bargaining position. Project-based foreign loans may, as is already seen, distort the loan-receiving country's priorities; it may lead to under-utilisation of domestic resources.

Foreign loans which are tied to projects would yield substantial advantages, if the following conditions are satisfied; the choice of projects should be done by government of the recipient country; choice of technology should also be done by the loan receiving country; there should be maximum utilisation of domestic resources whenever available so that import-content of the projects is limited to the absolute minimum; and as regards import-contents, they should be based on world tenders to be invited by the foreign loan-receiving country. If these conditions are satisfied, project-based foreign loans would go a long way in benefiting loan-receiving country and there will be minimum wastage of foreign exchange as that will not be spent on non-priority projects.

Untied Foreign Loans

Alan Carlin has defined untied foreign loan as "the loan whose disbursement is tied to the recipient's expenditure on a wide variety of items justified in terms of the total needs and development plan of the country, rather than to any particular project."[1]

India has been receiving non-project or untied foreign loans from United Kingdom and West Germany among other countries, to meet balance of payments deficits, for import of essential raw materials, capital goods and spares. Developing countries generally prefer untied foreign loans, because they can use such foreign loans in accordance with their plan priorities and development projects in various sectors of the nation's economy. The foreign loan-receiving country is also free to buy capital equipment and other essential goods from any source it desires and at competitive prices. There is no possibility of inter-governmental quarrels over the use of such untied loans. With the help of such

1. Alan Carlin, Project Versus Programme Aid From the Donor's View Point, *Economic Journal,* March 1967.

loans, a developing country is free to use technology that is in accord with the country's resource endowments. Naturally developing countries generally prefer untied foreign loans to tied foreign loans.

But there is the danger that untied foreign loans may be used in a wasteful way such as on sending delegations abroad, buying non-essential goods and services from abroad or establishing industries occupying low priorities in the economy of developing countries and catering to needs of elite classes and high level bureaucrats who happen to influence government's policies in developing countries. It cannot be said that untied foreign loans have always been used judiciously by India. Such use of untied foreign loans will not only be wasteful but would also pose a number of difficulties in future when the time for repayment of such loans arrives. This means only if most rational and appropriately planned use is made of untied foreign loans, then only will such untied foreign loans play their proper role in the process of development of LDCs and would be preferable to project-based or tied foreign loans.

17.7 TRADE OR AID?

Introduction: It should be made clear at the outset that here the term trade refers to international trade and the term aid refers to borrowing from foreign countries or raising loans, tied or untied, from foreign countries.

In recent years there appears to be a great amount of disappointment among developed countries regarding the role played by foreign capital or foreign loans in developing countries on the ground that according to creditor countries the enormous amount of foreign aid (loans and foreign investments in LDCs) poured into LDCs had failed to produce results expected by the lender countries. And, therefore, there has been a tendency to discount the role that can be played by foreign capital in LDCs in promoting their rapid economic development. On the other hand, LDCs believe that foreign capital received by them during the decades of development (i.e., 1960s and 1970s) was inadequate to meet their growing needs and, hence, the unsatisfactory results or outcome of foreign capital. And therefore, the UNCTAD adopted a resolution that developed countries should annually lend to the LDCs at least one per cent (after deducting payment of interest on past loans and instalment of the principal) of their national income. But developed countries are in no mood to reciprocate and their lendings have been declining an account for less than 0.5 per cent of their national income.

And, therefore, in recent years an idea is gaining ground in developing countries that 'trade' and not 'foreign aid' (by way of lending) would help rapid economic development of LDCs. This new approach has emerged because foreign capital inflow has not been coming in required amounts. Also, whatever foreign capital comes, a substantial part comes as 'tied' foreign loan and above all foreign loans impose the burden of payment of interest and amortisation of loans (i.e., repayment of the principal) Many LDCs are not in a position to build export surplus (after meeting their development needs) to pay interest on foreign loans and principal amount of the loans to developed countries in their own currencies.

And, therefore, the LDCs through the UNCTAD have been pleading for preferential treatment for exports from developing countries for manufactured and semi-manufactured goods and for exports of raw material in the markets of developed countries. In fact, the UNCTAD has succeeded in extracting some concessions by way of preferential treatment for export from LDCs to developed countries.

Trade is preferable to foreign loans provided developing counties like India make all out efforts to promote exports (through steps already discussed) and build up substantial export surplus which can be used to import needed capital goods and technical know-how. Trading and earning substantial export earnings is to be preferred to foreign loans because this does not involve burden of payment of interest and later principal in the form of foreign currencies. Also foreign countries cannot put any restrictions on the manner in which developing countries should use their export earnings.

Though countries like India which have been bringing about planned economic development since 1951 are in a position to talk in terms of trade in place of (foreign) aid (by way of loans from abroad), there are a number of LDCs which are very poor and are not in a position to export anything substantially at present. This means for such extremely backward countries foreign aid appears inevitable until they attain some degree of economic development and are in a position to export their goods and services. But for countries like India, trade and building up export surplus would be preferable to foreign loans. But it should be noted that foreign trade of even countries like India has been facing many obstacles and terms of trade are becoming more and more adverse. And, therefore, whatever the theoretical advantages of 'trade' over 'aid', a more realistic way for India at present appears both trade and aid.

Trade

(1) Trade occurs when two countries exchange goods and services for a given or agreed price.

(2) Trade can close the foreign exchange gap only if there is also an increase in domestic saving equal to the rise in export proceeds.

(3) In Trade, transfer of real resources can happen only if a country is allowed to charge a higher price for its exports than would otherwise prevail.

(4) Trade fosters growth through its dynamic effects.

(5) Trade is said to be disciplining. It penalizes countries following fraudulent policies by denying resources in terms of foreign investment.

Aid

(1) Pure aid is a grant; a gift of convertible currency for which the recipient country need not pay interest or make any repayment.

(2) Foreign aid can close a prospective foreign exchange gap without additional domestic saving by the recipient country.

(3) Receiving aid implies transfer of real resources to the recipient country.

(4) Aid can foster growth only if the resultant additional output is allocated so as to increase savings and reduce the trade gap.

(5) Aid sometimes allows perpetuation of ill-advised policies that turn out to be counter-productive to the recipient country's development.

17.8 MULTINATIONAL CORPORATIONS (MNCS) AND DEVELOPING COUNTRIES: INTRODUCTION

A multinational corporation is an industrial or commercial corporation or company or establishment with its head quarter in some developed country like the United States, the United Kingdom, or West Germany, etc., with its branches or subsidiaries in both developed and developing countries.[2]

It is observed that multinational corporations (MNCs) have their branches or subsidiaries not only in developing countries of LDCs in Asia, Africa and Latin America but also in developed counties in Europe, Australia and New Zealand.

The MNCs in developing countries generally operate in the following fields: various plantations like tea, coffee, coco and rubber, in mine extracting and refining or crude oil, pharmaceuticals, fertilisers, manufacture of various consumer goods and of capital goods, both for domestic consumption and for exports.

The MNCs are also found functioning in various services such as banking, insurance, shipping and tourism, etc.

Extent of Spread of the MNCs

During the post World War II period, the MNCs have come to dominate global investments as also international production, finance, trade and technology. Reliable data regarding the spread of the MNCs, their subsidiaries, extent of investment, profits etc. are not available. But in a pioneering study conducted in 1971 of 100 listed MNCs, it was found that their total production of goods and services (not sales) totalled 350 billion US dollars. Majority of those MNCs were US-controlled, followed by the United Kingdom and Holland as also other European companies from Sweden, etc. and from Japan.

Contribution of the MNCs to Development of LDCs

The MNCs have been playing a very significant role in the economic development of the LDC and have been conferring the following advantages to the LDCs:

(1) The MNCs have a very strong financial base and through direct investment in LDCs have been contributing to their economic development. As the rate of domestic savings in most LDCs is very low, the MNCs help the LDCs to push the rate of investment which is a vital aspect of development strategy. By themselves most LDCs would find it very difficult to push up the rate of investment to the required level or that may take very long time and until then the growth-rate would be very low which would mean perpetuation of poverty in LDCs.

---

2. The MNC can be defined from the economic, organisational or motivational point of view. The economic aspect of MNC lays emphasis on geographical size and extent of foreign investment. According to this aspect, a typical MNC is a corporation with net sales of 100 million dollars or more. Its geographical spread is over two or more countries and the extent of foreign investment varies from 25 to 100 per cent of the total investment. Also, from the geographical point of view a typical MNC treats the whole world or part of it as its areas of operation.

From the organisational point of view, a typical MNC tries to motivate a single overall objective for all its branches and the headquarters is the coordinating centre and authority. From the motivational point of view, a typical MNC highlights the corporate philosophy. There is less emphasis on nationalism and there is concern for the MNC as a whole rather than any particular branch, including the parent body.

From the organisational point of view, MNCs are classified into (i) Ethnocenteric (home-oriented), (ii) Polycentric (host-orinted) and (iii) Geocentric (world-oriented).

(2) Because of their strong financial base, MNCs can successfully undertake business risks which are inherent in the initial stages of industrialisation of LDCs. Because of their weak financial position, LDCs are not in a position to successfully undertake such risks which are great in industries like mining, oil exploration, etc.

(3) MNCs are in a position to develop and provide infrastructural facilities like means of transport and communication, power, technical institutes, etc. These are all essential for rapid economic development of LDCs.

(4) MNCs help development of modern skills in LDCs as also entrepreneurial, managerial and organisational capabilities and various other skills necessary for modernisation of the economies of LDCs which generally lack these abilities and skills.

(5) Research and Development (R&D) are the very foundations of economic development and progress. They require huge investment initially and there is no guarantee about the success of various experiments conducted for quite some time. The LDCs are not in a position in the initial stages to undertake research programmes because of huge investment needed or lack of capacity to invest such huge amounts. The R & D by the MNCs often result in discovering new products or new uses of existing natural resources contributing to their economic development.

(6) The MNCs transfer modern technologies to LDCs. Among various inputs, technology is the most important for increasing efficiency, productivity and consequent rapid economic development of LDCs.

(7) The MNCs adopt aggressive marketing and advertising strategy and thus help capture foreign markets into which goods and services from LDCs may enter and thus help acquire foreign currencies needed for developmental imports.

(8) The MNCs help fuller utilisation of natural and human resources of LDCs, help to raise level of employment and income and thus bring about rise in standard of living of people in LDCs.

(9) When MNCs enter LDCs, the latter are exposed to modern techniques and values which help bring about social and psychological transformation which is absolutely essential for rapid economic development of LDCs.

There is thus no doubt that the MNCs can and do contribute considerably to rapid economic and social development of LDCs which for centuries have been facing enormous problems of vast unemployment and mass poverty. The MNCs can act as catalysts and help LDCs to come out of the vicious circle of poverty in which they have got sunk for centuries.

Adverse Effects of MNCs on the Economies of LDCs

The MNCs, due to their strong bargaining strength, are in a position to exploit the LDCs. Some of the adverse effects of MNCs on the economies of the LDCs are as follows:

(1) Some of the US-based MNCs insist on 100 per cent equity holdings and ownership as they have done in the case of countries like Mexico, making enormous profits which are transferred annually to their mother-country.

(2) In the case of India, MNCs are allowed in some cases to operate joint ventures with equity holdings ranging from 25 per cent to 70 per cent, with a number of provisions which tend to

increase their profits. Thus, Coca Cola, a US-based company with a small investment of about one million US-dollars in its subsidiary in India used to send annually crores of rupees from India to US by way of profits. It refused to divulge its secret formula and hence Government of India had to ask the company to wind up its business in India. The same was true in respect of the US-based IBM business corporation dealing with computers and electronic goods.

Though Government of India has passed Foreign Exchange Regulation Act (FERA) compelling MNCs to gradually water down their equity-holding in their subsidiaries in India to less than 40 per cent, many MNCs played a trick of increasing their equities which were sold to Indians who are generally interested only in high rate of dividend generally given by MNCs, hardly ever attending general meetings and raising questions about some of their dubious dealings. With increase in capital base with the help of Indian citizens and acquiring huge funds in the shape of Indian rupees, those MNCs are now making more profits than before and have been sending larger profits to mother countries in their national currencies with adverse effects on India's balance of payments position. Thus, the FERA has become counter-productive.

MNCs generally pay relatively higher wages and salaries to their employees as compared to wages and salaries paid by purely Indian companies and industrial establishments. This leads to inequalities in wage and salary rates and demand for higher remuneration by employees in similar purely Indian industrial establishments. This often leads to rising cost of production, high prices in domestic markets, increasing inflationary pressures, decline in exports and adverse effects on India's balance of payments.

(4) The MNCs, when establishing a joint venture, often put a condition that the capital goods will be purchased only from the countries where their headquarters are located and also put conditions that a certain percentage of the goods produced by their subsidiaries in LDCs should be exported to mother countries at pre-determined prices. By taking advantage of these provisions in the collaboration agreements, capital goods are over-priced and exported goods are generally under-priced, thus depriving the LDCs of full benefits of direct foreign capital flowing into LDCs.

(5) Many MNCs with huge funds at their disposal buy purely domestic industrial companies and thus expand the field of their activities in LDCs with dominating and often controlling power in domestic markets so far as concerned commodities are concerned.

(6) MNCs generally transfer to LDCs obsolete technology which is often discarded in the mother country to transfer technology which is not appropriate to local resources and conditions in LDCs; or they bring in capital-intensive technology in a labour surplus country like India. Thus, the transferred technology by MNCs does not often result in increase in employment to any substantial extent in a country like India.

(7) The MNCs generally neglect imparting higher level skills and high technology to local personnel in their business establishments, keeping them as secret with themselves and thus denying the local the opportunities of training in high technology fields.

Concluding Remarks

Even though in certain counts, role of MNCs in developing countries can be unfavourable to the latter, it must also be appreciated that if appropriate precautions are taken, the MNCs can be agents of economic development and progress as also of modernisation of LDCs. The MNCs by establishing factories producing consumer and especially capital goods in LDCs, by imparting training in modern industrial techniques, management and organisational skills and by helping to exploit natural and human resources can help to solve the problem of unemployment and poverty that prevail in most of the LDCs, at least to some extent.

Guidelines to be followed in Case of MNCs: If full use is to be made by developing countries like India of the MNCs, the problem before them is how to avoid damaging or unfavourable consequences of MNCs and harness them as engines of development and growth.

India has long experience, both good and bad of MNCs and on the basis of her experience so far some guidelines can be laid down for restraining their unfavourable consequences and realising maximum advantage from them.

The MNCs should be asked to take Indian companies as major partners and it should be insisted that they impart to their Indian personnel proper and adequate training in sophisticated skills in all branches so that foreign personnel could got rid of within reasonable period of time and within the stipulated period. The MNCs should be paid a fixed royalty or fees and their patents should be bought in an outright way, instead of giving MNCs share in the profits or annual fees for using patented rights of manufacture.

Equity-holding by the MNCs should be so restricted that right of management of their subsidiaries in LDCs should never go into the hands of foreign management of the MNCs or in the hands of foreign personnel working in India or the parent company in their mother countries.

All joint venture agreements should specifically lay down that required capital goods would be purchased on global tender basis; that technology appropriate to resource-endowments of the country should only be made use of; that there should be maximum use of domestic resources and personnel who could be trained in required skills; that nationals should be employed in higher posts after giving them adequate training. The MNCs should be asked to pay more attention to R & D and should be compelled to invest part of their profits in R & D.

Prof. Streeten has emphasised that MNCs should be asked not to pay to their employees very high wage rates and salaries but should employ them on remuneration comparable to the prevailing wage rates in the country and especially in the neighbourhood.

The MNCs and foreign personnel should be duly taxed and it should be seen that only absolutely minimum foreign exchange is transferred to their mother countries. They should be asked to devote part of their profits on the development of infrastructure facilities.

The MNCs should be encouraged to establish their plants in industrially backward regions of LDCs, if necessary by providing certain concessions to them for this purpose.

The MNCs should be carefully watched to see that they do not attempt to influence through specially created lobbies economic and political policies of host countries and they should be asked to follow a specially prepared code of conduct for MNCs.

If these precautions are taken, MNCs can be effective engines of economic development and modernisation of societies in LDCs, goals which the LDCs by themselves will find very difficult to attain or may take very long time to do so.

ANNEXURE

Capital Movements (Short-term and Long-term)

Introduction

An attempt has been made in the following paras to analyse various concepts and theories regarding capital movements from one country to another as part of international trading transactions.

International movements of capital have been taking place for centuries and most of the presently developed countries developed their economies during the 18th and 19th centuries with the help of foreign capital. Foreign capital helped to transform mainly agricultural countries into industrially mature economies. One estimate by Bo Sodersten is that of outflow of foreign capital constituted roughly 10% of the value of international trade during the 45 years preceding World War I (1914-18).[3]

Though during the inter-War period (1919-1939) foreign exchange rules and controls or regulations hampered the movements of capital from one country to another to a considerable extent, during the post-World War II period flow of foreign capital, especially from developed to developing countries in Africa, Asia and Latin America, has gone up substantially. This movement of capital is taking place both on private account through industrial and commercial multinational corporations or companies or on government-to-government basis and through international monetary and financial institutions like the World Bank, International Monetary Fund, International Finance Corporation and the various regional international banks like the Asian Development Bank.

It would, therefore, be instructive to analyse various aspects of such capital movements from country - to-country, especially from developed to developing countries.

Types of International Capital Movements

The most usual classification of international capital movements is of the following types: (1) Short-term capital movement, and (2) Long-term capital movement.

Short-term Foreign Capital Movements

Short-term foreign capital movements generally take the form of credit instruments of less than 1 year's maturity. Credit instruments of 3-4 years' duration are generally classified as 'medium-term capital movements' and of longer period than 3-4 years as 'Long-term capital movements.'

Short-term international capital movement between, say the United States and India can take place through changes in claims of US resident on Indian residents in India, or liabilities of US residents owed to Indian residents and the Indian residents referred to above may include central banks of the two countries, commercial banks, other money market institutions, share and stock brokers, speculators, etc. Generally such short-term foreign capital movements take the form of commercial bank deposits, overdrafts, bills of exchange and such other short-dated credit instruments.

At this point it would be useful to point out that generally short-term capital movement manifests itself in financial aspects such as bills of exchanges, deposits with commercial banks, etc. (But the long-term foreign capital movements generally take the form of physical assets rather than financial claims.)

Short-term Foreign Capital Movements and Changes in Money Supply

Short-term foreign capital movements may result in some important changes in a country's money supply. Such changes in money supply may take the following forms: (1) Primary; (ii) Secondary; and (iii) Tertiary.

---

3. Bo Sodersten, *International Economics* (1971), pp. 121-123.

For example, when exports of a country exceed the country's imports there is net expansion of money supply in the hands of exporters. Reverse of this is true when a country's imports exceed her exports. Such expansion or contraction in money supply is a 'primary change' depending upon a country's balance of payments position.

As a consequence of short-term capital movements there might take place changes in reserve position of commercial banks which might lead to 'secondary' changes in money supply of a country. But it should be noted that secondary expansion or contraction in money supply of a country due to short-term foreign capital movements assumes that there are no excess reserves in the commercial banking system.

"If the central bank is functioning on a reserve basis and is ready to expand its open market investments when its reserves increase or contract when it loses reserves or when its foreign liabilities increase, the resultant changes in money supply can be termed as 'tertiary' effects of short-term capital movements from one country to another."

Short-term Capital Movements for Speculative Purposes

Under the 19th century gold standard, changes in rate of interest used to result in short-term movements of capital which played a significant role in bringing about adjustments in balance of payments of a country. Even at present, differences in rates of interest often result in short-term movements of capital to make speculative gains. This presupposes that the central bank, commercial banks and other sections of money market are willing to take risk and speculate on the basis of their expectations regarding changes in rates of interest in different countries.

Destabilising Short-Term Movements of Foreign Capital: When speculators deliberately undertake risks and that results in short-term foreign capital movements, such movements may be destabilising (or stabilising). Under such circumstances, an increase in discount rate would often result in capital outflow whereas a decline in discount rate would lead to an inflow of foreign capital. When there is rise in discount rate in a country and consequently there takes place short-term movement of foreign capital, such an outflow of capital is not a sign of strength indicating government's determination to protect a country's balance of payments position, but it may be a sign of weakness and very likely such a situation may eventually lead to currency depreciation.

Short-Term Foreign Capital Movements Under Paper Standard

It was observed during 1950-61 that even a 1% change in foreign exchange rate of the Canadian dollar used to induce 45 million US dollars worth movement of short-term capital; appreciation leading to capital outflows and depreciation to short-term capital inflows.

(It may be pointed out here that in the long-term foreign capital market, substantial long-term capital movements – i.e., capital flows–result because of differences in rate of interest and investors ignore changes in foreign exchange rates. This means that changes in long-term interest rates lead to long-term movements of capital which in turn may produce changes in exchange rates which in turn may lead to short-term capital movements among countries).

Long-Term Foreign Capital Movements

Long-term foreign capital movements may take any of the following forms: (I) Private corporations or individuals may purchase equity shares or bonds in another country where the foreigners wish to invest or private corporations or companies may be willing to provide machinery and industrial raw materials, etc. to companies incorporated and functioning in another country; and (ii) It may take the form of loans from international financial institutions like the World Bank and IMF, etc.

Distinction between Foreign and Domestic Investment

The following points of distinction should be noted in respect of foreign capital investment and domestic capital investment:

Foreign capital investment may increase capital-labour ratio resulting in upward shift in marginal product of labour and, therefore, in their wage rate, and declining marginal product of capital. And therefore, workers in lending countries may oppose shift of capital abroad because domestic investment of the same amount would have raised their marginal product and domestic wage rate.

J.M. Keynes has made the following distinction between foreign and domestic investment. A private investor has inevitably to run some risk when undertaking investment, whether at home or abroad. If a private investor makes a mistake when investing in his own country, there are atleast real or physical assets within the national boundaries; but these physical assets accrue to foreigners if private investor invests abroad. This is a real risk, if especially government resorts to confiscation without compensation as was done by Admin in Uganda. But on the whole, worthless investment is a worthless investment, whether at home or abroad, and assets of a company that has gone into liquidation may get some salvage value both at home and abroad. Most investors are generally skeptical about investing abroad and also much trouble has to be undertaken to obtain necessary information regarding investment opportunities in foreign countries. This places restriction on long-term capital movements from one country to another.

It is noticed at present that during post-World War II period, most foreign investments are undertaken through institutional channels. These institutions are very well informed about investment opportunities in different countries.

It is also observed that during the post-World War II period, unlike domestic capital flows, foreign investments, both borrowing and lending by private parties, banks or governments are strictly under government control of both lending and borrowing countries. In long-term capital movements these days political considerations have been proving a significant factor. Also major objective of government regulations, especially of capital outflows, is to guard against its adverse effect on balance of payments position.

And yet, we find that during post-World War II period, long- term capital movements, especially through international financial institutions like the World Bank and the IMF, etc. are substantially on the increase and so are government-to-government (i.e., bilateral) long-term borrowing and lending.

Tied and Untied Foreign Loans

Many developing countries are not in a position to convert foreign long-term capital into real capital assets by purely domestic efforts, may be because they lack necessary capital equipment or technical skills or capability, etc. And, therefore, often it is found that the lender country or company would tie up the loan with export of specific machinery or raw materials from the lending country. When the company or government from lending country knows that the borrowing company or country is legally compelled to purchase machinery and other capital equipment and other essential raw materials from the lending country, advantage is generally taken to push up prices of such capital equipment and other essential raw materials. And therefore, what is likely to happen in the case of tied loans is that even if the rate of interest charged on long-term foreign loans may be lower, higher cost of imports of capital goods would more than offset advantage of relatively cheaper foreign loans.

Borrowing Abroad to Pay Interest on Foreign Loans

Theoretically there is nothing wrong if a country borrows abroad to pay interest on foreign loans, provided such loans are invested productively and would yield an income out of which later on interest and part of principal can be paid. Trouble would start if all foreign loans are consumed rather than invested leading to creation of capital assets and increase in productivity and production.

Debt Servicing Ratio

During the post-World War II period, large number of developing countries have borrowed heavily from developed countries and are required to pay interest and instalment of the principal amount when they fall due. All this is called debt-servicing charge.

Generally debt-servicing charge (interest and amortisation) is measured in terms of percentage of current value of exports of borrowing country.

During recent years, debt-servicing charges of developing countries have risen in some cases alarmingly. In some cases more than a quarter of current export earnings of some developing countries are swallowed up by foreign debt-servicing charges.

It should be noted that there is no particular proportion or percentage of export earnings required to meet debt-servicing charges which can be called an ideal index. There are a number of critical factors that need to be taken into consideration. Some of the factors to be taken into account in this connection are: (i) whether foreign loans are invested productively or used for consumption purposes; (ii) whether or not substantial part of increased production due to foreign loans come to be exported or not, and whether or not export earnings have gone up or not due to foreign loans, (iii) whether or not as a consequence of foreign loans domestic economy has been in a position to reallocate from industries producing goods purely for domestic consumption to import-substitution industries, and (iv) whether or not the economy of the borrowing country is well managed. If care is taken in the above respects, temporary rise in debt-servicing charges in terms of percentage of export earnings of the borrowing country should not be a matter of concern. The main objective of countries borrowing from abroad should be to take all the necessary measures to so shape the domestic economy that along with increase in domestic production, there is also adequate increase in exports and export earnings of the borrowing countries enabling them to repay interest and the entire amount of capital borrowed from abroad within a reasonable period. This would call for both efficient management of long-term loans borrowed from abroad as also of the nation's economy as a whole.

CHAPTER

18 INTERNATIONAL TRADE AND ECONOMIC DEVELOPMENT

Structure:

18.1 HOW INTERNATIONAL TRADE FAVOURS ECONOMIC DEVELOPMENT

It is said that in the case of an open economy related to other countries through free international trade, there is likely to be faster economic growth or such economies would enjoy higher rate of economic development. The argument that international trade would serve as an engine of growth is based on the following considerations:

(1) Rapid economic development or economic growth requires most efficient use of the country's resources. This would mean that there will have to be division of labour, specialisation and production of goods on a larger scale. It is said that international trade based on the principle of comparative cost advantage permits the most efficient use of world's resources and the gains are shared by all the countries that participate in international trade.

(2) Prof. Bertil Ohlin has shown how international trade leads to equalisation of factor-prices. It would mean that the pattern of international trade is influenced by the pattern of factor-endowments. If there is an absence of international trade, relatively abundant factor in one country would be getting a low wage rate or low level of income, and the relatively scarce factor would be getting higher returns and thus enjoy some sort of quasi-rent. When international trade takes place, a country can export goods produced with the help of relatively abundant factor of production. This would create more demand for that factor of production. Thus in the case of developing countries where generally labour is abundant, export of labour-intensive goods would create larger demand for labour which would, therefore, be getting higher wage rate than the wage rate that would be prevailing if there were no international trade. Higher wage rate to abundant factor, namely, labour in developing countries would lead to higher per capita income and, therefore, higher rate of saving enabling higher rate of investment. Import of capital-intensive goods would relieve pressure on capital which is relatively a scarce factor which now can be utilised in the most efficient manner.

(3) J.M. Keynes has demonstrated how prosperity of one country brings prosperity to other countries participating in international trade. For example, during 1980s there was prosperity in Middle East countries because of the abnormal rise in prices of crude oil and petro-chemical goods. It is well-known how that prosperity gave boost to export of goods and services from India. It may be observed that autonomous increase in exports of a country has similar effect as are due to increase in investment. Through multiplier effect, larger export income, demand is created for many other goods produced in the country encouraging their production. It is possible that substantial increase in exports may create economies of scale which may help to push up growth-rate of the economy of developing country.

(4) Another most significant advantage of international trade is that it helps to widen the outlook of the people in developing countries. International trade brings developing countries in contact with developed nations. That helps to bring about radical changes in value-system as also technological demonstration effect. It helps to introduce a modern value-system in place of feudal value-system which generally prevails in developing countries which help in rapid economic growth and social development in those countries. Assimilation of modern ideas radiated from developed countries are conducive to relatively more rapid economic growth.

18.2 THE OTHER SIDE

It may be observed that the last two centuries and especially the period after World War II has witnessed phenomenal growth in international trade; and yet the economic gap between the developed countries and developing countries has been continually increasing. The developing countries have not been in a position to share the benefits of international trade, main benefits of which have gone to countries which are already developed or rich. Development has gone to countries which are already developed or rich. Developing countries have become victims of projectionist policies that are being followed by developed countries. And therefore, economists like Hans Singer and Dr. Prebisch have put forward the view that international trade has been retarding economic development of developing countries.

(1) In case economic relation between developed and developing countries is of colonial type, nature of exports and production of goods in developing countries would be such as would suit requirements of developed countries. This would mean that advantage of export growth would not percolate to other sectors of economies of developing countries. Instead, advantages of growth of exports from developing countries would be diverted to developed countries. Cheap imports of primary products by developed countries reduce production costs in industries in rich countries, increase profit margin and create more surplus funds for investment purposes. Thus, growing international trade has witnessed growing flow of resources from poor to rich nations.

(2) It is possible that some items increase in production of goods and in export may result in higher poverty. This immiserising growth may take place when supply of export goods by developing countries is inelastic (i.e., practically the same quantity to be produced whatever the price at which the commodity is sold in domestic or export market) and demand for such goods in developed countries is elastic (which means if the price of the goods is even slightly raised, there would be steep decrease in demand for the goods). This would result in sharp decline in prices of exportable goods of developing countries making terms of trade extremely unfavourable. This would mean that increase in the production of exportable goods in developing countries has resulted in a situation when increasing quantities of exportable goods from developing countries will be needed to import the same quantity of goods from developed countries. Under the above circumstances, increase in production of exportable goods and their increasing export might result in lower income for exporters from developing countries and thus lead to their immiserisation.

(3) It is also observed that with increase in international trade, there might take place increasing structural differences between rich and poor countries leading to international trade imbalances. It is common place knowledge that primary products of developing countries have competitive foreign markets. And therefore, technological advances in developing countries would result in lower cost of production and lower prices of primary products of developing countries. As against this, industries in developed countries generally are in monopolistic or oligopolistic position and they would succeed in retaining for themselves the advantages of technological advance in their countries, instead of passing those advantages to developing countries in the shape of lower prices of goods imported from them by developing countries. This would only widen the structural imbalance between the rich and poor countries; there would be increasing unfavourable terms of trade in the case of developing countries and developed countries would be enjoying increasing surplus at the cost of poor countries.

(4) It is observed that impact of economic growth on imports of rich and poor countries is extremely uneven. As poor countries have much higher propensity to import than rich countries and as imports constitute leakage in national income, the multiple income expansion comes to be diverted from poor to rich countries.

(5) With rapid technological advances, the principle of comparative cost advantage is no longer valid. Practically all types of goods, namely, agricultural commodities as also industrial goods, are being produced more cheaply in rich countries than in developing countries. This would imply that share of poor countries in world trade would be continually declining (as it has happened in the case of India) and developing countries will not be in a position to share the increasing prosperity of developed countries.

(6) With technological advancement, the so-called labour-intensive goods can now be produced by capital-intensive methods. This has disturbed the classical or traditional pattern of international trade and has made developing countries even more dependent on rich countries than before.

(7) Since the end of World War II there has been a tendency to form regional groupings, the classic example being that of the EEC. Through such regional groupings the rich countries have been discriminating against imports from developing countries. Thus, India has lost sheltered market in Britain because of preferential treatment given to Indian goods in the British Commonwealth under the Ottawa Agreement. With England joining the EEC that preferential treatment and sheltered markets for Indian goods in Britain have disappeared as the EEC has been adopting a common tariff on goods imported from non-member countries. Under the above circumstances developing countries have been trying to be more and more self-sufficient at least in respect of vital goods and services instead of depending for them on developed countries.

While all the above arguments are true, it does not mean that developing or poor countries have not all benefited from international trade. Certainly they have and but for international trade, economic growth of developing countries would have been possibly much slower and in the case of extremely backward countries practically impossible or would have taken long long time. The rich nations have reaped the major portion of gains from international trade; but the fact remains that poor nations would have been poorer in the absence of international trade. All that is suggested or the burden of all the above arguments is that while international trade generally benefits, the major share of benefits has gone to rich countries. It would have been more desirable if gains from international trade were to be more equitably shared between rich and poor countries.

18.3 IMMISERISING GROWTH

In normal circumstances, increase in domestic output in a country should make the country economically better off and increase the total welfare of people in the country. If it is a closed economy and the country does not carry on any international trade, increase in the country's national income would entirely depend on or be determined by increase in the total output.

When a country is not entirely isolated but carries on international trade with a number of countries, it is possible that rate of increase in that country's national income is not always proportionate to rate of increase in that country's domestic output. This is because in such a country because of increase in domestic output, there might be effect on terms of trade which must be taken into consideration to know if increase in the country's total output has brought about increase in welfare of that country.

When we think of an isolated country, we take into account only increase in domestic output, but when we consider the case of a country carrying on international trade, we will have to find out what quantities of imported goods a country is going to obtain in return of increase in quality of exports. If along with increase in domestic output terms of trade remain unchanged, it may be said that increase in national income (and therefore in national welfare) is equal to increase in domestic output. But if however, because of increase in domestic output, terms of trade have become unfavourable, it would mean that quantity of goods imported in exchange of a unit of exported commodity is now less than before and therefore, there is a certain loss of national income and therefore, of national welfare. This would mean that increase in national income (and therefore in national welfare) is slower than increase in total domestic output. If on the other hand, with the growth of national economy and increase in total domestic output and exports, terms of trade become more favourable than before, it would mean that per unit of exported goods larger quantity of imported commodity is now available and therefore, in such a case increase in national income (and in national welfare) is faster than increase in domestic output.

Prof. Edgeworth and Prof. Bhagawati have made an attempt to probe into the possibility of a type of growth which might result into making the country economically worse off rather than better off after the economic growth has been taking place. Such economic growth is referred to as 'immiserising growth.' Such immiserising economic growth shows that the loss caused by deterioration in terms of trade is more than the gain resulting from increase in output. And, therefore, the net effect might be decline in national income and in welfare of the community. For example, if pattern of economic growth is ultra export-biased and if it results in sharp decline in prices of exported commodities, that would make terms of trade so unfavourable that there is net decline in total availability of goods and services in the country with adverse effect on total welfare of the community consequent on development of such ultra export-biased industries in the country.

If increase in national production is exclusively confined to export sector of the economy and when national resources cannot be diverted to other sectors of the economy, it may be said that there is ultra export-biased economic growth. When supply and demand for exportable goods are inelastic, with economic growth, increase in production would be more than offset by deterioration in terms of trade. Because supply of exportable goods is inelastic, that would mean that the country is ready to sell those goods even at a lower price. If foreign demand for such goods is also inelastic, it would mean that demand would not increase, in spite of substantial decline in prices of exportable goods. As a consequence, prices of exported goods would decline to such an extent that even by increasing the amount of exported goods, total income from exported goods would decline and thus the country would become poorer. This would mean that ultra export-biased growth might result in immiserising growth.[1]

1. Prof. Edgeworth's model of immiserising growth appears to be over-simplified. This is because in practice, there is never complete specialisation by a country only in export industries and also there are several internationally traded goods. Bhagawati therefore, has refined the concept of immiserising growth and has demonstrated that even in the real world, such growth is possible. But to have such growth a number of conditions relating to demand and supply side must be fulfilled. In Bhagawati's concept of immisersing growth in a country where economic growth is taking place, production of importable goods must be declining. This appears unlikely, unless some non-reproduceable factor is used in the production of importable goods. If production of importables is not declining, immiserising growth can take place when the sum of elasticity of demand in country A for goods imported, elasticity of demand in country B for goods exported elasticity of supply in country for goods exported must be together less than unity. It is only then that economic growth in country A would make terms of trade so unfavourable that country A would grow poorer even with economic growth taking place in that country.

18.4 DEVELOPING COUNTRIES AND IMMISERISING GROWTH

Though in the real world it might be said that immiserising economic growth is a rare possibility, this concept is significant in drawing our attention to the fact that quite often gains of economic growth are likely to be largely offset by losses resulting from unfavourable terms of trade. Such situation is often faced by developing countries having international trading transactions with developed industrialised countries.

Conditions or sources of immiserising growth can be detected in the following tendencies in international trade:

(1) Economic growth in developing countries is ultra export-biased. Many developing countries are exporters of primary products and foreign capital is mostly invested in such export industries. This results in introduction of better technology, lower cost of production and lower prices of primary exportables. And, therefore, benefits of increase in export production are passed on to importing countries which are economically already developed.

(2) Developing countries do not generally possess mobility of factors of production and in spite of decline in prices of exportable goods resources cannot be re-allocated by diverting resources from export industries to other industries in the country. This happens because many developing countries do not have the skill of producing anything other than traditional exportable primary products. Also, as such countries do not have their own industries in their countries' primary products which they export are generally of no use for their own consumption. And therefore, supply of such primary exportable products tends to be highly inelastic.

(3) It is also observed that in developed countries demand for primary products exported by developing countries is generally inelastic. This is because even if developed countries are importing foodgrains from developing countries, their demand is subject to the Engel's law of family budgets. This law states that as income increases, there is not much increase in demand for essential goods like foodgrains. And, therefore, developed countries do not increase their imports of primary products from developing countries though levels of income are arising in those developed countries.

(4) There has been taking place another significant development. Developed countries have been using their advanced technology and factor endowments to produce cheaper substitutes like artificial fibres, rubber, plastic materials, etc. for goods they used to import from developing countries. As a consequence demand from developed countries for primary products of developing countries has been declining resulting in further decline in prices of exportable goods from developing countries.

(5) Developed countries have established a strong monopolistic position in respect of goods they export to developing countries. Prices of goods of developed countries exported to developing countries are not allowed to be determined by market forces of demand and supply; their prices are maintained at a fairly high level because of monopolistic position of industrial establishments in developed countries. This means benefits of technological advancements are not only not passed on to developing countries but in fact such advancement results only in further impoverishment of developing countries.

(6) Developing countries require several intermediate goods like essential industrial raw materials and capital goods and spares from developed countries as complementary to domestic

resources of production together producing final products. It so happens that demand for such intermediate goods is inelastic so that developing countries prefer to buy them from developing countries by paying high prices rather than allow domestic resources to lie idle without being used for productive purposes.

(7) Another factor that needs to be noted is that in the case of developing countries, income-elasticity of demand for imports is generally high. It is generally observed that in the case of developing countries, when level of national income goes on rising because of planned efforts at rapid economic development, an increasing portion of rising income comes to be spent on imported goods from developed countries. This naturally results generally in raising prices of imported goods from developed countries making terms of trade increasingly unfavourable to developing countries. From this it follows that absence or inability to adapt to changing situation on the part of developing countries is the main cause of immiserising growth via deteriorating terms of trade in the case of developing countries.

18.5 MEASURES TO CHECK IMMISERISING GROWTH OF DEVELOPING COUNTRIES

It is certainly true that developing countries do not want immiserising growth which instead of making their living conditions better off makes them worse than before such growth of their economies. But this should not mean that developing countries should have no growth at all as that might lead to immiserising them. The remedy lies not in abandoning the objective of growth but in preventing growth that is immiserising. With a view to prevent immiserising growth of developing countries, following measures are generally suggested:

(1) Developing countries should aim at more balance and diversified pattern of growth of their economies.

(2) Developing countries should make use of suitable technology according to their factor-endowments to produce different types of goods which are in domestic use or consumption. This, in other terms, means that they should not depend only on increasing export earnings to import various types of goods for domestic consumption.

(3) It may be observed that sometimes import-substitution is preferable to export promotion. If developing countries only concentrate on export promotion, as already seen, that might result in deterioration of terms of trade with increasing volume of exports but with declining export earnings. If however the emphasis is shifted to import-substitution, with declining demand for imports from developed countries, it is possible that prices of imported goods from developed countries might decline improving terms of trade in favour of developing countries.

(4) As a counteracting force against monopolistic position of export industries in developed countries, developing countries should form countervailing monopolies in primary products exported by them to developed countries. They should form their own monopolistic combinations to secure remunerative and rising prices for their exports of primary products to developed countries so that terms of trade do not go on deteriorating against them.

(5) International organisations like the UNCTAD should establish funds with which to stabilise prices of exportable commodities to developed countries, and possibly to make an effort to raise their prices in proportion to rise in prices of imported goods from developed countries to prevent terms of trade deteriorating against them.

(6) Ultimate answer to the problem of immiserising growth of developing countries lies not in seeking favours from developed countries but in becoming increasingly self-reliant by diversifying their economies so that prosperity of one sector of nation's economy automatically passes on to other sectors of the economy. This is possible only through systematic economic planning by developing countries aiming at all-round development of their economies consistent with their factor-endowment.

If the above measures are taken, it is possible for developing countries to have economic growth without immiserisation.

18.6 STATE TRADING

In the sphere of international trade, 'state trading' refers to government's participation in foreign trade of the country. It means government's complete or partial monopoly in international trade. It may be pointed out that though there used to be some state trading before World War I, it was not then of much significance. At present a substantial part of world trade is carried on through state trading.

Forms of State Trading

State trading may take various forms such as : (1) State itself may undertake functions like buying and selling operations in world markets as was done, for example, in the Soviet Union; (2) The State may establish autonomous corporations or agencies for undertaking foreign trade of the country, as is done by the State Trading Corporation of India. Such trading is entirely financed by the State treasury; (3) The State may grant sole rights under government regulations to private traders for exports and imports of some commodities.

In some countries, state control extends over to the entire foreign trade of the country (covering both exports and imports); in some countries, state trading is limited to only certain important commodities. Also, in some cases the state may buy and sell commodities along side private traders (as for example in the case of iron and steel in India). In such cases there may be healthy competition between the state agency and private traders in buying selling in world markets.

State Trading in Developing Countries

In developing countries, state trading is generally used to improve terms of trade. Developing countries generally export primary products; there is a large number of countries exporting primary products; there are in each country a large number of producers of primary products and mostly they are unorganized and therefore, their bargaining power is extremely limited. If foreign buyers are going to buy substantial quantities of primary products with strong bargaining power because they are well-organised, in such a situation generally terms of trade are found to be moving against developing countries. And therefore, state trading can be used as a countervailing power to improve terms of trade in world markets.

The extent to which state trading can improve terms of trade would depend upon the type of markets in which such trading transactions take place. For example, if the product is a standardised one and the number of selling countries is fairly large, then even state trading cannot exert much influence in making terms of trade more favourable. It may be said that the geographical location of a country, relative difference in transport cost and more importantly, the share of a country in the total exports of the concerned commodity greatly influence the bargaining power of the country, and therefore, terms of trade.

One advantage of state trading is that it can help stabilise domestic prices of the traded goods by eliminating speculative activities in foreign trade which plays significant part in disturbing domestic prices.

State trading enjoys wide discriminatory powers in the sphere of foreign trade. It can practise discrimination while selling goods in different foreign markets and discriminate with regard to supplies of goods.

State trading can be used as an effective instrument of export promotion. It is observed that various malpractices by private traders in the country's export trade bring bad name to the country in the world markets. State trading by fair dealings can build reputation and thus help promote exports of a country.

Another role which state trading can and does play is securing protection for some domestic industries. State trading by restricting imports of certain specified commodities can secure protection to import-substitution industries at home and help to bring about their development.

State trading, since it is not over-much concerned with profit which is the main concern in the case of private traders, can take steps to open up new foreign markets when private traders do not come forward for exporting of certain items or to certain countries.

Role of State Trading in a Planned Economy

State trading plays a very important role in a planned economy especially that of a developing country like India. State trading plays the following role in a planned economy:

(1) Developing economy like that of India requires effective mobilisation of financial resources for investment purposes. Profits made by state trading can be an effective method of mobilising resources. Taxes do not always reflect changes in prices and level of income of the people in a country. From that point of view state trading is a more flexible method of mobilising financial resources as it reflects the level of development.

(2) In the case of developing economies there is developmental disequilibrium in balance of payments. Development imports like capital goods, spares and industrial raw materials generally rise at a faster rate than that of exports from developing countries. If private importers are allowed to import these goods, being always in short supply, domestic importers will sell them at a very high premium making huge profits which are of the nature of unearned income or quasi-rent. State trading can help eliminate such unearned private incomes and make the funds available for development purposes.

(3) In the case of a planned economy, government cannot afford to depend upon private importers for the regular and timely supply of capital goods and other much needed materials for project implementation. This is because private importers are guided by personal profit motive. If developmental imports are delayed or their supply is irregular which is likely to happen if such imports are handled by private imports, the entire planning process will be endangered. This means there has to be concurrence or harmony between imports and development process. This can be established by state trading which thereby helps accelerate the process of development.

(4) In the case of state trading there is scope for bilateral trade agreements between governments of various countries. In such bilateral trade agreement, since generally exports balance imports, there is no problem arising out of availability or scarcity of foreign exchange. It thus eases the problem of deficits in balance of payments which is a recurrent feature in the case of developing countries.

Also, if there happens to be some surplus stock of some goods, bilateral trade agreement can help dispose of such surplus stocks.

(5) Since state trading means buying and selling fairly large quantities, there is generally enough scope for successful bargaining (thus getting higher prices for exports and imports at lower prices).

(6) State trading can be useful for promoting exports. Private traders may not have all the necessary information or they may not take the risk of entering new foreign markets for fear of loss. State trading can establish a network of its offices and exploit foreign markets more fully and thus help promote exports.

There is thus no doubt that state trading appears to be an essential part or element of economic planning in developing countries like India. State trading helps to bring about harmony between external sector and domestic sector of the economy. The strategic role which public sector plays in domestic industrial field and in the economy of a developing country is played by state trading in the international trade sphere. In a sense, state trading can be said to be an extension of the public sector playing its role in the external sector of the economy.

It needs to be pointed out that successful functioning of state trading would depend upon competence of government administrative machinery in charge of state trading. It is observed that generally the defects of bureaucratic administration make their appearance in state trading. There are delays and lack of initiative in managers and other personnel who have no share in profits made by state trading agency. There is absence of desire to take risks; there are lengthy negotiations; there is vast scope for corruption; and there is indifferent approach on the part of managers and other personnel. Thus, state trading is likely to suffer from all the defects generally observed in public sector undertakings. This means while potentially state trading can play a very useful role in the economy in developing countries, there will have to be evolved professional cadres of devoted managers and other personnel.

A few other points may be noted against state trading. Bilateral trading generally conducted by state trading would discourage multilateral trading with the result that exports may not get the highest price ruling in world markets and imports may not be from the cheapest markets. This is so especially because in bilateral trade agreements by state trading, along with economic factors political considerations also play a vital part. State trading eliminates competition and therefore, may give rise to monopoly in respect of vital goods and services handled by state trading; this might result in state trading making huge monopoly profits not justified by economic considerations. Further, state trading may find entry difficult in markets of countries which believe in capitalist economic philosophy. Thus, differences of political ideologies may deprive state trading of some major markets in the world.

State Trading Corporation of India (STC)

In India the State Trading Corporation (STC) was set up in May 1956 as a joint stock company. It had a paid-up capital of Rs. 1 crore wholly subscribed by the central government. Its share capital later rose to Rs. 7 crores. The STC has taken over certain international trading activities such as import of foodgrains, fertilisers, coal and steel, East African cotton and exports of short staple cotton, and products of cottage industries. The STC also sponsors negotiations on behalf of private importers and exporters.

Objectives of the STC of India: The main objectives of the STC of India are: (i) To organise and undertake trade with socialist countries; (ii) To render assistance to specialised export agencies like Handicraft and Handloom corporation by way of financial help and organisational advice; (iii) To promote exports of traditional items and also to introduce non-traditional items in world markets; (iv) To locate new markets of Indian products; (v) To organise production to meet export demand; (vi) To help private units in overcoming difficulties of procuring raw materials and other essential items; (vii) To render assistance to small-scale sector in exporting its products through sales promotion activities, attractive packaging and by providing credit facilities.

In the case of imports, the functions of the STC of India are as follows: (i) To ensure to have special trade agreements with other countries, adequate supply at the right time and to arrange for their proper distribution; (ii) To undertake import of commodities where bulk purchases would be advantageous; (iii) To undertake import of items where there can be high speculation and having a high margin of profit and to distribute them at fair prices; (iv) To undertake internal trade in certain items like imported cars as well as to undertake price support and buffer-stock operations in order to stabilise domestic prices of essential consumer goods.

It is said that since India has accepted a mixed type of economy, foreign trade by private traders should have a place in the economy; complete monopoly by the STC would make the organisation lethargic; there would be excessive bureaucracy in STC as private profit motive and private initiative are absent; many capitalist countries would like to trade with private traders in India and not through the STC and this would adversely affect international trade with capitalist countries like the United States and Great Britain.

ANNEXURE

Foreign Trade Multiplier

Foreign trade multiplier is also known as the export multiplier. Foreign trade multiplier operates like the investment multiplier of J.M. Keynes.

When there is an increase in exports of a country (with export prices remaining the same as before which means terms of trade remaining the same as before), there is increase in incomes of persons associated with export industries in the concerned country. This increase in the level of income of exporters creates increase in demand for all types of domestically produced goods and services. By how much demand for domestically produced goods will increase because of increase in level of income on account of increase in exports will depend mainly on two factors, namely, marginal propensity of the people in the country to save, and secondly marginal propensity of the people to import goods from abroad. It may be said that as a rule, smaller these two marginal propensities, larger will be the value of foreign trade multiplier and *vice versa.*

Working of foreign trade multiplier can be explained as follows. Let us assume that there takes place increase in volume of exports of a country (terms of trade remaining the same). To being with exporters of the country will sell more of their products to foreign countries and in return they will receive more income than before. With a view to meet increasing demand for exports, more factors of production in the country will be employed to produce more goods. This will result in raising level of income of the owners of factors of production engaged in the production of exportable goods. They, in turn, will begin to demand more of domestically produced goods for consumption because of rise in the level of their income. This process will go on continuing depending on as we saw, two factors, namely, people's propensity to save and their marginal propensity to import. And thus, as a result of initial increase in exports of the country, national income will increase by the value of the multiplier. It may again be emphasised that value of foreign trade multiplier or export multiplier will depend upon value of marginal propensity of the people in the country to save and their marginal propensity to import, there being inverse relationship between the two marginal propensities and value of foreign trade multiplier or export multiplier.

The Foreign Trade Multiplier

In national income theory the concept of multiplier is used to estimate the magnitude of change in income. It is defined as the ratio of change in income to the corresponding given change in expenditure. For example, if we write ΔI as the given change in investment expenditure and the resulting change in income as ΔY, then the multiplier denoted by k is given by

$$K = \Delta Y / \Delta I \quad \text{...(1)}$$

The word multiplier is used to signify that the change in income will be greater than the amount by which expenditure would initially change. The logic behind this is as follows: If for example one crore of investment expenditure is undertaken for building roads, initially it will increase the income only by the same amount as one crore would be given away as wages to the workers. (For simplicity we ignore the raw material cost). These workers would then spend the wages on various goods and services. This is induced rise in consumption expenditure. When output expands to meet this extra demand, employment and, hence, income will rise and industries affected thereby. When newly employed workers in the industries spend their income, output and employment will rise further, and more income will then be generated, more expenditure induced.

However, this process won't continue forever. This is because marginal propensity being less than one, consumption will increase with increase in income, but less than proportionately. Hence, every successive increment in income is smaller than the earlier one. This can be shown with the help of the following example.

Example: If expenditure increases by Rs. 1 crore with mpc of say 0.75, the first round of expenditure by those who earn rupees one crore of new income is Rs. 75 lakhs. Those who receive this income again spend 75% of it, which means Rs. 56.25 lakhs of new expenditure. This in turn gives rise to Rs. 42.19 lakhs of new expenditure and so on. However, note that at each step the increment is declining. This expenditure series will generate a convergent geometric series, whose sum will give the value of the multiplier, i.e.,

$$1 + 0.75 + 0.75*0.75 + 0.75*0.75*0.75... = 1/(1-0.75) = 4.$$

Thus the flow of investment expenditure of rupees one crore on road construction generates a series of income stream with each person, who receives a new flow of income, spending 75% of the new income and saving 25% UNTILL NATIONAL INCOME RISES BY Rs. 4 crore. In this case the multiplier is 4.

The Formal Derivation of the Multiplier for a Small Open Economy

When we consider an open economy the concept of multiplier gets slightly modified. This is because we have an additional autonomous component of exports and additional goods (imports) to spend on. Thus, national income becomes the sum of consumption, investment demand (for simplicity we are assuming that government does not spend anything) and Net Exports.

$$\begin{aligned} Y &= C + I + NX \\ &= cY + I + NX \\ &= I + cY + (X - mY) \qquad \text{...(2)} \end{aligned}$$

Investment is assumed to be autonomous, i.e., independent of the level of national income. The consumption expenditure that depends on the level of income is given by the marginal propensity to consume multiplied by the level of income, cY. As mentioned earlier part of the national income is also spent on imports, which is a leakage from the economy. This is given by mY, where m is marginal propensity to import. Exports primarily depend on Foreign Income and therefore can be treated as autonomous. Thus the equation 2 becomes:

$$Y = (I + X) + cY - mY$$

Substituting $A = I + X$

$$= A + (c-m)\,Y \qquad \text{...(3)}$$

Now suppose Y changes to Y' because of change in investment and exports. We can write the new equation as:

$$Y' = A' + (c-m)\,Y' \qquad \text{...(4)}$$

Subtracting 3 from 4, gives:

$$Y' - Y = (A' - A) + (c-m)(Y'-Y)$$

$$\Delta Y = \Delta A + (c-m)\,\Delta Y$$

$$\Delta Y\text{-}(c\text{-}m)\,\Delta Y = \Delta A$$

$$\Delta y\,(1-c+m) = \Delta A$$

$$\Delta Y = \Delta A/(1-c+m) \qquad \text{...(5)}$$

Equation 5 gives the formula for what is known as the "foreign trade multiplier." If we denote the foreign trade multiplier by 'k', then symbolically,

$$k = 1/\,(1-c+m)$$

As mentioned earlier any change in the autonomous expenditure, A, is going to bring about change in the equilibrium level of income by generating series of income and hence series of expenditure.

Note that higher the value of 'c,' higher will be the value of multiplier. Exactly opposite is true for 'm.' A higher value of 'm' will reduce the multiplier effect. This is quite obvious as 'm' signifies the increase in expenditure on imports for an increase in income. Hence a higher value of m signifies greater proportion of income spent on imports and therefore greater leakage from the economy.

Criticism of the Concept of Foreign Trade (Export) Multiplier

In the first place, the analysis or exposition of the concept of foreign trade multiplier is based on the assumption that both exports and investment are independent of changes in the level of national income. But in fact, this is not so. A rise or increase in a country's exports does not always lead to increase in national income. On the other hand, certain imports, say of capital goods, have the effect of bringing about increase in national income.

The second point of criticism is that foreign trade multiplier is assumed to be an instantaneous process without any time lags. This assumption is highly unrealistic.

In the third place, the analysis is applicable to a two-country model. In fact, there are more than two countries and that makes it difficult to analyse and interpret accurately repercussions of increase in exports of a country.

With all the above shortcomings, the concept of foreign trade (export) multiplier is a useful tool of economic analysis and is of great use in formulating foreign trade policy measures.

SECTION IV

THE WORLD ECONOMY

19 INTERNATIONAL COOPERATION

CHAPTER

Structure:

19.1 Importance of International Cooperation

19.2 Growth of International Cooperation

19.3 Marshall Aid Plan

19.4 Colombo Plan

19.5 Other Regional Economic Associations

19.6 New World Economic Order

19.7 Report of the Brandt Commission

19.8 Cofrontation between North and South

19.1 IMPORTANCE OF INTERNATIONAL COOPERATION

Unlike in the previous centuries, international cooperation has become a vital matter affecting the lives of all peoples in all the countries of the world. During the 20th century and especially after World War II, distance has been practically annihilated so that it is now possible to reach any place in the world within a day. Consequently, any significant development in any part of the world produces almost immediate repercussions in all other countries of the world. Thus, failure of crop in the United States might mean starvation and death to millions of people in Asia and Africa and war in far-off North Korea in 1950 sent price level in India shooting up; a new drug discovered by scientists in the United States or England might save lives of lakhs of children in the remotest villages in India; rise in crude oil prices in the Middle East countries upset balance of payments position of practically all the countries and sent prices in those countries skyrocketing; and nuclear war at any time hereafter would mean complete annihilation of entire mankind and in fact of all the animal world.

There are certain problems which in the 20th century, the entire humanity, irrespective of their nationality is facing. The problems of disarmament, nuclear proliferation, pollution, inflation, population control, control of epidemics and of new disease like Aids, world food supply, soil erosion and river water management, environmental problems, air-travel and sharing of radio wavelengths, fixing maritime boundaries, problems of international balance of payments, poverty in the Third World, scientific and technological research, conflict between North and South and between whites and blacks, problem of international drug-trafficking, are all problems which can be successfully tackled only on international or global basis. In fact, different countries of the world have come so close to one another that any talk by any county living in isolation and solving satisfactorily its own problems is theoretically and practically absurd. The shrinkage of the world and annihilation of distance have reduced the world community into a close-knit family. This means that most of the problems will have to be tackled at the international or global level as they cannot be solved at the national level alone. Without the cooperation of other nations, no nation will be in a position to solve the above problems confronting practically every nation. This, in brief, will explain the importance and in fact inevitability of international cooperation in the second half of the 20th century as also in future.

19.2 GROWTH OF INTERNATIONAL COOPERATION

It may be said that international cooperation began in the real sense of the term in the 19th century after the revolution in transport and communication in the western countries and especially after the opening of the Suez Canal in 1969. Various nations started cooperating in matters of postal services, in respect of sending communications by telegrams, in laying cables at the bottom of oceans and later on the 20th century in sharing radio wavelength, etc. Some sort of international political, economic and socio-cultural cooperation may be said to have taken a forward step with the establishment of the League of Nations after the end of World War I and establishment of various affiliates of that international organisation, namely, the International Labour Organisation (the I.LO) established at about this time which started laying down norms and conventions and making various recommendations in regard to labour problems after discussions with member-countries. The member-stages generally accepted those conventions and recommendations and tried to give effect to them.

But international cooperation may be said to have progressed in a very significant way only after the end of World War II. World War II (1939-45) had resulted in coordinated efforts among nations in their war-efforts, in coordination of supplies of war materials and other commodities, mobilisation of manpower and other resources, and above all in sharing of war sacrifices. This had naturally taught most countries lessons in international cooperation to achieve some common objectives.

19.3 MARSHALL AID PLAN

World War II left the West European countries almost completely devastated. It had also resulted in tremendous increase in industrial productive powers of the United States which, therefore, was seeking suitable markets for its goods of all kinds produced on a gigantic sale. Bringing about economic rehabilitation of Europe by mutual economic cooperation between the United States and West European countries was therefore thought to be in the interest of both the parties. The germ of idea of Marshall Plan was laid in 1947 when George Marshall (then secretary of state of the United States) said in a speech: "Europe's requirements for the next three or four years of foreign food and other essential products, principally from America, are so much greater than her present ability to pay that she must have substantial additional help to face economic, social and political deterioration of a very great character. Before the United States' Government could proceed much further in its efforts to alleviate the situation and help start the European world on its way to recovery, there must be some agreement among the countries of Europe as to the requirements of the situation and the part these countries themselves would take in order to give proper effect to whatever action might be undertaken by the Government. The initiative must come from Europe. The programme should be a joint one, agreed to by a number, if not all of the Europeans nations."

As the initiative in regard to Marshall Aid Programme was expected by the United States from the European countries, a conference of 16 European nations was held in Paris in July-September 1947. A programme was chalked out which aimed at (i) increasing production by each participating country by bringing foodgrains production back to the pre-war level, coal output to one-third above pre-war level; electricity output two-third above pre-war level; steel about two-thirds of the pre-war level; (ii) creating and maintaining internal financial stability; (iii) rendering maximum mutual help between the participating countries; and (iv) solving the problems of European trade deficit with the United States.

It was the greatest effort so far in international cooperation during peace time. It may be said to be a sort of international planning in some respects between the United States and West European countries. It helped on the one hand quick and fairly successful rehabilitation of the war-shattered economies of West European countries and, on the other hand, helped the United States to maintain its level of employment and output at the same level that was developed during World War II because of the availability of West European markets. Prosperous Europe would mean prosperous United States because of mounting demand for American goods and services. The gains of international cooperation were strikingly visible to all.

Thus, after World War II problems of reconstruction and development of international trade confronted the world. Attention therefore, came to be given to the need for laying the foundation of a new world order on the basis of sound structure of international cooperation.

19.4 COLOMBO PLAN

The Commonwealth structure underwent a radical change after India, Pakistan and Ceylon, formerly part of the British Commonwealth, became independent. The first Commonwealth Conference held in 1950 decided that one of the most important problems of the former Commonwealth countries was to bring about cooperative effort to aid Asian member countries in their post-war recovery and long-term economic development.

Initially the Colombo Plan was a purely Common Plan for cooperative planning and mutual assistance among members of the Commonwealth, namely, India, Pakistan, Ceylon, Singapore, British Borneo and the Federation of Malaya and non-Asian Commonwealth members, namely, Britain, Canada, New Zealand and Australia, the developed countries promising substantial aid for economic development of backward countries of the Commonwealth.

With the passage of time, it was realised that if the objective of the Colombo Plan is to be realised, the plan should not be limited to economic development of only Commonwealth countries but that the objective should be economic development of the whole of South and South-East Asia. In response to this change in perspective, a number of non-Commonwealth countries, namely, Burma, Cambodia, Indonesia, Japan, Laos, Nepal, the Philippines, Thailand and Vietnam joined. The United States also came in as an important member providing financial and technical assistance.

There were political rivalries among some of the Commonwealth countries as in the case of India and Pakistan, and therefore results out of this international cooperation were not spectacular. And yet the fact remains that a number of countries with different historical and cultural background, natural resources and different levels of economic development can come together in an international cooperative effort to solve the problems of poverty in South and South-East Asian region.

19.5 OTHER REGIONAL ECONOMIC ASSOCIATIONS

After the end of World War II a number of developing countries in Asia, Africa and Latin America became independent. They were all economically backward. Many of these newly independent countries formed regional blocks or associations for mutual cooperation for bringing about rapid economic development by exploiting their vast natural and human resources.

There is, for example, Latin American Free Trade Association (LAFTA), the Central American Common Market (CACM), the East African Community (EAC) and so on.

A number of developed countries have formed consortiums (like the Aid India Club) with the aim of helping developing countries like India, not only on bilateral but on multilateral basis also.

Not to be outdone by the capitalist countries of the West, the Soviet Union has also entered into agreements with developing countries of Asia, Africa and Latin America with a view to help them in the shape of financial and technical assistance.

If during 1950s and 1960, it was generally believed that international cooperation between developed and developing countries is necessary to bring about economic development of developing countries, it is now being increasingly realised that international cooperation among developing countries themselves can also go a long way in helping their development. Developing countries are at different levels of development as a consequence of their efforts at development during four decades. This cooperation among developing countries is also increasing because of two factors. There is a certain amount of disenchantment among developed countries that their financial and technical assistance for about two or three decades could not produce the desired impact because of lack of adequate efforts on the part of aid-receiving developing countries; and secondly, developing countries themselves have realised that it is no use depending upon developed countries to any great extent and they must cooperate among themselves to bring about their rapid economic development. The developing countries have been trying to obtain remunerative prices for their primary products like tea, coffee, tobacco, sugar, oil-seeds, rubber, leather, etc. through a specially created international agency, namely, the United Nations Conference on Trade and Development (the UNCTAD).

Many Asian countries are cooperating among themselves for specific projects which are mutually advantageous such as Asian Highway, Mckoyang River Valley Project and so on. The progress may be slow because of traditional rivalries among some of the Asian countries, lack of experience in the sphere of international cooperation, policy of divide and rule still followed by former imperial powers and lack of resources. But any way progress is being made in this, though slowly.

19.6 NEW WORLD ECONOMIC ORDER

Much of the debate on the New Economic Order for the world and the future world economy focuses attention on the economic development of developing or poor countries and what developed or rich countries should do to help this process of economic development of backward countries. Recently developed and developing countries are referred to as 'North' and 'South', respectively, and the debate is going on as to what the North should do to help the South.

Main Points of North-South Dialogue

The developed countries have tended to see the problems of economic development of developing countries in practical terms to improve the living conditions of the poor people in developing countries.

On the other hand, government of the poor or developing countries, according to the North, are insisting that "the discussion should focus on their demands for a new international economic order."

These demands of developing countries are set out in the Charter of Economic Rights and Duties of States adopted by the General Assembly of the United Nations in December 1974.

"In brief, the developing countries argue that they are at a disadvantage under the international economic order established after World War II, the main instruments of which are the General Agreement on Tariffs and Trade (GATT), the International Monetary Fund (IMF) and the International Bank for Reconstruction and Development (World Bank). Over the past two decades, they have called for massive transfers of resources, both directly on a government-to-government basis and indirectly through international commodity agreements."

The developing countries are emphasising that there should be a structural reform — a blend of political, economic and institutional changes. The developing countries are putting forward proposals that would change "the operation of the international system of trade and payments." Their proposals include an integrated programme for commodities to raise and stabilise commodity prices, commitments by developed countries to lower barriers to export from developing countries and to pursue policies to adjust their industrial structures to make room for such exports from developing countries, changes in international monetary system which would automatically provide developing countries with an expanding supply of international means of payment. 'a code of conduct' for multinational enterprise which would give the developing countries closer control of foreign investments, and finally, the commitments of industrial countries to targets for progressive industrialisation of developing countries, including transfer of technology on generous terms to developing countries.

19.7 REPORT OF THE BRANDT COMMISSION

A number of committees and commissions have discussed the problems of flow of resources from developed to developing countries, as for example the Pearson Commission.

In early 1980, the report of the Independent Commission on International Development Issues, under the chairmanship of Willy Brandt, was published. The Brandt Commission hoped to find a new approach without worsening the atmosphere of confrontation from which it was felt that the North-South dialogue had suffered in the past. The Brandt Commission Report assembled rather than improved the proposals that had been aired over the last decade or so. The Report served to focus political attention on the legitimate grievances of developing countries; but in giving new impetus to some of the proposals for a new international order, "it ignored for all intents and purposes the debate that was taking place over the issue during 1970s."

The main features of the Brandt Commission Report may be summarised as follows:

(1) There is a belief that the existing international economic order operates in favour of rich countries and in a way that frustrates and impedes the process of economic development of poor countries.

(2) There is a persistent belief in the efficiency and benevolence of governmental central planning and direction as the engine for economic development of countries. Developing countries have deep faith in central economic planning as the only effective instrument of rapid economic development.

(3) There is in developing countries a pervasive mistrust in the working of market mechanism or working freely of the forces of demand and supply; there is a belief that market mechanism will almost automatically produce wrong results. This belief implies also a belief in developing countries that competition is in itself harmful and should be replaced wherever possible by regulations. Indeed, there is a deep distrust of private enterprise, and collective institutions are preferred to individual ventures which are being worked for personal profit. There is a general distrust in the proposition that private enterprise could be the most efficient generator of economic growth and development of developing countries.

(4) There is a strong belief that establishment of new international institutions would contribute to the solution of the various problems faced at present by developing countries.

All these themes revolve around the central proposition that a necessary requirement for economic development in the Third World is a massive transfer of resources, financial, and technical, from rich countries to poor ones and that such transfers would promote sustained economic development and thus alleviate poverty in the Third World.

The Report states that the transfers suggested can be achieved in two ways: (i) First, there should be substantial increase in the amount of official aid on government-to-government basis or through international financial institutions, and there should be substantial modifications and relaxations of the rules and conditions regarding disbursement of funds by the World Bank and the IMF. (ii) There should be intervention by governments in the normal process of international trade designed to ensure that the developing countries both obtain a greater share of trade and receive more in payment than they would do in unregulated competition.

19.8 CONFRONTATION BETWEEN NORTH AND SOUTH

During 1950s and 1960s and in fact even during the major part of 1970s, a substantial amount of foreign assistance flowed into developing countries from developed countries and much of that was on government-to-government basis and through international financial institutions such as the World Bank and the IMF.

Since late 1970s there has however been a radical change in the attitude and approach of developed countries to the foreign aid they are to give to developing countries. The oil crisis of early 1970s, coming to power of conservative parties in the United States, the United Kingdom and in some other Western countries, disappointment over the results achieved in developing countries with the aid of foreign assistance etc. have brought about a radical change in the attitude of developed countries in respect of financial assistance they are to give on government-to-government basis and also by international financial institutions.

The rising inflation and unemployment in Western countries (around 8 to 10 of the total labour force) and coming to power in some of those countries of conservative governments resulted in reduction of the role of government in the sphere of economic activities of the community, lowering of tax rates to induce people to save and invest more in private sector industries, reducing government expenditure, especially on social welfare schemes, and increasing emphasis on private initiative, competition and private profit motive. Naturally, the governments of the United States and of United Kingdom on ideological and practical grounds want to cut down financial assistance, especially financial assistance at concessional rate of interest to developing countries. The two governments started questioning the role of World Bank and the IMF and other international financial institutions in bringing about economic development of poor countries. These governments are critical that financial assistance from them has only made developing countries neglect mobilization of domestic resources effectively. Those Governments are critical that financial assistance from developed countries is being used in India for the expansion of the public sector enterprises and spreading the doctrine of socialism. The Governments of the USA and the UK are, therefore, trying to reduce concessional loans to developing countries; they are bringing pressure on the World Bank and the IMF to do the same; they have been refusing trade and other concessions and are emphasising that developing countries like India should take loans from commercial banks in developed countries at market rates of interest and also allow foreign private capital increasing role in developing countries by liberalising their trade and other policies and by keeping their doors open to private foreign capital, instead of depending on concessional loans from Western countries. Naturally, this will mean paying higher rate of interest on foreign loans and increasing burden of debt-servicing charges. The flow of foreign assistance which was targeted at 1% of GNP of developed countries declined to around 0.4% and is likely to go down still further.

Thus, almost on every issue concerning the new international economic order — foreign aid, international trade, commodity agreements, enlarging resources of the World Bank and the IMF, role of government in the sphere of economic activities and of private sector and so on, the North and the South appear at present to be taking opposing stand which has been resulting in a sort of confrontation between the North and the South.

CHAPTER 20

INTERNATIONAL BANK FOR RECONSTRUCTION AND DEVELOPMENT (IBRD or the World Bank)

Structure:

20.1 OBJECTIVES OF THE WORLD BANK

The International Bank for Reconstruction and Development (the IBRD or the World Bank) came to be established by the International Economic Conference at Bretton Woods in July 1944. The World Bank started functioning from June 1946.

The objectives of the World Bank set forth in the Bretton Woods Agreements are as follows:

(1) To render assistance in the reconstruction and development of member-countries by facilitating investment of capital for productive purposes and help restoration of economies from enormous destruction brought about by the World War II (1939-45) (Reconstruction), and also to provide encouragement to the development of productive resources of less developed countries (hence the word 'Development' in the full title of the World Bank).

(2) To promote private foreign investment by means such as participation in loans or guarantee for loans made by private investors, as also to supplement private investment by its own (World Bank's) loans or finances.

(3) To promote long-term balanced growth of international trade and help achieve equilibrium in balance of payments position of member-countries by encouraging international investments for the development of productive resources and thereby rendering assistance in raising productivity, and standard of living of people in the member-countries.

(4) To make arrangements for loans or guarantees in respect of international loans so that large and small useful projects are rendered assistance.

The World Bank

The World Bank works as a partner in strengthening economies and expanding markets to improve the quality of life for people everywhere, especially the poorest. Unlike aid programs, the Bank doesn't make grants. The Bank lends money to developing countries — and the loans are repaid. Developing countries borrow from the Bank because they need capital, technical assistance, and policy advice.

Membership

The World Bank is an open partnership between the Bank's 180 member countries. The Bank is comparable to a global cooperative, which is owned by member countries. The size of a country's shareholding is determined by the size of the country's economy relative to the world economy. Together, the largest industrial countries (the Group of Seven or G-7)[1] have about 45 per cent of the shares in the World Bank — and they carry great weight in international economic affairs generally. Therefore, it is true that the rich countries have a good deal of influence over the Bank's policies and practices. The United States has the largest shareholding — about 17 per cent, which gives the United States the power to veto any changes in the Bank's capital base and Articles of Agreement (85 per cent of the shares are needed to effect such changes).

However, virtually all other matters, including the approval of loans, are decided by a majority of the votes cast by all members of the Bank. The Bank's Board of Executive Directors, which is resident at the Bank's headquarters in Washington, DC, represents all the members. Policies and practices

1. The G-7 members are Canada, France, Germany, Italy, Japan, the United Kingdom and the United States.

are regularly and frequently debated and decided upon by the Board, so every member's voice is heard. In fact, developing countries together have about half the votes in the Bank. Voting is generally rare because consensus is the preferred way of making decisions.

Only developing countries can borrow from the Bank. However, all members, including the richer nations, gain from economic growth in developing countries. A world increasingly divided between rich and poor is in no one's interest. The world certainly would benefit from increased trade and investment, higher incomes, fewer social tensions, better health and education, and environmental protection. The Bank's member countries — particularly the industrial countries — also benefit from procurement opportunities derived from World Bank financed projects.

Management

A resident Board of Executive Directors represents members at the Bank's headquarters in Washington, DC. The Board usually meets several times a week and oversees the Bank's business. A Board committee oversees regular audits of the Bank's work. The Board itself is answerable to a Board of Governors made up primarily of Finance Ministers and heads of Central Banks from member countries. The Governors meet once a year. The Bank also has an independent Operations Evaluation Department, which reviews Bank-financed projects and reports directly to the Board on the results of these evaluations.

20.2 CAPITAL STRUCTURE OF THE WORLD BANK

The World Bank commenced with an authorised capital of US dollars 10 billion, divided into 1,00,000 shares of US dollars 100,000 each. Of this authorised capital, US dollars, 9,400 million were actually subscribed.

As in June 1985, the authorised capital stock of the World Bank comprises of 7,16,500 authorised shares of the par value of SDR 1,00,000 each. Of those 58,154 had been subscribed. Thus, the subscribed capital of the World Bank is SDR 51,315 each. Ten per cent of the subscribed capital has been called and paid by member-countries. The remaining 90 per cent of the authorised capital is subject to call when the World Bank requires it to meet demand for loans or for guaranteeing loans to member-countries.

The World Bank's funding strategy or strategy for raising financial resources follow the four basic objectives: (1) To ensure availability of funds to the World Bank (by maintaining unutilised access of funds in markets in which the World Bank borrows); (2) To minimise the effective cost of loans to borrowers (through currency mix of the Bank's borrowings); (3) To have control over volatility in net income and overall loan charges (for which the Bank started in 1982 variable lending rates system that uniformly adjusts interest charges applicable to all outstanding balance on all loans); (4) To provide appropriate degree of maturity transformation between Bank's borrowing and lending.

20.3 BORROWING AND LENDING ACTIVITIES OF THE WORLD BANK

The World Bank gives loans primarily from its own medium and long-term borrowings in the international capital markets and Currency Swap Agreements (CSA). Under the CSA, proceeds of a borrowing country are converted into a different currency and at the same time a forward exchange agreement is executed providing for a schedule of future exchanges of the two currencies in order to recover the currency converted.

The World Bank can also borrow under the Discount-Note Programme, by placing bonds and notes directly with governments of member-countries, with government agencies and their central banks. Also, the World Bank offers issues to investors and in public markets through investing banking firms, commercial banks and investment banks.

The total borrowing of the World Bank under its various schemes in the fiscal year 1984 amounted to US dollars 9.8 billion. Also, a substantial amount of the World Bank's resources accrue from the Bank's retained earnings and repayment of loans borrowed earlier from the World Bank.

Lending

There are two types of Bank lending. The first type is for developing countries that are able to pay near-market interest rates. The money for these loans comes from investors around the world. These investors buy bonds issued by the World Bank. The second type of loan goes to the poorest countries, which are usually not creditworthy in the international financial markets and are unable to pay near-market interest rates on the money they borrow. The World Bank, therefore, cannot issue bonds to raise money that would finance lending to these countries.

Lending to the poorest countries is done by a World Bank affiliate, the International Development Association (IDA). More than 30 member countries periodically contribute the money needed to finance "credits" to borrowers. IDA credits are free of interest, carry a low 0.75 per cent annual administrative charge, and are very long-term — 35 or 40 years including 10 years grace. Countries with per capita incomes of less than $ 925 (in 1996 dollars) are eligible for IDA credits. In practice, most IDA credits go to countries, which are much poorer than this. However, again, the credits are repaid. They are not grants. IDA lends an average of about $6 billion a year to the world's poorest countries.

Lending Operations of the World Bank

Following are the ways in which the World Bank gives loans to its member-countries: (i) By granting loans out of its own funds; (ii) By participating in loans out of funds raised in the market of a member-country or otherwise borrowed by the World Bank; and (iii) By providing guarantee in part or in full for loans made by private investors through the usual investment channels.

It is stipulated that the total amount of outstanding loans or guarantees provided by the World Bank should not exceed 100 per cent of the Bank's unimpaired subscribed capital, reserves and surplus.

The World Bank gives loans or its guarantees on the following conditions: (i) The World Bank is satisfied that in the prevailing market conditions, the borrower is unable to obtain loans under conditions which the Bank considers reasonable; (ii) The loans are for reconstruction or development (except in special circumstances); (iii) If the central bank of the member-country gives full guarantee for repayment of the principal, interest on loan and other related charges; (iv) The project for which the loan from the World Bank is being sought is recommended by a competent committee after a careful study in its written report; and (v) The borrower is in a position to meet the Bank's obligations.

The World Bank gives medium-term loans and long-term loans usually running up to the completion of the project for which the Bank has given the loan. Long-term loans are repayable over a period of 20 years or less, with a grace period of 5 years. It is observed that interest rate charged by the World

Bank is calculated in accordance with guidelines related to its (i.e., Bank's) cost of borrowing. And, therefore, the World Bank loans carry different rates of interest. There is in addition an annual commitment charge of 0.75 per cent per year on the outstanding balances.

The total World Bank lending during 1999-01 amounted to US dollars 20,507.5 million.

The Changing Pattern of World Bank Lending

It might be noted that since the World Bank started functioning in 1946, roughly for the first two decades, the World Bank's lending was concentrated heavily upon providing capital for infrastructure projects such as roads and railways, generation and distribution of electricity, telecommunication, major irrational projects, development of ports etc.

But since 1970 onwards, the World Bank's loans for infrastructural projects started declining relatively and emphasis of the World Bank's lending changed to financing of educational systems in developing countries, loans for establishing institutions for financing industrial investment and provision of technical assistance for the selection and appraisal of industrial projects and help in preparing agricultural projects.

The World Bank's present lending strategy has been laying more emphasis on investments directly affecting welfare of the poor sections of the community in developing countries by helping them to raise their productivity and level of housing. For this purpose, the World Bank has been providing loans for financing agricultural projects and rural development projects, education, nutrition programmes, family planning projects, projects for provision of drinking water, low-cost housing and drainage and sewage systems in developing countries.

The World Bank's Special Action Programme

The World Bank started its Special Action Programme (SAP) in 1983. The idea behind the SAP is to assist member-countries to adjust to current economic environment. The SAP has the following four elements: (i) Expansion in lending for high priority operations that support structural adjustments, policy changes, production for exports, fuller use of existing capacity and maintenance of vital infrastructure; (ii) Accelerated disbursement of loans under the existing and new investment commitments to ensure timely implementation of high-priority projects; (iii) Expanding of advisory services on formulation and implementation of appropriate policies such as reviews of state enterprises, studies to strengthen development-oriented capabilities, studies to increase mobilisation of domestic resources, study of incentives for export promotion and diversification, and exploration of ways to strengthen debt-management capabilities; and (iv) Enlisting efforts by other donors for rapid disbursement of assistance in support-programmes of the World Bank and the IMF.

World Bank and the Private Sector

One of the Bank's top priorities is to help stimulate the private sector. That's because the private sector is the main source of economic growth — of jobs and higher incomes. The Bank encourages the private sector by advocating stable economic policies, sound government finances, and open, honest, accountable, and consistent governance, and by offering guarantees. In addition, it supports many sectors in which private sector development is making rapid inroads — finance, power, telecommunications and information technology, oil and gas and industry.

The Articles of Agreement prohibit the Bank from lending directly to the private sector.

However, a Bank affiliate — the International Finance Corporation — exists expressly to invest in private sector enterprises without such a guarantee. The IFC invested more than $ 8 billion in fiscal 1997. It also helps governments privatize state-owned enterprises, raises private finance for ventures, and advises on legal and regulatory issues.

Although lending is a fundamental part of the World Bank's work, the Bank does a lot more than just lend money. The Bank also routinely includes technical assistance in projects. This might cover advice on issues such as the overall size of a country's budget and where the money should be allocated, or how to set up village health clinics, or what sort of equipment is needed to build a road. The Bank funds a few projects each year devoted exclusively to providing expert advice and training. In addition, the Bank's Economic Development Institute trains people from borrowing countries how to create and carry out development programs.

20.4 THE WORLD BANK'S OTHER ACTIVITIES

The World Bank's other activities include items such as training, technical assistance, inter-organisational cooperation, economic research and studies, evaluation operations and settlement of investment disputes among member-countries of the World Bank and the IMF.

The World Bank set up Staff College in 1958. It is known as the Economic Development Institute (EDI). The EDI is meant for training senior officials of developing countries. The training is in macro-economic planning, pricing and development policies, management of agricultural research, training in rural health care, industrial policy, railway management and so on.

The World Bank renders technical assistance which is an integral part of the World Bank's programme of activities. This technical assistance is concerned with feasibility studies, engineering designs, construction supervision, management training, and diagnostic and institutional studies.

The World Bank also serves as executing agency in the case of projects financed by the United Nations Development Programme (UNDP).

An important function of the World Bank concerns inter-organisational cooperation based on formal agreements such as cooperative programmes between the FAO, the UNESCO, the WHO, the UNCTAD, the GATT, the United Nations Environmental Programme, the ILO, the Asian Development Bank (the ADB), etc.

The World Bank sets aside roughly 3 per cent of its administrative budget for economic and social research. These research programmes started in 1971. About 165 research programmes have already been completed and about 180 were in progress in 1985. The World Bank also renders assistance to research programmes in developing member-countries.

The World Bank helps borrowers of the Bank in post-evaluation of the Bank-assisted projects through its Operation Evaluation Department.

The World Bank has also set up 'International Centre of Settlement of Investment Disputes' between member-countries. For example, the World Bank successfully solved the problem of river water dispute between India and Pakistan and the Suez Canal dispute between Egypt and the United Kingdom.

20.5 CRITICAL APPRAISAL OF THE WORLD BANK'S PERFORMANCE

There are a number of achievements to the credit of the World Bank.

The World War II (1939-45) had almost completely devastated economies of West European countries that were involved in the war. It might be said that the World Bank played a significant role in the reconstruction of war-devastated economies of West European countries.

After the reconstruction of West European countries was practically completed, the World Bank has been helping not only developed but developing countries for the development of infrastructure facilities, development of basic and heavy industries and also for raising efficiency and productivity of their workforce and thus indirectly helping to raise their standard of living.

Areawise the World Bank loans in the fiscal year 1984 were as follows: Latin America and Caribbean countries (31%); East Asian and Pacific countries (24.5%); and South Asian countries (8.6%).

On the sectoral basis, during the fiscal year 1984, the World Bank loans were as follows: Agriculture and rural development (21%); energy (22%); transport (18%); water supply and sewerage (5%); and education (4%).

With all the above achievements of the World Bank, criticism against the role of the World Bank is made on the following grounds:

(1) One charge is that the rate of interest charged by the World Bank is very high as also its commitment charges on undistributed balances. Though the World Bank does not charge higher interest rates arbitrarily, the fact remains that developing countries consider the interest rates charged by the World Bank pretty high.

(2) Another serious criticism against the World Bank is that it has generally failed to meet growing financial needs of developing countries, taking into account the total requirements of capital for their economic and social development. Though with a view to increase World Bank's lending to developing countries, it established the International Development Association (the IDA) in 1960, the World Bank has generally not been successful in raising productivity of labour-force in the those countries and their level of living. This becomes clear from the fact that in the fiscal year 1984 the World Bank loans to the poorest countries amounted to a mere 2.3 per cent of the total World Bank loans in that year.

(3) The World Bank's lending principle is faulty as it links the amount of its loans to repaying capacity of the borrowing country, instead of linking of loans to potentials for development. The above principle of lending is very harsh from the point of view of poor and low-income countries that need financial assistance on a large-scale to develop their vast latent natural and human resources. What the World Bank should take into consideration is the fact that repaying capacity is the result of utilisation of the World Bank loans, and therefore, the potentials for development and potential for future repayment capacity of the poor countries should be taken into account while granting loans to them.

(4) Since 1980 the World Bank has introduced 'Structural Adjustment Loans' (SAL). Loans under SAL are meant to help countries to reduce deficits in their balance of payments while maintaining the tempo of economic development and growth. The SAL funds are used to give loans for general imports excluding luxury and military imports.

The criticisms is that since the introduction of SAL in 1980, the terms of loans by the World Bank have become tighter. The borrowing countries under the SAL are required to adopt an action programme set up in a letter of development policies such as liberalisation of international trade policy, reform of national budgeting, of debt management, revision of price policies, effective planning of public investment and more efficient management of public sector enterprises, etc. The second tranche of SAL is released only after the critical review by the World Bank officials of the SAL financed programme which must satisfy the officials of the World Bank.

20.6 THE WORLD BANK AND INDIA

India is one of the founder-members of the World Bank. In that capacity, India held a permanent seat on its Board of Executive Directors for a number of years. That position was threatened when China applied for membership of the World Bank.

The World Bank has been rendering substantial assistance to India in her efforts at planned economic development. This the World Bank does by granting loans, rendering expert advice in various spheres, and training Indian personnel at the Economic Development Institute (which was established to train senior officials of member-developing countries).

The World Bank has a Chief Mission at New Delhi and it conducts on behalf of the World Bank monitoring and consultation in respect of Bank-aided projects in India.

It needs to be emphasised that since its establishment, India happens to be the largest recipient of the World Bank financial assistance. The Bank since 1949 was committed to 84 loans to India totalling US dollars 7274.7 million till June 1984. In 1984 India borrowed 1.7 billion US dollars from the World Bank, and 670 million US doors from the IDA and about 2 billion US dollars from commercial sources.

The World Bank has been rendering assistance to India in respect of projects such as development of ports, oil exploration including Bombay High, gas-power projects, coal, iron, aluminium, railway modernisation, fertiliser plants, technical assistance and industrial development finance.

It was at the instance of the World Bank that the Aid India Consortium of 12 developed countries was established and it has been helping India substantially by granting loans and other assistance. The World Bank helped India to solve the almost intractable problem of the Indus Water dispute with Pakistan.

Thus, India has received substantial financial and non-financial assistance from the World Bank for the development of industries, energy, transport, agriculture, etc.

But the financial assistance from the IDA is shrinking and India will be forced to borrow more from the World Bank with considerable reduction in concessional finance which India used to receive from the International Development Association (the IDA). This means India will be forced to borrow more and more from the World Bank and will have to entail heavier financial burden as the terms of lending in the case of the World Bank are much stringent and harsher than in the case of loans from the IDA which offers loans at concessional rates of interest.

20.7 EVALUATION OF THE BANK'S LENDING OPERATIONS

Over the last ten years, the environment for the Bank's clients has changed dramatically. While official development assistance has declined, private capital flows have surged. However, they have been concentrated in a comparatively small number of countries. At the same time the role of civil society and that of the private sector have become more pronounced, governments have become more accountable for their actions, and all the players rely on the new capacity to share knowledge rapidly because of dramatic changes in technology. Considering these developments, the Bank has introduced new approaches to ensure that lending and advice the Bank provides is what the clients really need. One consequence is the reform process encapsulated in the Strategic Compact, which has the specific objective of making the Bank the most effective institution in the world in the fight against poverty. The Bank aims to reach this goal through a clearly defined business plan that will result in a higher level of service and greater volume of products to the clients by increasing the development effectiveness in four priority and related areas: refuelling current business activities; refocusing the development agenda; retooling the Bank's knowledge base and revamping institutional priorities. So the activities are more effective and show better development results for the clients, the portfolio of Bank-financed projects and programs are being improved. Projects at risk of not meeting their development objectives are being amended, redesigned, or refined to improve performance. In addition, a sample of new projects entering the portfolio is assessed for quality so that improvements can be initiated where necessary.

Before a project can be considered successful, it must have at least a 10 per cent rate of economic return. This rate is far higher than the minimum demanded by many bilateral donors, which require that their investments in development projects show a rate of economic return of half that amount — between 5 per cent and 6 per cent. Economic development and risk are often two sides of the same coin. If investments to raise living standards in developing countries were always free of problems, there would be little need for a World Bank or for other national and international development agencies. Indeed, the projects that are most needed often involve higher risks because they break new ground. Another inevitable source of uncertainty is that the Bank lends for the long-term; its loans are disbursed to borrowers over as many as 40 years.

In addition to the above evaluation criteria, all lending for projects is now evaluated after the Bank finishes its loan disbursements. This evaluation aims to enhance the Bank's internal and external accountability and "transparency." It also aims to provide a systematic, objective, and accessible record of accomplishment and supplies lessons from experience. Results and recommendations are reported to the Bank's Executive Directors and fed back into the design and implementation of policies and lending operations.

Economic Reform Programs

World Bank programs are designed to help the poor. The Bank has lent almost $400 billion since it started more than 40 years ago. The economic shocks of the 1970s and early 1980s-high interest rates, low commodity prices, and sluggish growth in the world economy hit many developing countries hard. Countries needed to make reforms in the way they ran their economies to encourage long-term and sustainable development: not spending more than a country can afford; ensuring that policy benefits the whole country rather than the elite; investing where scarce resources have most impact — for example, in basic education and health instead of excessive military spending; and in encouraging a productive private sector.

The Bank believes that far from being the victims of reforms, the poor suffer most when countries don't reform. What benefits the poor the most is rapid and broad-based growth. This comes from having sound macroeconomic policies and a strategy that favours investment in basic human capital — primary health care and universal primary education. Reform is not unique to developing countries. The long struggle to reduce the United States' budget deficit, a struggle mirrored in many other industrial countries, is also a form of economic reform or structural adjustment. Such changes can be painful. In the short-term, unemployment may rise. Workers in loss-making state enterprises may lose their jobs. Civil servants may be made redundant as a consequence of cuts in government spending. Groups of poor people are also particularly vulnerable, for instance, poor pregnant women and nursing mothers, young children and poor elderly people. Therefore, not surprisingly, Bank support for these developing countries carrying out structural reforms generally includes social safety nets and other measures to ease the temporary pain that poor people may experience. The Bank helps government's finance unemployment compensation, job creation schemes, and retraining programs. In addition, it helps government's target health and nutrition spending on the neediest people and also finances investments that are specifically designed to attack deep-seated poverty.

World Bank's Accountability

The Bank publishes a huge amount of information and is publicly accountable to the member countries. The sharing of information is essential for effective and sustainable development: it stimulates debate and broadens understanding of development issues, and it facilitates coordination among the many parties involved in development. It serves to strengthen public support for efforts to improve the lives of people in developing countries. The Bank believes that the quality of the work is enhanced when staff and government officials consult and share information with participants in development programs. In 1993, the Bank substantially expanded the range of documents prepared for operational purposes that are made available to the public, including a new Project Information Document (PID), which describes projects at the early stages of development. The Bank established a Public Information Centre, which anyone can visit or access on-line through the World Wide Web. The Bank's website, which helps the public obtain Bank documents with maximum ease. The Bank also issues about 500 research, policy, and other publications a year (including a detailed Annual Report) and produces numerous newsletters, fact sheets, press releases, and video and audio materials.

Nevertheless, there are, some constraints, on the Bank's openness. The Bank cannot, for example divulge information supplied by members in confidence, but this is now a very small portion of the material. To help get its material out and explain its work, the Bank has many direct links with public audiences. The Bank has extensive connections with non-governmental organizations ranging from "think tanks" to groups working in the field. Bank staff are encouraged to be open in their outside contacts. They frequently speak at conferences, address citizen's groups, and appear on radio and television. The Bank is also in contact with hundreds of journalists around the world through personal meetings, publications, telephone conversations, fax communications, and frequent press conferences. At the same time, its members, who in turn report to their parliaments and publics, hold the Bank's staff and management directly accountable.

20.8 WORLD BANK AND INDIA

As of October 2001, India is the World Bank's largest single borrower, with cumulative lending of more than US$56 billion in combined market-based loans from the International Bank for Reconstruction and Development (IBRD) and development credits from the International Development Association

(IDA), the World Bank affiliate that provides interest-free loans to economies with low per-capita incomes. Since 1950, the Bank has extended assistance to India for 424 projects, roughly equal in number from IBRD and IDA. Loans from the IBRD total approximately US$ 28.8 billion and credits from IDA total US$ 27.5 billion equivalent.

The Bank's Board of Executive Directors approved the 2001-2004 India Country Assistance Strategy in 2001.

The Bank's strategy provides the framework for analytical work, lending operations, and dialogue with other groups focused on India's development goals. The basic elements of this framework are as follows:

(1) **Strengthening the Enabling Environment for Development and Growth** involves the complementary tasks of improving government effectiveness and enabling the private sector to fully contribute to economic development.

Improving government effectiveness. There is a widespread consensus with India that fiscal reforms need to be accompanied by improvements in governance to tackle endemic problems such as inefficiency, corruption, and poor budgetary management. Because of strong partnerships and in-depth engagement, the World Bank can be most effective in those states where it has been most active. The Bank's structural adjustment loans can help to promote financial stability while states undertake reforms. Equally important, the Bank is integrating cross-cutting governance reforms into the design of lending operations and dialogue in sectors such as health, education, infrastructure and economic management. This type of sectoral support is aimed at improving the delivery of public services and strengthening government effectiveness.

Promoting private sector-led growth.

Four main goals have been set out:

(a) supporting the provision of adequate infrastructure — both through an expanded role for the private sector and through better public sector management and increased funding;

(b) accelerating rural growth through agricultural deregulation and expanded provision of rural infrastructure;

(c) improving competitiveness in industry and services, through dialogue at the national level on needed reforms, work on improving the investment climate at the state level, and support for restructuring and growth of internationally competitive firms from International Finance Corporation, the World Bank's private sector arm; and

(d) promoting financial sector development through selective interventions.

(2) **Supporting Pro-poor Interventions** is a central part of India's poverty reduction strategy to ensure that opportunities for improved livelihood are widely available across the entire spectrum of society, that the security of these livelihoods is promoted and that the constraints are removed that inhibit and exclude people from participating in and sharing the benefits of development.

Expanding Health and Education for All. The World Bank Group's strong support for the social sectors continues with a special focus on promoting gender equity. In education, the successful Bank-Government of India partnership in the District Primary Education Program is approaching a new phase. The Government has decided to replace the District Primary Education Program, which focuses on increased access to quality education for children in low literacy districts, with an expanded Education for All program. As a result, World Bank support is likely to expand from lower primary to include upper primary.

The Bank Group's health work focuses on improving health outcomes such as reduction of morbidity and mortality for infants and children, women and the general adult population. Bank assistance will be to improve health, population and nutrition policies, consolidate disease control efforts and strengthen public health capacity, upgrade health systems and promote interventions which improve health-related behaviour. With a focus on communicable and non-communicable diseases, this assistance increasingly builds capacity at the state level, pays greater attention to environmental health issues — such as air and water pollution, and focuses on the relative strengths of government, local communities, NGOs and the private sector.

Pro-poor rural development. The Bank's rural projects are designed not only to develop rural infrastructure, but to directly attack rural poverty, enhance social protection, and protect the natural resource base for the approximately 75 per cent of India's poor who live in rural areas. Interventions in this area are designed to be community-based, to target vulnerable groups (women, scheduled castes and tribes, the landless) and to support decentralization to and empowerment at the local level.

Major* Sectors in Current World Bank Lending to India
Lending totalled US$ 13,294 million as of October 2001 (US million)

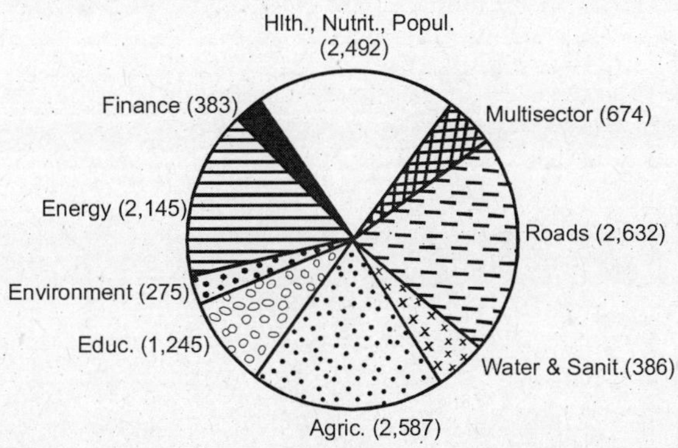

**Note:* Sum of sector components do not equal total lending as smaller lending for areas such as telecommunications and economic policy are not included.

** Note:* Sum of sector components do not equal total lending as smaller lending for areas such as telecommunicatons and economic policy are not included.

Lending by Volume in Millions of US Dollars – India

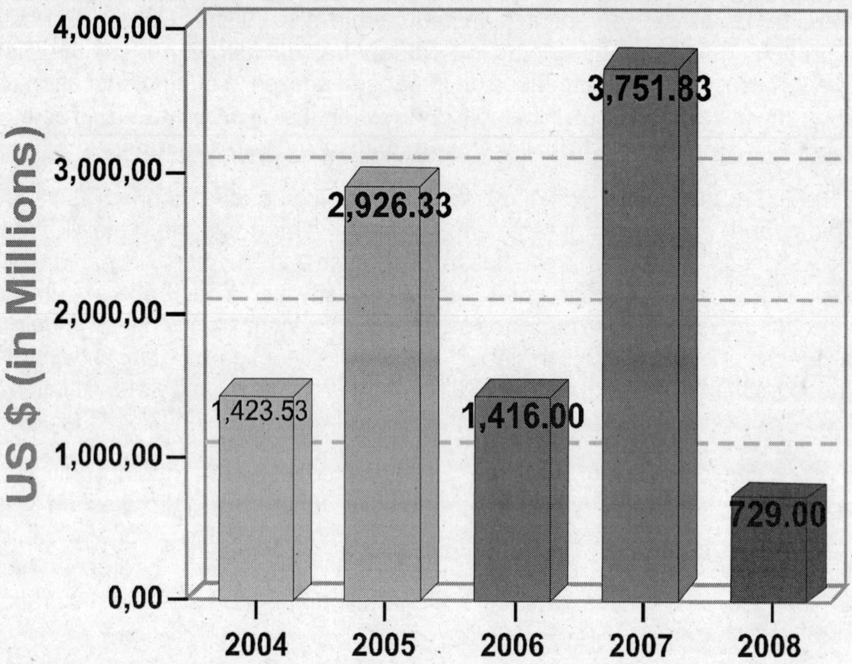

For the current Fiscal Year the chart shows total commitment amount to date. Data update frequency : Monthly

Lending by Volume in Number of Projects – India

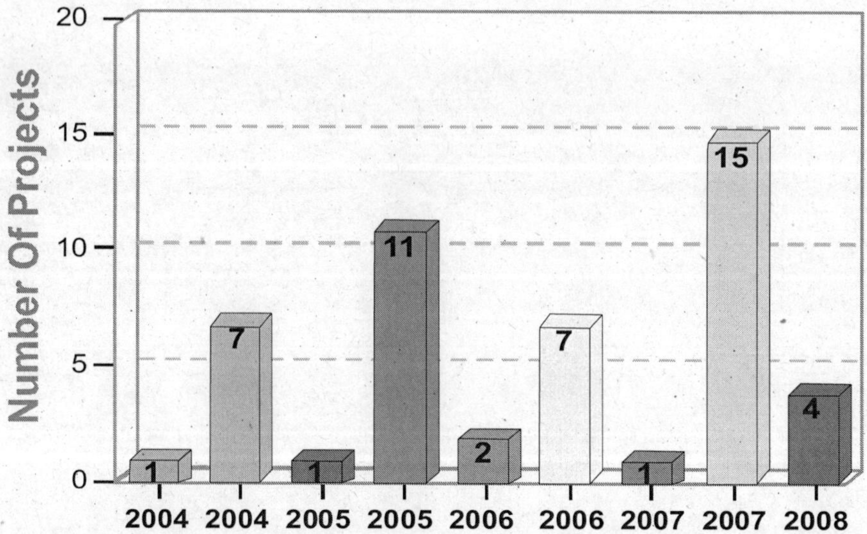

For the current Fiscal Year the chart shows the number of approved projects to date. Data update frequency : monthly

Current Lending by Sector in Millions of US Dollars approved in Current Fiscal Year* — India

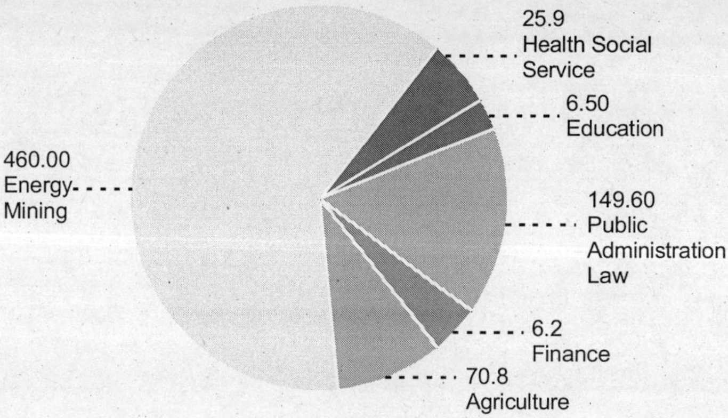

* World Bank Fiscal Year is from July 1 through June 30.

** Total commitment amount is the amount the Bank has agreed to lend to the project at the time of the project's approval

Data update frequency : monthly

Current Lending by Sector in Number of Projects – India

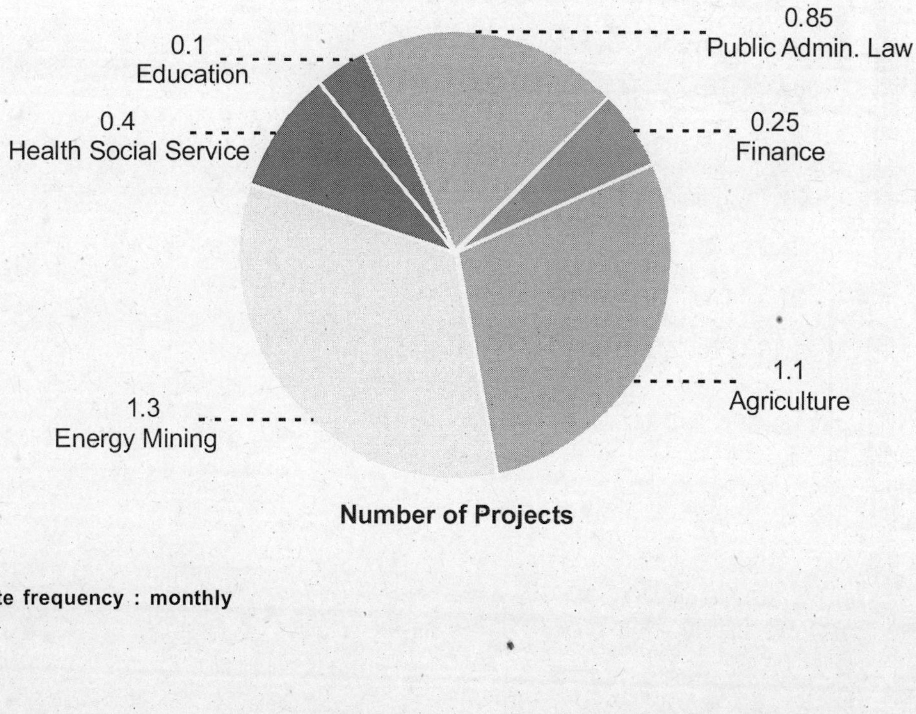

Number of Projects

Data update frequency : monthly

CHAPTER 21

INTERNATIONAL MONETARY FUND (IMF)

Structure:

21.1 INTRODUCTION

After the Great Depression (1929-33) there developed great rivalries of political and economic nature among the countries of the world, especially among the countries of Western Europe. These rivalries finally burst into World War II (1939-45). There was at that time urgent need of political and economic cooperation among the nations of the world with a view to avoid vast destruction for the type that resulted from World War II which was fought on a gigantic scale. The discussions on political and economic cooperation among nations started taking place among the statesmen of the world even as the war was being fought. And thus, for political cooperation, the United Nations Organisation came into existence. For economic and monetary cooperation two new international institutions that came to be established are the International Bank for Reconstruction and Development (the IBRD or the World Bank) and the International Monetary Fund (the IMF).

21.2 THE INTERNATIONAL MONETARY FUND (THE IMF) AND ITS OBJECTIVES

The Articles of Agreement of the IMF were formulated at Bretton Woods in the United States in July 1944. The IMF came into existence in December 1945 and it commenced its operations in March 1947.

The Objectives of the IMF

The following objectives of the IMF have been set forth in the Articles of Agreement:

(1) To promote international monetary cooperation through a permanent institution providing the machinery for consultation and collaboration on international monetary matters;

(2) To help bring about expansion and balanced growth of international trade and thereby contribute to the maintenance of high levels of employment and real income among member-countries;

(3) To promote exchange rate stability and thus help avoid competitive exchange rate depreciation;

(4) To provide facilities for multilateral conversions of national currencies and help removal of exchange controls and exchange restrictions; and

(5) To render help to member-countries to correct maladjustment in their balance of payment.[1]

1. It will be noted that while the IMF helps member-countries with short-term financial assistance to tide over temporary disequilibrium in balance of payments, the World Bank, on the other hand, helps member countries with loan-term capital for purposes of economic reconstruction and development. The IMF tries to facilitate smooth international trade through fixed or stable exchange rates, whereas the World Bank aims at expanding international trade by means of fuller utilisation of economic resources of member-countries. Thus, the objectives of the IMF and the World Bank are complementary to each other. Also, countries will have to be members of both the international institutions, namely, the World Bank and the IMF.

The IMF aims at promoting international monetary cooperation facilitating expansion and balanced growth of international trade thereby helping member-countries to utilise more efficiently their productive resources and help them to raise real income of the people in the member-countries, to promote exchange rate stability and avoid competitive exchange rate depreciation, to facilitate multilateral exchange rate system, to help shorten duration of disequilibrium in balance of payments of member-countries, and to create confidence among member-countries by providing it resources for correcting maladjustment in balance of payments thus ensuring national prosperity.

Organization of the IMF

The IMF is governed by its Board of Governors. Its business is conducted by:

an Executive Board,

a Managing Director,

a First Deputy Managing Director,

two other Deputy Managing Directors, and

a staff of International Civil Servants.

Board of Governors: The top link of the chain of command is the Board of Governors, which is composed of ministers of finance or heads of central banks (or other officials of comparable rank) from each of the IMF's 183 member countries. Apart from those Governors that are represented on the International Monetary and Financial Committee (see below), the Governors gather only on the occasion of the IMF-World Bank Annual Meetings to deal formally with IMF matters. During the rest of the year, they communicate the wishes of their governments for the IMF's day-to-day work through their representatives on the Executive Board.

The International Monetary and Financial Committee. The International Monetary and Financial Committee consists of 24 Governors representing constituencies or groups of countries, corresponding to those of the Executive Board (see below). It meets twice a year, on the occasion of the IMF-World Bank Annual and Spring Meetings, to advise the IMF on the functioning of the international monetary system.

Executive Board. The Executive Board consists of 24 Executive Directors representing the IMF's 183 member countries. The Board, which is based at IMF headquarters in Washington, D.C. is responsible for conducting the day-to-day business of the IMF and meets at last three times a week in formal session. At present, eight Executive Directors represent individual countries: China, France, Germany, Japan, Russia, Saudi Arabia, the United Kingdom, and the United States. The 16 other Executive Directors each represent groupings of the remaining countries. The Executive Board rarely makes its decisions on the basis of formal voting, but relies instead on the formation of consensus among its members.

Managing Director. The Managing Director is Head of IMF staff and Chairman of the Executive Board. The Executive Board appoints him.

The decision to establish the International Monetary Fund (IMF) was made at a conference held in Bretton Woods in July 1944. The IMF came into official existence on December 27,1945, with the signing of its Articles of Agreement. It commenced financial operations on March 1, 1947.

Current Membership: 183 countries.

Governing Bodies: Board of Governors, International Monetary and Financial Committee, Executive Board.

Managing Director: Horst Khöler, a German national.

Staff: Approximately 2,650 from 140 countries.

Accounting Unit: Special Drawing Rights (SDR).

Total Quotas: SDR 212.4 billion (US$ 265 billion).

The IMF Quotas

When a country becomes a member of the IMF, it is assigned a quota of subscription, its voting power and 'Drawing Rights.' The member-country's subscription-quota is based on its national income and its position in international trade. At the time of its establishment, the IMF quota ranged from 1 million US dollars for Ireland to 2,750 million US dollars for the United States. Every member-country was required to pay 25 per cent of its quota in gold or US dollars, and the balance in its national currency (which is kept with the central bank of the country in the name of the IMF). In order to increase the resources of the IMF, a general increase in member-country's quota by 50 per cent was made in 1959-60. The aggregate of the quotas of the IMF as on 30th April 1971 (including that of new member-countries) amounted to 28.5 billion US dollars compared to 21 billion US dollars a year earlier.

As we have seen, at the time of its establishment, each member-country was required to pay 25 per cent of its quota in terms of gold or US dollars. The practice of gold reserves by the member-countries with the IMF was discontinued from April 1978 and the IMF has been delinked from gold since then. At present, each member-country is allowed to maintain the par value of its currency and its quota in terms of the Special Drawing Rights.

21.3 FUNCTIONS PERFORMED BY THE IMF

It is the duty of the IMF to see that a member-country observes the provisions of the Bretton Woods Articles of Agreement; the IMF is a sort of guardian of 'good conduct' of member-countries in respect of their balance of payments. The IMF aims at reducing trade barriers like tariff and other international trade restrictions such as exchange controls. The IMF sees that no member-country will without the prior permission for the IMF impose restrictions on making payments or engage in discriminating arrangements or practise the system of multiple exchange rate. The IMF keeps watch on exchange rate policies adopted and followed by the member-countries.

The IMF also gives technical advice to its member-countries on monetary and fiscal policies and problems. It conducts research studies and provides technical experts to member-countries facing balance of payments problems. It also conducts short-term courses on monetary, fiscal and balance of payments for personnel from member-countries.

Exchange Rate Policy of the IMF

According to the Articles of Agreement, each country should express the par value of its currency in terms of gold or US dollar, the idea behind this being to create the regime of stable exchange rates with orderly and stable exchange rates. The IMF was obliged to agree to a change in the par value of plus or minus one per cent; a future change of plus or minus one per cent required the permission of the IMF. But since 1971, these provisions of the IMF have been changed. The IMF system of exchange rates has moved since 1971 from fixed or stable exchange rates to floating and flexible exchange rates.

Under the new system that is in operation since 1971, the member-countries are expected to establish and maintain par values of their currencies in terms of gold or US dollar. But the IMF, however, has no control over the guidelines for exchange rates by member-countries. It, however, lays down guidelines for exchange rate policies of the member-countries. This means the IMF undertakes international surveillance of exchange rate adjustment policies of its member-countries.[2]

IMF's Main Areas of Activity (Functions)

Surveillance. The IMF maintains a policy dialogue with each of its members through a process known as surveillance. Once a year, it appraises members' exchange rate policies within the overall framework of their economic policies in what is known as an Article IV consultation. Surveillance is based on the conviction that strong and consistent domestic economic policies will lead to stable exchange rates and a growing and prosperous world economy. The IMF also carries out multilateral surveillance, the results of which are summarized in the World Economic Outlook (prepared twice a year), and in the Global Financial Stability Report (prepared on a quarterly basis).

Financial assistance. The IMF provides credits and loans to member countries with balance of payment problems to support policies of adjustment and reform. As of February 28, 2002, it had credits and loans outstanding to 88 countries for an amount of SDR 61.7 billion (about US$ 77 billion). The IMF makes its financial resources available to members through a variety of financial facilities (loan programs). In addition to its regular facilities (Stand-By Arrangements; the Extended Fund Facility; the Supplemental Reserve Facility; Contingent Credit Lines; and the Compensatory Financing Facility), it also provides concessional assistance under its *Poverty Reduction and Growth Facility* (PRGF) and debt relief under the *Heavily Indebted Poor Countries (HIPC) Initiative.*

Technical assistance. The IMF offers technical assistance and training to help countries strengthen their human and institutional capacity, and design and implement effective macroeconomic and structural policies. Technical assistance is offered in several broad areas, including fiscal policy, monetary policy, and statistics.

21.4 LENDING OPERATIONS OF THE IMF

The IMF is an important international institution. The financial resources at its disposal come from quota subscriptions of the member-countries. Also, the IMF can increase its financial resources

2. "Surveillance of adjustment policies takes place with all members about once a year .... A team of four or five economists from the Fund headquarters visits the national capital to gather unpublished statistics, hear at first hand the motivation for recent policy changes and the authority's interpretation, of recent trends, and to discuss policy objectives with the competent authorities in the finance ministry, central bank and other agencies responsible for economic matters. The fruits of this consultation are incorporated in a lengthy background study and a shorter, more policy-oriented report on the discussion. The two resultant papers are then discussed at the Executive Board, where comments and advice are expressed to be relayed to the authorities of the country concerned."

by selling gold to its member-countries or by borrowing from governments or central banks of member-countries or from the Bank of International Settlements or if need be from the OPEC.

According to the provisions of the IMF, a member-country can borrow from the Fund by purchasing the needed foreign currencies in exchange of its own currency up to 125 per cent of its quota. However, during any one year, a country can borrow (i.e., purchase) foreign currencies only up to 25 per cent of its quota limit. The member-country borrowing foreign exchange from the Fund pays for it in terms of its own currency. But the borrowing country is expected to pay back the loan in foreign currency in which the country has borrowed (which means the country should buy back its currency in return of the foreign currency which it had borrowed before).

The IMF will grant loans to member-countries to correct disequilibrium in their balance of payments position; but such disequilibrium must be of a temporary type (as for example, due to crop failure on account of drought necessitating foodgrain imports of substantial quantities).

But if disequilibrium in the balance of payments position of a member-country is due to certain fundamental causes such as over-valuation of its currency, under such circumstances, the IMF will not be in a position to help the member-country by lending its financial resources, but will advise the government of the country to bring the value of its currency in line with values of other currencies.

Thus, the IMF gives short-term loans to member-countries to correct temporary disequilibrium (i.e., temporary deficits) in balance of payments position of member-countries.[3]

At the end of 1983-84 the member-countries made gross purchases from the Fund of SDR 10.2 billion. The bulk of these purchases (i.e., loans) were made under tranche conditionality. The IMF's aggregate commitments under the standby and extended facility arrangements amounted to SDR 18.6 billion.

---

3. The IMF has at its disposal a variety of facilities for, lending to its member-countries.

A member-country can draw in four 'credit tranches each of 25 per cent of its quota. The IMF has been continually raising the limit of borrowing by member-countries from the IMF. At present member-countries can borrow up to the equivalent of 450 per cent of their new quotas. Borrowing from the IMF upto the limit is allowed if the member-country is making serious efforts to correct disequilibrium in its balance of payments position.

(1) Compensatory Financial Facility (CFF): This was adopted in 1963 (and further liberalised in 1975) to meet balance of payments deficits arising out of temporary shortfalls in export earnings for reasons beyond the control of the borrowing country. Under this scheme, a member-country can borrow up to 125 per cent of the borrowing member's quota.

(2) Buffer Stock Facility (BSF): This facility was created in 1969 for financing commodity buffer stock by member-countries. This facility is equivalent to 50 per cent of the borrowing member's quota.

(3) Extended Financing Facility (EFF): This facility was created in 1974. Under this facility, the IMF provides funds to member-countries to meet their balance of payments deficits for longer periods and in amounts larger than under normal credit facilities. Under this facility loans are granted up to a period of ten years since 1981 and this facility is availed of by a number of developing member-countries. Thus, India could borrow 5.6 billion SDR under this facility (for a period of 3 years, beginning from 8th November 1981).

(4) Supplementary Financing Facility (SFF): This facility was created in 1977. This facility provides supplementary financing under extended or standby arrangements to member-countries to meet serious deficits in balance of payments position. Loans under this facility are being given to low-income developing member-countries of the IMF.

21.5 IMF AND THE ROLE OF GOLD

The original IMF Agreement fixed the par value of various currencies of member-countries in terms of gold (or dollar which was convertible into gold at the rate of one ounce of gold for 35 US dollars). Regarding the role played by gold in the functioning of the IMF standard, there are two diametrically opposite views. For example, Prof. Halm and Prof. Williams maintained that the gold provisions of the IMF were "not just window dressing," which meant that the IMF standard as originally conceived was related to gold standard or embodied the essential features of the gold standard. On the other hand, J.M. Keynes maintained that the IMF standard or provisions of the IMF, in fact, dethroned gold and it was "the exact opposite of the gold standard." It would be instructive to examine both these views critically before arriving at the final conclusion.

According to Halm and Williams, the IMF standard incorporates all the features of the international gold standard. For example, par values of national currencies are 'fixed' in terms of gold (or US dollar linked to and convertible into gold at the stated rate), and, therefore, the rate of exchange between any two currencies of the member-countries is determined in the same manner as in the case of gold standard. Thus, as in the case of gold standard, in the case of the IMF standard also, gold becomes 'a common denominator' for international trading transactions. Also member-countries of the IMF can buy or sell gold at the international price fixed by the IMF and the IMF may also buy gold from the member-countries at the fixed rate. It was pointed out that the IMF standard or the mechanism had the same monetary and price effects as in the case of international gold standard influencing central bank reserves of the member-countries in the same manner as movements of gold from one country to another when gold export and gold import points of the exchange rates in the case of the gold standard are touched. If a country begins to face a deficit in its balance of payments, and is forced to buy foreign exchange from the IMF, the volume of international currency with the central bank is reduced which in turn will reduce reserve position of commercial banks which are, therefore, forced to contract credit with the consequence that deflationary trends set in pushing up exports due to lower prices and thus the country moves in the direction of correcting adverse balance of payments. If on the other hand, a country has a surplus in its balance of payments, volume of international currency with it rises and so do reserves of commercial banks leading to expansion of credit, rise in prices and decline in its exports, thus gradually diminishing the surplus in the balance of payments position of the country. And, therefore, according to Halm and Williams, the IMF standard closely resembles the international gold standard and functionings of both the standards have close resemblances with one another.

J.M. Keynes and many others argued that the IMF standard differed from the international gold standard and was in fact exactly the opposite of it because of the following reasons:

Under the international gold standard, all countries must adopt gold standard, not only internationally but also domestically. Under the IMF scheme member-countries are not required to adopt gold standard domestically or internally (i.e., converting national currency into gold at a fixed rate and gold into national currency at the central bank of the country).

Under gold standard, exchange rate is rigidly fixed (and moves up and down within extremely narrow limits fixed by shipping, insurance and such other charges). But under the IMF standard, exchange rates are flexible; exchange rates can be altered to correct fundamental disequilibrium in balance of payments position of a country.

In the case of gold standard, there is a necessity of automatic adjustment of internal prices, wages and income of the country if it wants to remain on the gold standard. On the other hand, in the case of the IMF standard, what is required is adjustment in exchange rates in consonance or harmony with changing internal price and income trends in the country.

In the case of the IMF standard the deficit country is not required to adopt deflationary policy as would be required in the case of deficit country on gold standard. In fact, the IMF standard aims at removing deflationary tendencies in the economies of member-countries.

In the case of gold standard, it is the production and supply of gold that influence value of national currency that has adopted the gold standard. But in the case of the IMF standard, the Fund makes international currency available to member-countries and lends that to deficit countries. The financial resources of the IMF are not determined by the size of gold holdings as the creation of the SDRs has shown.

The IMF allows temporary exchange controls and restrictions to correct fundamental disequilibrium in the balance of payments position of member-countries; in the case of gold standard such restrictions are not allowed and if adopted would mean violation of the fundamental rules of the gold standard and would finally lead to the abandonment of gold standard.

Ellsworth has pointed out that the IMF Agreement "did not prescribe gold as the sole form in which reserves could be held", and therefore, the IMF standard cannot be said to have reintroduced the gold standard.

It is because of the above arguments that J.M. Keynes who was one of the architects of both the World Bank and the International Monetary Fund, maintained that the IMF standard or mechanism was "the exact opposite of the gold standard."

IMF and Gold

Before the Second Amendment of the *Articles of Agreement* in April 1978, the role of gold in the international monetary system was central and pervasive. The Second Amendment contained a number of provisions that, in combination, were intended to achieve a gradual reduction of the role of gold in the international monetary system and in the IMF. However, gold is still an important asset in the reserve holdings of a number of countries, and the IMF remains one of the largest official holders of gold in the world.

IMF's Total Gold Holdings

As of February 28, 2002, the IMF held about 103 million ounces (3,217 metric tons) of gold at designated depositories. The IMF's total gold holdings are valued on its balance sheet at SDR 5.9 billion (about $7.3 billion) on the basis of historical cost. Valued at current market prices, the IMF's holding amount to some SDR 24.7 billion ($30.7 billion).

The IMF acquired virtually all its holdings of gold through four main types of transactions under the original Articles of Agreement:

Subscriptions: The original Articles of Agreement prescribed that 25 per cent of initial subscriptions and quota increases was normally to be paid in gold. This represented the largest source of the IMF's gold.

Payment of Charges: Originally, all charges, i.e., interest on members' outstanding use of IMF credit, were normally payable in gold.

Purchases: A member wishing to obtain the currency of another member could acquire it by selling gold to the IMF. The major use of this provision was sales of gold to the IMF by South Africa in 1970-71.

Repurchases: Members could use gold to repay the IMF for credit previously extended.

Changes under the Second Amendment

The Second Amendment to the Articles of Agreement, which came into effect in April 1978, eliminated the use of gold as the common denominator of the post-World War II exchange rate system and as the basis of the value of the *SDR*. The Amendment also abolished the official price of gold and abrogated the obligatory uses of gold in transactions between the IMF and its members. It furthermore required the IMF, in its dealings in gold, to avoid managing its price or establishing a fixed price. Under the Amendment, members also undertook to collaborate with the IMF and other members with respect to reserve assets to promote better international surveillance of international liquidity.

The IMF's policy on gold is governed by the following principles:

As an undervalued asset held by the IMF, gold provides fundamental strength to its balance sheet. Any mobilization of IMF gold should avoid weakening its overall financial position.

Gold holdings provide the IMF with operational manoeuverability both as regards the use of its resources and through adding credibility to its precautionary balances. In these respects, the benefits of the IMF's gold holdings are passed on to the membership at large, to both creditors and debtors.

The IMF should continue to hold a relatively large amount of gold among its assets, not only for prudential reasons, but also to meet unforeseen contingencies.

The IMF has a systemic responsibility to avoid causing disruptions to the functioning of the gold market.

Profits from any gold sales should be used whenever feasible to create an investment fund, of which only the income should be used.

IMF's Use of Gold

The Articles of Agreement limit the use of gold in the IMF's operations and transactions. Transactions in gold require an 85 per cent majority of total *voting power*. The IMF may sell gold outright on the basis of prevailing market prices, and may accept gold in the discharge of a member's obligations at an agreed price on the basis of prices in the market at the time of acceptance. It does not, however, have the authority to engage in any other gold transactions, e.g., loans, leases, swaps, or use of gold as collateral, nor does it have the authority to buy gold.

Outflows of gold from the IMF's holdings occurred under the original Articles of Agreement through sales of gold for currency, and via payments of remuneration and interest. Sales of gold for currency were as follows:

Sales for Replenishment (1957-70): In the late 1950s and in the 1960s, the IMF sold gold on several occasions to replenish its holdings of currencies.

South African Gold and Mitigation: In the early 1970s, the IMF sold gold to members in amounts roughly corresponding to the amounts purchased earlier from South Africa. It also sold gold in connection with payments of gold for quota increases by some members, in order to mitigate the impact of these payments on the gold holdings of reserve centres.

Investment in U.S. Government Securities (1956-72): In order to generate income to offset operational deficits, some gold was sold to the United States and the proceeds invested in U.S. government securities. A significant buildup of reserves through income from charges prompted the IMF to re-acquire this gold from the U.S. government in the early 1970s.

Auctions and "Restitution" Sales (1976-80): The IMF sold approximately one-third (50 million ounces) of its then-existing gold holdings following an agreement by its members to reduce the role of gold in the international monetary system. Half of this amount was sold in restitution to members at the then-official price of SDR 35 per ounce; the other half was auctioned to the market to finance the Trust Fund, which supported concessional lending by the IMF to low-income countries.

Off-market Transactions in Gold: In December 1999, the Executive Board authorized off-market transactions in gold of up to 14 million ounces to help finance IMF participation in the *HIPC Initiative*. Between December 1999 and April 2000, separate but closely linked transactions involving a total of 12.9 million ounces of gold were carried out between the IMF and two members (Brazil and Mexico) that had financial obligations falling due to the IMF. In the first step, the IMF sold gold to the member at the prevailing market price and the profits were placed in a special account and then invested for the benefit of the HIPC Initiative. In the second step, the IMF immediately accepted back, at the same market price, the same amount of gold from the member in settlement of that member's financial obligations falling due to the Fund. The net effect of these transactions was to leave the balance of the IMF's holdings of physical gold unchanged.

21.6 IMF AND SPECIAL DRAWING RIGHTS (SDRS)

Introduction

The IMF maintained that international trade has been growing at a faster rate than supply of gold and other hard reserve currencies like US dollars. And, therefore, there is an urgent need to create additional reserve, "not because the world monetary system is in imminent danger without it, but because it would in a great measure establish world confidence in the system so as to permit fuller and freer non-inflationary growth of the world economy." And, therefore, to deal with the problem of international reserve and liquidity, ten leading members of the IMF (the big ten being the United States, West Germany, France, the United Kingdom, Canada, Belgium, Holland, Italy, Japan and Sweden) agreed to a new plan of international reserve known as Special Drawing Rights (SDRs).

And, therefore, in 1970, the IMF introduced a scheme for the creation and issue of Special Drawing Rights. The SDR is also known as 'Paper Gold.' The SDRs came to be created by the First Amendment to the Fund Articles of Agreement in 1969. The creation of SDRs as a reserve asset influences the level of world reserves with a view to solve the problem of international liquidity as the problem has become urgent due to rapid expansion of international trade. The SDRs are allocated to member-countries in proportion to their subscription to the IMF. For operational purposes, the IMF has opened the Special Drawing Account in the name of every member-country.

At the commencement, member-countries held SDRs as part of their reserves and they converted them into currencies when they were facing balance of payments difficulties. Then one SDR was equal to one US dollar (or equivalent to 0.888671 gram of gold).

When after 1973 the Fund abandoned the par value system and US dollar and other major currencies were allowed to float, it was decided to stabilise the value of SDR. Therefore, value of the SDR came to be calculated every day on the basis of a basket of 16 most widely used currencies of member-countries of the IMF. (These were currencies of the US, the U.K., West Germany, France, Japan, Canada, Italy, Netherlands, Belgium, Sweden, Australia, Spain, Norway, Denmark, Austria and South Africa). In 1978, currencies of South Africa and Denmark were dropped and those of Saudi Arabia and Iran were included in the basket of currencies. Each currency was given weightage in proportion to its importance in international trade and in world financial market.

With the Second Amendment in 1978, SDR became the international unit of account. In January 1981 with a view to facilitate proper valuation of a unit of SDR, the number of currencies in the basket in terms of which value of SDR was fixed, were reduced to five (namely, those of the US, West Germany, the UK, France and Japan). The currency composition in the basket of currencies and weightage to be given to each currency in the basket for the purpose of fixing value of a unit of SDR are to be revised every five years, beginning with January 1986 and this revision for value of SDR is to be based on value of exports and balances of currencies held with the Fund by member-countries.

SDR and Its Value

SDR is at present 'an international unit of currency.' The quotas of all the member-countries with the Fund are now valued in terms of SDR which is now an international monetary asset and as such SDR is held in the international reserve of the central banks of member-countries to finance their deficits or surpluses in their balance of payments position. At present, all transactions of the IMF such as its loans to member-countries, its liquid reserves, its capital structure are all expressed not in terms of gold or US dollars but in terms of SDRs.

Following are the three principal uses of SDRs:

(1) Under this arrangement, the IMF designates member-countries in the SDR scheme, with strong and favourable balance of payments position and heavy reserve position to provide their currencies in exchange of SDRs to other member-countries needing their currencies.

(2) The SDRs are used in all transactions with the IMF.

(3) Their use in transaction is by agreement. The IMF allows sale of SDRs for currency by agreement with another participating country in this scheme.

After the Second Amendment, the IMF allows the following additional uses, such as, 'Swap Arrangements' operation, granting and receiving of loans, settlement of financial disputes, as security for financial obligations and for granting of donations.

The IMF has allowed the World Bank and its associates (the Bank for International Settlements, the African Development Bank, the Arab Monetary Fund, etc.) to hold SDRs. Attempts are being made to make use of SDR as a unit of account in financial markets of the world and for private transactions.

During the initial period of 1970-72 the IMF created 9.3 billion SDRs and allocated them to 112 participants in the SDR scheme in proportion to their quota, for various uses mentioned above. Till

1978 total holding of SDRs amounted to 9.3 billion. In 1978 the IMF raised them by 4 billion SDR in each year, namely, 1979, 1980 and 1981. As a consequence, the total holdings of SDRs were 13.1 billion in 1979, SDRs 17.3 billion in 1980 and SDRs 21.4 billion in 1981.

Critical Appraisal of SDR Scheme

The SDR is a new form of international monetary reserve. The SDR scheme also aims at international liquidity that is urgently required to meet increasing need for it in view of continually increasing volume of international trade and to correct disequilibrium in balance of payments of member-countries.

The countries participating in SDR scheme receive SDRs under 'Transaction by Agreement' unconditionally. The participating countries under this scheme are not required to change their domestic economic policies as is expected under the IMF aid programme. It should be noted that payment and repayment of SDRs out of the Special Drawing Account in the Fund is easier and more flexible than under the IMF scheme.

In spite of the above advantages, the SDR scheme is criticised on the following grounds:

(1) The SDR scheme is unequitable as it favours rich and developed countries by making inequitable distribution of SDRs. This inequitable distribution of SDRs takes place because they are allotted to participating countries in proportion to their subscription quotas. This has resulted in smaller allocation of SDRs to developing countries which are in greater need of SDRs. Naturally, this relatively low allocation of SDRs to developing countries reduces their borrowing capacity.

(2) The SDR scheme is not linked to the needs for development finance for developing countries. In fact, need for international liquidity is greater in the case of developing countries because of their limited access to private banking and capital markets and limited capacity to hold foreign exchange reserves. Under such circumstances, there is need to create more SDRs with their distribution with unconditional liquidity to meet increasing needs of developing countries. But because of inflexible and unsympathetic attitude of the United States, this has not been possible, in spite of repeated requests from developing countries.

(3) And, therefore, it may be said especially from the point of view of developing countries that the IMF has failed in its objective of creating adequate international liquidity through the creation and equitable distribution of SDRs. In the face of this and terms of trade going against primary commodities and other products of developing countries, balance of payments problems are getting more and more acute and pressing for developing countries.

(4) It is said that the SDR scheme is still to prove its workability. It is probably too early to state that participating countries will develop enough confidence in 'the paper gold' and accept it as a trustworthy asset in place of or along with gold and hard currencies.

(5) It needs to be noted that it is too much to expect that mere creating of additional liquidity through creation of additional SDRs can solve problems of confidence in different forms of exchange reserves. It is absolutely essential that if the countries of the world are to successfully tackle their problem of balance of payments, they should be prepared to appreciate or depreciate their currencies when there appear persistent deficits or surpluses (as in the case of West Germany and Japan and deficits in the case of United States) in balance of payments. Only

when the problems of surplus and deficit in balance of payments of internationally trading countries are brought within manageable limits, can it be said that problem of international liquidity (through devices of creation of SDRs) might be successfully tackled. This means SDR scheme is still to prove its workability.

21.7 INDIA AND THE IMF

India happens to be one of the founder-members of the IMF. Until 1970 India's subscription quota was the fifth largest among the largest contributors and, therefore, India enjoyed the power to appoint a permanent Executive Director on the Board of Executive Directors. But after May 1970 the subscription quotas of Japan, Canada, and Italy increased and became more than that of India with the consequence that India has ceased to hold the position of a permanent Executive Director of the IMF.

At the commencement when India became a member of the IMF, par value of Indian rupee was fixed at 0.268601 gram of gold or 30.2 US cents. When the Indian rupee was devalued on 18th September 1949, its par value got reduced to 0.186621 gram of gold or 21 US cents (instead of 30.2 US cents till then). When Indian rupee was again devalued on 6th June 1966, par value of Indian rupee was further reduced to 0.118489 of gold or 13.33 US cents. Because the US dollar was devalued in May 1972, its par value has gone down. Since the Second Amendment of the IMF Agreement, like the other national currencies, exchange rate of Indian rupee has been floating and is at the present linked to SDR.

India happens to be one of the major beneficiaries of the IMF assistance. India has been getting financial assistance from various Fund facilities from time to time. Also, India has been paying regularly its debts borrowed from the IMF. Thus, between 1947 and 1955 India borrowed from the Fund 100 million US dollars twice to meet deficits in her balance of payments. Between 1957 and 1975 India borrowed from the IMF eight times, the total sum amounting to 1764 million US dollars.

India also received loans at concessional rates to meet deficits in her balance of payments amounting to SDRs 529.01 million between 1 July 1978 and 21st February 1981 under the IMF Trust Fund.

India received a loan of 5.6 billion US dollars (equivalent to Rs. 5220 crores) from the IMF in 1979. India started receiving this loan in installments beginning from November 1981. India had drawn US dollar 3.9 billion till April 1984 when it intimated to the IMF that it is not going to avail of the remaining amount of the loan.

The 5.6 billion US dollar loan was equivalent to 291 per cent of India's quota of SDRs 1717.5 million and that loan was financed by the Fund partly from its ordinary resources and partly from borrowed resources. Upto April 1982 the interest charged on the use of ordinary financial resources was 6.25 per cent and was raised to 6.6 per cent in May 1982. As regards the borrowed funds, the rate of interest charge upto December 1983 was 13.33 per cent and for the year ended April 1982, it was 14.56 per cent. The repayment period was between 4 and 10 years for loans from IMF's own resources and $3^1/_2$ years to 7 years in the case of loans from borrowed resources. The total interest burden on this 5.6 billion US dollar loan was expected to be very high, payment of interest and the principal together amounting to SDRs 10 billion. That was one reason why India after drawing 3.9 US dollars from the loan intimated to the Fund that it was not going to avail of the remaining part of the loan.

The worst part of this huge loan was the conditionality clauses imposed upon India. India was forced to change her export, import, monetary and other policies as per the guidelines laid down by the IMF while sanctioning the loan. This amounted to gross interference in domestic economic affairs of India and this was severely criticised by Indian economists and critics of Government of India.

In addition to substantial loans from IMF, India has also benefited from her membership of the IMF, by virtue of which India is also a member of the World Bank from which India has received long-term financial and other assistance for various projects. India has been getting advisory help from the Fund under the Fund surveillance conditionality. The IMF has also been providing short-term training courses to Indian personnel on monetary, fiscal, banking and foreign exchange and balance of payments policies.

India and the IMF

The last time that India knocked the doors of IMF for assistance was in 1991 on account of the balance of payment crises. However, since then as given by the following table there have been no outstanding loans or purchases as of April 30, 2002.

India's Financial Position in the Fund

As of April 30, 2002

I. Membership Status: Joined: December 27, 1945 **Article VIII**

II. General Resources Account:	**SDR Million**	**% Quota**
Quota	4,158.20	100.00
Fund holdings of currency	3,669.48	88.25
Reserve position in Fund	488.78	11.75
Holdings Exchange Rate		
III. SDR Department:	**SDR Million**	**% Allocation**
Net cumulative allocation	681.17	100.00
Holdings	9.57	1.40

IV. Outstanding Purchases and Loans: None

V. Latest Financial Arrangements:

Type	Approval Date	Expiration Date	Amount Approved (SDR Million)	Amount Drawn (SDR Million)
Stand-by	Oct. 31.1991	June 30,1993	1,656.00	1,656.00
Stand-by	Jan. 18, 1991	Apr. 17,1991	551.92	551.92
EFF	Nov. 09, 1981	May 01, 1984	5,000.00	3,900.00

VI. Projected Payments to Fund

(SDR Million; based on existing use of resources and present holdings of SDRs):

Forthcoming	2002	2003	2004	2005	2006
Charges/Interest	11.50	15.40	15.40	15.40	15.40
Total	11.50	15.40	15.40	15.40	15.40

India: Financial Position in the Fund

as of November 30, 2007

Summary of IMF member's quota, reserve position, SDR holdings, outstanding credit, recent lending arrangements, projected payments due to the IMF, and monthly historical transactions with the Fund.

I. Membership Status : Joined: December 27, 1945; Article VIII

II. General Resources Account:	**SDR Million**	**% Quota**
Quota	4,158.20	100.00
Fund holdings of currency	3,884,.81	93.43
Reserve Position	273.42	6.58
Holdings Exchange Rate		

III. SDR Department:	**SDR Million**	**% Allocation**
Net cumulative allocation	681.17	100.00
Holdings	2.07	0.30

IV. Outstanding Purchases and Loans: None

V. Latest Financial Arrangements:

Type	Date of Arrangement	Expiration Date	Amount Approved (SDR Million)	Amount Drawn (SDR Million)
Stand-By	Oct. 31, 1991	Jun. 30, 1993	1,656.00	1,656.00
Stand-By	Jan. 18, 1991	Apr. 17, 1991	551.93	551.93
EFF	Nov. 09, 1981	May 01, 1984	5,000,00	3,900.00

VI. Projected Payments to Fund 1/
(SDR Million; based on existing use of resources and present holdings of SDRs):

			Forthcoming		
	2007	2008	2009	2010	2011
Principal					
Charges/Interest		24.15	24.06	24.07	24.07
Total		24.15	24.06	24.07	24.07

1/When a member has overdue financial obligations outstanding for more than three months, the amount of such arrears will be shown in this section.

VII. Implementation of HIPC Initiative: Not Applicable

VIII. Implementation of Multilateral Debt Relief Initiative (MDRI): Not Applicable

Prepared by Finance Department

Disclaimer

The information provided is for your convenience and is not intended to replace other official IMF reports and statements.

21.8 CRITICAL ASSESSMENT OF IMF'S ROLE AND FUNCTIONING

As an international monetary institution, IMF has played an important and significant role in fulfilling its objectives. Since its establishment, the Fund has been supplying various foreign currencies to member-countries suffering from deficits in their balance of payments position. It needs to be noted that not only the developing but also developed countries have been taking advantage of the facilities made available by the Fund.

Another of its significant achievement has been that with rapidly increasing volume of international trade, the IMF by making suitable amendments in its Articles of Agreement has made an attempt to solve the problem of international liquidity by creating Special Drawing Rights (SDRs). In this respect, it has been flexible enough to meet the changing needs and requirements in the sphere of the international trade and balance of payments position of trading partners.

During 1950s and 1960s repayment of loans from the Fund had to be between 3 to 5 years; now loans from Extended Financing Facility of the IMF are between 4 and 10 years in the case of loans from IMF's own resources and 3½ to 7 years if the loan is from the Fund's borrowed financial resources.

And yet the IMF is subject to criticism on the following grounds:

(1) One criticism is that the IMF has been generally a conservative organisation and not flexible enough to make required changes quickly in the rapidly changing world of international trade.

(2) The second criticism is that the IMF is charging high rates of interest on loans given from its own financial resources. For example, if IMF loans are made available from the ordinary resources of the Fund, then 6.6 per cent interest rate is charged on such lendings from 1st May 1982. But if the loans by the Fund are from the Fund's borrowed resources, rate of interest charged is as high as 14.56 per cent from 30th April 1982.

(3) IMF has been insisting on stricter and stricter conditionality clauses over the last three decades which the borrower member-country must fulfill, if it is to get the required loan from the Fund.

For example, upto 1970 the IMF would insist on reduction in public expenditure for meeting deficit in balance of payments of borrower country.

From 2nd March 1979, in addition to the above, new conditionality clauses have been laid down by the IMF. These conditionality clauses include periodic assessment of the experience of borrowing countries with adjustment programmes. These conditionality clauses include also clauses emphasising increase in productivity and improvement in resource allocation in programmes which have acquired financial support from the Fund.

Another conditionality clause is regarding strengthening of borrower country's collaboration with the World Bank.

For example, when IMF sanctioned a loan of 5.6 billion US dollars to India in 1979, it laid down stringent conditions regarding performance criteria in implementing programmes, policies relating to savings, regarding exports and imports which were required to be liberalised. Thus, the IMF exercises considerable regulatory and supervisory role over economies of borrower member-countries. This makes nonsense of its declared objective or policy of non-interference in the domestic economic affairs of borrowing countries.

(4) Another criticism is that the Fund, instead of playing the central role in international monetary sphere, has been playing only a secondary role. For example, the Fund does not provide its facilities for short-term credit. The consequence of this is that the central banks of the Group of Ten (of the leading industrialised countries) have to enter into 'Swap Arrangements.' Under such an arrangement, countries exchange each other's currencies and also provide short-term credit to tide over temporary disequilibrium in balance of payments position. Such 'Swap Arrangements' have resulted in growth of Euro-Currency Market reducing the importance of the IMF.

(5) The IMF on the whole has failed in its objective of promoting exchange rate stability. The original objective was that there should be permitted only plus one per cent or minus one per cent in change of par values of exchange rates or what had come to be known as 'adjustable peg.'

But Bretton Woods system collapsed on 15th August 1971 when the United States stopped legal right of conversion of dollars into gold at the Federal Reserve System and decided not to interfere to maintain exchange rate stability. From then on different member-countries have been following different policies such as 'managed floating,' 'joint floating' and 'pegged exchange rates.' Thus, the IMF standard failed in 1971, one reason that is being attributed being the absence of adequate adjustment mechanism to solve the problem of balance of payments of member-countries.

(6) The IMF has failed to realise one of its main objectives of eliminating exchange restrictions. The policy and practice of foreign exchange controls have continued as before as also multiple exchange rates system under one guise or another in a number of member-countries.

(7) The IMF is accused of following discriminatory policy that favours developed countries and is against the interests of developing countries. No wonder, the IMF is nicknamed as 'Rich Countries' Club.' Though developing countries constitute a majority among member-countries of the IMF, policies of IMF are dominated by the rich countries, notably by the United States. Thus, the Fund has not been increasing its resources by creating SDRs and other resources that would enable the IMF to give loans of increasing amount to developing member-countries.

Concluding Remarks

In spite of these points of criticism, the fact is that the IMF has played a significant role in solving short-term balance of payments problems of developed as well of developing countries. What is more significant is that the IMF has shown itself to be flexible enough to keep itself moving with the changing environment in the sphere of international trade. For example, the original Article of Agreement was amended in 1978 legalising flexible exchange rates, raised quotas of member-countries to increase IMF's financial resources to enable it to lend more; and the Fund has succeeded in dethroning gold which used to hold the central place in exchange rate arrangements. The IMF has substituted the SDR in place of gold and is at present in a better position to tackle problems of international liquidity and balance of payments deficits. It may also be noted that the IMF has raised the limit of borrowing from 125 per cent of the subscription quota to 450 per cent of the quota which is in keeping with the needs of member-countries. As already stated, the IMF has been giving increasing financial assistance to developing countries through creating new lending facilities like Compensatory Financial Facility (CFF), Buffer Stock Facility (BSF), Extended Financing Facility (EFF) and Supplementary Financing Facility (SFF).

The significant role which the IMF has been playing becomes clear from the fact that the number of member-countries has increased from 44 in 1947 to 149 in 1986.

21.9 THE IMF AND RECENT CHANGES

In the financial year 2001, the IMF took steps to update its lending policies and review its policy conditionality. Following this the Executive Board approved some important changes in the IMF's lending facilities. Particularly the Executive Board took action to:

(1) Make the terms of the Contingent Credit Line (CCL) facility more attractive to potential users. CCL offers countries with sound economic policies a precautionary line of credit that can be quickly activated to help them counter contagion effects on their economies from financial crises elsewhere.

(2) Approve measures to encourage early repayment of IMF loans and discourage excessive use of IMF funds. These measures are taken with a view to reduce reliance on IMF for long-term financing and free up funds for use by other members.

(3) Strengthen its monitoring of country's economic policies after conclusion of IMF supported programs, particularly in cases where there is substantial credit outstanding to the IMF. This is to provide additional safeguards for IMF funds and helps preserve the achievements of IMF-supported programs.

Review of Conditionality in IMF Supported Programs: The IMF extends financing to a member country with balance of payments problems on the condition that the country has to put in place a program of policy adjustments to address its external payments problems. This is nothing but the IMF conditionality. However of late, the expanding scope of conditionality has raised concerns that excessively broad and detailed policy conditions may undermine a country's "ownership" of a policy program, which is essential for the program's successful implementation. This criticism seems to be well taken by the executive board of the IMF and according to the Annual Report 2001, a broad consensus seemed to have emerged, notwithstanding the indispensability of conditionality, about the need to streamline the conditionality and make it focussed to give greater scope for national ownership, while ensuring that the essential objectives of IMF supported programs were achieved.

21.10 PROBLEM OF INTERNATIONAL LIQUIDITY

Since 1960s the world has been facing a new problem in the sphere of international trade, namely, problem of international liquidity. International trade is expanding fairly rapidly since the end of World War II in 1945. Practically in the case of no country does the country's export exactly balance that country's imports and many countries have been facing deficits in their balance of payments position. Naturally, practically every country (except at present West Germany and Japan which are enjoying surpluses in their balance of payments position) has got to think of how to meet these deficits in their balance of payments in a manner that is acceptable to the creditor countries. The problem of international liquidity involves problem of finding assets or resources with which a country can satisfactorily meet its international obligations arising out of deficits in its balance of payments. (It may be noted that the Untied States has been facing deficits in its balance of payments over last many years and during the current year 1988-89 the deficit amounted to a monumental figure of more than 130 billion US dollars).

The concept of international liquidity can be made clear in the following way. International liquidity comprises of all the financial resources and facilities available to the monetary authorities of individual countries for financing deficits in their international balance of payments. The assets which constitute a part of such liquidity range from the assets readily acceptable to a country to resources which become available only after protracted negotiations. Thus, it includes the well-known components of 'official reserves', namely, gold held by central banks (gold held by private individuals and business does not constitute a part of official reserves and is accordingly excluded); foreign currencies held by central banks or treasuries; borrowing facilities available under swap and related credit arrangements of central banks and treasuries and other assets which are mobilisable when need arises.

International liquidity thus includes a wide variety of assets and financial resources acceptable to creditor countries from debtor countries, since creditor countries are not prepared to accept goods and services from debtor countries. Broadly speaking, these assets and resources comprising international liquidity may be classified under two headings : (a) owned reserves with the country and (b) borrowing facilities available to the country. The latter may be available automatically as with the International Monetary Fund, or may be available after protracted negotiations as in the case of foreign loans (i.e., loans from foreign countries).

Since international liquidity consists not only of existing assets but also of borrowing facilities on the basis of negotiations, it is very difficult to make an exact quantitative measurement of the existing resources available to settle international obligations.

Gold is an important commodity satisfying the requirement of international liquidity as that metal is acceptable to all countries in settlement of their debts. But the supply of gold in the world is increasing only by about 2% per annum and even granting that all that additional gold is available to governments for settlement of international claims, it is not adequate for the purpose as international trade is expanding annually at the rate of about 6%. Even if we include reserve currencies like the US dollar, the British pound, West German mark and Japanese yen which are generally acceptable to all countries in settlement of their international claims, all these together (i.e., gold with the central bank and treasury and reserve currencies with the government, i.e., those currencies which are hard currencies and which, therefore, are acceptable to all countries) are increasing relatively slowly and are not adequate to meet fully the mounting deficits in international balance of payments in large number of countries. This might lead to putting by countries all kinds of restrictions on international trade to avoid or to curtail international debt claims arising because import bills have been exceeding export earnings in the case of a large number of countries. Such restrictions on international trade would reduce total volume of international trade resulting in reduction in gains from international trade with adverse effects on the welfare of world community.

The World Bank in its report of the year 1976-77 expressed its concern over the growing restrictions being imposed on international movements of goods and protectionist trade policies being followed even by some developed countries.

There is another problem also. If in the absence of adequate stock of reserve gold, countries begin to store reserve currencies like the US dollar and British pound sterling for meeting their international payments obligations, there will be tremendous pressure on such reserve currencies resulting in their appreciation and causing considerable damage to economies of countries seeking their reserve currencies. Seeking US dollars and British pounds (and at present West German marks and Japanese yen at any cost) would mean that terms of trade would go against these countries and their total exports may bring less of those reserve foreign currencies than before.

International Monetary Fund and International Liquidity

The IMF is the main provider of international liquidity. By way of contribution of membership fees, etc. IMF has stock of various currencies and gold which it lends to member-countries to meet their short-term obligations arising out of balance of payments difficulties.

But as the existing financial resources were felt to be inadequate, the IMF raised the contribution of members by 50% in 1958 and thus IMF resources have been increased to meet growing requirements of international liquidity.

As even these resources were felt to be inadequate with the lapse of time when volume of international trade was growing as also deficits in balance of payments of a number of countries, in order to release pressure on the US dollar and British pound-sterling as reserve currencies, the IMF put into operation a scheme known as Special Drawing Rights (SDRs).

SDRs supplement gold reserves and reserve currencies constituting international liquidity. SDR is an international currency. In 1970, SDRs worth 3500 million dollars were brought into existence and in subsequent two years SDRs worth 3000 million dollars per year were created and distributed among member-countries. SDRs are supposed to possess international liquidity and are acceptable in settlement of international obligations. SDRs are distributed among member-countries on the basis of their contribution to IMF fund. Every member-country is obliged to accept SDRs upto a certain limit from a debtor country in settlement of its international obligations or debts. The debtor country in exchange for its national currency receives from the allotted SDRs, the needed amount of SDRs for settlement of its international obligations.

International liquidity problem has thus three aspects. As international trade among countries of the world is expanding rapidly, balance of payments problem is assuming bigger and bigger dimensions. This naturally requires increasing stock of assets and resources in the world as a whole to enable deficit countries to meet their international liabilities arising out of deficits in their balance of payments without putting many restrictions on international trade among countries and foreign exchange transactions (such as foreign exchange controls, etc.)

In the second place, this means that in future also supply of assets and financial resources constituting international liquidity should be flexible enough and should expand at an appropriate rate taking into consideration rate of expansion in international trade and expanding international payments obligations consequent on increase in the volume of international trade.

In the third place, total assets and resources (gold with the central banks, reserves of hard currencies with central banks and the treasuries, possible foreign loans and SDRs, etc.) should be appropriately distributed among different nations of the world. Many developing countries are not in a position to fully meet their international obligations and fill up deficits in their balance of payments (in spite of their quota of SDRs). It is, therefore, necessary to find ways so that there is creation of additional quantities of SDRs and their proper distribution among developing countries effectively helping them to meet fully their international obligations and thus helping them to accelerate rate of growth of their economies.

CHAPTER 22

INTERNATIONAL DEVELOPMENT ASSOCIATION (IDA), INTERNATIONAL FINANCE CORPORATION (IFC) AND THE ASIAN DEVELOPMENT BANK(ADB)

Structure:

Introduction

It was suggested in 1958 that a new international institution to be known as International Development Association (IDA) be established and administered by the World Bank.

The IDA started functioning from 8th November 1960.

22.1 AIMS AND OBJECTIVES OF THE IDA

The main objective of the IDA has been to provide financial assistance to less developed countries (LDCs) on soft loan basis which means on terms imposing a lower servicing charge on loans than on conventional loans by the World Bank to its member-countries.

In this connection, the Articles of Agreement concerning the IDA states: "...to promote economic development, increase productivity and thus raise standard of living in the less developed areas of the world included within the Association's membership, in particular by providing finance to meet their important development requirements on terms which are more flexible and bear less heavily on the balance of payments than those of conventional loans, thereby furthering the development objectives of International Bank for Reconstruction and Development and supplementing its activities.[1]

Thus, the IDA grants development loans on concessional and flexible terms than World Bank loans of conventional type. These loans from the IDA are for a period of 5 to 15 years or even more. The IDA provides a certain percentage of the cost of a project that is meant not only for meeting foreign exchange part of the project but also part of the cost of the project in local currency. Many countries which are unable to borrow from the World Bank (because their projects are not regarded as credit-worthy by the World Bank) are financed by the IDA. For example, such loans of IDA are for the purpose of water supply, construction of hospitals, housing and sanitary arrangements — objectives of projects for which World Bank loan facilities are not available.

The IDA loans bear a much lower rate of interest than those of the World Bank. In some cases, if warranted, IDA loans bear no interest at all but only administrative charge levied by the IDA. In a number of cases in recent years IDA has given loans to LDCs at ¾ per cent rate of interest.

Another important aspect of IDA loans is that the loans can be repaid in local currencies of borrowing countries. This ensures that the IDA loans do not have adverse effect on balance of payments of the LDCs.

22.2 MEMBERSHIP AND ORGANISATION OF THE IDA

It is provided that any member-country of the World Bank can become a member of the IDA, provided that a country is ready to subscribe to the IDA at the rate of 5 per cent of its existing World Bank share capital subscription quota. As on 30th June 1975, of the 125 member-countries of the World Bank, 114 countries were admitted as members of IDA. Of them 10 developed countries and 94 developing countries.

The organisation of the IDA is similar to that of the World Bank. Thus, IDA has its Board of Governors, Executive Directors and a President, all of whom are holders of these positions in the World Bank. They serve as ex-officio members in the IDA.

1. The World Bank, *Policies and Operations,* Washington (1960), p.16.

The initial subscription of member-countries to IDA amounted to 1,000 million US dollars. For the purpose of subscription and voting power, member-countries of IDA are divided into two parts. Part I consists of member-countries which are relatively more developed and which have paid their entire subscription quota in gold of freely convertible currencies which IDA can use for granting loans to LDCs. Part II consists of member-countries which are less developed; they are required to pay only 10 per cent of their subscription quota in gold or freely convertible currencies and the remaining 90 per cent in their own national currencies which cannot be used by IDA for granting loans without the previous consent of the member-country whose currency is going to be lent. It was also conceived that the IDA would be receiving additional financial resources from countries mentioned in Part I (i.e., developed countries) from time to time to augment IDA's financial resources and enable it to carry on its lending operations on a larger scale. During 1972-74, the Part I members of the IDA provided 2,410 million US dollars as supplementary resources. Since the establishment of the IDA, Part I countries have provided supplementary financial resources three times.[2]

22.3 THE WORLD BANK AND THE IDA

The World Bank and the IDA are complementary international financial institutions, both providing development assistance to member-countries.

But the difference between the two is that whereas the World Bank insists on the economic feasibility of projects to be financed by it and on the absorptive capacity of the member-countries seeking loans from it, the IDA loans on the other hand are designed to assist the LDCs. The second distinguishing feature is that as compared to the World Bank loans, IDA loans to LDCs are given on very easy terms and conditions, interest charged often hardly covering even administrative charges. Often loans are given for a period of upto 40 years or even for longer period in the case of extremely poor member-countries. Another distinguishing feature of the IDA is that unlike the World Bank loans, a substantial part of IDA loans is given as non-project aid. Naturally major share of the IDA financial assistance has gone to South Asian countries which are the major beneficiaries of the IDA.

Despite the complementary nature of the World Bank and IDA, approaches of the two to developing countries are different. Whereas the IDA along with the World Bank, provides substantial financial assistance to agricultural and transport projects, the IDA appears to have shown very little interest in projects in the field of power, industrial development and urbanisation.

22.4 PROGRESS OF THE IDA

As at the end of June 1975, the IDA had approved loans amounting to 8434 million US dollars, mainly for projects undertaken by countries mentioned in Part II. The IDA loans are given at very low rates of interest and terms and conditions of repayment are comparatively very easy. The IDA has charged ¾ per cent rate of interest on most of the loans which are generally repayable over a period of 40 years.

---

2. Some of the important Part I member-countries of IDA are: the United States, the United Kingdom, France, the Netherlands, Federal Republic of Germany, Canada, Australia, Sweden, Japan (and other 11 members). Some of the Part II important member-countries of the IDA are: India, China, Pakistan, Brazil, Argentina, Indonesia and 88 others.

   As on 30th June 1975, total subscription and supplementary resources of IDA amounted to 10,774 million US dollars (expressed in US dollars at the prevailing rates of exchange). Of this nearly 97 per cent were provided by Part I member-countries and only about 3 per cent by Part II or developing member-countries. But Part I member-countries while contributing 97 per cent of the financial resources of the IDA enjoy only 69 per cent of the total voting power. This implies that Part II member-countries are enjoying proportionately greater decision-making power in the functioning of IDA. The United States and the United Kingdom have together subscribed around 50 per cent of the financial resources of the IDA, whereas the two countries together enjoy only about a third of the total voting power.

The IDA loans have been given to LDCs for the development of agriculture, industry, education, communication, population control and so on.

Major share of IDA loans has gone to South Asian countries, followed by East African countries and West African countries. It needs to be noted that IDA has treated countries in the South Asia region more favourably than LDCs in other regions of the world.

The IDA and India

India has been a member-country of the IDA right from its establishment. Up to the end of June 1975, India received from IDA loans amounting to 3441.7 million US dollars for her 70 projects. Loans to India from IDA amounted to nearly 40 per cent of the total credits (i.e., loans) approved by the IDA.

Some of the development projects in India helped by the IDA are: Rajasthan Canal Command Area Project, Chambal Command Project, Madhya Pradesh and Rajasthan Dairy Development Project, Development of Drought Prone Areas, Sindri Fertilizer Corporation, Godavari Barrage, etc., India has been the single largest beneficiary of the IDA.

IDA and Recent Developments

The IDA commitments to India in the fiscal years 1987 and 1988 amounted to 678 million US dollars and 717 million US dollars, respectively. India's share in the total lending by the IDA to all countries was 16 per cent in the fiscal year 1988. This was much lower than in the previous years (i.e., 19.9 per cent in the fiscal year 1986 and 19.4 per cent in the fiscal year 1987). This continued decline in the percentage in the share of India in soft loans granted by the IDA has been a cause of concern as such decline adds to India's debt servicing burden.

22.5 INTERNATIONAL FINANCE CORPORATION (IFC)

Introduction

After the establishment of the World Bank, the need for establishing another international financial institution was keenly felt. The World bank gives financial assistance (i.e., loans) only to its member-countries. This provision discouraged private foreigner investors. And, therefore the United States suggested in December 1954 that a new corporation be established that may promote foreign private investments. The Work Bank prepared the draft of the IFC which came into existence on 20th June as "an autonomous international institution designed to stimulate growth in its developing member-countries, by investing in productive enterprises in association with private capital and management and without any government guarantee."

Objectives of the IFC

The main objectives or functions of the IFC are as follows:

(1) The IFC makes investments in productive private enterprises in association with private investors and without government guarantee as regards repayment of loans in cases where sufficient private capital is not forthcoming on reasonable terms and conditions.

(2) The IFC makes an attempt to bring together investment opportunities domestic and foreign private capital as also experienced management.

(3) The IFC thus makes an attempt to promote investment flow of private capital.

(4) The IFC renders assistance for the development of capital markets in LDCs.

Membership and Capital Resources of the IFC

The IFC is affiliated to the World Bank, which means the membership of the IFC is open to all the member-countries of the World Bank.

The management of the IFC is about the same as that of the World Bank. Thus, Governors and Executive Directors of the World Bank represent member-countries in the IFC and serve the IFC in similar capacities. The President of the World Bank is the Chairman of the Board of Directors of the IFC. It is on the recommendation of the Chairman that the Board of Directors of the IFC appoints its President. This means that the activities and functioning of the IFC are fully controlled by the World Bank authorities, though the IFC maintains a separate account of its own.

Ownership and Management

IFC has 175 member countries, which collectively determine its policies and approve investments. To join IFC, a country must first be a member of the IBRD. IFC's corporate powers are vested in its Board of Governors, to which member countries appoint representatives. IFC's share capital, which is paid in, is provided by its member countries, and voting is in proportion to the number of shares held. IFC's authorized capital is $ 2.45 billion. Statement of Capital Stock and Voting Power. The Board of Governors delegates many of its powers to the Board of Directors, which is composed of the Executive Directors of the IBRD, and which represents IFC's member countries. The Board of Directors reviews all projects. The President of the World Bank Group, James D. Wolfensohn, also serves as IFC's president. IFC's Executive Vice President, Peer Woicke, is responsible for the overall management of day-to-day operations. Although IFC coordinates its activities in many areas with the other institutions in the World Bank Group, IFC generally operates independently as it is legally and financially autonomous with its own Articles of Agreement, share capital, management and staff.

The World Bank and the IFC

The IFC differs from the World Bank in the following three important respects:

(1) The IFC functions like a private investment firm, with a compact and competent staff of engineers, investment experts, lawyers, accountants, etc. Also the IFC hires outside consultants to deal with special technical problems like market surveys, etc.

(2) The IFC has the option of making fixed interest loans or make investments of equity-type nature and deal directly with private enterprises.

(3) The World Bank has substantial funds to make great impact on economies of member-countries. But the role of the IFC is that of a catalyst. The IFC employs its limited resources in conjunction with private investment capital for the expansion of private industrial enterprises in developing countries.

The authorised capital of the IFC is 100 million US dollars (of 1960 or equivalent of gold) and is subscribed by members in amounts in proportion to their subscriptions to the capital stock of the World Bank. The capital base of the IFC can be broadened if three-fourth majority of members of the IFC so desire. As on 30th June 1975, the IFC'S share capital amounted to about 107 million US dollars of which the contributions (in US dollars) were as follows: The United States (35.17 million), The United Kingdom (14.4 million), France (3.81 million), West Germany (3.65 million), India (4.43 million), Brazil (3.65 million) and Japan (2.77 million)..

In addition the IFC can borrow from the World Bank to the extent of four times its subscribed capital for its lending activities.

Investment Policy of IFC

The President of the IFC has explained the guiding principles of the IFC as follows: The Corporation (i.e., IFC) is to make investments in private sector enterprises in member-countries, particularly in less developed countries. It is envisaged that the IFC's investments will never be more than half of the capital needed for the venture. The rate of interest in each case would be a matter of negotiations depending upon risks and on other terms of investment. In general, it would be reasonable to expect that loans would normally run between 5 to 15 years. For several reasons the IFC's investments are likely to be in the industrial rather than in other fields.

Loans of the IFC are generally made on the following guiding principles:

(1) At least local entrepreneurs provide half of the total cost of the concerned project;

(2) As a matter of general policy, IFC does not invest in projects in developed project;

(3) The project to be aided by the IFC should generally be in the field of manufacturing, mining and processing;

(4) In each case, rate of interest would be determined by negotiations depending upon risk involved and other terms and conditions of investment;

(5) The IFC would evaluate projects from their profit-making capacity (as would normally be done by a private capitalist investor);

(6) The IFC enjoys the option of converting loans into capital stock of a project and appoint its members on the Board of Directors of the borrowing private enterprise;

(7) The IFC reserves the right to sell such capital stock at any time and to any party;

(8) Loans of the IFC would normally be for a period of 5 to 15 years;

(9) The IFC would grant loans to a project only if it is satisfied that the enterprise has experienced and competent management;

(10) The role of the IFC is to supplement and not to compete with private capital in areas where the IFC is providing finance;

(11) The IFC does not require guarantee of the government of the country where the project is located to be aided by the IFC. But in case the concerned government objects to a project, the IFC would not grant loan to such a project. Until June 1971, IFC had invested 577.8 million

US dollars in 172 industrial projects in 47 LDCs. The IFC investment in India then amounted to 27.3 million US dollars in various projects, some of the important ones being Kirloskar Diesel Engines, Lakshmi Machine Ltd., Suari Agro-Chemical Ltd., KSB Pumps Ltd., etc.

By June 1975 gross commitments of the IFC had risen to 1262 million US dollars. This amount was sanctioned for 249 enterprises in 57 LDCs.

Of the total amount disbursed by 30th June 1975, 48 per cent was provided by the United States, 23 per cent by Japan, 11 per cent by the European Economic Community, and about 15 per cent from IFC's own resources.

Of the total amount committed by 30th June 1975, 43% was allotted to Latin American countries, 24% to Asian countries, 19% to European countries, 9% to African countries and around 5% to Middle East countries.

Major part of the IFC loans have gone for promoting development of industries such as iron and steel, cement, textiles, paper, chemicals and allied industries in member-countries.

By 30th June 1975 India had received 52 million US dollars for 11 private sector projects.

Funding of IFC's Activities

IFC's equity and quasi-equity investments are funded out of its net worth: the total of paid in capital and retained earnings. Of the funding required for its lending operations, 80 per cent is borrowed through public bond issues of private placements. The remaining 20 per cent is borrowed from the IBRD.

IFC Financial Products: IFC offers a wide variety of financial products to private sector projects in developing countries. IFC offers:

- Loans for IFC's own account : A-loans
- Equity Finance
- Quasi-Equity Finance: C-loans
- Syndicated Loans: B-loans
- Risk Management Products

Intermediary Finance: IFC can provide a mix of financing that is tailored to meet the needs of each project. However, the bulk of the funding, as well as leadership and management responsibility, lie with private sector owners. IFC operates on a commercial basis. It invests exclusively in for-profit projects and charges market rates for its products and services. There is no standard application form for IFC financing. A company or entrepreneur, foreign or domestic, seeking to establish a new venture or expand an existing enterprise can approach IFC directly. As a rule, the enterprises IFC finances must be majority private sector owned and controlled. Exceptions can be made for state-owned enterprises, which are in the process of being privatized. Although IFC does not take any government guarantees for its financing, IFC's work often requires close cooperation with government agencies in developing countries.

Resource Mobilization: Mobilizing funds from private investors and lenders for private sector projects in developing countries is one of IFC's most essential functions. IFC actively seeks partners for joint ventures and raises additional finance by encouraging other institutions to make investments in IFC projects. The Corporation's unique strengths include:

- A capacity to act as a catalyst. By mobilizing capital from institutions that would not invest without IFC's involvement, the Corporation greatly increases the leverage of its limited resources.
- A large network of company contacts and a special ability to match sponsors and partners with investors.
- A capacity to pioneer transactions that are first-of-their kind to a particular market.

IFC operates on a commercial basis. It invests exclusively in for-profit projects and charges market rates for its products and services.

Securitization, Underwriting and Private Placements: The cornerstone of IFC's finance mobilization efforts is the B-loan program for syndicated loans. In addition, IFC is at the forefront of developing innovative products and instruments that channel investor funds to the private sector in developing countries. For example, IFC helped established the first specialized securitization and credit enhancement institution in Indonesia. As corporations in developing countries find that their financing requirements increase, some attempt to fill these needs by issuing securities in international capital markets. Through securitization, IFC can help these companies raise funds.

Portfolio Investment: IFC also works to promote foreign portfolio investment in developing countries by establishing and investing in a wide range of funds, such as private equity funds and debt funds that invest in emerging market securities issues. For example: IFC launched the first local currency emerging market corporate debt fund. As an alternative method for investor to gain access to emerging markets, IFC promotes index funds. Investments in venture capital funds help channel flows to companies that are generally unlisted and that might not receive the notice of large investors. It should be noted that through IFC's mobilization efforts, both small and large companies in the developing world are able to gain access to longer-term finance, many for the first time. Accessing financing from international capital markets help them to enhance their competitiveness in more open economies around the world.

Multilateral Investment Guarantee Agency

The Multilateral Investment Guarantee Agency (MIGA) was created in 1988 as a member of the World Bank Group with an objective to promote foreign direct investment into emerging economies and to improve people's lives and reduce poverty. MIGA tries to accomplish these objectives by offering political risk insurance (guarantees) to investors and lenders, and by helping developing countries attract and retain private investment.

MIGA is led in its mission by four guiding principles:

- Focusing on clients — serving investors, lenders and host country governments by supporting private enterprise and promoting foreign investment;
- Engaging in partnerships — working with other insurers, government agencies and international organizations to ensure complementarity of services and approach;

- Promoting development impact — striving to improve the lives of people in emerging economies, consistent with the goals of host countries and sound business, environmental, and social principles; ensuring financial soundness — balancing developmental goals and financial objectives through prudent underwriting and sound risk management.

MIGA Membership

MIGA membership, which currently stands at 154, is open to all World Bank members. The agency has a capital stock of SDR 1 billion. In March 1999, MIGA's Council of Governors adopted a resolution for a capital increase of approximately $850 million. The agency received another $150 million in operating capital from the World Bank.

MIGA's guarantee coverage requires investors to adhere to social and environmental standards that are considered the world's best. Without World Bank Group involvement, projects often go ahead without adequate safeguards. MIGA both supports and draws on the extensive resources of the World Bank Group, applying available pool of knowledge of emerging economies to the projects it guarantees. MIGA's unique strengths also derive from its structure as an international organization that acts as an umbrella of deterrence against government actions that could disrupt investments, and allows it to influence the resolution of potential disputes. MIGA's potential capacity to serve as an objective intermediary can enhance investor confidence that an investment going into an emerging economy will be protected against non-commercial risks.

Concerns about uncertain political environments and perceptions of political risks often inhibit investment, with foreign direct investment (FDI) often going to a handful of countries and leaving the world's poorest economies largely ignored. MIGA is supposed to work as an important catalyst, increasingly promoting FDI — a key driver of growth — into developing countries through its guarantees, technical assistance, and legal services.

Since its inception, MIGA has issued more than 500 guarantees for projects in 78 developing countries. As of June 2001, total coverage issued exceeded $ 9 billion, bringing the estimated amount of foreign direct investment facilitated since inception to more than $ 41 billion. The agency mobilized an additional $ 153 million in investment coverage in fiscal 2001 through its Cooperative Underwriting Program (CUP), encouraging private sector insurers into transactions they would not have otherwise undertaken, and helping the agency serve more clients. MIGA's technical assistance services also play an integral role in catalyzing foreign direct investment by helping developing countries around the world define and implement strategies to promote investment. MIGA develops and deploys tools and technologies to support the spread of information on investment opportunities. The agency uses its legal services to further smooth possible impediments to investment. Through its dispute mediation program, MIGA helps governments and investors resolve their differences, and ultimately improve the country's investment climate. MIGA complements the activities of other investment insurers and works with partners through its co-insurance and re-insurance programs to expand the capacity of the political risk insurance industry's income. To date, MIGA has officially established 18 such partnerships.

Criticism of the IFC

Following are the main points of criticism brought against IFC:

(i) The IFC charges normally 6½ to 8% interest which is too high for a number of LDCs to pay.

(ii) The IFC insists that interest on loan and the principal be paid by borrowing countries in US dollars which many LDCs are not in a position to do.

(iii) The financial assistance rendered by IFC often falls short when compared to capital requirements of projects in LDCs.

In spite of the above points of criticism, there is no doubt that the International Finance Corporation has been contributing significantly to industrial development of a number of developing countries.

22.6 ASIAN DEVELOPMENT BANK (ADB)

Introduction: The World Bank had been trying to set up regional development banks and some regional banks have been established for developing countries in Latin America, Africa and Asia.

The Economic Commission for Asia and Far Fast (ECAFE) had made in 1963 a suggestion for a regional development bank for Asian countries. Representatives of the major Asian countries met at Manila in December 1965 to finalise the proposal and the Asian Development Bank came to be formally established in December 1966.

Objective and Functions of the ADB

The basic objective behind the establishment of the ADB is "to promote economic development of and mutual cooperation among the countries of Asia." The ADB's objective is to help accelerate the process of economic development of developing countries in the Asian region.

To realise the objective the ADB performs the following functions:

(1) To promote investment of public and private capital for economic development of Asian countries;

(2) To channelise investible funds of the ADB for the implementation of those projects which are important for the development of major sectors of the country's economies;

(3) To render assistance to member-countries in coordinating their programmes and policies of economic development and at the same time to promote inter-regional trade and cooperation among countries of the Asian region;

(4) To promote technical assistance for the execution of projects; and

(5) To mobilise funds for economic development of member-countries by extending cooperation of the World Bank, ECAFE and other United Nation's bodies and public as also private institutions located among member-countries.

Membership, Capital Resources and Organisation

The membership of the ADB is open to all countries in Asia, but for procuring additional and substantial financial and other resources, many developed countries of other regions are also admitted as members of the ADB.

By the end of June 1975, the ADB had 27 Asian members and 14 non-regional members, thus making a total of 41 members.

The authorised capital (in terms of US dollars) for the ADB was 3366 million US dollars as on 31 December 1974. The subscribed capital on that date was 2770 million US dollars.

Besides subscribed capital, the ADB has also raised additional financial resources through borrowings. By December 1972 the total amount of outstanding borrowings by the ADB was 293 million US dollars, about 30% of this being borrowings from Japan in yens.

At the time of the establishment of the ADB, member-countries were asked to deposit only 50% of their subscribed capital in their national currencies. The Board of Governors is free to call the remainder of the member-countries subscribed capital, whenever the ADB needs additional funds for carrying on its lending activities.

Some of the important non-regional members of the ADB are: United States, the Untied Kingdom, West Germany and Canada. Japan is the principal subscriber to the ADB, apart from contributing substantial share capital of the ADB.

Out of the total voting power, 20% has been allocated among member-countries equally, whereas the remaining 80% has been allocated on the basis of subscribed share capital by each member of ADB.

The management of the ADB is entrusted to the Board of Governors constituted by representatives of the member-countries of the ADB. The Board of Governors meet once a year, whereas for routine decision-making and carrying on the ADB's lending and other operations, a ten-member Board of Directors has been constituted.

In April 1974 there came to be established a fund known as the Asian Development Fund. It is a multi-purpose fund, the proceeds of which are to be utilised for providing concessional loans to the relatively poorer member-countries of the ADB. Ten member-countries had subscribed 245.4 million US dollars to the Asian Development Fund by December 1974.

Lending Operations of the ADB

The ADB provides loans to its member-countries keeping in view the following considerations:

(1) Larger portions of ADB loans should be given to relatively poorer among developing countries in Asia;

(2) The government of the borrowing country has approved the loan by ADB being given to the private or public sector enterprise;

(3) The Chairman of ADB has received a detailed report of the project for which the ADB is to provide loan;

(4) The ADB while giving loan also takes into consideration prospects of loans which the applicant may receive from other than ADB source.

(5) Generally the ADB loans are to be used within the markets of member-countries for purchase of essential goods, etc.; but the Board of Directors with a two-third majority can allow the ADB loan to be used in markets of non-member countries; and

(6) The ADB will function strictly keeping in view the sound principles of banking.

During 1968-73 the ADB approved loans totalling (in terms of US dollars) 1376 million US dollars to 21 countries for 189 projects. Of these, industrial development projects were given a quarter of the total loans; 24% of loans were given for development of transport and communication projects; 26.5% for electrical power projects; 12.5% for agricultural development projects; 11.2% for water supply projects and 1% for educational projects.

During 1974 the ADB sanctioned loans worth (in terms of US dollars) 547.7 million of which 186.9 million were for industrial development projects; 134 million for agricultural development projects; 76.55 million for power projects; and 81.5 million for transport and communication projects. There appeared an evident shift in the sectoral allocation of ADB's lending policy in 1974.

If the period of 1968-74 is considered, of the total approved, 17.5% were given to South Korea; 12.5% to the Philippines; 10.63% to Malaysia; 9.4% to the Republic of China; and 8.5% to Singapore. This means that more than 50% of the total loans sanctioned were given during this period to East Asian countries. India did not ask for any loan during this period; but Bangladesh received 9.5% of the total loans during this period.

The ADB charges $8^1/_4$% interest on its loans, though at the time of its establishment the rate of interest charged was 6.78% which was raised to $7^1/_2$% in May 1970 and to $8^1/_4$% in September 1974.

Criticism of the Role and Functioning of the ADB

Following are the main points of criticism that are generally made in regard to the role and functioning of the ADB:

(1) Though the ADB is a financial institution concerned solely with development problems of Asian countries, it is alleged that the role and working of the ADB is greatly influenced by strategies and interest of the United States. This becomes clear from the fact that majority of Asian countries that received financial assistance from the ADB are allies of the United States (e.g., South Korea, the Philippines, Singapore which have fairly developed economies). The borrowers of the ADB have generally been supporters of the United States in international affairs. It is for this reason that the Soviet Union has not become a member of the ADB.

(2) It is alleged that the rate of interest charged by the ADB is high and the proportion of concessional loans from the ADB has been generally low. And, therefore, ADB has not been in a position to provide substantial financial assistance to poorer Asian developing countries which should have been the main objective of the ADB. And, therefore, the LDCs from Asian region are forced to borrow from some other international agencies than the ADB.

(3) Generally, ADB provides 'tied loans' and compels borrowing countries to use those loans only for specified projects. Naturally, this reduces scope or area for the development of LDCs for which ADB was established in the first instance.

(4) Generally, ADB loans were given to private sector projects. The ADB has shown very little interest in the development of public sector which has been playing a major role in the development of LDCs in Asian countries.

There is thus need to re-examine the role and functioning of the ADB in the light of the above criticism.

India and the ADB

India is the third largest shareholder in ADB among its regional members. Overall, India is the fourth largest shareholder.

Number of shares held: 224,010 (6.45% of total shares).

Votes: 238,733 (5.50% of total membership, 8.39% of total regional membership).

Overall capital

Subscription: US$ 2.81 billion

Paid-in capital

Subscription: US$196.97 million

Loans and Technical Assistance

ADB approved seven loans totalling US$1.5 billion in 2001 to rehabilitate and reconstruct areas damaged by the Gujarat earthquake, develop the western transport corridor and the West Bengal corridor, establish a private sector infrastructure facility at the state level (two project loans), and implement the Madhya Pradesh power sector development program (program and project loans).

ADB approved 12 technical assistance grants, of which 8 were for advisory purposes on capacity building for earthquake rehabilitation and reconstruction of housing, conducting the Madhya Pradesh integrated water resource management study, enhancing the corporate finance capability of the National Highways Authority of India, assessing the role of mortgage-backed securities, determining the impact on poverty reduction of financial sector policies and reforms, and improving the accounting system of the Calcutta Municipal Corporation. Four were technical assistance grants to prepare the Kerala power sector development program, Madhya Pradesh State road sector and integrated urban development projects, and public-private partnership on the National Highway Corridor. Five of the technical assistance grants approved in 2001 were funded by the United Kingdom.

Cumulative ADB lending to India as of 31 December 2001 was US$ 10.45 billion.

Breakdown of cumulative ADB lending to India, as of 31 December 2001. **Sector**	**Loan (number)**	**Loan Amount (US$ million)**	**%**
Energy	20	3,741.8[a]	35.8
Transport and Communications	15	2,605.6	24.9
Social Infrastructure	13	1,400.0[b]	13.4
Finance	11	1,330.0	12.7
Multisector	6	1,200.0	11.5
Industry and Non-fuel Minerals	4	175.9	1.7
Total	69	10,453.3	100.0

(a) Adjusted after termination of the private sector loan to Balagarh Power Co., Ltd. amounting to US$25 million.

(b) Adjusted after termination of two loans under the Housing Finance II: Housing and Urban Development Corporation (US$100 million), and Housing Development Finance Corporation (US$ 80 million).

Table 22. 1. India: Economic Indicators, 2002-2006

Economic Indicator	2002	2003	2004	2005	2006
Per capita GNI (US$)	470	530	630	720	...
GDP growth (% change per year)	3.8	8.5	7.5	9.0	9.2
CPI (% change per year)	3.4	5.4	6.4	4.4	5.5
Unemployment rate (%)	...	...	...	...	...
Fiscal balance (% of GDP)	-9.6	-8.5	-7.5	-7.4	-6.4
Export growth (% change per year)	20.3	23.3	28.5	23.4	20.0
Import growth (% change per year)	14.5	24.1	48.6	32.0	26.2
Current account (% of GDP)	1.2	2.3	0.4	-1.1	-2.1
External debt (% of GNI)	20.8	18.9	18.0	15.6	...

... = data not available, CPI = consumer price index, GDP = gross domestic product, GNI = gross national income.

Sources: ADB. 2007. *Asian Development Outlook, 2007,* Manila

ADB. 2007. Statistical Database Systems.

Table 22.2 India: 2006 Loan, TA, and Grant Approvals

($ million)

Loans				
Sovereign	**Non-sovereign**	**TA**	**Grants**	**Total**
1,260.00	275.00	30.57	5.00	1,570.57

Cumulative Lending (as of 31 Dec. 2006) : $ 16,448.21 million

Cumulative Disbursements (as of 31 Dec. 2006) : $ 8,856.54 million

Table 22.3 India: Cumulative ADB Lending as of 31 December 2006

Sector	Loans (no.)	Amount ($ million)	%
Agriculture and Natural Resources	1	46.11	0.28
Energy	29	5,125.80	31.16
Finance	14	2,460.00	14.96
Health, Nutrition and Social Protection	1	20.00	0.12
Industry and Trade	8	185.90	1.13
Law, Economic Management and Public Policy	5	850	5.17
Multisector	15	2,280.00	13.86
Transportation and Communication	24	4,979.20	30.27
Water Supply, Sanitation and Waste Management	3	501.20	3.05
Total	100	16,448.21	100.00

Total may not add due to rounding.

The core focus of ADB's operational strategy in India is poverty reduction through infrastructure-led growth. ADB's current operational strategy for India was laid down in the Country Strategy and Program (CSP) 2003-with updates in 2004 and 2005-and the Country Operations Business.

Plan (COBP) in 2006 to reflect the evolving priorities of the Government of India. The three pillars of ADB's strategy are inclusive and broad-based growth, social development, and good governance.

The relevance of this strategy is borne out by the high priority the Government gives to programs, such as Bharat Nirman, National Highway Development Program, Pradhan Mantri Gram Sadak Yojana (Rural Roads Development Program), Power for All by 2012, and the National Urban Renewal Mission. More than 75% of ADB's India program has traditionally focused on infrastructure.

In line with the Government's focus on agriculture, rural development, and sustainable water use, ADS has initiated.operation in these areas since 2004-2005. The first such loan, the Chhattisgarh Irrigation project for $46.1 million, was approved In 2004. In December 2006, it approved the $1 billion Rural Cooperative Credit Restructuring and Development Program loan for revamping India's cooperative credit system.

Impact of Assistance

Poor roads are among the main causes of poverty in India, and an impediment to realizing the economic potential of rural areas. The Government's Rural Roads Program (Pradhan Mantri Gram Sadak Yojana) aims to provide all-weather roads to poor rural areas, where nearly 70% of the population lives. In 2003, ADB approved a loan assistance of $400 million for the program, and made $750 million available in 2005 (as an MFF loan). The program is in its sixth year of implementation and has successfully improved nearly 87,314 kilometers of rural roads. ADB's assistance to the program is expected to encourage growth in agricultural incomes and employment by improving marketing of farm inputs and outputs, and enhancing access to health and educational facilities.

The $85 million Karnataka Urban Infrastructure Development Project (KUIDP, Loan 1415-IND, December 1995-June 2004) has met its objective of improving basic urban services and infrastructure (water supply, sewerage, drainage, solid waste, urban roads, and capacity building of the municipal corporations) in the four main towns surrounding Bangalore. More than 1.5 million people-mainly the urban poor and those with low income-benefited from the Improved services constructed under the project. More than 17,500 low-income homes were fitted with personal toilets and water connections. More than 20 local non-government organizations were engaged to undertake a number of community-based interventions in public health. This was ADB's first effort at urban development in India and the lessons learned have been incorporated into subsequent urban development projects in Karnataka and elsewhere.

The Madhya Pradesh Power Sector Development loan (December 200 1-December 2006) has helped separate the generation, transmission, and distribution companies of the State Electricity Board, improving the viability of the state power sector through rationalization of tariffs, financial restructuring, and improved cost recovery through expanded metering. The loan has also helped establish the legal and regulatory framework for encouraging private sector participation. Power sector reforms will help to spur economic growth in Madhya Pradesh and indirectly lower poverty. A follow-up Madhya Pradesh Sector Investment Program (MFF $620 million) was approved at the end of March 2007.

Reform of India's vast cooperative credit structure-a key priority of the current government — is critical for facilitating inclusive growth. The $1 billion Rural Cooperative Credit Restructuring and Development Program, approved in 2006, aims at supporting government efforts and strengthening rural finance institutions.

Contributions to Special Funds Resources

India has contributed to the Technical Assistance Special Fund (TASF) US$ 2.81 million, which provides grants to borrowing members to help prepare projects and undertake technical or policy studies.

Cofinancing

ADB arranges cofinancing from official, commercial, and export credit sources as additional resources for project financing. Cofinancing arrangements in 2001 amounted to US$ 1.4 billion for 25 loan projects and US$ 86.5 million in untied grant financing or 34 technical assistance projects. At the end of 2001, cumulative cofinancing arrangements (beginning in 1970) amounted to US$ 36.2 billion for 580 loan projects and US$ 425.3 million for 430 technical assistance grants.

Share in ADB's Procurement Contracts

Each year, ADB provides loans to fund projects and activities in its Asian and Pacific developing members and several billion US dollars' worth of contracts to procure goods and consulting services.

From 1 January 1997 to 31 December 2001, ADB approved US$ 31.30 billion in loans for 315 projects and US$ 790.75 million in technical assistance for 1,360 projects. As of 31 December 2001, the cumulative totals were US$ 93.16 billion in loans for 1,683 projects in 38 countries and US$ 2.04 billion for 4,748 technical assistance projects, including regional technical assistance projects.

Procurement contracts for goods and related services, civil works and consulting services under loan and technical assistance operations totalled US$ 3.54 billion in 2000 and US$2.70 billion in 2001. Cumulative procurement as of 31 December 2001 was US$ 62.62 billion. Most contracts were awarded on the basis of international competition, which is open to firms and individuals from any ADB member countries, regional or non-regional.

ADB Governors and Executive Directors for India

The Honorable Yashwant Sinha, Minister of Finance, is the Governor for India in ADB. *Mr. C.M. Yasudev,* Secretary, Department of Economic Affairs, Ministry of Finance, is the Alternate Governor for India in ADB. *Mr. P. Mankad* is the ADB Executive Director for India. Mr. Mankad, who is from India, was Finance Secretary; Industry Secretary; and Chairman, Foreign Investment Promotion Board, Ministry of Commerce and Industry, Government of India.

Mr. M. Saiful Islam is the ADB Alternate Executive Director for India, effective 1 April 2002. Mr. Islam, who is from Bangladesh, the constituency that Executive Director Mankad and Alternate Executive Director Islam represent on ADB's Board of Directors also includes Bangladesh, Bhutan, Lao People's Democratic Republic, and Tajikistan.

CHAPTER 23

REGIONAL ECONOMIC COOPERATION

Structure:

23.1 INTRODUCTION

Developments in modern industrial techniques require and make possible production of goods and services on a very large-scale — one car per minute, thousands of newspapers per hour, millions of calculations per hour, reaching from any place to any other place in the world in a single day and so on. Development of such modern techniques of production necessitate expanding markets (i.e., markets larger than mere national markets) and also increasing purchasing power with the people. Logically it follows that if nations by themselves constitute geographically and monetarily smaller markets than required by modern techniques of production, then the only remedy to fully exploit production potentialities of modern techniques would be to bring about geographical expansion of markets which would be economically viable units. Realisation of this fact led many national leaders to think in terms of regional economic cooperation or formation of economic groupings to enable fuller exploitation of rapidly advancing modern techniques of production.

There are also political reasons behind the thinking of forming regional economic groupings. The two devastating wars in the first half of the 20th century led some West European leaders to think in terms of United States of Europe based on close economic cooperation and inter-dependence so that there would be no political or economic cause for fighting with one another (as France and Germany did in 1870, 1914-18 and 1939-45).

There were two other considerations making West European leaders think in terms of regional groupings. For quite some time the Soviet Union was thinking in terms of world dominance through the spread of international communism. It was feared that if West European countries remain scattered and divided national states, successful resistance to the Soviet aim of spreading communism in the whole of Europe and later on in the whole world cannot be successfully resisted. This also led democratic leaders of West European countries to think in terms of unified Europe to successfully resist the possible onward march of international communism.

There is also another reason, though not openly mentioned. The United States of America, compared to West European nations, is geographically a vast country with variegated and abundant supply of practically all types of agricultural and industrial resources unmatched by any single West European country. Also, during World War I and World War II the United States was away from the main theatre of those devastating wars which engulfed practically the whole of Western Europe. While in the 19th century there was the West European economic domination in the world, the consequence of World War I and World War II was that the United States emerged as supreme economic power and as the most powerful industrial nation in the world. It was rightly felt that the United States, industries which produce on a very large-scale would just dominate West European markets as also markets in other countries in the world. If this unrivalled US industrial supremacy is to be successfully matched and if industries are to be established to successfully compete with those in the United States, it was felt that such an effort could succeed only if European countries unified their economies. Thus, economic and political considerations led to the formation of European Economic Community (the EEC) and subsequently to the formation of other regional groups of sovereign nations, mainly for economic cooperation among members of such regional groupings of national states.[1]

1. The vision of the creation of the European Economic Community was provided by two French Statesmen, Jean Monnet and Robert Schuman with the cooperation of the West German Chancellor Konard Adenauer.

23.2 TYPES OF ECONOMIC COOPERATION

During the Post-World War II period, there have evolved various types or forms of economic cooperation. Economic cooperation among nations may take any one or a combination of the following forms:

(1) Customs Union; (2) Economic Union; (3) Free Trade Area; (4) Partial or Sectoral Integration; and (5) Long-term Trade Agreements.

The above classification of economic cooperation among nations is based on the degree of economic cooperation contemplated among nations.

(1) *Customs Union:* According to the Article XXIX of the Articles of Agreement of the GATT a 'Customs Union, is defined as "The substitution of a single customs territory for two or more customs territories, so that : (i) Duties and other regulations of commerce ... are eliminated with respect to substantially all trade between the constituent territories of the Union or at least with respect to substantially all the trade in products originating in such territories, and (ii) The same duties and other regulations of commerce are applied by each of the members of the Union to the trade of territories not included in the Union."[2]

Following the above definition, Prof. J.E. Meade has defined the Customs Union as the one in which "there is complete freedom for the movement of goods and services between... the partner countries of a Customs Union: Complete freedom of movement of goods and services within the territories of member-countries or a common tariff applicable to all the member-countries of the Customs Union and a common tariff adopted by all the member-countries of the Customs Union with respect to the rest of the world."

(2) *Economic Union:* Economic Union is a case of complete integration of economies of different national economies. Economic Union may be defined as "... the complete economic integration of a group of countries in which capital, labour, commodities and services move without any restrictions, and the economic activities and policies of the constituent countries are harmonised, coordinated and collectively operated." In an ideal type of Economic Union all the member countries forming the Economic Union follow the same taxation, commercial, industrial and other policies; there is a common currency; all constituent countries constitute one market and there is allowed completely unrestricted movement of factors of production, notably labour and of commodities.

The Benelux (Belgium, the Netherlands and Luxembourg) is a classical example of Economic Union. Another example of Economic Union is European Economic Community (the EEC), though full integration of the economies of all the member-countries is still to be achieved.

The basic features of Economic Union are: The customs union; complete abolition of all restrictions hampering movements of labour, capital and services in the areas of all the member-countries; there is common transport policy; common agricultural policy; common policy and measures to remedy the balance of payments difficulties and problems of member countries; the establishment of a development bank; formulation of rules ensuring competition among all the member-countries and common currency and common monetary and fiscal policy.

2. Article XXIV — Articles of Agreement of GATT.

It is generally not possible to establish Economic Union straight away. As in the case of European Economic Community, Economic Union comes to be evolved only by stages, one step leading to another, finally leading to the establishment of Economic Union. As the constituent member-countries would be having their own vested individual interests and policies to protect them, it would take some time before the interests of different constituent member-countries get harmonised and they merge into Economic Union.

(3) *Free Trade Area:* 'Free Trade Area' may be defined as "a group of two or more customs territories in which duties and other restrictive regulations of commerce are eliminated substantially on all the trade between the constituent territories in products originating in such territories."

The difference between 'Customs Union' and 'Free Trade Area' is that in a Customs Union, the constituent members adopt a common tariff policy applicable to the countries not in the Customs Union; but in the case of Free Trade Area, the constituent-members adopt uniform tariff rates for the member-countries but each member-country may adopt different individual tariff in respect of countries not in the Free Trade Area.

For example, Free Trade Areas are (1) European Free Trade Association (EFTA). For some years England did not join the European Economic Community, and as a counter measure to the EEC, England took the lead in establishing EFTA which is also known as 'The Outer Seven.' Members of the EFTA are: England, Norway, Sweden, Switzerland, Austria, Portugal and Denmark. Finland joined the EFTA as an associate member in 1961. (2) Latin American Free Trade Association (LAFTA).

Compared to Customs Union, Free Trade Area may be preferred by constituent members because of the absence of common external tariff. This would enable constituent members freedom to adopt separate tariff and trade policies in respect of countries which are not members of Free Trade Area, while at the same time having a common tariff within the area of constituent members.

(4) *Partial or Sectoral Integration:* 'Partial or Sectoral Integration' may be defined as "the establishment of a common market for a particular or specific product or products." The example of such a partial or sectoral integration is the European Coal and Steel Community (E.C.S.C.). In the case of a partial or sectoral integration, by mutual agreement among the member-countries, import and export duties on specific commodities or commodity as also all discriminatory practices, quantitative restrictions, export subsidies and all types of restrictive practices that would prevent competition among member-countries forming such a partial or sectoral integration in respect of such a commodity or commodities are eliminated.

(5) *Long-Term Trade Agreement:* Long-term trade agreement or contract is a type of bilateral arrangement in regard to a specific commodity or commodities entering into trade between the two participating countries. In case of such an arrangement, long-term means any period exceeding one year. For example, India entered into long-term trade contract with Japan whereby India supplied to Japan iron ore for a period of five years on conditions agreed in the bilateral contract, or India's bilateral contract with the Soviet Union whereby the Soviet Union agreed to supply raw cotton and India was to weave it into cloth and send back the entire quantity of cloth, the Soviet Union paying to India the entire amount of value-added in converting raw cotton into cloth. India has entered into such long-term trade contracts or arrangements

with a number of countries in respect of specific commodity or commodities. The main advantage of such a long-term trade contract or arrangement is that it helps to stabilise export prices of a specific commodity or commodities and thus by helping to avoid fluctuations in export prices in respect of specified commodity or commodities, help to ease pressure on balance of payments position of the participating countries. Also, if the long-term contract is for a fairly long period (i.e., 5 years in the case of supply of iron to Japan), it helps to plan the production of such a commodity or commodities on long-term basis and thus helps the general planning process by increasing export earnings, at least in respect of specified good or goods. But one possible disadvantage is that if price escalation clause is not provided for in the long-term contract, the exporting country cannot take full advantage of upward fluctuations in prices of the concerned commodities in regard to which the long-term contract or agreement is entered into.

23.3 THEORY OF CUSTOMS UNION

The term 'Customs Union' refers to a block of many countries trying to remove barriers on trade of goods between member-countries forming the customs union and thus helping economic integration.

It is observed that after the end of World War II, several nations in different parts of the world made an attempt to explore the possibilities of regional economic cooperation. The most significant move in this direction resulted in the formation of the European Economic Community (the EEC). With the establishment of the EEC, six Western nations (now twelve) decided to create a free trade block of the member-countries of the EEC and at the same time decided to have a common tariff against imports of goods from non-member countries.

Since then economists have started paying increasing attention to static and dynamic effects of customs union.

Prof. Viner made an attempt to throw light on probable impact of customs union on the welfare of people in member-countries of the customs union.

While analysing such effects, note must be taken of the fact that every customs union is a mixture of free trade (within member-countries) and protection (in regard to imports from non-member countries). Customs union is practising free trade in the sense that there are no restrictions on movement of goods and services or import of goods and services from partners of customs union. At the same time, customs union represents policy of protection because there are tariffs and other quantitative trade restrictions on imports from non-member countries.

The favourable and unfavourable effects of customs union are mainly the result of this mixture of policies of free trade and protection.

Historically, before the formation of a customs union like the EEC, most of the countries had tariffs on foreign goods to divert demand from imported goods to domestically produced goods. This means that after the formation of customs union, tariffs on goods from non-member countries continued, but tariffs on goods from member-countries of the customs union were abolished. It allowed free trade in the markets of member-countries of the customs union. It is argued that if it is possible to have free trade for the entire world economy, there should at least be a beginning in the direction of free trade for a particular region in the world.

Prof. Viner has made an attempt to explain effects of customs union in terms of trade diversion and trade creation.

Every customs union results in a certain volume of trade diversion. Free trade diversion can be of two types: (1) Trade is directed from non-member countries to the member-countries of the customs union. In this case though goods of non-member countries may be cheaper in terms of comparative cost advantage, people in the customs union have to buy goods of member-countries at higher prices because of common tariff imposed on imports from non-member countries, making those goods dearer.

Trade is also diverted from a particular country joining customs union to its other member-countries. This may happen because when customs union is formed, there is no protection to domestic producers against competition of producers of similar goods from other member-countries. Therefore, if domestic goods are costly, people in the country would buy similar cheaper goods from other member-countries. When there is trade diversion in this manner, there may be loss of welfare of the community because people do not get advantage of buying goods in the cheapest markets in the world.

At the same time, because there is no tariff on goods of member-countries, government incur loss of revenue which indirectly means that the terms of trade have become unfavourable for a particular member-country.

However, according to Prof. Viner, loss resulting from trade diversion may be compensated by gains arising out of trade-creation. When customs union is formed, tariffs on goods from member-countries of the customs union are abolished. As a consequence consumers might get those goods comparatively cheaply and that may lead to larger consumption and increase in demand for those goods. Such additional consumption gives more satisfaction to people. It is also possible that because free trade takes place among member-countries of customs union, inefficient producers may disappear and resources are released to more efficient units of some other member-country which enjoys advantages arising out of such trade creation.

23.4 DYNAMIC EFFECTS OF CUSTOMS UNION (AS ALSO OF ECONOMIC UNION)

Though the title indicates that the dynamic effects of 'Customs union' are to be analysed here, since 'Economic Union' includes 'Customs Union' the economic effects or consequences of Customs Union are equally true or hold good in the case of Economic Union, possibly much more so than in the case of Customs Union.

Before the formation of a Customs Union, say of two countries, countries A and B were pursuing independent customs policy, thus A imposing its own customs duty on goods imported from country B, and country B doing the same in respect of imports from country A, and both the countries A and B were following their own independent customs or tariff policy in regard to C (i.e., rest of the world). When countries A and B form a Customs Union, customs and other trade barriers between countries A and B are removed, and the two countries A and B also pursue a common customs or tariff policy in regard to C (i.e., the rest of the world). Such a Customs Union leads to trade diversion between countries A and B and also between countries A and B and C (i.e., rest of the world), and there is effect on prices of goods traded among A, B and C and on the welfare of peoples in countries A and B. These effects are known as 'effect of the formation of a Customs Union.

Prof. W.M. Corden and Prof. T. Scitovsky and many others have given greater emphasis on or importance to dynamic effects of the formation of a Customs Union (which as stated above, are also the dynamic effects of the formation of Economic Union).

Following are the main effects of the formation of a Customs Union:

(1) *Increasing Competition:* Formation of a customs union, say of countries A and B, provides stimulus to increasing competition. As internal tariffs are removed in countries A and B, markets for their goods and services expand, and competition increases among producers in countries A and B. The monopolistic and oligopolistic industrial establishments that have become inefficient in the sheltered markets of countries A and B (before they formed a customs union) will be exposed to increasing competition and this would undermine their monopolistic or oligopolistic power over their markets.

In the same way industrial and commercial firms operating below optimum level or size will be exposed to increasing competition in wider markets made up of markets of countries A and B. Naturally, this will lead to restructuring of the industrial establishments providing stimulus to their managerial and technological improvements, leading to reduction of costs and prices. T. Scitovsky has to draw attention to this significant dynamic effect of the promotion of the European Economic Community.

(2) *Movements of Factors of Production:* When countries A and B form a customs union (and, therefore, a common market) there will be free and unrestricted movement of labour, capital and entrepreneurs in the common market. This leads to increase in their efficiency, and rise in growth rates of the economies of countries A and B.

(3) *Emergence of Economies of Scale:* With the formation of a customs union, there is expansion in size of markets. Thus, markets of countries A and B, instead of remaining independent markets with their own tariffs, fences, etc., now constitute a single, and therefore, a wider market. This will lead to increasing specialisation, expansion in the sizes of industrial and commercial establishments and to reaping benefits of both internal and external economies. Thus, Prof. Lipsey has pointed out that as a result of the formation of a customs union, the union market expands and that will lead to the growth in size of industrial establishments thereby leading to the realisation of economies of scale.

(4) *Technological Advancement and Progress:* Expansion of markets, increased specialisation and competition will provide stimulus to innovations and technological advancement which with increasing competition in the larger markets consequent on the formation of a customs union becomes possible and essential even for survival. Industrial and commercial units reaping the economies of scale in the larger markets will be in a position to push upto their sales, expand their production, earn increasing profits and provide increasing amount of funds for research and development. This will lead to faster technological advancement and growth of economies of countries forming a customs union.

(5) *Effects on Investment:* It would be difficult to estimate the effect of formation of customs union on investment, namely, whether there would be increase in investment or not. Formation of customs union may lead to increase in investments in some industries which are specialising more and more and expand to take advantage of expanded markets. But it is also possible that some of the import-competing industries in countries A and B before the formation of the

customs union will be closed down leading to disinvestment in such industries. "But since most firms in a customs union can be counted on not to lie down and roll over when faced with keener rivalry, a substantial net increase in investment seems almost certain. Moreover, if the forces generating increased efficiency operate as expected, aggregate income will rise, savings will increase, and aggregate investment will be larger. With expanding markets giving a lift to confidence, the proportion of income saved and invested will be raised."

Also, foreign firms operating in the area of the customs unions, may also increase their investment to take fuller advantage of expanded markets consequent on the formation of customs union. Also, foreign firms which were formerly exporting their goods to countries A and B, may now set up their industrial establishments in the now expanded custom area to take advantage of tariff-free trade and to avoid disadvantage of facing a common tariff to be imposed by countries A and B now forming customs union.

(6) *Effects on Economic Growth-Rate:* Expanded markets, increase in competition, increase in scale of production, in economies of scale, in efficiency and in technological advancement and in investment are all sure to result in higher growth-rate of countries forming the customs union than when they were functioning as independent countries.

Thus, on the whole there will be substantial advantages as a consequence of the formation of a customs union.

As stated already, all these advantages would also follow from the formation of Economic Union of two or more countries.

23.5 EUROPEAN ECONOMIC COMMUNITY (EEC) ALSO KNOWN AS EUROPEAN COMMON MARKET (ECM)

One of the most significant and constructive developments as a result of the devastating World War II (1939-45) was the realisation on the part of most West European nations of the futility of such a war, both for victors and the vanquished, and the necessity of establishing long-term economic (and also political) cooperation among nations in the neighbourhood in particular, as they are potential enemies of one another.

Thus, even before the end of the World War II in 1945, Belgium, the Netherlands and Luxembourg formed a Customs Union in 1944. Other economic cooperation agreements followed after the end of World War II : The Organisation for European Economic Cooperation (O.E.E.C.) in 1948; the European Coal and Steel Community (ECSC) formed in 1952; and the European Payments Union (E.P.U.) formed in 1955. But the most important among them all was the establishment of the European Common Market (ECM) or the European Economic Community (EEC).

The devastation caused by the World War II gave rise to various post-war problems of reconstruction and development. The importance of cooperation among the former warring nations came to be appreciated. The success of the European Coal and Steel Community demonstrated the increasing scope for supra-national organisation. The post-War experiences in the field of economic cooperation finally led to the Treaty of Rome in 1957. The Treaty of Rome signed on 25th March 1957 led to the establishment of 'The European Economic Community' (EEC) usually called 'The Common Market.' The various institutions envisaged in the Treaty of Rome started functioning from 1st January 1958. The main objective of the Treaty of Rome has been to bring about gradual integration of the economic policies of the member-countries of the EEC and of all their economic resources.

The Constitution of the EEC

(1) *The Executive Commission:* This is a very important and unique institution. This is so because of its independent position in relation to national governments of member-countries of the EEC.

The Executive Commission is responsible for initiating, evolving and implementing the EEC's economic policies. The Executive Commission is responsible for ensuring that national governments of the member-countries implement the agreed Community policies. This Commission has the power to issue orders which are binding on the national governments and it also enjoys the power in certain cases of over-ruling national policies of national governments of member-countries. There are 14 Commissioners who are appointed by national governments of EEC member-countries. The Commissioners have to take on oath which binds them to be independent of their governments' policies. One of the important achievements of the Executive Commission is in the anti-trust field. The Commission has brought about successful suits against multinational corporations on charges of adopting monopolistic policies within the geographical limits of the European Economic Community.

(2) *The Council of Ministers:* The Council of Ministers is the inter-governmental decision-making body. The foreign ministers of the EEC member-countries are entrusted with the responsibility of taking major decisions on political issues (which are invariably involved in economic policy matters). The foreign ministers are also called upon to decide on technical matters and provide policy guidelines on questions on which other ministers fail to agree. Who among the ministers of the EEC member-countries meet depends upon the nature of the issue that is to be decided. All issues are decided by the Council of Ministers and are majority decisions; but generally all important matters are decided unanimously, as far as possible.

(3) *European Parliament:* The European Parliament is a consultative body of 142 members of the country's national parliament. According to the Treaty of Rome, the European Parliament is to be elected by direct suffrage, though France and other countries are opposed to this idea. The European Parliament holds eight sessions per year.

(4) *The Court of Justice:* The Court of Justice which is based in Luxembourg settles all disputes arising out of different provisions of the Treaty of Rome. The Court of Justice of the EEC has the power to overrule decisions by the national courts on questions relating to the EEC policies and disputes arising out of them.

(5) *The Economic and Social Committee:* This is essentially a consultative body representing employers, workers, and various professionals from the member-countries of the EEC.

(6) *The Monetary Committee:* The Monetary Committee performs the function of advising the Executive Commission and the Council of Ministers on international monetary problems. The Monetary Committee comprises of national experts and central bank officials of the member-countries of the EEC.

In addition there are a number of important committees such as the Committee of Permanent Representatives (of ambassadors of different member-countries of the EEC) which first examines various legislative measures which are often decided in this committee only going for the formal approval to the Council of Ministers; the D'avignon Committee (which is an inter-governmental body to discuss foreign policy questions), etc.

Great Britain, Ireland and Denmark formally joined the EEC on 1st January 1973, making the EEC the world's second largest trading block, next only to the United States.

The nine members of the EEC appear to have determined to accelerate the process of European integration. As the nine members are proceeding towards monetary and economic union, the EEC is required to make many political decisions of vital importance. This appears inevitable. Thus, to the proposed economic union, political dimension appears to have been added. Naturally, political policies of the EEC member-countries will have to be properly coordinated before the political union of the EEC member-countries is envisaged and accomplished. The EEC proposes to achieve economic union of the member-states sometime in the 1990s.

Main Provisions of the Treaty of Rome

The main provisions of the Treaty of Rome have provided for a customs union which would have a common external tariff (at the level of the average of the previous tariffs of the six member-states). There is also the important provision of the abolition of all tariffs and all other quantitative restrictions between member-states of the EEC. These tariff changes were to be brought about within 12 to 14 years and the above provisions were given effect to by 1971 which was the deadline for abolition of internal tariffs. In fact, that objective was realised only within 11 years. By July 1968 all internal tariffs on industrial goods were abolished and common external tariff came to be adopted by the EEC.

Another important provision of the Treaty of Rome is promotion of economic integration of the EEC member-countries. To achieve this objective mere abolition of internal tariffs and adoption of common external tariff would not be enough, if tax systems, monetary policies, public expenditure policies and policies regarding balance of payments continue to be different in the case of different member-countries of the EEC. This would make impossible economic integration of the EEC member-states.

It was, therefore, felt that national policies in the above fields of the EEC member-countries must be properly harmonised. With a view to accomplish economic integration, the Treaty of Rome has made provision for the following: (i) Abolition of all obstacles and restrictions on movement of labour and capital in the Common Market area; (ii) adoption of a common transport policy; (iii) adoption of a common agricultural policy; (iv) ensuring effective competition and to see that it is not restrained; and (v) adoption of procedure to make possible coordination of economic policies to remedy balance of payments problems of the EEC member-countries.

The Treaty of Rome has made provision for the setting up of a 'Special Aid Fund' and a 'Special Investment Fund.' These funds will be concerned with the problems of the relatively backward regions in the EEC member-countries. Programmes will be undertaken for education and retraining of workers who might be unemployed as a consequence of competition among member-states of the EEC.

Agreement on common agricultural policy has been posing some serious problems. Because of the post-World War II food-shortages, scarcity of foreign exchange to import required quantities of foodgrains from the United States, because of political pressure from farmer lobby particularly in France, most European countries had imposed a variety of import restrictions and adopted price support policies in respect of agricultural commodities in their countries. Harmonisation of those different agricultural policies of the EEC member-countries has been posing serious problems. Even to this day, there does not appear to be a satisfactory solution to the problem of harmonisation of agricultural policies of different EEC member-countries. Though the Treaty of Rome made provision of some general principles on which to have a common agricultural policy, the EEC appears to have as yet found no solution to the problem of common agricultural policy which still poses a serious problem for the EEC.

Role of the EEC

The enlarged EEC accounts for nearly 40% of the world trade. The special trading relations of the EEC would encompass about 50 countries. Tariffs in the EEC member-countries have come to be gradually abolished. This has provided strong stimulus to the mutual trade among the EEC countries.

Naturally, the trading activities of such a huge monopolistic block comprising of industrially developed West European countries is bound to have global implications for and impact on the economy of the world.

The EEC secured in 1958 nearly 30% of its imports from member-countries; this figure rose to 38% in 1964; and by 1972 value of this intra-trade in manufactured goods was around 50% higher than it would have been if the EEC had not been established. Abolition of tariffs in EEC member-countries has had its impact on efficiency of industries in the EEC countries. Because of this, prospects of exports from the EEC to the rest of the world improved considerably. The intra-trade of the EEC as a share of world trade rose from 9% in 1960 to 14% in 1970. But the share of the EEC imports from developing countries declined from 35% to 30% during the same period.

Improvement in efficiency and productivity and in trade has brought about reduction in the level of unemployment in EEC member-countries, and average earnings of people in the EEC member-countries have been rising substantially.

The EEC as a whole has maintained strong balance of payments position with a surplus on current account, the surplus amounting to nearly 25,000 million US dollars during the period 1958-69. (On the contrary, in the case of the United Kingdom during the same period when she was not a member of the EEC, there was a small cumulative deficit in her balance of payments on current account). The EEC may be said to have become the world's largest importer and exporter and the EEC's share in total world trade has been continuously rising.

Great Britain's entry into the EEC in January 1973 put an end to her special trading relations with Commonwealth countries. Exports from and to Great Britain from Commonwealth countries which used to get and receive preferential treatment have been stopped. The Commonwealth preferences to exports from India to Great Britain as also from other Commonwealth countries have practically disappeared compelling those countries to divert their exports and find new substitute markets.

Britain's Entry into the EEC

For quite sometime, Britain did not join the EEC as she had many reservations about becoming a member of the EEC. It was only in 1961 that Britain made application for membership of the EEC. It was only since 1st January 1973 that Britain has become a full member of the EEC.

Britain's entry into the EEC was held up for quite sometime because of differences arising out of Commonwealth preferences which Britain wanted to retain and the EEC wanted Britain to abolish. Also, the EEC member-countries wanted Britain to open up her markets to French agricultural commodities and impose common tariff. On the other hand, Britain wanted to retain agricultural tariff which was prevailing then as a result of which she could import most of the agricultural requirements from the Commonwealth countries free from any tariff and, therefore, at comparatively low prices. Also, the French opposition to Britain's membership of the EEC was motivated by political considerations.

Finally on 1st January 1973 Britain became a full member of the EEC. The conditions of membership were as follows: (i) Britain, like other member-countries of the EEC, will contribute her share of funds to the common budget and to the special aid fund of the EEC; (ii) Britain will open up her markets to French agricultural commodities and a common tariff will be imposed on agricultural imports by all the members of the EEC; (iii) Britain's industrial tariff between Britain and other members of the EEC will be completely abolished in 5 stages so that Britain's prevailing industrial tariffs will be removed completely by July 1977. Britain along with other members of the EEC should adopt a common tariff in the case of industrial commodities imported from non-EEC countries; and (iv) Britain will give up the system of Commonwealth preferences.

23.6 IMPACT OF THE EEC ON INDIA

Britain's joining the European Economic Community became a matter of grave concern for India. This was because of the Commonwealth preference system. Britain had been one of the largest markets for Indian goods which enjoyed preference there over imports from non-Commonwealth countries into Britain. For example, 37% of her tea, 26% of her woollen carpets, 24% of cotton piece goods and 21% of India's leather goods used to enjoy duty-free entry into Britain or without having to face other tariff from India to Britain and non-tariff restrictions from Britain. It was feared that these exports from India to Britain would naturally suffer a severe setback once Britain became a member of the EEC from January 1973.

Not only the Commonwealth preference to those Indian exports to Britain stopped but Britain also terminated Indo-UK trade agreement of 1939 under which India's exports enjoyed Commonwealth preferences. These preferences were expected to be stopped after 1974 when Britain's tariff would become the same as that of the EEC.

It was expected that Indian exports worth about Rs. 75 crores annually could thus get adversely affected. Indian exports to Britain of tobacco, cotton textiles and yarn, oilcakes, cardamom, jute goods, coir goods and cashew kernels were all expected to be adversely affected because of the abolition of the Commonwealth preferences from 1st January 1974.

Also, India's trade relations with other EEC member-countries would get adversely affected as the EEC would be adopting a common tariff without leaving any scope for India to enter into bilateral trade agreements with individual EEC countries, and also because they would all be trading among themselves without any tariff.

Britain's joining the EEC has compelled India to enter into commercial agreements with the EEC. Also, India was compelled to restructure her exports, because Britain joined the EEC. How much India can export to the EEC would depend upon two basic factors : Whether and to what extent the EEC would have alternative and better sources of supply in the case of commodities exported by India; and secondly, elasticity of demand for Indian goods in the EEC market.

Another factor that is of significance is that as the EEC starts its move towards political union (which happens to be the final objective in the formation of the EEC), India will be compelled to seek new satisfactory political relationship with the EEC, mainly because India has over the decades developed close economic and political relations with the Soviet Union and East European block of the communist countries and this may or may not be viewed with favour by some of the EEC countries.

But there is the other side to the picture. India can take advantage of the vastly enlarged trading market in the shape of EEC, if she successfully enters into trading agreements with EEC. Since Indian goods will stop getting Commonwealth preferences, Indian industries will have to strive hard to improve efficiency and quality of her goods and services. This kind of competition would do immense good to Indian industries which have been growing for long under one type of protective shelter or another. India's exposure to EEC should motivate Indian industries and agricultural products to be more competitive in the world market as also in EEC market.

It will be observed from Table no. 23.1 that India could successfully take advantage of the large EEC market and boost her exports over the years.

Table 23.1

India's Exports to EEC and Imports from EEC

	1970-71		*1980-81*		*1985-86*	
	Exports	*Imports*	*Exports*	*Imports*	*Exports*	*Imports*
The EEC	282.29	320.07	1447.43	2638.92	1996.30	5211.34
of which						
Belgium	20.33	11.51	144.48	295.86	228.65	926.61
France	17.98	21.33	146.94	280.30	199.99	615.12
F.R.G.	32.31	107.47	384.75	693.77	506.98	1542.16
Netherlands	13.98	19.09	152.04	214.50	171.42	292.16
U.K.	170.44	126.76	394.88	730.99	538.23	1248.76

It would be observed that compared to 1970-71, India's exports to the EEC went up substantially and her imports from the EEC have risen much more rapidly. Also, compared to India's exports in 1980-81 to some of the important member-countries of the EEC, they appear to have declined substantially in 1985-86; her imports from those countries have been gradually rising. India is thus facing huge annual deficit in her commodity trade with European Economic Community.

23.7 European Free Trade Association (EFTA)

When attempts were being made to establish European Economic Community, Britain was initially reluctant to join the EEC. As a counter measure to EEC, Britain prepared a scheme to neutralise the adverse effects of the double tariff policy of the EEC on her (Britain's) foreign trade and her balance of payments.

In November 1960, Britain, Denmark, Norway, Sweden, Portugal, Switzerland and Austria signed the Draft Agreement constituting the European Free Trade Association (EFTA).

As in the case of the EEC, those seven member-countries of the EFTA abolished all tariffs on trade conducted within the area of EFTA. But as regards trade with countries outside the EFTA, the seven member-countries of the EFTA decided that every member of the EFTA was free to adopt her own independent tariff policy with respect to their trade with non-EFTA countries. Further, unlike the EEC, labour and capital from one member-country to another member-country of the EFTA were not freely mobile. This meant that the EFTA was a loose economic organisation of seven European countries providing tariff concessions to mutually traded goods. By stages all tariffs within the member-countries of the EFTA came to be removed.

It should be clear that Britain took the lead in forming the EFTA mainly for her own advantage. Britain imports most of her foodgrains and industrial raw materials from other countries. It is to her advantage to procure these goods at minimum prices. British exports had been enjoying preferential tariff from the Commonwealth countries and was thus getting foodgrains and industrial raw materials cheaply from them in return of her exports. Britain took the lead in forming the EFTA so that she could also obtain low cost goods from the member countries of the EFTA and could export maximum quantities of her manufactured goods to them. Thus, the formation of the EEC consisting of rich European countries compelled Britain to integrate other European countries into the EFTA as a counter to the EEC.

From the above account it should be clear that the EFTA was established basically for the benefit of Britain. For example, Britain was not prepared to have complete economic integration with the EFTA countries; only tariff concessions which were to the great advantage of Britain were provided to the EFTA member-countries, whereas Britain was free to follow her own Commonwealth preferential tariffs and her own tariff policy with the non-EFTA countries. As Britain joined the EEC in January 1973 as a full member, the EFTA for all practical purposes has lost its significance as its leader was compelled by circumstances to joint the EEC as a full member.

23.8 ESTABLISHMENT OF THE EUROPEAN UNION

Following the UK's entry, the Paris summit in December 1974 reached an agreement to establish the European Regional Development Fund, whose purpose was to help close the gap between the most disadvantaged and the most favoured regions within the Community. The same summit conference took some important decisions, which further lead to the establishment of the European Council and the European Parliament.

On March 1979 the European Monetary System came into effect. It compensated to some extent for the failure of the earlier aspiration to achieve a full economic and monetary union by 1980s. The EMS is based on a European Currency Unit (ECU) and comprises an exchange and intervention mechanism, credit facilities and a media to ease the path of the less prosperous Community countries.

By January 1986, Greece, Spain and Portugal had taken their places in the Community. The later years saw two important developments, which had profound effects on the European Community. One was the collapse of Russia leading to a general downfall of communism and the West and East German Unification. Following these events a summit meeting in Dublin agreed to establish a second Inter Governmental Conference, to run parallel to that on economic and monetary union (EMU), to recommend changes which would lead to 'political union' within the Community.

The European Council met at Masstricht in December 1991 to consider a draft treaty based on the work of the two Inter Governmental Conferences. After two days of hard bargaining the Treaty of European Union was approved. The Masstricht treaty undoubtedly represents the most important development in the EC's history since the signing of the treaty of Rome. Not only did it set out a detailed time-table for achieving economic and monetary union, at the latest by 1999, and provide for the development of common foreign and defense policies, but also introduced a new concept of EC institutions.

Objectives of the EU according to the Treaty of the European Union

The Union has set itself the following objectives:

To promote economic and social progress and a high level of employment and to achieve balanced and sustainable development, in particular through the creation of an area without internal frontiers, through the strengthening of economic and social cohesion and through the establishment of economic and monetary union, ultimately, including a single currency in accordance with the provisions of this Treaty;

To assert its identity on the international scene, in particular through the implementation of a common foreign and security policy including the progressive framing of a common defence policy, which might lead to a common defence, in accordance with the provisions of Article 17;

To strengthen the protection of the rights and interests of the nationals of its Member States through the introduction of a citizenship of the Union;

To maintain and develop the Union as an area of freedom, security and justice, in which the free movement of persons is assured in conjunction with appropriate measures with respect to external border controls, asylum, immigration and the prevention and combating of crime;

To maintain in full the *acquis communautaire* and build on it with a view to considering to what extent the policies and forms of cooperation introduced by this Treaty may need to be revised with the aim of ensuring the effectiveness of the mechanisms and the institutions of the Community.

Though, the following years were not so smooth as far as the ratification of the treaty in member countries parliament, the treaty finally came into force on November 1st 1993, ten months later than planned. Since then the European Community has been generally regarded as the European Union. The treaty established three pillars for the European Union. Pillar One embraced the three existing European Communities treaties (the ECSC, EC and Euratom). Pillar Two contained the common foreign and security policy (CFSP) and Pillar Three provided for cooperation between the member states on justice and home affairs.

The post 1995 period saw accession of more countries like Australia, Finland and Sweden. It also saw the launch of Euro, the currency of the European Union, in January 1999. Following the launch Austria, Belgium, Finland, France, Germany, Ireland, Italy, Luxembourg, The Netherlands, Portugal and Spain adopted the Euro as their official currency. Later in January 2002, the Euro coins and notes entered into circulation in the twelve participating Member States: Austria, Belgium, Finland, France, Germany, Greece, Ireland, Italy, Luxembourg, the Netherlands, Portugal and Spain.

Foundations of the European Integration

To summarise we can say that the European integration is based on four founding treaties:

The Treaty establishing the European Coal and Steel Community (ECSC), which was signed on 18 April 1951 in Paris, entered into force on 23 July 1952, and will end on 23 July 2002;

The Treaty establishing the European Economic Community (EEC);

The Treaty establishing the European Atomic Energy Community (Euratom), which was signed (along with the EEC Treaty) in Rome on 25 March 1957, and entered into force on 1 January 1958. These Treaties are often referred to as the "Treaties of Rome." When the term "Treaty of Rome" is used, only the EEC Treaty is meant;

The Treaty on European Union, which was signed in Masstricht on 7 February 1992, and entered into force on 1 November 1993, created the political Union amongst the Member States and brought about considerable changes to the existing Treaties. The treaty created the European Union, a concept comprising the European Communities (which had also been amended to the term European Community on the same occasion), as well as other forms of cooperation.

Moreover, the founding treaties have been amended on several occasions, in particular when new Member States acceded in 1973 (Denmark, Ireland, United Kingdom), 1981 (Greece), 1986 (Spain, Portugal) and 1995 (Austria, Finland, Sweden). There have also been more far-reaching reforms bringing major institutional changes and introducing new areas of responsibility for the European institutions:

The Merger Treaty, signed in Brussels on 8 April 1965 and in force since 1 July 1967, provided for a single Commission and a Single Council of the then three European Communities;

The Single European Act (SEA), signed in Luxembourg and the Hague, and entered into force on 1 July 1987, provided for the adaptations required for the achievement of the Internal Market;

The Treaty of Amsterdam, signed on 2 October 1997, entered into force on 1 May 1999; it amended and renumbered the EU and EC Treaties. Consolidated versions of the EU and EC Treaties are attached to it. The Treaty of Amsterdam changed the articles of the Treaty on European Union, identified by letters A to S, into numerical form;

The treaty of Nice, signed on 26 February 2001, will amend the existing Treaties. The treaty is actually an agreement on the institutional issues which had not been settled at Amsterdam and which had to be resolved before enlargement, and on a series of other points not directly connected with enlargement. It will enter into force once the 15 Member States have ratified it according to their respective constitutional procedures. The ratification process is already under way and will continue into 2002.

References: Leonard Dick (1998), Guide to the European Union, The Economist, Sixth Edition & Europa online — the official website of the European Union.

24 CHAPTER GENERAL AGREEMENT ON TARIFFS AND TRADE (GATT) AND THE UNITED NATIONS CONFERENCE ON TRADE AND DEVELOPMENT (UNCTAD)

Structure:

24.1 INTRODUCTION

During the period of World War II (1939-45) discussions were going on regarding economic policies to be followed after the war to bring about economic reconstruction and development. It was felt that there was need for establishing a body for nations after the war to guide policies in the sphere of international trade. There was a proposal to set up International Trade Organisation (ITO) with the objective of promoting world trade and economic development. But, most nations did not agree on the scope of the proposed ITO. And therefore, the proposal to set up the ITO did not materialise. In its place, the General Agreement on Tariffs and Trade (GATT) was signed at the Hawana Conference in 1947. Originally intended as a purely temporary arrangement, GATT however developed into a permanent institutional organisation. Since its establishment in 1947, the membership of the GATT has gone up from 23 to around 140 made up of both developed and developing countries. New members can be admitted with the consent of two-third members of the GATT. Members of the GATT must accept the code of conduct prescribed by the GATT. While most of the leading trading countries like the United States, the United Kingdom, West Germany and France are members of GATT, the Soviet Union, China and most of the Eastern bloc socialist countries are not members of the GATT.

24.2 IMPORTANT PRINCIPLES OF THE GATT

The GATT agreement is based on the following four principles:

(1) There will be non-discriminatory trade among member-countries of the GATT;

(2) Tariff should be the only instrument to influence international trade;

(3) There should take place consultations among member-countries before action is taken by any member-country that might harm trade of other member-countries; and

(4) There should be provided arrangements for negotiations for tariff reductions.[1]

24.3 OBJECTIVES OF GATT

The general objective of GATT is to enable member-countries to enter into reciprocal and mutually advantageous arrangements to bring about substantial reduction in tariff as also reduction or removal of other barriers to international trade and, if possible, elimination of discriminatory practices in the sphere of international trade.

In other words the general objectives of the GATT are:

(1) To bring about improvement in the standard of living of people in member-countries;

(2) To encourage full employment and steady and growing level of real income and effective demand;

---

1. The GATT Agreement consists of the following four parts:

Part I lays down the main obligations of the contracting parties;

Part II provides a code of fair trade;

Part IIII prescribes conditions of membership and withdrawal of membership; and

Part IV which came to be incorporated in 1965 is concerned with the expansion of international trade of developing countries. (It is, for example, stated in this Part IV that the LDCs need not offer reciprocal reductions of duties and they can also impose quotas, if necessitated by their balance of payments position).

(3) To bring about expansion of world trade and world production; and

(4) To enable full use of the world's resources.

The above objectives are very general in nature and the GATT does not aim at achieving the above objectives directly. The above general objectives are to be achieved "through evolving a pattern of world trade based upon multilateral trade and non-discriminatory tariffs with the ultimate objective of reducing these tariffs to a minimum, consistent with the national objectives of the countries concerned." The GATT Agreement recognises that trade barriers are necessary under certain circumstances and, therefore, it is decided that tariffs and trade barriers (imposed mostly during the period of World War II) are to be reduced and not altogether eliminated. Also, reduction in tariffs and elimination of trade discrimination are to be reciprocal and on mutually advantageous basis. The GATT has stated explicitly that "The developed contracting parties should not expect reciprocity for commitments made by them in trade negotiations to reduce or remove tariff and other barriers to the trade of less developed contracting countries."

The GATT proposes to achieve the above objectives through the following methods:

(1) *Principle of 'Most Favoured Nation Clause' or Elimination of Discrimination:* 'The Most Favoured Nation Clause' is to be adopted to avoid discrimination in international trade. This clause means that each member-country of GATT shall be treated as well as the most favoured nation. Any particular trade concession offered by a member-country to her trading partner should also be available to all the member-countries of the GATT at the same time. This means that any tariff concessions resulting from bilateral trade negotiations are in effect multilateral concessions as any tariff reduction bilaterally agreed upon are available to all member-countries of the GATT.

But there are several 'Escape Clauses.' The developing countries are assured the right to discriminate under certain circumstances. For example, dumping and export subsidy might be countered by trade measures only against the offending country. Special concessions are allowed for trade with former colonies of developed Western countries.

(2) *Quantitative Restrictions on Imports:* The GATT rules, as a matter of principle, prohibit the use of import quota fixation. But the following three important exceptions are allowed to this rule: (i) Countries which are facing balance of payments difficulties may use the device of import quota fixation; but this quota fixation should be limited to the extent necessary to stop a serious decline in foreign exchange reserves; and for the adoption of import quota fixation, the IMF is to be consulted; (ii) Underdeveloped countries may resort to quota-fixation but only under procedure approved by the GATT. Also, developing countries, when the use of tariff is not possible or applicable, may adopt quota-fixation to protect domestic industries; and (iii) Quotas may be applied to agricultural and fishery products, if domestic production is subject to equally restrictive controls.

(3) *Tariff Negotiations and Reduction of Tariff:* The GATT recognises that tariffs are often an important obstacle to international trade. And, therefore, the GATT would encourage negotiations for the reduction of high tariffs. The negotiations for tariff reduction are to be conducted on a reciprocal and mutually advantageous basis, taking into consideration the varying needs of individual contracting parties. The GATT makes provisions for taking into consideration the

needs of developing countries for a more flexible use of tariff protection to assist economic development and special needs of developing countries to main tariff also for revenue purposes.

The important rules relating to tariff negotiations are: (i) Reciprocity and mutuality and (ii) reduction of tariff or imposing tariffs at low rates.

24.4 THE GATT CONFERENCES

So far eight GATT conferences were held.

The GATT conference at Brussels in 1964 is known as the Kennedy Round.

It is said that the first and the Kennedy Round in 1964 achieved the maximum results — first conference because at the end of World War II tariffs were relatively high; and the Kennedy Round, because the United States announced across the board reduction in tariffs, following the enactment of the United States Trade Expansion Act in 1962.

The first round of tariff negotiations was held at Geneva in April 1947. The concessions exchanged in the negotiations in the first round of tariff negotiations took the form of (i) Complete elimination of certain duties and of preferences; (ii) reduction of duty preferences; (iii) the binding of duties at the existing levels; and (iv) the binding of duty-free treatment. At this conference, the participating countries completed 123 sets of bilateral negotiations.

It was at Annecy that the second GATT conference was held in 1949. This GATT conference was called primarily to facilitate extension of the GATT to countries which could not participate at the Geneva conference in April 1947. By this time 10 additional countries had joined the GATT increasing the strength of GATT to 33. In this second Conference 147 sets of bilateral negotiations covering around 500 items came to be completed.

The third GATT Conference at Torquay in 1950-51 saw 6 new countries become members of the GATT. The third conference could not be said to have been a success because only 147 out of total of around 400 negotiations could be successfully completed. At this conference the United States which had already offered a number of tariff concessions, did not offer any more tariff concessions.

It was in Geneva in 1956 that the fourth conference of GATT was held. At this conference, the United States went to the limit of negotiating power granting concessions in respect of her imports valued at 900 million dollars and obtained concessions on exports valued at 400 million dollars. But no country was satisfied and several countries withdrew from the negotiations at the fourth conference of the GATT.

It was in Geneva in 1960-61 that the fifth GATT conference was held. The developing countries expressed the view at this conference that their reciprocity was practically exhausted as a consequence of the application of the principle of reciprocity in previous conferences. The developing countries also pointed out that industrialised countries had avoided negotiations on products which were of vital interests to developing countries. The LDCs emphasised that the conference could be successful only if the industrialised countries were prepared to grant unilateral tariff concessions. This view of developing countries was strongly supported by Prof. Haberler's Report.

The Kennedy Round (1964)

The GATT sixth conference held in May 1964 at Brussels is known as the Kennedy Round. President Kennedy suggested at this conference all round reduction in tariffs. The main objective was reducing tariffs between the United States and the EEC and the EFTA. It might be recalled that historically the United States had been strongly in favour of protection mainly as a means of safe-guarding standard of living of people in the United States against cheap labour in the rest of the countries of the world.

Though the trade agreements of the United States between 1934 and 1962 did allow for negotiated tariff reductions, there was a legislative provision relating to 'the peril point' principle, according to which the peril points were to be established for setting limits below which tariffs could not be lowered by the President of the United States without the approval of the Congress. The Trade expansion Act of 1962 abolished the 'peril point principle' and empowered the President of the United States to reduce all import duties up to a maximum of 50 per cent. While the United States had agreed already to a number of tariff concessions, they could not be compared to tariff concessions offered by the United States at the 6th conference of the GATT held at Brussels. The initiative in this respect came from President Kennedy and, therefore, the 6th GATT conference at Brussels came to be known as 'The Kennedy Round.'

The sixth GATT conference was attended by 50 nations and 37 nations made duty reductions covering 40 million US dollars. The United States agreed to reduce tariffs on two-thirds of her total imports by an average of 30 per cent; in some cases reduction in US tariff being of the order of 50 per cent or even more.

At the Kennedy Round, the ECM also reduced tariff on an average by 35 per cent; the United Kingdom by 38 per cent; Japan by 30 per cent and Canada by 24 per cent. These cuts in tariffs announced at the Kennedy Round were not to be implemented at once but were to be given effect to over a period of next 5 years (i.e., during 1964-68).

When the recommendations of the Kennedy Round came to be fully implemented, the duties imposed on manufactured goods by the leading industrial countries were to be in the range of only 5 to 15 per cent.

It may be pointed out that the incidence of tariff reductions announced at the Kennedy Round varied considerably among commodity groups. For example, chemicals, paper and other manufactures were subject to maximum cuts, whereas iron and steel, textiles, fuels and tropical products received tariff reductions relatively on a smaller scale.

The developing countries were expecting specially favourable treatment in regard to exports of particular goods which were of interest to them. But they were disappointed in this respect at the outcome of the Kennedy Round.

The progress of the Kennedy round was limited to tariff duty reductions mainly on manufactured goods. But on the whole, the Kennedy Round was a remarkable achievement. But it needs to be noted that though the Kennedy Round aimed at considerable tariff reductions, there are many non-tariff barriers to international trade that continue to this day hampering smooth and expanding flow of international trade.

Tokyo Round (1973-79)

Ninety-nine countries, i.e., countries representing ninety per cent of the world trade participated in this round. However, the economic climate during the Tokyo round was far from encouraging as the world economy suffered from stagnation, non-tariff barriers proliferated and trade relations between the major players in world trade, namely, the U.S., European Community and Japan were strained (Södersten & Reed 1994).

Nonetheless, after a heated debate on how should reduction in tariffs be done was resolved, tariff liberalisation went forth smoothly. Tariffs were reduced on the thousands of industrial and agricultural products and some 33,000 additional tariff lines were bound (Hoekman and Kostecki 2001). The total value of trade affected by this reduction was around US$ 300 billion, measured in 1981 imports. On an average there was a 37% reduction in Pre-Tokyo round tariff levels.

The Tokyo round also effected adoption of some important agreements. These included the formal incorporation of preferential tariff and non-tariff treatment in favour of developing countries and a number of codes dealing with specific products. Negotiations on codes included subsidies and countervailing measures, technical barriers to trade (product standards), government procurement, customs valuations, import licensing procedures, anti dumping, bovine meat, dairy products and civil aircraft.

Though, Tokyo round was the first round in which developing countries participated in strength and with cohesion, Srinivasan (2000, pp. 26-27)[2] argues that the round produced outcomes that were not in their long-term interests. This is because the developing countries' demands continued to be driven by the import substitution ideology. Hence, the demand for preferential treatment and therefore, a permanent status of inferiority under the "special and differential clause." Had they participated vigorously on equal footing with the developed countries and had they been outwardly oriented, the Tokyo round could have boosted their growth significantly. The growth experience of East Asian Countries gives ample reason to believe so.

The Uruguay Round (1986-94)

Uruguay round, the most recently concluded round of trade negotiations was the last one to be held under the auspices of the GATT. It was also comparatively more complex, included a larger number of participants, and took much longer to conclude. In addition, to policies affecting trade in goods, trade policy measures affecting investment, trade in services, and intellectual property rights were included in the negotiations. This round led to further liberalisation of international trade, the reintegration of agricultural trade and textiles and clothing in the trading framework and a significant expansion of GATT disciplines. This led to the creation of a new GATT, which made the formal amendment of the GATT 1947 unnecessary and at the same time ensured that the results of the round were a Single Undertaking and hence applied to all. The most significant outcome of this round was the establishment of the WTO to oversee the functioning of GATT, the GATS, and the agreement on TRIPS.

The average tariff on the manufactured products of industrial countries, weighted by the volume of trade in the products concerned, saw a reduction of almost 40 per cent from 6.4% to 4%. It will be interesting to note that the weighted average duty before the creation of GATT (1947) was 35% and at the time of the Dillon round was 15%.

---

2. Srinivasan T.N. (2000), *"Developing Countries and the Multilateral Trading System,"* Oxford University Press.

The proportion of such goods entering developed countries from all sources subject to no MFN tariffs was also to more than double from 20% to 44% and the proportion subject to tariffs exceeding 15% would fall from 7% to 5%. Developing countries' exports facing tariffs greater than 15% would fall from 9% to 5%. The percentage of bound tariffs on such goods would increase from 78% to 99%. The corresponding increase for developing countries will be from 21 per cent to 73%. This rise might seem dramatic but it is tampered by the fact that the tariffs had already been bound at fairly high levels.

Another important feature of the Uruguay Round was the agreement on agriculture. This agreement claimed to provide a framework for long-term reform of agriculture trade and domestic policies over the years to come. It makes a decisive move towards the objective of increased market orientation of agricultural trade. The most important component aspect of the agreement is however the requirement that all non-tariff barriers be replaced by tariffs that initially provide the same level of protection. Much is made out of this agreement to create a fear psychosis among the developing countries that they would eventually lose control over their agriculture and hence starve. However, this is not really true. Even under this agreement a country is allowed to retain import restrictions until the end of the implementation period under some carefully and strictly defined circumstances. Moreover, developing countries are afforded special and differential treatment that in effect exempts them from the commitment to liberalise with respect to any agricultural product that is a predominant staple in their traditional diet (Srinivasan 2000, p. 39).

Thus, Uruguay Round contributed significantly to liberalising international trade and bringing agriculture in the multilateral trading framework. However, the most important result of the round was the establishment of a formal institutional framework for multilateral trade, the WTO.

The GATT and Developing Countries

The LDCs are facing a number of problems in the field of international trade such as protection to agriculture and to their industries, instability in prices of primary products exported to developed countries, decline in the share of world trade, adverse and worsening terms of trade *vis-a-vis* developed countries, recurring deficits in balance of payments, increasing foreign debt burden and servicing charges and so on.

The LDCs get several advantages as members of the GATT. For example under the GATT Article XVIII, LDCs get some special concessions; they are provided some special facilities such as (i) concessions to promote a particular industry; (ii) permission to impose quantitative restrictions for safe-guarding their external financial position and for ensuring and build up of adequate foreign exchange reserves for implementing the development programmes; (iii) permission to use quantitative and other similar measures necessary to improve their balance of payments positions; and (iv) to introduce necessary measures and trade steps for the establishment of an industry for their economic development.

The GATT, realising the difficulties of the LDCs in trade matters, appointed a Group of Exports in 1957 to report on the trends in international trade with special reference to the failure of the trade of the LDCs to develop as rapidly as that of the developed countries, excessive short-term fluctuations in prices of primary products, etc. The Group of Experts submitted its report in 1950 and that report is known as Haberler Report. As a consequence of that report, the GATT decided to undertake its ambitious trade expansion programme for LDCs.

It must however be said that the progress has been very slow. Many trade restrictions by developed countries inconsistent with the provisions of the GATT still continue to be in operation. It is observed that the concerned developed countries refuse to set the date by which they would reduce or abolish trade restrictions as per the objectives of the GATT.

The GATT has carried out many studies to assess the likely trade implications of development plans of LDCs and to examine potential role of export sector of individual developing countries with a view to improving their development plans, familiarising the LDCs with one another's import requirements and export targets. These studies of GATT are carried out in combination with the World Bank and other international agencies concerned with foreign assistance so as to improve the coordination of foreign aid to and trade efforts by the LDCs.

24.5 THE GATT AND INDIA

India has been taking part in tariff negotiations arranged by the GATT. India has been consistently presenting trade problems faced by developing countries of whom she has become the main spokesman.

But to make her voice in the GATT negotiations more effective, it is necessary that a developing country like India must acquire sufficient and effective competitive strength *vis-a-vis* developed countries, through measures such as strict internal economic discipline, rapid industrial development, development of aggressive salesmanship and above all by containing inflationary pressures which alone can enhance her competitive strength, apart from improving quality of her manufactured goods.

24.6 DEFECTS OF GATT ARRANGEMENTS

The following defects or deficiencies have been observed in the functioning and the role of the GATT since its establishment:

(1) There is no doubt that the GATT provides a forum for multinational negotiations on the basis of reciprocity and mutual advantage as also machinery for discussions and settlement of trade disputes among member-countries of the GATT. However, the GATT only prescribes a code of conduct in international trade sphere. This means the GATT does not possess authority to enforce the recommendations. Also, the escape clauses in the GATT Agreement have been very frequently used by member-countries to justify protection and such other international trade barriers which the GATT aims at removing.

(2) Membership of the GATT is of diverse nature and economic and political motives of different countries have got mixed up making successful negotiations on trade matters very difficult. Because of the diversity among member-countries and different economic and political objectives and motives, it has become practically impossible to evolve and implement general rules of trade conduct or present a common front by developing countries before the developed countries so as to bring effective pressure on them and extract due concessions and favourable treatment.

(3) Recommendations regarding the principles of non-discrimination and of reciprocity have posed some problems. Reciprocity implies that there must be a trade bargain between two member-countries, while offering non-discrimination means that the negotiating countries must have strong competitive position in world markets. This means while on the one hand, domestic industries must have strong competitive strength (to enable them to follow the principles of non-discrimination), on the other hand, domestic industries in developing countries need protection from industries in developed countries and their manufacturers.

(4) The GAAT has provided or adopted the practice of negotiations on commodity-to-commodity basis. This principle has gone against the interests of developing countries which are mainly exporters of primary products, the terms of trade continuously moving against them.

(5) While the GATT emphasises the principle of multilateral negotiation which is supposed to be superior to bilateral negotiation, the reciprocity principle requires bilateral negotiation in which developed countries enjoy negotiating advantage when bargaining bilaterally with a developing country.

(6) The most serious defect of the GATT is that the organisation cannot be said to be a world representative body as its membership is denied to communist countries like the USSR, China and East European countries, or because they have not become members of the GATT. And, therefore, the GATT is often sarcastically referred to as 'The Rich Countries' Club' wherein the United States and West European countries exercise a dominant position and voice in all trade negotiating matters generally to the detriment of developing countries.

(7) Due to the above defects, the GATT has not done much or could not do much to solve the international trading problems of developing countries and this has led to the establishment of the United Nations Conference on Trade and Development (UNCTAD) to pay special attention to international trading problems of developing countries in the world.

24.7 UNITED NATIONS CONFERENCE ON TRADE AND DEVELOPMENT (UNCTAD) — THE BACKGROUND

During the 1960s there was growing awareness among the countries of the world about the necessity of global efforts to reduce the growing disparities between the rich and poor or developing countries in Asia, Africa and Latin America. The United Nations declared 1960s as 'The United Nations Decade of Development.' This was indeed an encouraging sign for developing countries. And thus, on 30th December 1964, the United Nations Conference on Trade and Development (the UNCTAD) came to be established as a permanent organisation of the United Nations. The UN session also adopted the objective of a minimum of 5 per cent annual growth rate for the developing countries at the end of the decade and called upon the developed countries to help developing countries to realise the above objective.

By 1960s many developing countries had emerged as independent nations free from the shackles of their former imperial masters. They were all former colonies of West European nations which ruled over them for centuries. There was, therefore, discontent among them on account of persistence of their colonial pattern of international trade supplying agricultural goods and industrial raw materials to developed countries and also providing ready markets for manufactured goods from developed countries. Naturally, after they became independent, these nations launched programmes of rapid industrialisation of their backward economies by adopting policy of protection and erecting other protective barriers against industries in developed countries mostly from the Western Europe and the United States. This became necessary because demand for primary products in world market is income-inelastic. This meant that mere specialisation in the production of primary products would not help and there will have to be a diversified and well-developed industrial structure to supplement the predominant agricultural structure prevailing in those countries. It was also seen that secular terms of trade were deteriorating against primary products of developing countries *vis-a-vis* manufactured goods of developed countries. Naturally developing countries made an attempt to bring about their rapid industrialisation in their countries.

But it was soon realised that such an objective and policy were beset with a number of difficulties. It was realised that international trade alone cannot be the main instrument of economic development of backward countries; and yet international trade has an important role to play in the development process of former colonies.

Developing countries require large investments for their economic development, especially for rapid industrialisation. This necessitates large imports, especially for capital goods and technical know-how from developed countries. But during 1950s export earnings of developing countries were growing very slowly compared to their requirements of foreign currencies. This meant that there would be recurring deficit in balance of payments of most of the developing countries. During 1950s this gap was filled mostly by foreign loans. But the requirements of imports were much larger than could be met by export earnings and foreign loans. On the other hand, there arose demand for more foreign loans. But it was also realised that the real value of increasing foreign loans was decreasing because of conditions attached to foreign loans. Also repayment of foreign loans and their servicing charges would soon require larger export earnings. All this emphasised that there is need to expand world trade in which developing countries should have an increasing share. It was also realised that the GATT had failed to provide representation to developing countries on the GATT and pay adequate attention to their needs and demands dominated as that organization was by the United States and West European countries.

It was under such circumstances that the United Nations Conference on Trade and Development (the UNCTAD) came to be established in 1964 and it emerged as a permanent organisation of the UNO with its own permanent secretariat. The UNCTAD is to consider problems of developing countries like financing of international trade, commodity prices, trade in manufactured and semi-manufactured goods from developing countries, problems of invisible exports from developing countries to developed countries, implications of the emergence of regional economic groupings like the EEC and the balance of payments problems faced by developing countries and so on. It was decided that the UNCTAD should meet once in four years.

24.8 ROLE AND FUNCTIONS OF THE UNCTAD

Following may be said to be the role or functions of the UNCTAD:

(1) The UNCTAD is to promote international trade, especially with a view to promote economic development of countries which are at different stages of economic development and with varying social organisations.

(2) The UNCTAD is to formulate principles and policies regarding international trade and related problems of economic development and suggest steps to implement them.

(3) The UNCTAD is to facilitate coordination of the activities of the UNCTAD and other institutions of the United Nations so as to promote interests of developing countries in the matter of international trade.

(4) The organisation is to initiate action with competent organs of the UNO for negotiations and adoption of multilateral trade negotiations and arrangements.

(5) The UNCTAD is to serve as a centre for harmonising trade and other development issues faced by developing countries and regional economic groupings.

Organisation of the UNCTAD

The UNCTAD is a permanent organisation or body of the UNO. Membership of the UNCTAD is open to all members of the UNO (i.e., to both developed and developing countries). The procedural matters are decided by a simple majority and matters of substantive nature by two-third majority. The permanent organisation of the UNCTAD is 'The Trade and Development Board.' It meets twice a year. This Board has the following four organs which meet once a year: (1) Commodities, (2) Manufactures, (3) Shipping and Invisibles, and (4) Finance, related to international trade.

The headquarters of the UNCTAD is in Geneva. The conference is a plenary body with over 140 members and as already seen meets once in four years.

The UNCTAD I

The first conference of the UNCTAD resulted in the emergence of 'the Group of 77.' The Seventy-Seven developing countries presented a united front and drew attention to the seriousness of their trading problems. The UNCTAD I marked the beginning of a new era in the sphere of international trade and development of developing countries. The result was that the developed countries were forced to accept new principles of international trade and new approach to the problems of development of developing countries.

The UNCTAD laid down general principles in respect of measures necessary to help development of backward countries through international arrangements for market access, remunerative prices for primary products, increasing aid without military and political strings, encouraging regional groupings of developing countries, and preference to exports from developing countries without the application of the principle of reciprocity. These principles were only in the nature of recommendations.

The UNCTAD I recommended that international economic policies should be directed towards the attainment of an international division of labour and specialisation in conformity with the needs and interests of the developing countries.

All countries should participate in creating conditions for rapid increase in export earnings of developing countries. Developed countries should progressively reduce and in appropriate cases eliminate trade barriers and other restrictions that hinder free trade in products which are of special interest to developing countries. All countries should cooperate to increase and stabilise export earnings from primary products and secure remunerative prices for primary products. It was recommended that developed countries should grant concessions to all developing countries without requiring trade or other concessions from them. It was recommended by the UNCTAD I that "new preferential concessions both tariff and non-tariff, should be made to developing countries as a whole and such preferences should not be extended to developed countries." It was recommended that regional economic groupings of developing countries should not adversely affect expansion of exports from developing countries either individually or collectively." The UNCTAD I recommended that "each developed country should transfer annually 1 per cent of its Gross National Product to developing countries." Developed countries should also soften the terms and conditions of their loans to developing countries to reduce burden on them of both the principal and servicing charges.

At the UNCTAD I some policy decisions were also taken to implement some of the above recommendations. But on the whole progress in regard to implementation of the recommendations made by UNCTAD I was extremely slow. For example, no progress was made between 1964-68 in regard to granting of non-reciprocal preferences for exports from developing countries and in respect of the objective that 1 per cent of the GNP of developed countries should be given as foreign aid to developing countries. In fact, during 1964-68 there was an overall deterioration in regard to foreign aid. The practice of tying foreign loans continued as before. The share of developing countries in the total world trade continued to decline and so also the growth-rate in world trade of primary commodities which is of primary importance to developing countries.

On the success side, it might be said that the Kennedy Round of tariff negotiations in 1964 saw the first practical application of the principle of non-reciprocity recommended by the UNCTAD I. Also, agreement was reached on the outline of a facility to create Special Drawing Rights in the IMF as a supplement to the world resources consisting of gold and key currencies. The UNCTAD I can also take credit for liberalisation in 1966 of the IMF facility for compensatory financing for fluctuations in export trade of primary products of developing countries.

But the evolution of an effective international primary commodity policy continues to face numerous difficulties and problems.

The UNCTAD II

"The Group of 77" met in Algiers in October 1967 and issued what is known as 'The Charter of Algiers' with a detailed programme of action. This programme was to be taken up by the UNCTAD II for consideration and action.

The Algiers Charter drew attention to the need for commodity agreements (especially in respect of sugar and coca), buffer stock operations and provision of initial funds for that purpose by international financial institutions and developed countries, need for guaranteeing by developed countries a market share for primary products (which have to compete with those in developed countries), grant of non-discriminatory, non-reciprocal tariff preferences for all manufactured and semi-manufactured products exported by developing countries and the target of 1 per cent of GNP to be attained by 1970.

The UNCTAD II met in New Delhi in Feb-March 1968, developing countries being in a very optimistic mood expecting too much out of the deliberations at the UNCTAD II.

But the UNCATD II was marked by increasing disagreements and prolonged discussions mostly without arriving at any specific results. The main reason for the internal disagreements was the political nature of the discussions at the conference. Other reasons for the disappointing results of the UNCTAD II were the gold crisis, balance of payments problems faced by the United States and the United Kingdom, deep involvement of the United States in Vietnam war, recession in the United States, movements towards liberalisation in the socialist block countries, and fluid political and economic situation in West Asia. Developed Countries took full advantage of the disagreement and dissension among developing countries as the Group of 77 failed to present a united front to confront the developed countries which always happen to form a close union and pursue a joint policy. Significantly Dr. Prebisch, the main architect of the UNCTAD since its inception, resigned soon after the session of the UNCTAD II, because of frustration with the way the UNCTAD had been functioning so far.

On the whole, the UNCTAD was termed a failure, because it failed to make any contribution to the evolution of international development policy, though the UNCTAD II did manage to achieve a few gains in matters of tariff preferences, commodity agreements, recognition by developed countries of their responsibility to help development of developing countries, progress in regard to commercial credit to add to the flow of foreign resources, in regard to land-locked backward countries which were expected to be helped by international financial institutions in the matter of development of transport and communication facilities, increasing realisation of the need to extend and develop trade among member-developing countries themselves, and the concept of resolving differences among developing countries by mutual negotiations rather than by confrontation.

The UNCTAD III

The UNCTAD III was held at Aantiago (the Chilean capital) during April-May 1972 in which economists from 140 countries and around 3000 politicians participated. The main point of discussion was the widening economic gap between the rich and poor countries. Mr. Robert McNamara, the President of the World Bank, laid emphasis on the need for a policy to reduce the widening gap between the per capita incomes of peoples in rich and poor countries. He stated that whereas the average per capita income in developed countries was 2400 US dollars and would be raised to around 3600 US dollars by 1980, the per capita income in LDCs would be only around 180 US dollars and would be only 280 dollars by 1980.

The UNCTAD III unanimously approved a resolution which recommended the following decisions: (i) The developed countries should continue rendering assistance to the LDCs in diversifying the latters' economies; (ii) developed countries should give special consideration to commodity agreements; (iii) special consideration should be given by developed countries to the development of shipping and port facilities in developing countries to reduce transport costs at present incurred by developing countries; (iv) special consideration should be given to further promote exports from developing countries; and (v) the World Bank should devote greater share of their development resources to developing countries.

At the UNCTAD III there was also taken the unanimous decision to render assistance to the 23 poorest countries in the world and help reduce the gap that exists between these poorest countries and the other developing countries. It is however, not known to what extent this recommendation has been implemented and with what effect. But one good thing that came out of this was that developing countries realised that they must reduce and if possible get rid of their dependence on developed countries for self-development. Mutual economic cooperation among developing countries themselves to help their process of socio-economic development came to be emphasised at the UNCTAD III.

The UNCTAD IV

The UNCTAD IV was held at Nairobi in May 1976. Prior to that the Group of 77 (now consisting of 110 developing countries) met at Manila in Philippines to prepare a programme of action for protecting their international interests. It was decided at Manila that developing countries should press for the participation of the UNCATD IV for "restructuring the commodity trade, creation of a common fund for maintaining buffer stocks of their primary products, for softening of terms and conditions of foreign aid."

The representatives of developing countries at the Nairobi conference showed serious concern for the widening gap between the rich and poor nations. One estimate was that 7.2 trillion US dollars would be required to reduce over the next 50 years the gap in personal income between the rich and poor nations. The prevailing ratio between the 30 per cent of the total world population living in developed countries and the 70 per cent living in developing countries was estimated at 40:1.

It was recommended that with a view to contain fluctuations in the prices of primary commodities exported by developing countries, a common fund of 6000 billion US dollars should be created. It was argued that only such an integrated plan would stabilise export earnings of developing countries and help develop their economies. The fund was proposed to be utilised for providing finance for creation and maintenance of buffer stocks of primary products generally exported by developing countries. It was proposed that both the producing countries and consuming countries should subscribe to the fund which should serve as the anchor of integrated commodity programme intended to stabilise commodity prices to help developing countries to bring about economic development.

Some representatives of developing countries pleaded for a general moratorium on foreign debt with a view to rescue developing countries out of the present plight of foreign debt.

It might be noted that representatives of developing countries could not convince representatives of developed countries about the merits of their proposal, though the latter agreed to provide some debt relief by arranging debt-rescheduling in the case of poor nations. Henry Kissinger, representing the United States, expressed his doubt about the utility of the common fund to finance buffer stock of primary products. He warned developing countries against using any pressure tactics to get through their proposals and warned that the United States would "resist confrontation" and would ignore unrealistic proposals. But he was willing to consider issues like tariff negotiations and foreign aid proposals.

In the end it was agreed that the question of integrated commodity programme and debt relief be reviewed thoroughly by representatives of both developed and developing countries with a view to evolve a programme acceptable to both the groups of countries and it was proposed to do that by March 1977.

In subsequent meetings of the UNCTAD more or less the same resolutions were passed and recommendations made all with very little practical achievements.

UNCTAD and Recent Developments

Trade and Development Report of the UNCTAD for 1988 has suggested that there is a need to reduce claims of commercial banks by 30 per cent in the case of highly-indebted middle income countries to solve their external debt problem. But the industrialised countries and their group expressed strong opposition to this suggestion. At their Toronto Summit held in June 1988, heads of seven industrialised countries declared their desire to provide debt relief to the poorest and heavily indebted countries. The relief provided will be in the form of either concessional interest rates, usually with shorter maturities, or longer repayment periods at commercial rates or partial write-off of debt service obligations during the consolidation period or a combination of any of these elements.

Conclusion of an agreement on Generalised System of Trade Preferences among the developing countries of the Group of 77 marks an important achievement in the realm of South-South Cooperation. The Agreement was adopted at the Ministerial meeting of the participating countries in Belgrade in April 1988. Annexed to this Agreement is the list of tariff concessions exchanged amongst 48 participating countries of the Group of 77 in the first round of negotiations. India has exchanged tariff concessions with 14 countries. The tariff concessions exchanged in the first round have been only modest in terms of trade and product coverage. But the significant achievement lies in the conclusion of the Agreement which provides a framework for exchange of trade concessions among developing countries and for promoting trade and economic cooperation among themselves. The Agreement is expected to come into force shortly as it is in the process of ratification by participating countries.

CHAPTER 25

THE WORLD TRADE ORGANISATION

Structure:

The World Trade Organisation (WTO) was set up on Ist January 1995. It builds on the organisational structure of the GATT and its secretariat. It is the legal and institutional foundation of the multilateral trading system (Blackhurst 1998)[1]. The key principle to which the GATT contracting parties subscribed and is also the founding principle of the WTO is the 'principle of open and non-discriminatory trade.'

The Punta del Este Ministerial Declaration that launched the Uruguay Trade round did not contain any proposal regarding the establishment of an international organisation to manage the implementation of the negotiations. However, it was the Canadian proposal made in 1990, supported later by the EU, to set up a Multilateral Trade Organisation, which could be deemed as the impetus behind the establishment of WTO. The proposal was motivated by a desire to create a single institutional framework for world trade.

The obligations and commitments of the members of the WTO are contained in *The Results of the Uruguay Round of Multilateral Trade Negotiations, which* was formally adopted in Marrakech in April 1994. It comprises of twenty nine individual legal texts and twenty eight additional ministerial declarations, decisions, understandings that spell out further obligations and commitments, together with 26,000 pages of computer print out detailing each member's schedule of tariff concessions and schedule of service commitments. Every member of WTO, in contrast to GATT has to submit schedules on tariff concessions and service commitments (Blackhurst 1998, p. 32). With the exception only of the least developed countries, every member has to accept in its entirety a common set of rules and disciplines covering goods, services, and intellectual property.

25.1 SCOPE OF THE WTO

Four Annexes to the WTO define the substantive rights and obligations of members. Annex 1 has three parts: Annex 1A entitled Multilateral Agreements on Trade in Goods, contains GATT 1994 (the GATT 1947 was amended by a large number of Understanding and Supplementary Agreements negotiated in the Uruguay Round); Annex 1B which contains the GATS; and Annex 1C, the Agreement on TRIPS. Annex 2 contains the Understanding on Rules and Procedures Governing the Settlement of Disputes (DSU) — the WTO's common dispute settlement mechanism Annex 3 contains the Trade Policy Review Mechanism (TPRM), an instrument for surveillance of member's trade policies. Finally, Annex 4 — entitled Plurilateral Trade Agreements — consist of Tokyo Round codes that were not multilateralised in the Uruguay Round and that therefore only bind the signatories. All the agreements in the Annexes 1-3, according to the Article II WTO, are the integral part of the WTO Agreement, and are binding on all the members (Hoekman and Kostecki 2001, p. 51)[2].

1. Blackhurst R. (1998), "The Capacity of the WTO to Fulfill its Mandate", in Krueger Anne O. ed., *"The WTO as an International Organisation",* Oxford University Press.
2. Hoekman Bernard M. & Kostecki Michel M., (2001), *"The Political Economy of the World Trading System — The WTO and Beyond,"* Oxford University Press, Second Edition.

The main differences between the GATT and the WTO

GATT was adhoc and provisional. The General Agreement was never ratified in members' parliaments, and it contained no provisions for the creation of an organization. The WTO and its agreements are permanent. As an international organization, the WTO has a sound legal basis because members have ratified the WTO agreements, and the agreements themselves describe how the WTO is to function.

The WTO has "members." GATT had "contracting parties", underscoring the fact that officially GATT was a legal text.

GATT dealt with trade in goods. The WTO covers services and intellectual property as well.

The WTO dispute settlement system is faster, more automatic than the old GATT system. Its rulings cannot be blocked.

Source: WTO, "Trading into the Future" (available on www.wto.org).

25.2 FUNCTIONS OF THE WTO

The WTO's prime objective is to help trade flow smoothly, freely, fairly, and predictably. It does this by:

Administering trade agreements

Acting as a forum for trade negotiations

Settling trade disputes

Reviewing national trade policies

Assisting developing countries in trade policy issues, through technical assistance and training programmes

Cooperating with other international organizations like the IMF and the World Bank to achieve greater coherence in global economic policy making.

25.3 STRUCTURE OF THE WTO

In order to achieve these complex objectives the WTO has to have an effective organizational structure. This especially becomes important given the number of members involved, multiplicity of members' interests, and their domestic political compulsions.

The WTO has more than 130 members, accounting for over 90% of world trade. Over 30 others are negotiating membership. Decisions are made by the entire membership. This is typically by consensus. A majority vote is also possible but it has never been used in the WTO, and was extremely rare under the WTO's predecessor, GATT. The WTO's agreements have been ratified in all members' parliaments.

The WTO's top-level decision-making body is the Ministerial Conference, which meets at least once every two years. Below this is the General Council (normally ambassadors and heads of delegation in Geneva, but sometime officials sent from members' capitals), which meets several times a year in the Geneva headquarters. The General Council also meets as the Trade Policy Review Body and the

Dispute Settlement Body. At the next level, the Goods Council, Services Council, and Intellectual Property (TRIPS) Council report to the General Council.

Numerous specialized committees, working groups and working parties deal with the individual agreements and other areas such as the environment, development, membership applications and regional trade agreements. The first Ministerial Conference in Singapore in 1996 added three new working groups to this structure. They deal with the relationship between trade and investment, the interaction between trade and competition policy and transparency in government procurement. At the second Ministerial Conference in Geneva in 1998, ministers decided that the WTO could also study the area of electronic commerce, a task to be shared out among existing councils and committees.

25.4 SECRETARIAT

The WTO Secretariat, based in Geneva, has around 500 staff and is headed by a director-general. It does not have branch offices outside Geneva. Since the members themselves take decisions, the Secretariat does not have the decision-making role that other international bureaucracies are given. The Secretariat's main duties are:

to supply technical support for the various councils and committees and the ministerial conferences,

to provide technical assistance for developing countries,

to analyze world trade, and

to explain WTO affairs to the public and media.

The Secretariat also provides some forms of legal assistance in the dispute settlement process and advises governments wishing to become members of the WTO. The annual budget is roughly 122 million Swiss francs.

The main actors in day-to-day activities are officials affiliated with the delegations of members. To WTO — as was the GATT 1947 — is therefore something of a network organization (Blackhurst 1998). A schematic representation of the structure of WTO is given in the following diagram:

Decision-Making in the WTO

Decision-making Rule	*Type of Issue*
Unanimity	Amendments concerning general principles such as non-discrimination
Three-quarters majority	Interpretations of the provisions of the WTO and waivers of WTO disciplines for members
Two-thirds majority	Amendments to the WTO relating to issues other than general principles; accession
Consensus as a rule	Where not otherwise specified, Decisions of the Dispute Settlement Body, Waiver of obligations subject to transition period, and Addition of a plurilateral trade agreement.

Source: Blackhurst (1998) and Hoekman & Kostecki (2001).

Dispute Settlement Procedures

The effective resolution of trade disputes is essential for smooth working of the trading system. The Dispute Settlement Mechanism is the unique feature of the WTO and the dispute settlement procedures are binding. Such a system is especially important from the point of view of developing countries, which would find it difficult to oppose the unilateral actions by large traders that would arise in the absence of multilateral dispute settlement mechanisms.

The use of WTO dispute settlement mechanism is mandatory for all disputes concerning agreement that have been concluded. A member may use unilateral instruments to initiate consultations, but if it is decided to pursue the case it must first submit the case to the WTO (Article 23.2 DSU). Only in situations where a member doesn't abide by the ruling, instruments of unilateral retaliation can be used. However, they also have to be authorised by the WTO.

Disputes arising under any WTO agreement are dealt with by Dispute Settlement Body (DSB), which has the authority to establish panels, adopt panel reports, scrutinize implementation of recommendations and authorize retaliatory measures if the losing party to a dispute does not abide by the panel's recommendations (Hoekman & Kostecki 2001, p. 76). The WTO council itself functions as the DSB. The rules by which the process of dispute settlement is carried out are laid down in Uruguay Round Dispute Settlement Understanding (DSU).

25.5 SETTLEMENT OF DISPUTES: STEPS[3]

Settling disputes is the responsibility of the Dispute Settlement Body (the General Council in another guise). The Dispute Settlement Body has the sole authority to establish "panels" of experts to consider the case, and to accept or reject the panels' findings or the results of an appeal. It monitors the implementation of the rulings and recommendations, and has the power to authorize retaliation when a country does not comply with a ruling.

First stage: consultation (up to 60 days). Before taking any other actions the countries in dispute have to talk to each other to see if they can settle their differences by themselves. If that fails, they can also ask the WTO director general to mediate or try to help in any other way.

Second stage: the panel (up to 45 days for a panel to be appointed, plus 6 months for the panel to conclude).

If consultations fail, the complaining country can ask for a panel to be appointed. The country "in the dock" can block the creation of a panel once, but when the Dispute Settlement Body meet for a second time, the appointment can no longer be blocked (unless there is a consensus against appointing the panel). Officially, the panel is helping the Dispute Settlement Body make rulings or recommendations. However, because the panel's report can only be rejected by consensus in the Dispute Settlement Body, its conclusions are difficult to overturn. The panel's findings have to be based on the agreements cited. The panel's final report should normally be given to the parties to the dispute within six months. In cases of urgency, including those concerning perishable goods, the deadline is shortened to three months. The agreement describes in some detail how the panels are to work. The main stages are:

3. The material included in this section is based on the WTO document, "Trading into Future." Its freely downloadable from the official website of the WTO (www. wto. org.).

Before the first hearing: each side in the dispute presents its case in writing to the panel.

First hearing: the case for the complaining country and defense: the complaining country (or countries), the responding country, and those that have announced they have an interest in the dispute, make their case at the panel's first hearing.

Rebuttals: the countries involved submit written rebuttals and present oral arguments at the panel's second meeting.

Experts: if one side raises scientific or other technical matters, the panel may consult experts or appoint an expert review group to prepare an advisory report.

First draft: the panel submits the descriptive (factual and argument) sections of its report to the two sides, giving them two weeks to comment. This report does not include findings and conclusions.

Interim report: The panel then submits an interim report, including its findings and conclusions, to the two sides, giving them one week to ask for a review.

Review: The period of review must not exceed two weeks. During that time, the panel may hold additional meetings with the two sides.

Final report: A final report is submitted to the two sides and three weeks later, it is circulated to all WTO members. If the panel decides that the disputed trade measure does break a WTO agreement or an obligation, it recommends that the measure be made to conform with WTO rules. The panel may suggest how this could be done.

The report becomes a ruling: The report becomes the Dispute Settlement Body's ruling or recommendation within 60 days unless a consensus rejects it. Both sides can appeal the report (and in some cases both sides do).

25.6 APPEALS

Either side can appeal a panel's ruling. Sometimes both sides do so. Appeals have to be based on points of law such as legal interpretation — they cannot reexamine existing evidence or examine new evidence. Each appeal is heard by three members of a permanent seven-member Appellate Body set up by the Dispute Settlement Body and broadly representing the range of WTO membership. Members of the Appellate Body have four-year terms. They have to be individuals with recognized standing in the field of law and international trade, not affiliated with any government. The appeal can uphold, modify, or reverse the panel's legal findings and conclusions. Normally appeals should not last more than 60 days, with an absolute maximum of 90 days. The Dispute Settlement Body has to accept or reject the appeals report within 30 days — and rejection is only possible by consensus.

Actual Working of the Dispute Settlement System

The actual functioning of the DSB is much in line with the expectations, though the use of DSB over years has also highlighted some flaws in the system. Over 160 requests for consultations were bought to the WTO in the first five years of its operation (which is almost three times more on a per annum basis than under the GATT). Out of the total cases about 30 per cent were brought by or against the developing countries. Some developing countries even successfully contested action of large players as in the case of Costa Rica *vs.* Us regarding the latter's restriction on cotton textiles. The following table gives the compilation of the users of the Dispute Settlement during the period April 1994-March 1999.

Table

The largest share of cases involves allegations of violation of the principles of non-discrimination (MFN or national treatment)[4]. About half of all the cases involve one or both of these rules. The second largest chunk of cases pertains to the violation of the prohibition on use of QRs.

Shortcomings of the Dispute Settlement Procedure

Some of the major problems that emerged were related to the implementation of the DSB rulings and attempts to use the process to address issues where countries have strongly divergent regulatory regimes, especially in the area of public health and safety (e.g., the EU Bananas case and Hormones case). Moreover, even if a ruling is given by the DSB, the ability to enforce it is very asymmetric.

The other major shortcoming is the cost of the process can be significant. This especially is pertinent for the developing countries. It is often noted that the big players like the US and the EU are better equipped in terms of legal talent, are well briefed by export interests, and have a world wide network of commercial and diplomatic representation that feed their system with the relevant data (Hoekman & Kostecki 2001, p. 91). The developing countries often lose on these grounds. They not only lack the adequate technical and legal talent but also lack the resources to hire them privately. India can be exception to this as it has talent as well as resources. What it lacks is the political will and bureaucratic efficiency to utilise the available resources.

The threat of retaliation will have credibility only in the case of large players. The small countries cannot effectively threaten as their import barriers will have little impact on the target market while being costly in welfare terms to itself.

One of the potentially very troublesome issues is the issue of non-violation disputes. These disputes are an important avenue for countries to contest WTO legal measures that have serious consequences for their economies. However, the problem with non-violation cases is the generality of the language "nullification or impairment", which creates great ambiguity about what would be an appropriate way to analyse these cases and to determine when one nation had some sort of right of relief from another nation (Jackson 1998)[5]. One such issue is that of the Competition Policy. If any country brings a non-violation case based on competition policy, then any ruling in favour of the complainant will be directed towards 'law making' rather than 'law applying.' This would be clearly inconsistent with the clause in the DSU which supposedly restrains panels from "changing the rights or obligation of parties."

4. See Appendix at the end of the chapter for a detailed explanation of the Principles of Non-discrimination.

5. Jackson John H. (1998), "Designing and Implementing Effective Dispute Settlement Procedures: WTO Dispute Settlement, Appraisal and Prospects," in Krueger Anne O. Ed., *"The WTO as an International Organisation,"* Oxford University Press.

Negotiating Forum

How do members of the WTO having diverse interests and attitudes come together and decide upon any contentious issues surrounding international trade? Here we realise the importance of the WTO as negotiating forum. Negotiations are the impetus behind a multilateral trading system. They are important to decide upon rules and procedures related to trade, to periodically reduce trade barriers and to resolve trade conflicts. The WTO is basically a permanent negotiating forum in which trade issues may be discussed and agreed upon against the background of the agreements already reached.

The first eight trading rounds and the ministerial meetings of Geneva (1982), Brussels (1990) and Marrakech (1994) were held under the auspices of the GATT. The following table gives the results of ministerial meetings held under the asupices of the WTO:

Name of the Meeting	*Period and Number of Parties*	*Subject and Modalities*	*Outcome*
Singapore	1996 / 130 members	Proposals to discuss labour standards, competition and investment policy, procurement and trade facilitation in WTO; Elimination of barriers to trade in information technology products; pursue negotiations on basic telecom and financial services.	Information Technology Agreement (ITA). Creation of working groups on competition and investment policy and procurement. Labour standards rejected as subject for negotiation.
Seattle	1999/ 135 members	Launch of a new MTN. Major issues included developing country concerns on Uruguay Round implementation, modalities of agricultural liberalization, and competition, investment and labour standards.	Failure to agree on a MTN or on a work program. Members pursue only the 'built-in' agenda inherited from the Uruguay Round.
Doha	2001/135 members	Launch of new MTN. Implementation related issues and concerns; Liberalisation of agriculture and services; Market access for non-agricultural commodities; trade related intellectual property rights; competition policy; Transparency in government procurement.	Decision on Implementation related issues and concerns which addresses a number of complaints of the developing countries with respect to the implementation of the Uruguay Round (UR) Agreement; Declaration on the TRIPS Agreement and Public Health, which weakens some of the provisions of the TRIPS Agreement; Doha Ministerial Declaration, which outlines the work program for the new round.

Cancun	2003 / 135	Lack of democracy, market access for South, dumping, unfair trade, patent rules, try to introduce new issues before Doha round is settled	Imbalanced, non-democratic, free trade promotion, social environment issues, failedto give importance to sustainable develeopment.
Hong Kong	2005 / 135	Market access, reduce tariffs, domestic support, end direct payments, EU to end subsidies, Singapore issues, Govt. procurement, transparency in investment, competition etc.	Agricultural development, NAMA, non-reciprocal preferences, need to ensure commensurably high levels of ambition.

Source: Hoekman & Kostecki 2001, Panagariya (2002)[6] & WTO Ministerial Declaration 2001.

Conclusion

World Trade Organisation signifies the political economy aspects of the multilateral trading system. It is an international organisation based on a sound legal framework. Though, many drawbacks have been evident in the process of negotiations, it has been effective in fostering an environment of trust amongst the members, by providing a much needed forum for international trade negotiations and settlement of disputes.

6. Panagariya Arvind (2002), "India at Doha: Retrospect and Prospect", *Economic and Political Weekly*, January 26.

APPENDIX

Principles of Non-discrimination

The Most favoured Nation Principle

Central to the global trading system in goods is the unconditional most favoured nation (MFN) principle enshrined in Article I of GATT 1994. According to this provision, if country A grants a concession to country B as a part of a bargain, it must automatically grant the same concession to all other WTO members even if the latter offer no concession in return. Thus, a member country must treat all WTO members at par with its most favoured trading partner. An immediate implication of this provision is that a country must charge the same tariff rate of imports irrespective of its origin (leaving aside the possibility that the imports may have come from a non-member). If applied without exception, this provision has the virtue that it ensures a single tariff rate on each product in a country. The resulting tariff regime is not only transparent but also economically efficient from the global standpoint. Being non-discriminatory, it also gives reason for political discord across trading partners.

Being a compromise among competing interests, the WTO agreements admit a variety of violations of the MFN principle. Article I itself accommodates the trade preferences that existed prior to April 10, 1947. But more extensive violations of the MFN principle have come from preferential trade areas (PTAs) under three sets of provisions (see below for more details). First, GATT Article XXIV permits the formation of free trade areas (FTAs) and customs union (CUs) whereby two or more WTO members eliminate trade barriers among them but not on outside countries. Under an FTA, such as the North American Free Trade Agreement (NAFTA), each member retains its own external tariffs while under a CU, such as the European Community (EC), the members adopt a common external tariff on each product. These arrangements naturally introduce discrimination between union member and outside countries. Second, the Enabling Clause, introduced in 1979, allows two or more developing countries to exchange partial trade preferences with one another. In these cases, internal tariffs neither be eliminated entirely; nor is it required that substantially all products be covered.

The Enabling Clause also permits one-way preferences by developed to developing countries. These preferences, as exemplified by GSP, may be partial and can be granted on selected products. Finally, in the past, the GATT contracting parties have granted waivers from the application of Article I. The United States-Canada Automotive Products Agreement of 1965, which established a free trade area between the two countries in the automotive sector, operated under such a waiver. During 1971 to 1981, GSP also operated under a similar waiver.

Violations of the MFN principle also happen in the application of safeguard measures. For instance, when anti-dumping duties are imposed, they apply only to those firms or countries found guilty. This automatically induces discrimination in trade policy. Any time that safeguard actions take the form of quantitative restrictions, no matter how they are administered, discrimination is likely to result. Voluntary export restraints, which limit imports from specific countries only, are outright discriminatory. Countries may also discriminate across trading partners by classifying imports to place similar products coming from different partners into categories subject to different tariff rates. But such discrimination can be challenged successfully in the WTO at least so long as the products can be shown to have similar characteristics.

National Treatment

While Article I of GATT 1994 is designed to eliminate discrimination among imports from different WTO members, Article III aims to eliminate discrimination against imported goods *vis-à-vis* domestically produced goods once they cross the border. It stipulates that once imports have entered the territory of a member country, they must be treated no less favourably than similar domestically produced goods. Article III explicitly states that products from other member countries should not subject to internal taxes or other charges in excess of those applicable to similar domestically produced goods. At least equal treatment to imports must also be given with respect to all laws, regulations, and requirements affecting their internal sale, purchase, transportation, distribution, or use. Also prohibited under the national treatment provision are any internal quantitative restrictions that discriminate against imports. For instance, producers cannot be required that a minimum proportion of an input used in production be of domestic origin. Such "domestic content" requirements have been a source of contention, especially when imposed on foreign investors. The UR Agreement on TRIMs now explicitly recognizes that the domestic content requirements violate Article III of GATT. The national treatment provisions do not apply, however, to laws, regulations, or requirements governing the procurement of goods by government agencies for governmental use. A code on government procurement was signed by a plurality of the members in the Tokyo Round. While future negotiations may try to extend this code, appropriately modified, to the entire WTO membership, at present, government Procurement is exempt from Article III. In recent years technical standards are fast becoming effective means of discrimination in favour of domestic producers of manufactured goods. The standards can be set in such a way as to make it costly for foreign producers to comply. Likewise, unduly strict inspections of imports for health, safety reasons may raise the costs of imports unnecessarily. The UR Agreements on TBTs (Technical Barriers to Trade), and SPS (Sanitary and Phytosanitary) measures have recently tried to address some of these concerns. The Agreement on TBTs explicitly states that WTO members shall "ensure that neither technical regulations, nor standards themselves nor their application have the effect of creating unnecessary obstacles to international trade." The Agreement on SPS similarly requires that sanitary and phytosanitary measures "should be applied only to the extent necessary to protect human, animal or plant life or health and should not arbitrarily or unjustifiably discriminate between Members where identical or similar conditions prevail."

Source: Panagariya Arvind, *"Core WTO Agreements: Trade in Goods & Services and Intellectual Property", Article posted on his personal website.*

SECTION V

INDIA'S INTERNATIONAL TRADE

26

CHAPTER

INDIA'S INTERNATIONAL TRADE

Structure:

After studying the theoretical aspects of international trade and finance, it would be interesting to know what is happening to international trade of India over the years. As has been mentioned earlier the new economic policy of 1990-91 has brought in its wake a sea change in the orientation of the Indian economy. Prior to this policy India was a largely inward oriented economy. After 1991, however, we have become increasingly outwardly oriented. What does this mean in terms of volume of exports and imports? What has happened to the composition and direction of India's trade? What is the state of our balance of payments? These are some of the questions for which we seek answers for in this chapter.

26.1 VOLUME OF INDIA'S TRADE

After independence and especially since the commencement of the planning era in the country in 1950-51, volume of India's foreign trade (total of Exports and Imports as a percentage of GDP as well as in absolute value) is seen continuously rising. However, one has to point out some important features of this rise. Trade as percentage of GDP doubled from 7.5% to roughly 15% during the period 1970-1988, i.e., in 19 years. But in the later period it doubled to 30% in just 12 years (1989-2000). This difference in growth rate is generally attributed to the liberalisation policies of 1985-88 and then the post 1991 ones. What are these changes that caused trade to rise as a proportion of GDP? Why is Trade gaining importance in the Indian Economy? The answers to these questions can be found in the following policy changes that have been brought about since 1991. Before that a brief word about the crisis of the 1990 which paved the way for these changes.

India's Economic Crisis of 1990s

The crisis of 1990-91 was indeed a major one. Foreign exchange reserves were barely enough to pay for even 15 days' imports. Was this because of import liberalisation of mid eighties? Many people would like to say so. But this is not really the picture that is conveyed by the data. Import liberalisation did lead to increase in imports in some categories. However, the worsening trade gap accounted for only small part of the increase in the current account deficit. In fact imports rose more than indicated by the customs figures as a result of public imports such as military equipment but these have little to do with import liberalisation; rather it has more to do with the overall level of government expenditure (Joshi & Little 1994).

The crisis of the 1990 had its origin in the policy stance taken in the post second oil shock period. At that stage, exports stagnated on account of real exchange rate appreciation and there was deterioration in the fiscal position. Both the domestic and foreign debt increased rapidly. As a result, the underlying macroeconomic situation in 1985/86 was unsatisfactory. Thus, the major drawback of the macroeconomic policy lay in the neglect of the warning signals evident in 1985-86 on the fiscal front. Fiscal deterioration was allowed to continue. As a result, the current account deficit continued to worsen and domestic and foreign debt continued to increase at a dangerous rate. By the end of the decade, the macroeconomic fundamentals were out of tune. Even a strictly temporary shock like the Gulf War was enough to trigger a full-scale crisis.

Recent Trade Policy Changes

- *Reduction in Taxes and Subsidies on Exports and Imports:* As noted in the introductory chapter there has been a continuous decline in the import duty 1991 onwards. It came down from the level of 150% in 1991 to a meagre 25% in the year 2002. There also has been rationalisation in the other duties, multiple rates, and slabs, which was carried out through subsequent budget proposals.

- *Removal of Quantitative Restrictions:* The EXIM policy of 2001 completed the process of removal of QRs on the BOP grounds by dismantling the restrictions on the remaining 715 items. QRs on 714 items were removed via EXIM policy 2000. This included 58 items that were reserved for the SSI sector.

- *Exchange Rate Adjustment:* Initially the replenishment licensing system was widened into a broad-based system of incentive licences (Exim scrips) to exporters. The system was then moved towards the Liberalised Exchange Rate Management System (LERMS), whereby 60 per cent of export earnings could be converted to rupees at the open market rate, allowing a dual rate system to operate. This was the first step towards full convertibility of rupee in the current account. After 199 steps have been taken to achieve this full convertibility in the current account thereby doing away with the dual rate system. Currently the exchange rate of the rupee against the US $ is broadly market determined with temporary shocks in demand for and supply for foreign exchange taken care of by the RBI, thereby containing the excessive volatility in the foreign exchange market.

We have already seen the behaviour of Trade to GDP ratio over the years in the introductory chapter. The following table gives the absolute value of exports and imports for a fairly long period. We can easily see both imports and exports picking up considerably after 1990-91. In fact compared to the period 1980-81 to 1989-90, exports grew faster by an additional 2 per cent in the period 1990-91-1999-2000 and imports grew by a difference of 6 per cent. In the post 1990 period both the exports and imports grew by almost 17 per cent.

Table 26.1

Volume of India's Foreign Trade

Rs. Cr.

Year	*Exports*	*Imports*	*Trade Balance*
1949-50	485	617	–132
1950-51	606	608	–2
1951-52	716	890	–174
1952-53	578	702	–124
1953-54	531	610	–79
1954-55	593	700	–107
1955-56	609	774	–165
1956-57	605	841	–236
1957-58	561	1035	–474
1958-59	581	906	–325
1959-60	640	961	–321
1960-61	642	1122	–480
1961-62	660	1090	–430
1962-63	685	1131	–446

1963-64	793	1223	–430
1964-65	816	1349	–533
1965-66	810	1409	–599
1966-67	1157	2078	–921
1967-68	1199	2008	–809
1968-69	1358	1909	–551
1969-70	1413	1582	–169
1970-71	1535	1634	–99
1971-72	1608	1825	–217
1972-73	1971	1867	104
1973-74	2523	2955	–432
1974-75	3329	4519	–1190
1975-76	4036	5265	–2419
1976-77	5142	5074	68
1977-78	5408	6020	–612
1978-79	5726	6811	–1085
1979-80	6418	9143	–2725
1980-81	6711	12549	–5838
1981-82	7806	13608	–5802
1982-83	8803	14293	–5490
1983-84	9771	15831	–6060
1984-85	11744	17134	–5390
1985-86	10895	19658	–8763
1986-87	12452	20096	–7644
1987-88	15674	22244	6570
1988-89	20232	28235	–8003
1989-90	27658	35328	–7670
1990-91	32553	43198	–10645
1991-92	44041	47851	–3810
1992-93	53688	63375	–9687
1993-94	69751	73101	–3350
1994-95	82674	89971	–7297
1995-96	106353	122678	–16325
1996-97	118817	138920	–20103
1997-98	130100	154176	–24076
1998-99	139752	178332	–38580
1999-2000	159561	215236	–55675
2000-01	203571	230873	–27302
2001-02(P) (April-Dec.)	**154445**	**181753**	**–27308**

Source: Economic Survey 2001-2002.

26.2 COMMODITY COMPOSITION OF EXPORTS AND IMPORTS

Given the fact that India's foreign trade has been generally rising, more so after the year 1991, we can now turn to the commodity composition of this increasing trade. Following two tables describe the share of various commodities in exports and imports generally. It should be noted at this point that in general merchandise trade (trade in tangibles) forms a major part of our current account even today. Hence it will be worthwhile to have a closer look at what is happening inside our merchandise basket.

Exports

Exports of India are broadly classified as:

(1) Agriculture and allied products which include coffee, tea, oil cakes, tobacco, cashew nuts, spices and so on.

(2) Ores and minerals include manganese ore, mica and iron ore.

(3) Manufactured goods include textiles and ready-made garments, jute manufactures, leather and footwear, handicrafts including pearls and precious stones, etc.

(4) Mineral fuels and lubricants (not very significant).

One is ought to think that India being a developing country, will primarily export commodities with less value addition, i.e., agricultural commodities. However, the data reveals a different truth.

- *Agriculture and allied products* do not contribute more than 14% of our exports today and have generally shown a decreasing tend over the years.
- Instead, *manufactures,* which are supposed to be more value adding than the agricultural products, have formed a major part of our export basket and have shown a rising trend, though not phenomenal. This implies increasing diversification of the Indian economy.
- However, we should not think that we export highly sophisticated engineering goods as manufactures (with an exception of computer software). Ready-made garments and gems and jewellery are the commodities, which contribute significantly to our manufactured goods (almost 30%), with rest of the commodity groups contributing 2-5% each.
- One interesting export item is the iron ore. This in a way reflects our incapacity to process the ore domestically and export steel instead. Another way of interpreting this is that it might be actually cheaper to export iron ore and import steel, rather than processing it domestically to get steel.

Imports

Imports are generally classified as Bulk imports and Non-bulk imports. Bulk imports consist mainly of petroleum, crude and products. Other items to get classified as bulk are cereals and pulses, edible oils and sugar and other bulk items comprising of fertilizers etc. Non-bulk items are further classified into three components: (1) Capital goods and (2) export related items like pearls, organic and inorganic chemicals, cashew nuts etc. (See Table no. 26.3 for data according to this classification).

Following the classification of Table no. 26.3 we can say the following about imports:

Table 26.2

Share of Major Exports

	1993-94	*1994-95*	*1995-96*	*1996-97*	*1997-98*	*1998-99*	*1999-2000*	*2000-01*	2003-04	2004-05	2005-06	2006-07
I. Agriculture and Allied products	18	16	19.2	20.3	18.8	17.3	15.2	13.5	12.5	10.5	10.2	9.9
II. Ores and Minerals	4	3.8	3.7	3.5	3	2.6	2.5	2.6	4.0	5.5	5.2	4.0
III. Manufactured goods	75.5	78.1	75.4	74.1	75.8	77.8	80.7	78	76.9	74.3	72.0	69.0

Source: Economic Survey — various issues.

Table No. 26.3

Share of Major Imports

	1991-92	*1992-93*	*1993-94*	*1994-95*	*1995-96*	*1996-97*	*1997-98*	*1998-99*	*1999-00*	*2000-01*
I. Food and Allied Products	2.2	3.2	2.4	5.1	3.6	3.8	4.5	6.1	5.8	3.7
II. Fuel (POL main)	29.8	30.1	26.7	23.2	23	28.5	22.6	17.6	27.4	33.2
III. Fertilizers	4.9	4.5	3.5	3.7	4.6	2.4	2.7	2.3	2.8	1.5
IV. Paper board, manufacture and News print	1	0.8	1	0.9	1.3	1.3	1.2	1.1	0.9	0.9
V. Capital Goods	21.8	20.4	26.7	26.5	23.1	20.1	18.2	16.6	12	11
VI. Others	23.6	24.1	26.8	24	23.5	25.5	32.3	35.9	32.8	29.8
VII. Unclassified	16.6	17	12.9	16.7	20.9	18.5	18.6	20.4	18.3	19.9

Source: Same as table no. 26.2

- **POL:** Petroleum imports continue to be a significant proportion of total imports. With the domestic production levelled an ever increasing demand for fuel, this is somewhat expected.

- **Capital Goods:** The second important item is the capital goods imports. This does not necessarily mean that the domestic capacity to produce our own means of production is limited, but it might make sense to import if significant gains in terms of time and money saved are to be reaped (law of comparative advantage at work!). Economists point out that easy imports of inputs might significantly boost exports. This was markedly true of good export performance from 1985/86 to 1989/90 (Joshi & Little 1994)[1]. The remaining share goes to items grouped under others and unclassified.

- Imports of edible oils (non-POL bulk item) have recorded a significant growth after 1990-91. It increased from Rs. 326 crores in 1990-91 to Rs. 7,589 crores in 1998-99 (included under Food and Allied Products in the following table).

If one looks at the structural changes in imports since independence, they reveal following important points[2].

(1) Rapid growth of industrialisation seems to be necessitating imports of capital goods and raw materials.

(2) Imports of food grains and consumer goods are seen declining due to country becoming self-sufficient in food grains and other consumer goods through agriculture and industrial growth.

(3) Share of non-bulk imports (capital goods and export related items) is seen rising and that of bulk exports (POL and bulk consumption goods) declining over the period 1970-71 to 1998-99. In 70-71 non-bulk imports were 50 per cent of the total imports. On the other hand in 1998-99 it rose to 69 per cent.

---

1. Joshi Vijay & Little I.M.D. (1994), *India: Macroeconomics and Political Economy 1964-1991,* The World Bank, Washington D.C., pp 183-184.

2. Based on Datt Ruddar & Sundaram K.P.M. (2001), *Indian Economy,* S. Chand and Company Ltd. pp. 732-733.

Table no. 26.4
Share and Percentage Change of Major Imports

Commodity Group	(Percentage share)				(Percentage change)'			
	2004-05	2005-06	2005-06 Apr.-Oct.	2006-07 Apr.-Oct.	2004-05	2005-06	2005-06 Apr.-Oct.	2006-07 Apr.-Oct.
1	2	3	4	5	6	7	8	9
I. Food and allied products, of which	**3.5**	**2.5**	**3.0**	**2.3**	**16.7**	**– 4.7**	**11.0**	**– 3.5**
1. Cereals	0.0	0.0	0.0	0.0	371	36.7	13.6	30.5
2. Pulses	0.4	0.4	0.4	0.4	–20.4	41.3	50.9	11.6
3. Cashew Nuts	0.4	0.3	0.4	0.3	34.5	17.5	27.8	–9.8
4. Edible Oils	2.2	1.4	1.7	1.3	–3.0	–17.9	–6.1	–1.1
II. Fuel, of which	**29.6**	**32.1**	**32.2**	**36.2**	**50.3**	**44.8**	**40.5**	**42.2**
5. Coa	I2.9	2.6	2.6	2.4	126.8	21.0	30.6	21.1
6. POL	26.8	29.5	29.6	33.7	45.1	47.3	41.4	44.0
III. Fertilizers	**1.1**	**1.3**	**1.4**	**1.8**	**96.8**	**59.4**	**87.8**	**62.6**
IV. Paper board manufactures & newsprint	**0.7**	**0.6**	**0.7**	**0.7**	**10.6**	**29.8**	**41.1**	**35.2**
V. Capital goods, of which	**13.0**	**15.8**	**10.7**	**12.1**	**39.3**	**62.5**	**53.8**	**43.1**
7. Machinery except elect. & machine tool	6.7	7.4	6.5	7.2	42.9	49.0	54.4	38.8
8. Electrical machinery	11	1.0	1.0	1.1	37.1	25.9	26.7	37.5
9. Transport equipment	3.9	5.9	18	2.1	34.1	104.2	64.9	49.1
10. Project goods	0.5	0.6	0.6	1.0	50.5	48.0	92.3	117.1
VI. Others, of which	**48.3**	**43.7**	**48.2**	**44.4**	**31.0**	**21.1**	**46.5**	**16.6**
11. Chemicals	6.2	5.7	6.1	55	48.6	23.2	422	12.9
12. Pearls, precious, semi precious stones	8.4	6.1	7.5	4.1	32.2	–3.1	36.8	-31.3
13. Iron & steel	2.4	3.1	3.4	3.3	77.2	71.3	114.5	21.0
14. Non-ferrous metals	1.2	12	1.2	1.4	38.1	40.8	49.1	43.9
15. Professional Instruments, optical goods, etc.	1.4	13	1.4	1.3	24.4	28.9	43.8	18.5
16. Gold & Silver	10.0	76	9.0	8.6	62.6	1.5	43.4	20.8
GRAND TOTAL	**100.0**	**100.0**	**100.0**	**100.0**	**42.7**	**33.8**	**44.4**	**26.4**

*In US Dollar terms.
Source: DGCI&S, Kolkata.

26.3 DIRECTION OF INDIA'S TRADE

Table 26.5

Destination of India's Exports

Country/Region	*1991-92*	*1992-93*	*1993-94*	*1994-95*	*1995-96*	*1996-97*	*1997-98*	*1998-99*	*1999-2000*
U.K.	6.6	6.5	6.2	6.4	6.3	6.1	6.2	5.7	5.9
Germany	7.1	7.7	6.9	6.6	6.2	5.8	5.4	5.6	4.8
Other EC/EU	13.1	14	12.9	13.6	13.9	13.2	13.4	14.7	13.8
U.S.A.	17	18.8	18	19.1	17.3	19.8	19.5	21.8	23
Japan	9.8	7.7	7.8	7.7	7	6	5.6	4.9	4.5
USSR	9.1	3.2	2.9	3.1	3.3	2.4	2.6	2.1	2.6
Other East Europe	2	1.1	0.9	0.5	0.6	0.5	0.5	0.6	0.5
OPEC	7.7	9.6	10.7	9.2	9.7	9.7	10.1	10.5	10.1
Other LDCs	20.2	20.3	24.2	29.9	25.7	26.9	28.0	24.6	25.0
Others	5.8	11	9.4	9.8	10	9.8	8.7	9.6	9.8

Source: Economic Survey, various issues.

The above table shows the destination of India's exports over the years. It can be easily noted that U.S.A. has emerged as the major destination for our exports followed by U.K., Germany and Japan. However, as a group the developing countries top the list. USSR as destination seems to be losing out over the years.

Nevertheless, during the financial year 2001-2002, Switzerland has emerged as the fifth largest trading partner (after USA, UK, Belgium and Germany). Notably Indo-China bilateral trade has displayed robust growth expanding by around 26 per cent during 2000-01.

An analysis of the sources of imports (data not reported) reveal a lower share of imports from OECD countries, from 43% in 1999-00 to 39.9 %, as imports from this region declined by 5.6 per cent in 2000-01. However, over the years we have been sourcing our imports significantly from the OECD countries, which happen to be exporters of capital goods. Whereas the share of Eastern Europe has been maintained, shares of imports from OPEC and Developing countries have increased to 5.7 % and 19.1 % respectively, during the year 2000-2001. This is quite expected given the increase in the share of fuel in total imports of late.

Following can be said to be salient features of direction of India's trade:

- New Trade Partners: Before Independence, U.K. was the principal trading partner for India, accounting for 34 per cent of India's exports and imports. In the later period scenario seemed to have changed with other developed countries like Germany and Japan also accounting for some share of India's exports and imports. However, as mentioned above USA has emerged as a major trading partner, especially after 1990s.
- Trade with other OECD countries, namely, Australia, and Switzerland also shows an increase, especially after 1990s.
- OPEC countries continue to be prominent source of imports because of India's dependence on petroleum.

Table 26.6
Direction of Exports : Exports by Regions and Countries

Countries/Regions	2004-2005 (US$ Million)	2004-2005 (Rs. Crores)	2005-2006 (US$ Million)	2005-2006 (Rs. Crores)	Change (4) over(2) (Per cent)	Share (Per cent)	April-Sept. 2005-06 (US$ Million)	April-Sept. 2005-06 (Rs. Crores)	April-Sept. 2006-07 (US$ Million)	April-Sept. 2006-07 (Rs. Crores)	Change (10) over (8) (Per cent)	Share (Per cent)
(1)	(2)	(3)	(4)	(5)	(6)	(7)	(8)	(9)	(10)	(11)	(12)	(13)
I. EUROPE	**19,673.5**	**88,395.8**	**24.716.5**	**109,428.6**	**25.6**	**24.06**	**11,644.07**	**50,824.26**	**13,475.27**	**61,879.26**	**15.73**	**22.00**
(a) EU Countries (25)	**18,118.3**	**81,408.3**	**22,948.4**	**101,600.6**	**26.7**	**22.34**	**10,801.15**	**47,145.07**	**12,608.63**	**57,899.60**	**16.73**	**20.59**
1. UK	3.681.1	16,539.7	5.146.0	22,783.1	39.8	*5.01*	*2,398.02*	*10.466.90*	2,679.93	*12,306.40*	11.76	4.38
2. Germany	2.826.3	12,698.8	*3.517.0*	*15,570.9*	24.4	3.42	1,646.43	7,186.39	1.955.68	*8,980.58*	18.78	3.19
3. Belgium	*2,509.7*	11,276.5	2.853.1	12,631.8	13.7	2.78	*1,350.74*	5.895.72	*1,605.60*	*7,373.01*	18.87	2.62
4. Italy	*2.286.0*	*10,271.3*	*2.490.0*	*11,023.9*	8.9	2.42	*1,160.77*	*5,066.57*	*1.693.70*	7,777.58	45.91	2.77
5. Netherlands	*1,604.9*	*7,210.9*	2.456.1	10,874.0	*53.0*	2.39	*1,106.98*	4,831.75	1,166.07	5.354.66	5.34	*1.90*
6. France	*1,680.9*	7,552.7	*2,047.6*	*9.065.3*	21.8	1.99	*1,057.26*	4,614.77	*1.077.69*	4,948.81	1.93	1.76
7. Spain	1,389.4	6,242.6	1.562.8	6,919.0	12.5	1.52	737.75	*3,220.14*	*880.35*	*4,042.60*	19.33	1.44
8. Greece	*306.3*	1,376.4	559.2	2,475.6	82.5	*0.54*	*219.06*	956.14	*330.86*	1.519.33	*51.04*	*0.54*
9. Denmark	*305.7*	1,373.7	*401.5*	1,777.6	31.3	*0.39*	193.62	845.13	224.69	1,031.78	*16.04*	*0.37*
10. Sweden	241.8	*1,086.4*	*320.3*	1,418.0	32.5	0.31	152.23	664.45	173.06	794.7	13.68	0.28
11. Ireland	*212.0*	952.5	274.8	1.216.8	29.7	*0.27*	112.35	490.38	107.83	495.16	*-4.02*	0.18
12. Portugal	223.2	1,002.7	251.3	1,112.8	12.6	0.24	121.33	529.58	174.05	799.23	43.45	*0.28*
13. Poland	176.3	792.1	*223.0*	987.3	26.5	0.22	97.31	424.73	143.65	659.67	47.63	0.23
14. Finland	143.5	645.0	202.2	895.3	40.9	0.20	103.03	449.69	96.24	441.93	-6.59	0.16
15. Austria	117.2	526.4	130.1	575.9	*11.0*	*0.13*	68.79	300.27	64.54	296.38	-6.18	0.11
16. Malta	31.5	141.5	120.5	533.5	282.6	*0.12*	76.36	333.29	8.23	37.81	-89.22	0.01
17. Czech Republic	*88.0*	395.4	95.4	422.2	8.4	*0.09*	47.28	*206.35*	43.38	199.2	-8.24	0.07
18. Hungary	108.1	485.7	83.6	370.0	-22.7	0.08	46.78	204.17	43.25	198.61	-7.54	0.07
19. Slovenia	63.4	284.7	75.9	335.9	19.7	0.07	*40.94*	178.69	49.74	228.39	21.48	0.08
20. Lithuania	*30.6*	137.5	33.1	146.6	8.2	0.03	15.91	69.43	18.91	86.83	18.88	0.03
21. Cyprus	29.4	132.0	31.8	140.9	8.3	*0.03*	14.58	63.64	16.36	75.1	12.18	0.03
22. Latvia	17.4	78.3	*28.0*	123.9	*60.6*	0.03	*12.09*	52.75	20.43	93.8	*69.03*	*0.03*
23. Slovak Rep.	23.9	107.2	21.1	93.3	-11.6	*0.02*	10.49	45.77	12.15	55.77	15.84	0.02
24. Estonia	*10.2*	46.0	13.7	60.8	34.1	0.01	5.48	23.92	10.14	46.54	84.92	0.02
25. Luxembourg	11.6	52.3	10.5	46.3	-10.2	0.01	5.61	24.47	12.13	55.71	116.35	0.02
(b) Other WE countries, of which	**1,381.8**	**6,208.5**	**1,614.0**	**7,145.5**	**16.8**	**1.57**	**767.93**	**3,351.86**	**755.03**	**3,467.13**	**-1.68**	**1.23**
1. Turkey	723.7	3,251.7	999.9	4,427.0	38.2	*0.97*	*453.30*	1.978.58	*475.03*	2.181.37	4.79	*0.78*
2. Switzerland	540.9	*2,430.3*	474.1	*2,099.2*	-12.3	*0.46*	241.18	*1,052.72*	205.63	944.25	-14.74	0.34
3. Norway	103.8	466.4	126.8	561.5	22.2	*0.12*	66.94	292.17	66.35	*304.67*	-0.88	0.11
(c) East Europe, of which	**173.4**	**779.0**	**154.2**	**682.5**	**-11.1**	**0.15**	**74.99**	**327.34**	**111.61**	**512.54**	**48.83**	**0.18**
1. Romania	*106.0*	476.1	83.4	369.4	-21.3	0.08	43.30	188.98	61.16	*280.87*	41.27	0.10
2. Bulgaria	24.8	111.2	23.4	*103.5*	-5.6	0.02	10.20	44.51	15.23	69.95	49.39	0.02
3. Union of Serbia & Montenegro	9.3	41.6	8.2	36.5	*-11.0*	*0.01*	3.54	15.44	4.31	19.81	21.97	0.01
II. C.I.S. & BALTICS STATES, of which	**1,094.2**	**4,916.5**	**1,237.8**	**5,480.3**	**13.1**	***1.20***	**589.79**	**2,574.34**	**692.69**	**3,180.89**	**17.45**	**1.13**
1. Russia	631.3	2,836.4	729.9	3.231.5	15.6	*0.71*	*350.90*	1,531.63	419.17	1,924.86	19.45	*0.68*
2. Kyrghyzstan	49.6	222.7	27.8	123.0	*-44.0*	0.03	14.53	63.44	22.24	*102.12*	53.02	0.04
3. Ukraine	207.7	933.4	255.6	1.131.6	23.0	0.25	114.21	498.5	131.26	602.77	14.93	0.21
4. Uzbekistan	21.4	95.9	23.8	105.2	11.3	0.02	11.98	52.31	14.51	66.65	21.11	0.02

- Importance of Eastern Europe (USSR) as export destination as well as import source declined phenomenally.
- Developing countries as a source of imports and destination of exports have shown rising importance in the post 1990 period.

26.4 INDIA'S BALANCE OF PAYMENTS

We have already seen the theory and accounting principles underlying the balance of payments. We also had a cursory look at the India's balance of payments. This section expands on the theme further by looking at the changes happening in the balance of payments. We do this in two ways: One look at the historical evolution of our balance of payments by plan periods and secondly analyse the changes happening in the BOP especially after 1990-91. Given a background of BOP crises this becomes really important and relevant.

Table 26.7

India's BOP according to the Plan Periods:

Year	*Trade Deficit*	*Net Invisibles*	*Balance of Payments*	*3 as a % of 2*
1	*2*	*3*	*4*	*5*
First Plan (1951-56)	–542	500	–42	92.2
Second Plan (1956-61)	–2339	614	–1725	26.5
Third Plan (1961-66)	–2382	431	–1951	81.1
Three Annual Plans (1966-67, 67-68, 68-69)		52	–2015	2.5
Fourth Plan (1969-74)	–1564	1664	100	106.4
Fifth Plan (1974-79)	–3179	6221	3052	195.7
1979-80	–3374	3140	–234	93.1
Sixth Plan (1980-85)	–30456	19072	11384	62.6
Seventh Plan (1985-90)	–54204	13157	–41047	24.3
1990-91	–16934	–435	17369	–2.6
1991-92	–64495	4258	–2237	65.6
Eighth Plan (1992-97)	–149004	86090	–62914	57.7

Source: Datt & Sundaram (2001).

Seventh Five Year Plan and Balance of Payments Position

There is no doubt that domestic economy has recorded a remarkable recovery in the year 1988-89 after severe drought of 1987-88; but the strains on India's balance of payments position have not only continued during the period of the Seventh Five Year Plan (1985-90) but have got intensified. The external payments position has continued to remain difficult throughout the period of the Seventh Five Year Plan so far on account of several factors such as deceleration in the rate of growth of domestic crude oil production, intensification of protectionist tendencies in developed countries, the bunching or repayment obligations to the IMF and others and the unfavourable climate for concessional financial assistance from international financial institutions like IDA. The situation got aggravated during 1988-89 because of mounting import bill, reflecting a spillover of essential imports necessitated by the severe drought of the previous two or three years. There was also buoyant import demand associated with a strong economic recovery in 1988-89 and the sharp rise in international prices of metals, chemicals and edible oil in 1988.

The merchandise trade account continues to show a large deficit, with net invisible earnings playing a progressively smaller role in financing the trade deficit. Invisible earnings played an important role in earlier years and they used to offset a substantial part of trade deficit. It might be said that on an average net invisibles neutralised over sixty per cent of trade deficit over the period of the Sixth Five Year Plan (1980-85). This ratio (of invisibles financing India's trade deficit) which was as high as 72 per cent of the trade deficit in 1980-81, came down to 57 per cent of the trade deficit in 1984-85. During 1985-86 and 1986-87, the first two years of the Seventh Five Year Plan (1985-90), the net invisibles could offset only about 38 per cent of India's trade deficits in those years. Net invisible earnings have lost their buoyancy in recent years largely on account of rising interest payments on past foreign debts. Correspondingly, net inflows on capital account of balance of payments have been playing an increasing role in financing trade deficit, leading to substantial build-up foreign debt and also foreign debt servicing charges.

Government of India has accorded a high priority to improving India's balance of payments position by accelerating growth-rate in India's exports, move efficient import-substitution and economic and efficient utilisation of scarce foreign exchange resources. Strong performance in India's exports in 1987, 1988 and the current year reflects the response to earlier policy measures announced by Government of India to promote exports. The trade performance in 1987-88 was satisfactory as in rupee terms India's exports increased by 26.4 per cent in 1987-88 over that in 1986-87. This buoyancy has continued during the first nine months of 1988-89 with the rupee value of India's exports showing an increase of 24.4 per cent over the comparable period of 1987-88.

However, India's imports have grown at a rate of 27.4 per cent in April-December 1988. The main reasons for this sharp increase in India's imports have been higher imports of essential commodities such as foodgrains and edible oils necessitated by previous year's drought, strong recovery of the Indian economy during 1988-89, unusually high prices in international markets for metals and edible oils and exchange rate variations. Thus, the DGCI & S data reveal growth in non-oil imports by 33.4 per cent during the first nine months of 1988-89; and therefore the provisional trade deficit in April-December 1988 at Rs. 6,601 crores was higher by Rs. 1,688 crores over the deficit of Rs. 4,913 crores during the corresponding period of 1987.

First Five Year Plan (1951-56)

During the period of the First Year Plan, India's balance of payments position was much more satisfactory than was anticipated. The Plan had anticipated an annual balance of payments deficit varying from Rs. 180 crores to Rs. 200 crores. In fact, the entire balance of payments deficit for the whole period of First Five Year Plan amounted to only Rs. 42.3 crores.

The reasons for this favourable position in the balance of payments position during the period of the First Five Year Plan were the modest nature of the First Five Year Plan, emphasis on completing the on-going projects rather than undertaking new projects, good monsoon and satisfactory position in agricultural sector which meant that there was no necessity to spend much foreign exchange on import of foodgrains and agricultural raw materials for industrial sector. There was substantial increase in agricultural and also industrial production in the country, thanks to fairly satisfactory monsoon.

Second Five Year Plan (1956-61)

The Second Five Year Plan was more ambitious, the main objective being rapid industrialisation of the country with emphasis on the development of basic and heavy industries like iron and steel, chemicals, fertilisers, transport equipment and heavy machinery. Naturally, such a nature of the Second Five Year Plan necessitated heavy imports of capital equipment and essential industrial raw materials. Also, during the period of the Second Plan, because of the generally unsatisfactory nature of monson, substantial imports of foodgrains and other agricultural raw materials were required to be made. The consequence of all those developments was that there developed foreign exchange crisis due to recurring and substantial trade deficit (of Rs. 2339 crores) with the result that during the period of the Second Plan, balance of payments deficits amounted to a substantial high figure of Rs. 1712.6 crores as compared to only Rs. 42.3 crores during the period of the First Five Year Plan.

Third Five Year Plan (1961-66)

During the period of the Third Five Year Plan India's balance of payments position remained unsatisfactory and fairly tight. The balance of payments deficit during the period of the Third Plan amounted to Rs. 1972.5 crores. The main reasons for this unsatisfactory balance of payments position were increasing import of machinery, of spare parts and such other maintenance imports, of industrial raw materials, etc. There was also heavy import of defence materials and equipment consequent on Chinese aggression in 1962 and Indo-Pakistan conflict in 1965. There was also decline in India's exports of traditional goods like cotton textiles and jute manufactures. In addition to these there was also increasing payments due on account of foreign debt servicing.

Three Annual Plans (1966-67, 1967-68 and 1968-69)

Increasing balance of payments deficits so also increasing foreign debt servicing charges compelled India as a measure to correct deficit in her balance of payments to take the drastic step of devaluation of her rupee in June 1966. But in spite of the devaluation of the Indian rupee (which made Indian goods and services cheaper in foreign markets and foreign goods and services dearer in Indian markets) and in spite of encouragement to exports, India's balance of payments position continued to be serious. This was because of the failure of monsoon for successive years, necessitating large imports of foodgrains during the period of the first two annual plans (namely, 1966-67 and 1967-68), while the usual imports of machinery and maintenance imports continued as before.

During the Third Annual Plan (i.e., in 1968-69) India's exports increased by about 13.5% while her imports declined only marginally. With better foodgrains production and better performance in the export sector, India's overall balance of payments position did not improve as value of her imports rose and of exports declined as a consequence of devaluation of the Indian rupee in 1966. As a result, deficit in India's balance of payments during the period of the Three Annual Plans amounted to Rs. 1982.4 crores.

Fourth Five Year Plan (1968-74)

During the period of the Fourth Five Year Plan, the average annual growth rate of India's exports was fairly high being 12.8%. Despite this substantial growth-rate in India's exports, her balance of payments for the period of the Fourth Plan resulted in deficit of Rs. 2231 crores. This was because a severe and widespread drought in the country forced India to import substantial quantities of foodgrains at relatively high prices. Also, world prices of items like petroleum products, steel, non-ferrous metals, newsprint, etc. rose substantially and to this were added increasing foreign debt-servicing charges. All these factors resulted in balance of payments deficit of Rs. 2231.0 crores during the period of the Fourth Plan.

Fifth Five Year Plan (1974-79)

For the first time since the planning era commenced in India, her overall balance of payments position might be said to have been fairly satisfactory. During the Fifth Five Year Plan period as a whole there was a surplus of Rs. 1404.3 crores in India's balance of payments.

The reasons for this happy position were: Continued rise in India's commodity exports and steep decline in her imports of foodgrains and of fertilisers due to their improved domestic production. For example, in 1976-77 while India's exports went up by 27% over the previous year's, her imports declined by 3.6%. There was also large net increase in value of India's exports of invisibles on current account (i.e., of various services). But in the last year of the Fifth Five Year Plan (i.e., in 1978-79) India's imports went up substantially, whereas her exports slackened a little due to recessionary trends in world markets as also the general protectionist trend in Western countries.

Sixth Five Year Plan (1980-85)

The Sixth Five Year Plan anticipated that balance of payments deficit would be around Rs. 9663 crores during the entire period of the Sixth Plan. But the balance of payments position turned out to be much better than anticipated. During the period of the Sixth Plan, the deficit in balance of payments on current account was only Rs. 6,400 crores.

The relatively less deficit in balance of payments on current account was attributed to (i) considerable saving in the imports of crude oil consequent on its increased domestic production which increased from 11.8 million tonnes in 1979-80 to 29 million tonnes in 1984-85, so that of the total consumption of petroleum in the country, 73% used to be imported in 1980-81, that percentage declined to 31 in 1984-85. The net share of petroleum and petroleum imports in India's total import bill declined from 42% in 1980-81 to 21% in 1984-85. (ii) India could check growth in her imports considerably by making significant improvement in the functioning of her infrastructure facilities by import-substitution in respect of cement, non-ferrous metals and steel and improvement in production of foodgrains in which India became practically self-sufficient, any imports of foodgrains that were made were generally for maintaining buffer-stock at reasonably safe level. (iii) It was noted that net earnings from invisibles increased substantially from the estimated amount of Rs. 8,700 crores to Rs. 14,600 crores during the period of the Sixth Plan. (iv) There were large capital-inflows to the tune of Rs. 11,114 crores from non-resident Indians living abroad consequent on various concessions offered to them for investment of their funds in India.

It was due to the above factors that as compared to the estimated balance of payments on current account during the Sixth Plan period of Rs. 9,063 crores, actual deficit turned out to be Rs. 6,400 crores.

Seventh Five Year Plan and Balance of Payments Position

There is no doubt that domestic economy has recorded a remarkable recovery in the year 1988-89 after severe drought of 1987-88; but the strains on India's balance of payments position have not only continued during the period of the Seventh Five Year Plan (1985-90) but have got intensified. The external payments position has continued to remain difficult throughout the period of the Seventh Five Year Plan so far on account of several factors such as deceleration in the rate of growth of domestic crude oil production, intensification of protectionist tendencies in developed countries, the bunching or repayment obligations to the IMF and others and the unfavourable climate for concessional financial assistance from international financial institutions like the IDA. The situation got aggravated during 1988-89 because of mounting import bill, reflecting a spillover of essential imports necessitated by the severe drought of the previous two or three years. There was also buoyant import demand associated with a strong economic recovery in 1988-89 and the sharp rise in international prices of metals, chemicals and edible oil in 1988.

The merchandise trade account continues to show a large deficit, with net invisible earnings playing a progressively smaller role in financing the trade deficit. Invisible earnings played an important role in earlier years and they used to offset a substantial part of trade deficit. It might be said that on an average net invisibles neutralised over sixty per cent of trade deficit over the period of the Sixth Five Year Plan (1980-85). This ratio (of invisibles financing India's trade deficit) which was as high as 72 per cent of the trade deficit in 1980-81, came down to 57 per cent of the trade deficit in 1984-85. During 1985-86 and 1986-87, the first two years of the Seventh Five Year Plan (1985-90), the net invisibles could offset only about 38 per cent of India's trade deficits in those years. Net invisible earnings have lost their buoyancy in recent years largely on account of rising interest payments on past foreign debts. Correspondingly, net inflows on capital account of balance of payments have been playing an increasing role in financing trade deficit, leading to substantial build-up of foreign debt and also foreign debt servicing charges.

Government of India has accorded a high priority to improving India's balance of payments position by accelerating growth-rate in India's exports, more efficient import-substitution and economic and efficient utilisation of scarce foreign exchange resources. Strong performance in India's exports in 1987, 1988 and 1989 year reflects the response to earlier policy measures announced by Government of India to promote exports. The trade performance in 1987-88 was satisfactory as in rupee terms India's exports increased by 26.4 per cent in 1987-88 over that in 1986-87. This buoyancy has continued during the first nine months of 1988-89 with the rupee value of India's exports showing an increase of 24.4 per cent over the comparable period of 1987-88.

However, India's imports have grown at a rate of 27.4 per cent in April-December 1988. The main reasons for this sharp increase in India's imports have been higher imports of essential commodities such as foodgrains and edible oils necessitated by previous year's drought, strong recovery of the Indian economy during 1988-89, unusually high prices in international markets for metals and edible oils and exchange rate variations. Thus, the DGCI & S data reveal growth in non-oil imports by 33.4 per cent during the first nine months of 1988-89; and therefore the provisional trade deficit in April-December 1988 at Rs. 6,601 crores was higher by Rs. 1,688 crores over the deficit of Rs. 4,913 crores during the corresponding period of 1987.

Eighth Plan Period

For the first time in forty years, net invisibles turned negative to the tune of Rs. 435 crores in the year 1990-91. This removed the cushion available in the earlier periods to neutralise the trade deficit.

During the eighth plan period trade deficit had certainly widened. It reached a record level of Rs. 52,561 crores in 1996-97 showing a threefold increase compared to the 1990-91 level. Invisibles neutralised the trade deficit to the extent of 58 per cent, which was commendable compared to the performance in the seventh plan period and the year 1990-91. The total trade deficit for the eighth plan period was Rs. 1,49,004 crores as compared to the projected Rs. 69,490 crores.

Ninth Plan Period

Ninth plan period is different in one important respect from other plan periods. It entails major trade policy changes. To be precise this change is the removal of quantitative restrictions on imports and movement towards tariff regime instead. This will be a sea change given the much restricted trade policy of the period prior to the 1990s.

Considering the period 1997-98 to 2000-01 (4 years), the trade deficit is to the tune of Rs. 2,56,018 crores neutralized to the extent of 73 per cent by the invisibles, which is certainly not a discouraging scenario. For this period the total BOP deficit on the current account is Rs. 69,434 crores, which is only slightly higher compared to that of the eighth period.

Impact of the Removal of QRs on Imports

Considerable apprehensions from certain corners were voiced over the deleterious effects of removal of QRs on the Indian economy. It was argued that it would lead to immediate surge in imports making the BOP position vulnerable. Secondly it would also affect certain sections of the economy (mainly farmers) adversely. Detailed studies might have to wait as that would require some more time to pass by. But some tinkering with the available data of imports of what are deemed as sensitive items (total 300 items) like milk and milk products, fruits and vegetables, poultry, coffee, spices etc. do not show any phenomenal surge following the removal of QRs. (Economic Survey 2001-02, p. 141). The total imports of these sensitive items (in Dollar terms) during the first nine months of the financial year 2001-02 have increased by only 2.1 per cent, due mainly to higher imports of edible oils, cotton and silk, spices, rubber and marble granite. Import data on the full financial year 2000-01 on 714 items, restrictions on which were removed with effect from 31.3.2000, do not reveal any surge in their imports.

External Debt of India

Debt of a country can be classified into two categories, viz., internal debt commonly known as domestic debt and external debt i.e., debt taken from foreign sources. Monitoring external debt especially became important after the East Asian economic crisis, which among other factors, was primarily precipitated by unsustainable level of external debt.

There was a considerable controversy about the exact magnitude of India's external debt as figures reported by the government differed from those given in World Debt Tables.

This difference in figures was because of the differences in definitions adopted by the respective agencies while compiling the figures. However, since 1992-93 we get data compiled on the scientific methodology of the RBI and hence these discrepancies have vanished.

Salient Features of External Debt

According to the report on external debt prepared by the Ministry of Finance in May 2000, four basic facts emerge from the changing profile of India's external debt.

(1) The level of debt has been relatively stable in the last decades, showing only a modest increase.

(2) The debt portfolio is characterised by high share of concessional and low share of short-term debt.

(3) There has been a sustained improvement in key debt indicators showing considerable investment in external indebtedness position of the country.

(4) When compared to other emerging economies, India's indebtedness position is relatively comfortable and has improved over time.

Stock of External Debt

India's external debt stood at US $ 100.38 billion at the end of September 2001 slightly higher than the March 2001 figure of US $ 99.61 billion. Despite this marginal increase in the stock of the external debt, indebtedness position of the country has shown improvement in the recent years. Thus, the debt-GDP ratio shows a decline from 38.7% in 1992 to just 21% by September 2001. (See the following table).

Table 26.8

India's External Debt Outstanding (US $ billion)

Categories	*End March*							
	1991	*1992*	*1995*	*1998*	*1999*	*2000*	*2001*	*End Sept. 01*
Long-term debt	75.3	78.2	94.7	88.5	92.6	94.4	96.1	97.6
Short-term debt	8.5	7.1	4.3	5	4.3	3.9	3.5	2.8
Total	83.8	85.3	99	93.5	96.9	98.3	99.6	100.4

External Debt-Key Indicators (ratios as per cent)

Total external debt to GDP	28.7	38.7	30.8	24.3	23.6	22.2	22.3	21
Short-term to total debt	10.2	8.3	4.3	5.4	4.4	4.0	3.5	2.8
Short-term debt to foreign currency assets	382.1	125.6	20.5	19.4	14.5	11.2	8.8	6.7

Source: Economic Survey 2001-02.

Following features of India's External debt in the 1990s are revealed by the above table:

- The short-term debt declined from US $ 8.54 billion in end March 1991 to US $ 3.46 billion at end March 2001. This means a decline in share of short-term to total debt from 10.2% to 3.5% during this period. Thus, there is a fall in the absolute value of the short-term debt as well as proportion of total debt over the years. Given the volatility associated with such kind of debt, this is certainly a welcome development.
- Short-term debt, as a proportion of foreign currency assets was a whopping 382.1 %, which certainly implies unsustainability. This position has bettered over the years with the decline in this ratio to 6.7%.
- Total external debt as proportion of GDP, which shows the magnitude of external debt in relation to domestic output, has also declined in the late 1990s (even below the 1991 level) after registering an increase in 1995.

India's External Debt in International perspective

International comparison shows that India's indebtedness position *vis-à-vis* other emerging economies has improved over the years. In 1991, in terms of absolute level of debt, India stood third after Brazil and Mexico. In 1999 this position improved considerably and India stood tenth amongst the top fifteen debtor countries with a 'less' indebtedness classification[3]. In terms of present value (PV) of external debt, India also ranks as the tenth largest debtor country. Moreover, according to World Bank's Global Development Finance 2001, India has the highest share of concessional debt (36 % at end March 2001) among the top 15 debtor countries of the world. This implies significant savings in terms of debt servicing over the years.

Creditor Classification

At the end of December 1999, the total multilateral (excluding IMF) debt at US $ 31.1 billion accounted for 31.4 per cent of the total external debt. This share has remained steady at around that level since end-March 1996. The share of bilateral debt (excluding Rupee debt) in total external debt, declined from 20.5 per cent at end-March 1996 to 17.9 per cent at end-March 1999. The share of total debt from official sources, which includes multilateral, bilateral, IMF and Rupee debt has been gradually declining in recent years and stood at 54.3 per cent of the total debt at end-March 1999 before increasing to 54.8 per cent at end-December 1999. This shows that the share of private creditors in the total debt has been gradually rising in recent years.

3. Countries are classified as having 'less', 'moderate', or 'severe' level of indebtedness. In 1991 India's indebtedness was classified as 'severe.'

Table 26.9
India's External Debt Outstanding

(Rs. crore)

	As at End-March										End-June		End Sept.
	1991	1997	1998	1999	2000	2001	2002	2003	2004	2005	2006R	2006R	**2006-QE**
I. MULTILATERAL	40,386	105,066	116,904	129,682	137,132	145,105	155,633	142,683	131,105	138,915	145,503	153,678	**165,212**
A. Government Borrowing	38,429	94,824	104,218	114,531	120,321	127,886	138,023	129.727	120,073	127,782	133,800	141,701	**142,237**
(i) Concessional	25,849	63,418	70,560	78,979	84,051	89,008	96,177	102,559	101.490	105,114	105,853	111,859	**111,627**
a) IDA	25,221	62,343	69,392	77,725	82,721	87,753	94,848	101,122	100,065	103,671	104,457	110,392	**110,160**
b) Others	628	1,075	1.168	1,254	1,330	1,255	1,329	1,437	1.425	1.443	1,396	1,467	**1,467**
(ii) Non-concessional	12,580	31.406	33,658	35,552	36,270	38,878	41,846	27,168	18,583	22,668	27,947	29,842	**30,610**
a) IBRD	12,161	24,354	25,438	25,747	25,343	26,376	28,012	19,069	14,074	16,500	19,625	20,848	**21,149**
b) Others	419	7,052	8,220	9,805	10,927	12,502	13,834	8,099	4,509	6,168	8,322	8,994	**9,461**
B. Non-Government Borrowing	1,957	10,242	12,686	15,151	16,811	17,219	17,610	12,956	11,032	11,133	11,703	11,977	**22,975**
(i) Concessional	0	0	0	0	0	0	0	0	0	0	0	0	**0**
(ii) Non-concessional	1,957	10,242	12,686	15,151	16,811	17,219	17,610	12,956	11,032	11,133	11,703	11,977	**22,975**
a) Public Sector	303	4,738	8,765	10,716	12,183	12,386	12,729	9,255	7,916	8,000	8,509	8,742	**10,780**
(i) IBRD	303	3,341	5,217	6,349	6,931	7,114	7,298	4,378	4,402	4,462	4,594	4,726	**4,777**
(ii)Others	0	1,397	3,548	4,367	5,252	5,272	5,431	4,877	3,514	3,538	3,915	4,016	**6,003**
b) Financial Institutions	1,270	2,391	2,171	2,723	3,099	3,368	3,736	3,177	2,902	2,789	2,629	2,689	**6,523**
(i)IBRD	872	1,618	1,011	1,057	999	1,017	1,049	525	381	252	630	649	**639**
(ii)Others	398	773	1,160	1,666	2,100	2,351	2,687	2,652	2,521	2,537	1,999	2,040	**5,884**
c) Private Sector	384	3,113	1,750	1,712	1,529	1,465	1,145	524	214	344	565	546	**5,672**
(i)IBRD	330	1,639	1,321	1,312	1,173	1,148	929	298	0	0	0	0	**0**
(ii)Others	54	1,474	429	400	356	317	216	226	214	344	565	546	**5,672**
II.BILATERAL	27,378	62,891	67,104	74,304	79,278	74,519	74,762	79,921	77,084	74,174	70,272	73,463	**72,297**
A. Government borrowing	23,065	49,092	51,420	57,106	60,920	56,802	56,302	60,243	58,121	57,458	54,593	57,004	**56,053**
(i) Concessional	23,065	48,165	50,583	56,425	59.380	55,504	55,418	59,688	57,742	57,207	54,468	57,004	**56,053**
(ii) Non-concessional	0	927	837	681	1.540	1,298	884	555	379	251	125	0	**0**
B. Non-Government borrowing	4,313	13,799	15,684	17,198	18,358	17.717	18,460	19.678	18,963	16,716	15,679	16.459	**16,244**
(i) Concessional	514	3.409	1.770	2.738	4,022	5.579	6.885	8,013	8.876	7,472	6,949	7,292	**7,153**
(a) Public Sector	0	1,054	192	526	1,488	2,962	4,278	5,152	5,759	5,653	5,285	5.527	**5,442**
(b) Financial Institutions	514	2,355	1,578	2.212	2,534	2,617	2.607	2,861	3,117	1,819	1,664	1.165	**1,711**
(c) Private Sector	0	C	0	0	0	0	0	0	0	0	0	0	**0**
(ii) Non-concessional	3,799	10,390	13,914	14,460	14,336	12,138	11,575	11,665	10,087	9,244	8,730	9,167	**9,091**
(a) Public Sector	2,957	5,216	5,360	5,197	4,752	3,715	4,822	5,116	4,851	4,354	3,628	3,892	**3,703**
(b) Financial Institutions	527	2,436	4,216	4,363	4,151	3,568	3,708	3,571	3,119	2,844	2,386	2,499	**2,393**
(c) Private Sector	315	2,738	4.338	4,900	5,433	4,855	3,045	2,978	2,117	2,046	2,716	2,776	**2,995**
III. IMF	5,132	4,714	2,622	1,218	113	0	0	0	0	0	0	0	**0**
IV. EXPORT CREDIT	8,374	21,044	25,783	28,812	29,564	27,625	26,110	23,750	20.553	21,798	24,075	25.375	**26,024**
(a) Buyers' credit	2,230	11,184	15,433	18,097	18,734	17,336	16,147	13,421	11.061	12.900	16.011	17,030	**17,849**
(b) Suppliers' credit	933	4,791	5,453	5,532	5,582	5,401	5,144	5,139	4,471	3,923	3,328	3,388	**3,301**
(c) Export credit component of bilateral credit	1,390	4,189	4,399	4,905	5,165	4,828	4.819	5,190	5,021	4,975	4,736	4,957	**4,874**
(d) Export credit for defence purchases	3,821	880	498	278	83	60	0	0	0	0	0	0	**0**
V. COMMERCIAL BORROWINGS	19,727	51.454	67,086	89,019	86,963	113,839	113,908	106,843	95,611	118,243	119,763	143,322	**149,180**
(a) Commercial bank loans #	13,200	29,968	39,419	43,892	44,015	46,169	48,683	46,929	50,346	60,448	73,111	83,875	**87,725**
(b) Securitized borrowings ##	5,840	17,320	23,786	41,464	39,564	64,769	62,714	57,495	41,567	54,152	43,299	55,399	**57,439**
(c) Loans/securitized borrowing etc., with multilateral/ bilateral guarantee + IFC (W)	687	3,521	3,451	3,430	3,271	2,901	2,511	2,419	3,698	3,643	3,353	4,048	**4,016**
(d) Self-Liquidating Loans	0	645	430	233	113	0	0	0	0	0	0	0	**0**

Table 26.9
India's External Debt Outstanding

(Rs. crore)

	As at End-March										End-June		End Sept.
	1991	1997	1998	1999	2000	2001	2002	2003	2004	2005	2006R	2006R	**2006-QE**
VI. NRI & FE (B&O) DEPOSITS@ (Above one year maturity)	20,030	39,527	47,050	50.048	59,120	77,273	83,712	110,022	135,618	143,267	156,715	164,298	**168,025**
(a) NRI deposits	19,843	39,527	47,050	50.048	59,120	77,273	83,712	110,022	135,618	143,267	156,715	164,298	**168,025**
(b) FC (B&O) Deposits@@	187	0	0	0	0	0	0	0	a	0	a	a	**0**
VII. RUPEE DEBT*	25,199	26,978	23,204	20,077	19,218	17,345	14,807	13,405	11,856	10,070	9,064	8,833	**8,827**
(a) Defence	22,875	24,590	20,976	18,004	17,290	15,573	13,198	11,946	10,539	8,887	7,992	7,789	**7,783**
(b) Civilian	2,324	2.388	2,228	2,073	1,928	1,772	1,609	1,459	1,317	1,183	1,072	1,044	**1,044**
VIII. TOTAL LONG-TERM DEBT (I TO VII)	146,226	311,674	349,753	393,160	411,388	455,706	468,932	476,624	471,827	506,467	525,392	568,969	**589,565**
IX. SHORT-TERM DEBT	16,775	24,153	19,929	18.137	17,162	16,919	13.396	22,180	19,251	32,922	39,199	41,960	**48,616**
(a) NRI deposits (up to one year maturity)@	7,018	13,547	8,657	8,852	5,983	4,463	4,724	9,320	1,321	0	0	0	**0**
(b) FC (B&O) Deposits (up to one-year maturity)@@	328	0	0	0	0	0	0	a	0	0	0	0	**0**
(c) Others (trade-related)**	9,429	10,606	11,272	9,285	11,179	12,456	8,672	12,860	17,930	32,922	39,199	41,960	**48,616**
of which, short-term debt over 6 months	4,976	10,606	11,272	9,285	11,179	12,456	8,672	12,860	17,930	32,922	39,199	41,960	**48,616**
X. GRAND TOTAL (VIII+IX)	163,001	335,827	369,682	411,297	428,550	472,625	482,328	498,804	491,078	539,389	564,591	610,929	**638,181**

QE: Quick Estimates.
R: Revised
IFC (W): International Finance Corporation (Washington D.C.).
FC (B&O) Deposits Foreign Currency (Banks & Others) Deposits

#. includes Financial Lease since 1996.

##: includes India Development Bonds (IDBs), Resurgent India Bonds (RIBs). India Milleniurn Deposits (IMDs), also includes Foreign Currency Convertible Bonds (FCCBs) and net investment by 100% FII debt funds FCCB debt has been adjusted since End-March. 1998 after netting out conversion onto equity and redemptions.

@ Figures include accrued interest.

@:@ The Scheme was discontinued in July, 1993.

*: Rupee denominated debt owed to Russia and payable through exports.

**: Does not include Suppliers' credits of up to 180 days.

Source: Ministry of Finance (Department of Economic Affairs), Ministry of Defence, Reserve Bank of India, Securities & Exchange Board of India.

Measures to Improve India's Balance of Payments Position

Introduction: Since the foreign exchange crisis during the second half of 1950s, Government of India has been taking measures to reduce, and if possible, eliminate deficits in India's balance of payments (on current account). Broadly, these measures have concentrated on three fronts: (1) measures to promote exports; (2) measures to promote import-substitution (i.e., measures to reduce imports); and (3) measures to increase flow of external assistance (i.e., funds especially from non-resident Indians living abroad).

(1) Measures to Promote Exports: An important step to reduce deficit in India's balance of payments is to promote India's exports to the maximum possible extent. Even otherwise, India needs to maximise export earnings as stimulus to economic development.

With a view to promote exports, Government of India, has been taking the following steps: (i) Introduction of intensive schemes for import of capital goods, maintenance spares, etc. at concessional rate of import duty or even duty free in the case of export units of various industries; (ii) adoption of fiscal measures such as concession in direct taxes in the case of export units, drawback and duty exemption in the case of export units, cash compensatory support scheme; (iii) duty-free import of capital goods, plants and equipment, raw materials etc. meant for 100% export-oriented industries, units in India; exemption from excise and other duties in the case of indigenously available capital goods and raw materials, etc. meant for 100% export-oriented industries; (iv) special rail and shipping facilities for export of goods; (v) introduction of scheme of liberalisation for India's export by abolishing or reducing export duties on commodities to be exported; (vi) measures to grant liberal credit facilities for Indian exports (through, for example, the Import-Export Bank of India); (vii) establishment of a number of organisations dealing with specific commodities for promoting their exports.[4]

There is no doubt that since independence India's exports are getting diversified over the years. Though export promotion measures are being taken for quite some time, it is observed that in the case of some commodities like jute and tobacco, there are some demand constraints which are making substantial and sustained increase in their export difficult. These commodities are confronted by protectionist policies of developed countries and jute manufactures by substitutes like plastic bags and metallic containers, etc. for storing grains and such other commodities. In the case of India, there are a number of items which are facing supply constraints which are due to high cost of production, competitive prices of foreign goods and generally low quality. Commodities which are generally facing supply constraints are iron ore, engineering goods, chemicals, sugar, light electrical goods, iron ore, marine products, plastics, coffee, cashewnuts, agricultural products, etc.

There are some products which so far as their exports are concerned are confronted by both demand constraints and also supply constraints. Goods belonging to this category are: leather and leather goods, ready-made garments, handicrafts, textiles, carpets, etc.

---

4. For example, Government has built elaborate organisational structure for promoting exports. The organisational structure is composed of the following organisations: (a) Export Promotion Councils (for most of the export products) to conduct market surveys, arrange exhibitions and trade fairs; (b) Commodity Boards which are responsible for production, development and export of certain specific commodities; (c) Export Houses which are specialising in export trade; (d) Central Advisory Council of Trade to advise government relating to export and import policy and programmes, operation of import and export controls, organisation and development of commercial services, and organisation and expansion of export production, the Federation of Indian Export Organisation, the Trade Development Authority entrusted with the task of inducing and organising entrepreneurs mainly in the small-scale and medium-scale sector to develop their individual export capabilities: (e) The Indian Institute of Packaging; (f) The Indian Institute of Foreign Trade; (g) The Export Credit and Guarantee Corporation of India; (h) The Export Inspection Council; (i) Trade Fair Authority of India; and (j) The State Trading Corporation (STC).

In the case of Indian goods facing demand constraints in foreign markets, steps that need to be taken to further increase their exports are: Enlarging their scale of production to enjoy economies of scale enabling reduction in their prices to make them competitive in foreign markets, improving their quality, introducing attractive packaging and adopting aggressive marketing strategy.

In the case of Indian goods where supply constraints are hampering further increase in their exports, major constraints are small-scale of their production, inadequate supply of goods, raw materials, inadequate supply of energy and transport facilities, etc. All these constraints must be removed if their exports are to increase further. 'Export-Marketing' is a weak aspect of India's export sector. Indian exporters often do not take advantage of exhibitions held in foreign countries, they often lack knowledge of policy-changes that have taken place in foreign countries with which they are trading because of late receipt of relevant information. There is thus urgent need to establish an organisation to provide comprehensive and up-to-date export market intelligence to Indian exporters. The performance of Indian trade missions in this regard is generally disappointing.

Establishing Free Trade Zones is an important export-promotion measure. There are in India at present six Free Trade (Zones) at Kandla, Santa Cruz, Madras, Noida (in U.P.), Falta (in West Bengal), and Cochin. The main advantages of free trade zone are freedom of import of capital goods under Open General Licence (OGL) and duty free blanket permission of business visits abroad, grant of approval for establishing industrial units, etc. at a single point and tax-holiday for a period of five years for newly established industrial units.

Another export strategy is 'Counter Trade.' Under this scheme, payments for import of capital goods and essential raw materials are made through equivalent export of domestically manufactured goods to the participating country.

There is at present in India a plethora of organisations and schemes meant to promote Indian exports with very little coordination among them. What is needed is a compact organisational structure with adequate authority to promote Indian exports and a dynamic export strategy which should cover an appropriate marketing strategy of proper pricing, competitive production, distribution set-up abroad and overseas promotion.

It needs to be noted that India's export sector should not be viewed in isolation. There should be an integrated development plan for exports which should be a part and parcel of overall general development plan for the country. In India export sector is for too long being viewed in isolation with slender or no proper coordination with the production sector of Indian economy.

In addition, special attention needs to be paid to India's export sector by taking steps such as removing disabilities from which Indian exporters suffer because of undue restrictions on import of essential goods, removing obstacles in the expansion of capacity for exports, streamlining existing cash compensation and other tax-concession schemes and procedures with a view to remove disabilities from which Indian exporters have been suffering for long, removing some of the physical and fiscal controls at present restraining promotion of exports, adoption of government policies to make exports at least marginally more profitable to exporters than selling the same goods in domestic markets, steps to capture new foreign markets and expand them, and above all maintaining adequate links with technological developments which are taking place to increase export capability which is being obstructed to a great extent because of the continued use of obsolete technology (for example as compared to developments in this regard in South Korea).

The Seventh Five Year Plan (1985-90) has been trying to implement some of the above proposals and measures vigorously. The Seventh Plan has placed greater emphasis on import of high technology in the export sector to improve productivity. At the same time, with a view to see that import of high technology is not very costly, steps are to be taken to develop progressively local technological capabilities.

The Government has also been taking steps to highlight the importance of the export potentialities of service sector, particularly tourism for which there is vast potential in India. Public and private sectors are taking coordinated measures to provide increasing facilities for foreign tourists.

Import Policy : Import-Substitution

Import-substitution is another important measure to reduce deficits in India's balance of payments. India has been following the policy of import-substitution in the form of domestic production of consumer goods of all types as also capital goods (instead of importing them as before). There is increasing emphasis on Research and Development to help promotion of import-substitution. Though India has been producing and is almost self-sufficient in consumer goods, there is still a large number of goods like petroleum and petroleum products, non-ferrous metals, edible oil, etc. which India has been importing and which cost a great deal in foreign exchange. For example, edible oil bill is annually around Rs. 800 crores. This can be and must be reduced; the same is the case in respect of fertilisers in which India should try to be self-sufficient.

The import-substitution policy of the Government has resulted in the development of a number of industries in the country. Thus, around 300 commodities which used to be imported before 1950 are being completely substituted by domestically produced goods. Some of the import-substitution industries developed in India are: cement-manufacturing machinery, sugar mill machinery, printing machinery, paper-manufacturing machinery, railway wagons, railway engines, commercial vehicles, bulbs and tubes, cars and jeeps, two-wheelers (like motorcycles and mopeds), sewing machines, bicycles, electric fans, refrigerators, tyres and tubes, different types of chemical fertilisers, T.V. sets and transistors and various types of electronic goods like calculators and computers. India has not only been producing these goods which used to be mostly imported before 1950, but she has become practically self-sufficient in most of them and in fact has been exporting some of these goods not only to developing countries but even to developed countries.

Till the middle of 1970s, India used to import substantial quantities of foodgrains. But as a result of the Green Revolution, production of foodgrains has gone up from around 50 million tonnes in 1950 to around 150 million tonnes and is expected to be around 170 million tonnes in 1989-90. India has practically become self-sufficient in foodgrains and if some small quantities are being imported now and then, this is mainly to maintain buffer-stock of foodgrains at a safe level.

But a note of warning needs to be sounded in regard to the policy of import-substitution and development of import-substitution industries. Care should be taken to see that import-substitution does not lead to development of industries producing high-cost, low-quality goods under excessive protection. In some fields of import-substitution, such a development appears to have taken place. This should be corrected as early as possible.

Concluding Remarks

By way of conclusion it may be said that there appears to have emerged a fairly comprehensive and co-ordinated policy for the promotion of India's export, reduction of her imports and thus bring about reduction and if possible elimination of deficits in her balance of payments on current account and succeed in establishing equilibrium in the sphere of international trade. What is needed is effective implementation of the policy and various measures formulated in this sphere.

India's balance of payments position has for long remained rather critical. Some relief was provided by relieving pressure on India's balance of payments because of capital inflows, both repatriable and especially non-repatriable (i.e., to be paid in Indian currency after maturity) from non-resident Indians (NRIs) into India from 1982-83 onwards. As figures in Table 26.6 would show, the repatriable and non-repatriable capital inflows from NRIs went on rising from Rs. 60 crores and Rs. 3 crores, respectively, in 1982-83 to Rs. 423 crores and Rs. 58 crores, respectively, in 1986-87.

But because of decline in crude oil prices from 1985 onwards, demand for Indian labour, technicians and projects in OPEC, capital inflows into India from NRIs have started declining in recent years creating additional pressure on India's balance of payments.

ANNEXURES

Table 1

Principal Exports

Quantity : Thousand tonne
Value: Rs. crore & US $ Million

		1998-99			1999-2000			2000-2001		
		Qty.	Rs. or	$ million	Qty.	Rs.cr.	$ million	Qty.	Rs. or	$ million
1	2	21	22	23	24	25	26	27	28	29
I.	**Agricultural and allied products: of which**	—	26104	6205	—	25016	5773	—	28535	8246
I. 1	Coffee	193.6	1728	411	190.1	1435	331	184.9	1185	259
I. 2	Tea and mate	210.4	2265	538	179.3	1785	412	202.3	1978	433
I. 3	Oil cakes	3487.8	1942	462	2594.2	1638	378	2417.2	2045	448
I. 4	Tobacco	88.9	762	181	131.5	1009	233	108.4	871	191
I. 5	Cashew Kernels	77.3	1627	387	94.1	2461	568	83.8	1883	412
I. 6	Spices	209.8	1633	388	234.9	1767	408	244.9	1619	354
I. 7	Sugar and molasses	22.6	24	6	143.7	40	9	769.1	511	112
I. 8	Raw cotton	41.9	207	49	15.9	78	18	30.2	224	49
I. 9	Rice	4963.6	6281	1493	1896	3126	721	1534.4	2943	644
I. 10	Fish and fish preparations	311.2	4369	1038	390.7	5125	1183	502.6	6367	1394
I. 11	Meat and meat preparations	—	788	187	—	819	189	—	1470	322
I. 12	Fruits, vegetables and pulses (excl. Cashew Kernels, processed fruits & Juices)	—	931	221	—	1247	288	—	1608	352
I. 13	Miscellaneous processed foods (incl. processed fruits and juices)	—	546	130	—	668	154	—	1094	240
II.	**Ores and minerals (excl. Coal) of which**	—	2827	672	—	3005	693	—	4139	908
II.1	Mica	49.6	43	10	46	42	10	63.2	64	14
II.2	Iron ore (million tonne)	22.2	1615	384	15.7	1175	271	20.2	1634	358

III.	**Manufactured goods of which**	—	109787	26096	—	127532	29431	—	160771	35192
III.1	Textile fabrics & manufactures (excl. Carpets hand-made) of which	—	35581	8457	—	40178	9272	—	49831	10908
III.1.1	Cotton yarn, fabrics, made-ups etc.	—	11661	2772	—	13388	3090	—	16030	3509
III.1.2	Ready-made garmenets of all textile materials	—	18364	4365	—	20649	4765	—	25478	5577
III.2	Coir yarn and manufactures	—	317	75	—	200	46	—	221	48
III.3	Jute manufacture incl. twist & yarn	141.4	582	138	—	544	126	—	933	204
III.4	Leather & leather manufactures Incl. leather footwear, leather travel Goods & leather garments	—	6847	1580	—	6890	1590	—	8914	1951
III.5	Handicrafts (incl. carpets hand-made) of which	—	4950	1177	—	5058	1167	—	5097	1116
III.5.1	Game and Jewllery	—	24945	5929	—	32716	7550	—	33734	7384
III.6	Chemicals and allied products @	—	14211	3378	—	17389	4013	—	22850	5002
III.7	Machinery, transport & metal Manufactures including iron and steel*	—	18479	4393	—	22251	5135	—	31870	6976
IV.	**Mineral fuels and lubricants (incl. coal)#**	—	594	141	—	3399	784	—	8821	1931
V.	**Others**	—	441	105	—	609	141	—	1305	286
VI.	**Total**	—	**139752**	**33218**	—	**159561**	**36822**	—	**203571**	**44560**

@ Chemicals and allied products figures relate to "Basic Chemicals" and "Plastic Linoleum Products."

* Also includes electronic goods and computer software.

During 1990-91, 1995-96, 1997-98, 1998-99, 1999-2000 and 2000-01, Crude oil exports amount to Rs. Nil.

Source: DGCI&S.

Table 2
Principal Imports

Quality : Thousand tonne
Value: Rs. crore & US $ Million

		1998-99			1999-2000			2000-2001		
		Qty.	Rs. cr.	$ million	Qty.	Rs. cr	$ million	Qty.	Rs. cr	$ million
1	2	21	22	23	24	25	26	27	28	29
I.	**Food and five animals chiefly for food (excl. Cashew raw) of which:**	NA	NA	NA	NA	NA	NA	NA	NA	NA
I.1.	Cereals and cereal preparations	1850.8	1210	228	1620.3	961	222	69.9	90	20
II.	**Raw materials and intermediate Manufactures**	NA	NA	NA	NA	NA	NA	NA	NA	NA
II.1	Cashewnuts (unprocessed)	243.3	969	230	256	1198	276	249.7	962	211
II.2	Crude rubber (including Synthetic and reclaimed)	131.7	612	146	128.1	621	143	119.1	695	152
II.3	Fibres of which :	NA	NA	NA	NA	NA	NA	NA	NA	NA
II.3.1	Synthetic and regenerated Fibres (man-made fibres)	56.0	291	69	33.5	184	42	42.6	275	60
II.3.2	Raw wool	55.0	490	116	61.4	492	114	53.7	458	100
II.3.3	Raw cotton	57.4	381	91	237.4	1254	289	212.3	1185	259
II.3.4.	Raw Jute	99.5	86	20	137.4	139	32	67.3	84	18
II. 4	Petroleum, oil and lubricants	—	26919	6398	—	54649	12611	—	71497	15650
II. 5	Animal and vegetable oils and fat of which:	NA	NA	NA	NA	NA	NA	NA	NA	NA
II.5.1	Edible oils	2621.9	7589	1804	4196	8046	1857	4267.9	6093	1334
II.6	Fertilizers and chemical products of which:	NA	NA	NA	NA	NA	NA	NA	NA	NA
II.6.1	Fertilizers and fertilizer Mfg.	8081.1	4248	1010	9921.2	5560	1283	7423.4	3034	664
II.6.2	Chemical elements and compounds	—	1640	390	—	1563	361	—	1542	338

Table 2 (contd.)

1	2	21	22	23	24	25	26	27	28	29
II.6.3	Dyeing, training and Colouring material	—	780	185	—	841	194	—	874	191
II.6.4.	Medicinal and pharmaceutical Products	—	1615	384	—	1616	373	—	1723	377
II.6.5	Plastic material, regenerated Cellulose and artificial resins	2843	676	—	3118	720	—	—	2551	558
II.7	Pulp and Waste paper	1063.8	991	236	1204.1	1106	255	1050.9	1290	282
II.8	Paper, paper board and Manufctures thereof	603.2	1957	465	641.8	1938	447	585.6	2005	439
II.9	Non-metallic, mineral manufactures of which	NA	NA	NA	—	710	164	—	797	174
II. 9.1	Pearls, precious and semi-precious stones, unworked or worked	—	15820	3760	—	23556	5436	—	22101	4838
II.10	Iron and steel	204.1	4474	1064	1910.2	3832	884	1613.6	3569	781
II.11	Non-ferrous metals	—	2513	597	—	2370	547	—	2462	539
III.	**Capital goods***	—	32304	7678	—	25878	5972	—	25281	5534
III.1.	Manufactures of metals	—	1599	380	—	1755	405	—	1786	391
III.2	Non-electrical machinery** Apparatus and appliances including Machine tools	—	14267	3391	—	17301	3993	—	16915	3703
III.3	Electrical machinery, Apparatus and appliances**	—	1771	421	—	1897	438	—	2227	487
III.4	Transport equipment	—	3358	798	—	4925	1137	—	4353	953
IV.	**Others (unclassified)**	NA	NA	NA	NA	NA	NA	NA	NA	NA
V.	**Total**	—	**178332**	**42389**	—	**215236**	**49671**	—	**230873**	**50536**

NA Not available.

* From the year 1987-88 onwards, Capital goods Include Project Goods.

** From the year 1991-92 onwards, Items III.2 & III.3 exclude electronic goods.

Source: DGCI & S.

Table 3

India's External Debt (as at the end of March)

Items	*Rupees Crore*						*US & Million*					
	2000	*1999*	*1998*	*1997*	*1996*	*1995*	*2000*	*1999*	*1998*	*1997*	*1996*	*1995*
I. Multilateral	136585	129673	116904	105066	98173	89819	31317	30534	29553	29218	28616	28542
A. Government Borrowings	119722	114531	104218	94824	89428	82223	27447	26967	26344	26369	26059	26127
(i) Concessional	82864	78979	70560	63418	60425	55963	18997	18596	17836	17636	17576	17777
(a) IDA	81590	77725	69392	62343	59349	54897	18705	18301	17541	17337	17263	17438
(b) Others	1274	1254	1168	1075	1076	1066	292	295	299	299	313	339
(ii) Non-concessional	36858	35552	33658	31406	29003	26260	8450	8371	8508	8733	8483	8350
(a) IBRD	25924	25747	25438	24354	23721	22442	5943	6062	6430	6772	6938	7136
(b) Others	10934	9805	8220	7052	5282	3818	2507	2309	2078	1961	1545	1214
B. Non-Government Borrowings	16863	15142	12686	10242	8745	7596	3870	3567	3209	2849	2557	2415
(i) Concessional	0	0	0	0	0	0	0	0	0	0	0	0
(ii) Non-concessional	16863	15142	12686	10242	8745	7596	3870	3567	3209	2849	2557	2415
(a) Public Sector	12184	10711	8765	4738	4628	3248	2797	2523	2216	1318	1353	1033
IBRD	6933	6349	5217	3341	2942	2013	1592	1495	1319	929	860	640
Others	5251	4362	3548	1397	1686	1235	1205	1028	897	389	493	393
(b) Financial Institutions	3101	2720	2171	2391	2464	2559	711	641	550	665	721	813
IBRD	999	1057	1011	1618	1643	1605	229	249	256	450	481	510
Others	2102	1663	1160	773	821	954	482	392	294	215	240	303
(c) Private Sector	1578	1711	1750	3113	1653	1789	362	403	443	866	483	569
IBRD	1172	1312	1321	1639	1244	1610	269	309	334	456	364	512
Others	406	399	429	1474	409	179	93	94	109	410	119	57
II. Bilateral	78748	74297	67104	62891	65740	63761	18056	17498	16969	17494	19213	20270
A. Government Borrowings	60819	57106	51420	49092	53119	52965	13943	13447	12998	13652	155535	16841
(i) Concessional	59280	56425	50583	48165	52078	52965	13590	13286	12786	13394	15232	16841
(ii) Non-concessional	1539	681	837	927	1041	0	353	161	212	258	303	0
B. Non-Government Borrowings	17929	17191	15684	13799	12621	10796	4113	4051	3971	3842	3678	3429
(i) Concesisonal	4025	2738	1770	3409	3088	1896	924	645	448	948	903	603
(a) Public Sector	1489	526	192	1054	376	654	342	124	49	293	110	208
(b) Financial institutions	2536	2212	1578	2355	2712	1242	582	521	399	655	793	395
(c) Private Sector	0	0	0	0	0	0	0	0	0	0	0	0

Table 3 (contd.)

tems	Rupees Crore						US & Million					
	2000	1999	1998	1997	1996	1995	2000	1999	1998	1997	1996	1995
(ii) Non-concessional	13904	14453	13914	10390	9533	8900	3189	3406	3523	2894	2775	2826
(b) Public Sector	4590	5190	5360	5216	5602	6120	1053	1223	1358	1453	1631	1943
(b) Financial Institutions	4108	4362	4216	2436	2197	1883	942	1028	1067	678	639	598
(c) Private Sector	5206	4901	4338	2738	1734	897	1194	1155	1098	763	505	285
III. International Monetary Fund	113	1218	2622	4714	8152	13545	26	287	664	1313	2374	4300
IV. Trade Credit	29006	28810	25783	21044	18432	20876	6652	6789	6526	5861	5376	6629
(a) Buyer's Credit	18188	18099	15433	11184	7216	6227	4171	4265	3908	3116	2101	1977
(b) Supplier's Credit	5581	5534	5453	4791	5382	6432	1280	1304	1380	1335	1567	2042
(c) Export credit component of bilateral credit	5154	4901	4399	4189	4529	4604	1182	1155	1112	1165	1325	1464
(d) Export credit for defense purposes	83	276	498	880	1305	3613	19	65	126	245	383	1146
V. Commercial Borrowings	84475	89521	67086	51454	47642	40915	19373	21096	16986	14335	13873	12991
(a) Commercial bank loans	43391	43891	39419	29968	23120	18384	9951	10343	9981	8349	6731	5837
(b) Securitised borrowings (incl. /IDBs and FCCBs)$	37736	41964	23786	17320	19790	16935	8654	9889	6022	4825	5751	5377
(c) Loans/securitised borrowings, etc., with multilateral/bilateral guarantee and IFC (W)	3235	3433	3451	3521	3050	2998	742	809	874	981	888	952
(d) Self liquidating loans	113	233	430	645	1682	2598	26	55	109	180	503	825
VI. NRI and FC (B&O) Deposits (above one year maturity)	63585	52382	47050	39527	37802	39006	14582	12344	11913	11012	11011	12383
VII. Rupee Debt*	19128	20078	23204	26978	28150	30315	4386	4731	5874	7511	8233	9624
(a) Defence	17211	18005	20976	24590	25602	27603	3947	4243	5311	6847	7488	8763
(b) Civilian*	1917	2073	2228	2388	2548	2712	439	488	563	664	745	861
VIII. Total Long-term Debt (I to VII)	411640	395979	349753	311674	304091	298237	94392	93279	83485	86744	88696	94739
IX Short-term Debt	17629	18616	19929	24153	16637	13448	4043	4387	5046	6726	5034	4269
(a) NRI Deposits (upto 1-year maturity)	6449	9331	8657	13547	9896	7176	1479	2199	2192	3773	2883	2278
(b) Others (trade related)**	11180	9285	11272	10606	6741	6272	2564	2188	2854	2953	2151	1991

Table 3 (contd.)

tems	Rupees Crore						US & Million					
	2000	*1999*	*1998*	*1997*	*1996*	*1995*	*2000*	*1999*	*1998*	*1997*	*1996*	*1995*
X. Gross Total	429269	414595	369682	335827	320728	311685	98435	97666	93531	93470	93730	99008
(a) Concessional Debt	165297	158220	146117	141970	143741	141139	37897	37258	36944	39489	41944	44845
(b) Concessional Debt as per cent of total	38.5	38.2	39.5	42.3	44.8	45.3	38.5	38.1	39.5	42.2	44.7	45.3
(c) Short-term Debt as per cent to total	4.1	4.5	5.4	7.2	5.2	4.3	4.1	4.5	5.4	7.2	5.4	4.3
Memo Items:												
Debt Indicators												
1. Debt Stock GDP Ratio (per cent)	22.0	23.5	24.4	23.8	26.3	30.0	22.0	23.5	24.4	23.8	26.3	30.0
*2. Debt-Service Ratio (per cent)	16.0	18.0	19.0	21.2	24.3	26.2	16.0	18.0	19.0	21.2	24.3	26.2

$ Includes net investments by 100 per cent FRR debt funds.

* Debt owed to Russia denominated in Rupees and converted at current exchange rates. payable in exports.

* Includes Rupee suppliers credit from end-March 1990 onwards.

** This does not include suppliers credit of up to 180 days for which no estimates are available.

Notes: Multilateral loans do not include revaluation of IBRD pooled loans and exchange rate adjustment under IDA loans for pre-1971 credit. Debt-service ratio from the year 1992-93 includes the revised private transfer contra-entry on account of gold and silver imports.

Source: Reserve Bank of India – Annual Report (various issues).

Table 4

India's External Debt Outstanding

(Rs. crores)

	End-March											End-September	
	1991	*1992*	*1993*	*1994*	*1995*	*1996*	*1997*	*1998*	*1999*	*2000*	*2001 R*	*2000*	*2001 P*
I. MULTILATERAL	40,386	68,262	77,758	82,199	89,819	98,173	105,066	116,904	129,682	137,132	145,103	141,482	151,162
A. Governmental Borrowing	38,429	63,787	72,286	75,617	82,223	89,428	94,824	104,218	114,531	120,321	127,889	124,618	133,598
(i) Concessional	25,849	40,990	48,206	50,250	55,963	60,425	63,418	70,560	78,979	84,051	89,009	87,449	93,583
(a) IDA	25221	40,017	47,167	49,238	54,897	59,349	62,343	69,392	77,725	82,721	87,753	86,166	92,236
(b) Others	628	973	1,039	1,012	1,066	1,076	1,075	1,168	1,254	1,330	1,256	1,283	1,347
(ii) Non-concessional	12,580	22,797	24,080	25,367	28,260	29,003	31,406	33,658	35,552	36,270	38,880	37,169	40,015
(a) IBRD	12,161	21,134	21,602	22,518	22,442	23,721	24,354	25,438	25,747	25,343	26,377	25,575	26,921
(b) Others	419	1,683	2,478	2,849	3,818	5,282	7,052	8,220	9,805	10,927	12,503	11,594	13,094
B. Non-Government Borrowing	1,957	4,475	5,472	6,582	7,596	8,745	10,242	12,686	15,151	16,811	17,214	16,864	17,564
(i) Concessional	0	0	0	0	0	0	0	0	0	0	0		
(ii) Non-concessional	1,957	4,475	5,472	6,582	7,596	8,745	10,242	12,686	15,151	16,811	17,214	16,864	17,564
(a) Public Sector	303	1,424	1,777	2,786	3,248	4,628	4,738	8,765	10,716	12,183	12,380	12,090	12,590
(i) IBRD	303	962	1,300	2,158	2,013	2,942	3,341	5,217	6,349	6,931	7,108	7,154	7,036
(ii) Others	0	462	477	628	1,235	1,686	1,397	3,548	4,367	5,252	5,272	4,936	5,554
(b) Financial Institutions	1,270	2,345	2,883	2,718	2,559	2,464	2,391	2,171	2,723	3,099	3,371	3,240	3,564
(i) IBRD	872	1,720	1,791	1,667	1,605	1,643	1,618	1,011	1,057	999	1,017	1,026	1,020
(ii) Others	398	625	1,092	1,051	954	821	773	1,160	1,666	2,100	2,354	2,214	2,544
(c) Private Sector	384	706	812	1,078	1,789	1,653	3,113	1,750	1,712	1,529	1,463	1,534	1,410
(i) IBRD	330	628	709	953	1,610	1,244	1,639	1,321	1,312	1,173	1,147	1,190	1,119
(ii) Others	54	78	103	125	179	409	1,474	429	400	356	316	344	291
II. BILATERAL	27,378	47,603	50,258	54,580	63,761	65,740	62,891	67,104	74,304	79,278	74,364	79,482	79,460
A. Government borrowing	23,065	40,371	42,220	45,387	52,965	53,119	49,092	51,420	57,106	60,920	58,800	61,434	60,660
(i) Concessional	23,065	40,371	42,220	45,387	52,965	52,078	48,165	50,583	56,425	59,380	55,502	60,152	59,793
(ii) Non-concessional	0	0	0	0	0	1,041	927	837	681	1,540	1,298	1,282	867
B. Non-Government borrowing	4,313	7,232	8,038	9,193	10,796	12,621	13,799	15,684	17,198	18,358	17,564	18,048	18,800
(i) Concessional	514	928	1,243	1,453	1,896	3,088	3,409	1,770	2,738	4,022	5,411,	4,289	6,737
(a) Public Sector	0	0	0	190	654	376	1,054	192	526	1,488	2,794	1,641	3,855
(b) Financial Institutions	514	928	1,243	1,263	1,242	2,712	2,355	1,578	2,212	2,534	2,617	2,648	2,882
(c) Private Sector	0	0	0	0	0	0	0	0	0	0	0	0	0